# MARGINALIZATION IN THE MIDST OF MODERNIZATION

## A Study of Sweepers in Western India

# Marginalization in the Midst of Modernization

*A Study of Sweepers in Western India*

TAKASHI SHINODA

MANOHAR
2005

First published 2005



ISBN 81-7304-647-6

*Published by*
Ajay Kumar Jain for
Manohar Publishers & Distributors
4753/23 Ansari Road, Daryaganj
New Delhi 110002

*Typeset by*
A J Software Publishing Co. Pvt. Ltd.
New Delhi 110005

*Printed at*
Lordson Publishers
Delhi 110007

*Distributed in South Asia by*
FOUNDATION BOOKS
4381/4 Ansari Road, Daryaganj
New Delhi 110002
and its branches at Mumbai, Hyderabad,
Bangalore, Chennai, Kolkata

# Contents

*Preface* 9

INTRODUCTION: INDIAN SOCIETY AND THE SWEEPER CASTE 11

Scope of the Study 11
Geography and History of Gujarat 13
Castes in Gujarat 14
Under British Rule 14
After Independence 15
The Backwardness of the Scheduled Castes 16
Caste Studies: A History 19
Castes in General 19
The Bhangis 23
The Organization of the Study 27

1. SCAVENGERS IN GOVERNMENT REPORTS 43

Introduction 43
An Outline of the Reports 43
Report of the Scavengers' Living Conditions Enquiry Committee (The Barve Committee) 44
Background 44
Contents of the Report, Members of the Committee 45
Report of the Scavenging Conditions Enquiry Committee (The Malkani Committee) 45
Background 45
Contents of the Report, Members of the Committee 46
Report of the Committee to Study the Working and Service
Conditions of Sweepers and Scavengers (The Pandya Committee) 47
Background 47
Contents of the Report, Members of the Committee 48

Report of the Task Force for Tackling the Problems of Scavengers and Suggesting Measures to Abolish Scavenging with Particular Emphasis on Their Rehabilitation (The Basu Task Force) 49
Background 49
Contents of the Report, Members of the Committee 50
Evolution of Scavengers and Their Customary Rights 51
Evolution of Scavengers 51
Before British Rule 51
During and After British Rule 51
Customary Rights of Scavengers 52
The Development of Customary Rights 52
Problems associated with Customary Rights 54
Scavenging Work 55
The Labour Process 55
Collection of Human Waste from Dry Latrines 55
Transportation of Human Waste 57
Disposal Depots for Human Waste 58
Recommendations in Government Reports 59
Employment Conditions and Trade Unions 62
Wages 63
Terms of Employment 66
Working Hours and Holiday Provisions 67
Recruitment and Promotion 69
Trade Unions 70
Development of Sanitary Administration and Abolition of Customary Rights 70
Sanitary Administration System 70
The Abolition of Customary Rights 72
Dry Latrines and Scavenger Population 75
Conclusion 78

2. DIFFERENTIALS IN SOCIO-ECONOMIC DEVELOPMENT AMONG THE SCHEDULED CASTES 83

Scheduled Castes in Gujarat 83
Geographical Distribution of the Major Scheduled Castes 85
Differentials in Socio-economic Development among the Scheduled Castes 88
Land Holding 88
Occupational Structure 90
Educational Structure 98

The Bhangis and Traditional Occupations 104

3. SANITARY FACILITIES AND SWEEPERS 115

Introduction 115
Development of the Municipal Administration System and Urban Sanitary Conditions 115
Municipal Administration System and Expansion of the City 115
Development of the Municipal Administration System 116
Expansion of the Municipal Area and Population Growth 118
Sanitary Facilities: Historical Development 120
Before British Rule 120
During and After British Rule 121
Sanitation Facilities and their Management 123
The Sewage System: An Outline 123
Disposal of Human Waste and Sewage System 126
Cesspools, Septic Tanks and Sewage Removal 126
Provision of Latrines and their Maintenance 130
Rubbish Collection and Disposal 132
The Municipal Sanitation Section 137
Its Labour Organization 137
Problems Relating to Labour Management 139
Conclusion 140

4. EMPLOYMENT POLICIES OF THE CONSERVANCY DEPARTMENT 144

Introduction 144
Sweepers and Awards 144
The Shah Award, 1948 145
The Jeejeebhoy Award, 1958 147
The Thakore Award, 1976-1980 149
The Barot Award, 1984-1992 154
Sweepers and Employment Policy 158
The Waiting List 159
Compensatory Appointment 161
Sweepers and Trade Unions 164
Awards and the Trade Unions 165
Trade Unions in the Early 1990s 167
The Ahmedabad Municipal Nokar Mandal 168
The Ahmedabad City Sweepers' Association 170
The Gujarat Municipal and Panchayat Kamdar Association 171
The Ahmedabad Municipal Kamdar Karamchari Union 172

All India Safai Mazdoor Congress (Gujarat Branch) 173
Conclusion 174

5. MOBILITY OF SWEEPERS EMPLOYED BY THE AHMEDABAD MUNICIPAL CORPORATION 181

Introduction 181
Sweepers and Other Related Workers in the Municipal Corporation 182
An Analysis of Mobility 184
Distribution of Workers by Zone, Sex and Age Group 184
An Analysis of Permanent Workers by Sex and Age Group 185
Conservancy Department 186
Refuse Department 202
An Analysis of Temporary Workers by Sex 208
Conclusion 210

6. THE SOCIO-ECONOMIC CONDITION OF SWEEPERS 213

Introduction 213
Employment and Working Conditions 214
Legal Developments 214
Public Sanitation Facilities 224
Treatment Facilities for Liquid Waste 224
Treatment Facilities for Solid Waste 226
Employment Conditions 227
Labour Unions 229
Working Conditions 230
Occupational Structure 231
Education 237
Income 242
Debt 246
Conclusion 249

7. EPILOGUE: SOCIAL DEVELOPMENT OF SWEEPERS: PROSPECTS AND CHALLENGES 253

Scope of the Present Study 253
Prospects for the Bhangi Liberation Movement 255

*Bibliography* 267

*Index* 275

# Preface

In the early 1990s, a good many Japanese scholars of various disciplines organized a study group on the system of untouchability in India. It was a good opportunity for me to take part in the study group. The association helped deepen my understanding of the various issues of untouchability through workshops and publications. Among the many untouchable castes, I was particularly interested in the socio-economic conditions of the sweeper castes for the very reason that they have continued their association with their traditional occupation, i.e. sweeping, despite various changes in the set-up of India after Independence. Notably, the job of the sweeper has been perceived as one of the most wretched occupations in India. While, other untouchable castes have tended to abandon their traditional occupations in the course of time, which was by and large beneficial for their socio-economic development, why have sweepers continued on with their association with sweeping? This was the question which first prompted me to do research on them.

The study can be divided in two parts. The first is an analysis of documents related to sweepers, which include various committee, commission, and task force reports at the level of central government as well as state governments. A lot of awards to solve industrial disputes at the level of local bodies are also dealt with. These materials supplemented by census and other related statistics are used to trace how institutional changes affected the socio-economic life of sweepers. The second is made up of first hand data and information collected in the course of field survey conducted in several local bodies in the western part of India. The field survey was aimed at analysing both the service and labour conditions of sweepers employed by the local bodies. Thus, this study is made up of the weft of institutional reform and the warp of the analysis of its impact on service and labour conditions of sweepers, woven together through an analysis of group and individual mobility. By doing so it attempts to show the direction in which the sweepers are moving. It can be expressed in one line as 'marginalization in the midst of modernization' as the title of this book indicates.

This book would not have been published without guidance and cooperation extended by my teachers, friends and fellow researchers in

India and Japan. I am deeply indebted to Dr. Ishwarbhai Patel of Safai Vaidyalaya, for his kindness and cooperation from the outset of my research. Prof. S.P. Kashyap supported me in various ways while I was associated with the Sardar Patel Institute of Economic and Social Research. My special thanks are due to the late Prof. Pravin Visaria, Prof. Sudarshan Iyengar, Prof. Rakesh Basant and Prof. B.B. Patel for their support when I was accommodated in the Gujarat Institute of Development Research as a visiting scholar. I am grateful to Dr. Anil Gumber who assisted me at every stage of my research without which I could not have completed this work. Also, my sincere thanks are due to my friends in Ahmedabad, Achyut Yagnik, Makrand Mehta, Indira Hirway, Leela Visaria, Amita Shah, Jeemol Unni, Kalpana Mehta, Arti Oza, Dharmishta Joshi, Uma Rani, R. Parthasarathy and Keshab Das. I shall be ever grateful to the staff at the eight local bodies, i.e. Ahmedabad, Dehgam, Viramgam, Dholka, Sanand, Bareja, Bavla and Sola, for pleasantly responding to my irritating demands. I am particularly thankful to Mr. P. Basu, the then Commissioner, Mr. P.U. Asnani, the then Deputy Commissioner, Mr. Z.A. Sacha, Mr. Rajendra Shah, Mr. D.J. Patel of the Ahmedabad Municipal Corporation for their valued cooperation.

Last but not least, I would like to express my hearty gratitude to all the interviewees, the sweepers, the trade union members and social activists, who despite their own personal inconvenience came forward with all enthusiasm and spared quite a lot of their precious time. It is really an appreciable gesture on their part to have sat with me answering questions which would not bring immediate relief to any of their problems.

This book is a translation of my work, *Indo no Seisonin Kasuto Kenkyu* (in Japanese), published by Shunjusya in 1995. The translation of the book was aided by a Grant-in-Aid for Publication of Scientific Research Result (Grant-in-Aid for Scientific Research, Ministry of Education, Culture, Sports, Science and Technology, Japan) and translated by Ms Gaynor Sekimori. I am grateful to the Ministry of Education and Gaynor Sekimori for their help and cooperation.

TAKASHI SHINODA

# Introduction
# Indian Society and the Sweeper Caste

## Scope of the Study

The caste system, together with the family system and the village community, has long been considered an important factor characterizing Indian society. Caste is here understood to be an endogamous group following a specific occupation, and, despite fluctuations in ranking and social status between *jatis* (sub castes), caste remains the unchanging social regulator in India. In recent years, however, particularly after India's Independence in August 1947, a number of changes affecting the system as a whole have brought into existence a social transformation that cannot be understood in terms of the existing framework. It is therefore desirable to seek a new understanding of the functioning of the caste system and its power to regulate society.

The present social transformation is extremely complicated. The Constitution of India,[1] at the centre of whose drafting was Bhimrao Ramji Ambedkar (1891-1956) provided for positive treatment in favour of the historically discriminated groups, with a number of reserved seats guaranteed in parliament, higher education and the public service. The Indian Government has designated as recipients of this reservation policy[2] the Scheduled Castes, comprising 16.48 per cent of the population (1991), and the Scheduled Tribes (8.08 per cent of the population). Further, recognition of a third category, Other Backward Classes,[3] and the application of the reservation policy to it is at the discretion of individual states. Because the reservation policy acts against fair competition, it has been called protective discrimination, reverse discrimination and compensative discrimination. Though there are certain problems with the policy, such as underutilization of seats and the level of skill of policy recipients, it has, overall, been a major factor in bringing those groups into broader political participation and in breaking down the traditional caste and class structure. Tensions with Caste Hindus dissatisfied with the reservation policy have increased and both national and state governments have fallen as a direct result of the issue.[4]

Many changes have, in addition, been brought about to the caste system through the land reforms and industrial policies initiated by the states since Independence. Though the land reform laws have been criticised as being full of loopholes, they have been successful in redistributing land among the lower classes to an extent, while the Green Revolution has led to a differentiation among the higher castes. In the process of this transformation, there has been seen the development of trans-caste organizations based on class, as well as of a large number of caste-centred organizations (Caste Associations).[5] Besides providing educational opportunities for their members and acting as mediators for marriages among them, Caste Associations have also functioned as political pressure groups and as a force for caste participation in elections. Caste Federations too emerged, comprising castes of different social and economic status, and the ensuing collaboration among caste associations and other religious groups has resulted in an entirely new situation, one unknown before Independence.

The introduction of universal suffrage gave socially and economically backward communities a completely new opportunity for active political participation. Today what is important is not whether a community is backward or advanced, but how many voters it commands. Universal suffrage promoted a reorganization of leadership within backward groups and opened the way for populous castes to develop politically.

Though institutional reforms such as the reservation policy, land reforms and universal suffrage were a severe blow to the traditional caste system, the backwardness of historically discriminated groups has not automatically been swept away. The factors that make up backwardness, therefore, must be overcome in the wake of the institutional reforms. The key to this is the raising of the educational and occupational levels of such communities within the new framework. In this connection, it is necessary to have a clear understanding of how the household and the community mobilize their resources and what obstacles either encounters.

The Scheduled Castes are made up of a large number of sub-castes (*jatis*), and these, as well as regional differences, give rise to a wide variation in the level of development. This study focuses on the Bhangi, the sweeper caste, considered the most backward of any group in the Scheduled Castes, and examines the nature of, and factors in, its backwardness, and the impact of institutional reforms and reform movements on this backwardness. Though I shall deal briefly with the sweeper caste of India as a whole, the bulk of this study will be concerned with Gujarat in western India. My methodology combines historical (documentary) research and field study in Gujarat.

## Geography and History of Gujarat

Gujarat, already an important base for sea-trade between the Arab world and South-East Asia before the arrival of the Portuguese in India, was one of the most commercialized regions in the Indian subcontinent. Diu and Surat prospered through the spice trade in the fifteenth and sixteenth centuries,[6] and Surat in particular was prized as a trading port by the Mughal Empire. Gujarat came under the control of the Mughals in the sixteenth century, and then passed into the hands of the Marathas in the eighteenth century. The British East India Company, which as a result of the Battle of Plassey in 1757 had achieved supremacy over the other European powers vying for a stake in India, concluded the Treaty of Basain with the Maratha Gaekwad in 1803, thereby gaining a foothold in Gujarat. Until the middle of the nineteenth century the Company ruled virtually the entire area of Gujarat either directly or indirectly. Gujarat, which was part of the Bombay Presidency, consisted, for administrate purposes, of a British District, a State Agency and a number of Princely States.[7] With Independence in 1947, these administrative units were reconstituted. For a time, Kutch and the Peninsula Saurashtra were designated Part B and Part C states respectively, but in 1956 they were incorporated, with mainland Gujarat, into Bombay State. The bilingual Bombay State, combining both Marathi and Gujarati speaking populations, was divided into the present Maharashtra and Gujarat States in May 1960.[8]

Gujarat State is made up of twenty-five districts (but when the original Japanese version of this book was written, there were nineteen districts only. The following narrations are based on the divisions of nineteen districts.).[9] It may be divided into either two or five regions, based on common geographical and cultural factors. The two regions are peninsular (Saurashtra and Kutch) and mainland Gujarat. The great Rann of Kutch stretches across much of Kutch and so farming and population are concentrated in the south of the region. Kutch is hemmed in by desert in the north-west, but is connected to Sind by means of harbours such as Mandvi on the Gulf of Kutch. Its connections with Sind are deep, not only through trade, but culturally as well. The peninsula has a curving coastline, which looks out onto the Gulf of Kutch, the Arabian Sea and the Gulf of Khambhat (Cambay). It is connected to other regions by the harbours of Jamnagar, Porbandar and Bhavnagar. Historically relatively free of Mughal and Maratha control, it developed its own culture based on a large number of politically independent small and medium-sized kingdoms, collectively called Saurashtra (the land of innumerable small states). Mainland Gujarat is considerably different geographically from the peninsular region. In the east a highland area runs north-south which is the source of a number of rivers, including the Mahi, the Tapi and the Narmada, which flow into the Gulf of Khambhat. Besides the harbour towns of Khambhat, Bharuch and Surat, which played a very important role in the development of Gujarat, there are a number of inland cities, such as Ahmedabad and Vadodara, which were significant in the region's modern growth. Subjected to domination and intervention, from both within and without India, they contributed much to the development of external and internal Indian trade. Though mainland Gujarat has far more variety than the peninsular region, it remains a well-defined area in relation to it.

The five regions into which Gujarat also can be divided are Kutch (one district), Saurashtra (six districts), North Gujarat (three districts), Central Gujarat (five districts) and South Gujarat (four districts). North Gujarat is the most backward area of mainland Gujarat. Central Gujarat, centring on the districts of Ahmedabad, Kheda and Vadodara, has in recent times become the most advanced region of Gujarat, with a good balance of agriculture, industry and commerce. The area south of Kheda stretching into South Gujarat is the granary of the state. The harbours of Surat and Bharuch are the main cities of the south. Though their importance as ports waned with the growth of Bombay, Surat in particular has revived in recent years as a commercial and industrial centre. With Kheda, South Gujarat is the richest agricultural region in the state, and agriculture there is largely dependent on workmen from the Scheduled Tribes living in the highlands.[10]

## Castes in Gujarat

### *Under British Rule*

The highest ranking castes in the nineteenth century when Gujarat was under British rule were the Brahmans, the Baniyas and the Rajputs. Though certain *jatis* of Brahmans, such as the Anavil, were powerful landholding groups, in general Gujarati Brahmans were not as politically and economically powerful in proportion to their numbers as were the Brahmans of northern and southern India. This was one reason for the fluidity between sects and castes within the caste structure.

The Baniya caste was made up of Jains and Vaishnava Hindus and had a powerful influence on politics and the economic life. Because of the Baniya's high social position, a segment of middle and lower castes tried to identify themselves not only with the Kshatriyas but with the Vaisyas in the course of Sanskritization in Gujarat. The Baniyas were active all over western India, though their most important base was Bombay.

The Rajputs were members of the domain lord stratum who ruled a large number of small and medium sized kingdoms over a broad area of the peninsula and part of the plains with certain Kolis and Muslims at the beginning of the nineteenth century, when the East India Company was gaining a foothold in Gujarat. Britain recognized their territorial rights, but the political and economic power of the Rajputs has been drastically reduced as a result of the establishment of the land settlement.

At the beginning of the twentieth century there was increased fluidity between castes and religious sects within the caste structure. The Patidar (also called Kanbi) had been a middle-ranking agricultural caste, which was actively associated with a peasant's movement in the course of noncooperation movement advocated by Mohandas Karamchand Gandhi (1869-1948) and Vallabhbhai Jhaverbhai Patel (1875-1950). As a result the Patidar attained political strength. Their economic base was expanded, from the 1860s, due to the cultivation of raw cotton, and, through to the 1880s, due to the expansion in area of cultivation, and was strengthened due to occupational diversification and active migration by the middle of the twentieth century.[11]

### *After Independence*

The various changes, which occurred after Independence, caused the very framework of the caste structure to shake. The series of land reforms, though not thoroughgoing, dismantled the privileged economic base of the old landed class, particularly the Rajputs, and encouraged a favourable framework for the Patidars. In response to this new situation, the Rajputs established in 1948 the Gujarat Kshatriya Sabha as a flagship for the Kshatriyas as a whole, in an effort to incorporate the populous Kolis into their fold.[12] This action was in response to the introduction of universal suffrage. Because of the definite success of the strategy, the Scheduled Castes and the Backward Classes at once accelerated moves to identify themselves with the Kshatriyas.

The establishment of the Kshatriya Sabha saw the beginning, in the post-Independence period, of alliances among religious sects and castes in elections and on the political front. The socially and economically weaker groups used the voting power of their members to achieve political leadership at the State, District and Taluka level. Thus for example, in the state assembly elections of 1980, M. Solanki gained power through a political alliance of Kshatriyas, Scheduled Castes, Scheduled Tribes and Muslims, and governed successfully until 1985.[13]

Already in the 1960s tension between the Kshatriyas and the Patidars was a motivating factor in government, and since 1975 rivalry between the alliance of low-ranking associations and the high-ranking castes centring on the Patidars and the Baniyas has been a keynote in state politics. The comeback of the higher castes, which had lost political control temporarily, took a violent form in the anti-reservation agitation of 1985.[14]

### The Backwardness of the Scheduled Castes

The Scheduled Castes lack many of the necessary conditions for social development as a group, and it is this lack which constitutes their backwardness,[15] moulded by historical conditions, such as the caste and landholding systems. The necessary conditions for both backwardness and progress have of course changed with the times. The post-Independence reservation policy, for example, stressed the reservation of parliamentary seats to ensure a certain political strength, and the reservation of seats in higher education and the public service to encourage social respect and economic power.

Under British rule the colonial authorities specified categories such as Depressed Classes and Backward Classes and made them the object of preferential treatment.[16] The categories of Scheduled Castes and Tribes as defined in Articles 341 and 342 of the Indian Constitution have their origins in the Government of India Act of 1935. The establishment of such categories prior to Independence had an ideology of Divide and Rule as their background but in the Constitution, the Scheduled Castes and Tribes were considered as an integral part of the Indian people. On top of this a number of institutional measures were put in place to strengthen the backward groups politically, socially and economically. Of these, the most important were the law prohibiting discrimination, the reservation policy and the Twenty-Point Programme, all embodying a policy of aid to the weak.[17] In addition, the execution of the series of land reform measures and the introduction of universal suffrage also contributed both directly and indirectly to the political, social and economic strength of the backward groups.

Following the prohibition of discrimination against the Untouchables in the Constitution, the Untouchability Offences Act was passed in 1955 (renamed The Protection of Civil Rights Act in 1976). This was an epoch-making law which prescribed punishments for acts of discrimination. However in Gujarat as in other places, there were many problems surrounding its enforcement.[18] The focus at that time of the anti-discrimination movement regarding the backward classes, and the Scheduled Castes in particular, was on guaranteeing access to common water facilities and the right to temple entry.[19] Both involved serious human rights issues about. The state government gave financial help so that the Scheduled Castes could be assured of their own access to a water supply, and by the 1970s restrictions on access to common water facilities had been alleviated, even in villages. The question of temple entry, however, directly involved the religious beliefs of caste Hindus and there was strong resistance. Even today temple entry is not completely free.[20]

Urban life has developed in constant contradiction of the restrictions on the Untouchables, which means that most problems regarding them are generally to be found in villages. As a result of both institutional and socio-economic changes, such as the expansion of primary and lower secondary schooling in rural areas, the increase in the radius of people's activities as a result of an improved road network, the growth of opportunities to work outside the village, the penetration of mass media, many of the restrictions placed traditionally on the Untouchables have weakened or disappeared. In particular, restrictions in facilities or places of a public nature, like schools, shops, factories and transport, have been greatly relaxed.[21]

Furthermore, tenancy legislation and laws restricting the size of land that can be owned, which form the basis of land reform, have limited how much land the dominant agricultural castes can accumulate and have made it possible for previously tenanted and surplus land to be distributed among the Scheduled Castes. Land management by the Scheduled Castes has been generally poor, according to reports, by a lack of capital and economic skills, but all the same, the redistribution of land, on however small a scale, has brought about a considerable shaking of the traditional order in rural villages.[22]

Political participation by the Scheduled Castes has changed greatly since Independence. Because of their numbers, universal suffrage and the reservation policy have become weapons in their political advancement. They now send representatives to all levels of government, national (both houses), state, and, with the introduction of the Panchayati Raj,[23] also to local bodies like the Village Panchayat, the Panchayat Samiti and the Zila Parishad. However, as more than half the seats reserved are not taken up and the Scheduled Castes are easily beaten during political bargaining with the Caste Hindus, they have not yet acquired the political power proportional to their population. Nevertheless, their political participation has dealt a blow to the very foundations of the traditional power structure.[24]

Such institutional changes have guaranteed to a certain extent the basic human rights and political interests of the Scheduled Castes. Further, the literacy ratio between the Scheduled Castes and other groups has decreased, as has the ratio of the number of workers in non-agricultural jobs. The conditions for social development for the various groups are, however, different today from those that prevailed before Independence, and the deciding factors now are education and occupation. It is vital for the social advancement of the Scheduled Castes that the stratum of their students in higher secondary education is broadened, as also the number of their members working in more highly regarded occupations, such as white collar jobs, the public service and finance. The Scheduled Castes have as yet made little impact on the occupations that hold the key to such social advancement and it is difficult to say that there is as yet any lessening of the difference in this area between the advanced groups and the Scheduled Castes.

Backwardness as an obstacle to social development is not limited to economic poverty; other factors include a low standard of education, a narrow choice of occupation, a poor living environment, and customs and beliefs which hamper change.[25] Untouchability, which includes social and occupational regulations, is also a formative factor in backwardness. The various factors work together to prevent the social advancement of a group or a household.

Though benefited by the land reforms to some extent, land holding by the Scheduled Castes in rural areas is generally on a very small scale. As a result, the Scheduled Castes tend to make up a large proportion of agricultural labourers and their income level is low. Their fragile economic base hinders the upgrading of educational and occupational levels. In urban areas, by contrast, school attendance by members of the Scheduled Castes has increased dramatically in recent years, but while a greater proportion are working in the public service and in manufacturing industries, few have advanced to high positions.

Institutional measures, such as the Reservation Policy, have played an important role to bring about a change in the social position of the targeted groups themselves, rather than create particular beneficiaries within the groups. Putting aside the question of beneficiaries through the measures, the Scheduled Castes must, to escape from their backwardness, construct for themselves an influential position as economic groups. To do so, it is important how they utilize their organization and resources. Improving social position as a group is not the same as increasing the social standing and position of the individual household; nevertheless both actions are in a broad sense complementary. For example, social and economic advancement at household level among the higher ranking castes is not achieved apart from caste ties. It relies on the support provided among individual caste members as well as caste associations in the form of information, trust, and human resources.[26] In this regard, the Scheduled Castes have hardly any forms of mutual support and even the organization of caste members has been fraught with difficulties. While the middle-ranking castes organized a large number of associations to cope with the situation under British rule and after Independence, very few such associations emerged from within the Scheduled Castes.[27] The social advancement of the Backward Classes depends on the effective employment of institutional measures and the systematization of their own resources.

There are considerable differences in advancement among the various groups constituting the backward classes. Differences in social and economic conditions between the Scheduled Castes and the Scheduled Tribes are particularly conspicuous. Furthermore, there are large differences in levels of education and occupation even among groups within the Scheduled Castes and Tribes. In Gujarat, the Scheduled Castes consist of 30 subgroups, of which the most advanced are the Vankar and the Chamar, while among the 40 groups of the Scheduled Tribes, the most advanced are the Dhodia and the Chaudhari.[28] Since Independence differences between the advanced and backward groups have been growing. As a result, there has been a demand from within the groups that there should be a reexamination of recipient groups of the reservation policy. There remains, too, within the advanced groups of the Scheduled Castes a strong attitude towards the untouchability of the backward groups such as the Bhangi. This attitude may appear more extreme even than discrimination by Caste Hindus. It is an important social issue which must be resolved together with the eradication of backwardness among the Scheduled Castes.

## Caste Studies: A History

### *Caste in General*

The study of caste began at a comparatively recent period. The word itself derives from the Portuguese *casta*. Even in premodern times foreigners visiting India reported caste related characteristics as being one aspect of Indian society. These descriptions were, however, very fragmentary.[29] More organized reporting came after England began governing India in the nineteenth century. In the latter half of that century, England began conducting censuses and compiling gazetteers as a function of colonial government. The census provided a table of the population differentiated by caste and religion.[30] The official classification and ranking of castes, as can be seen from the numerous petitions seeking a change in classification, gave much impact on the local society.[31] The gazetteers contained both census results and the historical background of the castes and sects. Survey and Settlement Reports, made for the purpose of tax collection, and Administration Reports also refer to caste and sect. Further, in 1901, the government organized an ethnographic survey[32] and detailed reports concerning sub-castes, sects, customs, and rituals were published into the 1920s.

Descriptions of caste by government officials and private individuals in the late nineteenth and early twentieth centuries were very influential in moulding the image of India among the European intelligentsia. However it must also be remembered that the writers themselves tended to interpret what they saw in terms of the current European understanding of Asia and India. As a result, Indian society was deemed to be stagnant and static.[33] Caste was also understood in similar terms in the course of controversy on the origin of caste, participated by officials and Indologists from the late nineteenth to the first half of the twentieth century.[34]

Monographs about the Untouchables began to appear in the twentieth century, of which a pioneering work is the study of the Chamars made by G.W. Briggs.[35] His work mainly covered the Chamars in northern India, and included references to economy, society, ritual and beliefs incorporating the findings from census reports and gazetteers. Still, Briggs remained trapped within a static understanding of society.

With Independence and the establishment of the Indian Constitution, a political and social framework regarding the Untouchables came into being which was quite different from what had gone before. As with caste studies as a whole, the study of the Scheduled Castes not only exhibited a new growth but also occupied a greater proportion of the studies being made.[36] The introduction of American sociology also contributed to the expansion of the field.

In the early 1950s, a number of village surveys were published by leading scholars. Their analyses focused on caste and class at village level, on intracaste hierarchies, and on trends in social change in terms of division of labour. In doing so they drew a distinction between their research and the type done before Independence, based on census reports, gazetteers and ethnological studies.[37] In this new atmosphere, the work of W.H. Wiser, unremarked before Independence, was re-evaluated, and the *jajmani* system that he had described became established as a sociological concept.[38] M.N. Srinivas' concept of 'Dominant Caste'[39] was similarly derived from village surveys.

Particularly important among the post-Independence institutional reforms were universal suffrage, the land reforms, and the reservation policy. Universal suffrage brought about an explosion in caste communal mobility and, while strengthening linkages between castes on the political stage, accelerated associations and joint struggles among castes to further their political interests. From the middle of the 1950s throughout the 1960s, research on caste associations, caste federations and the general elections expanded.[40] With the introduction of the Panchayati Raj as the key of rural development, the Scheduled Castes were able to send representatives to organs of local self-government, such as the village and district Panchayats. Now that the Panchayati Raj system has taken firm root, there is presently a great increase in studies dealing with the impact of the Panchayati Raj in local society as well as with associated issues.[41]

Circumstances relating to land holding differ greatly from state to state. However, the tenancy laws and the ceiling acts have limited the accumulation of land by the dominant agricultural castes, and have made it possible for previously tenanted and surplus land to be distributed among the Backward Classes, including the Scheduled Castes. Economic surveys analysing the impact of land reform began to appear in the 1950s and most of them referred also to land holding by the Scheduled Castes.[42]

More important in terms of group mobility by the Scheduled Castes than the land reforms was the reservation policy. Concrete research into its impact began appearing in the latter half of the 1970s. Though studies had formerly been done on reservation in higher education and the public service, no methodology had been constructed to evaluate its institutional impact, which made it easy merely to fall into a discussion of the pros and cons of the policy. *Competing Equalities* (1984) of Marc Galanter, a pioneer in the field and a scholar with a thorough knowledge of the Constitution and the law, has considerably deepened the legal and sociological understanding of Indian society.[43]

Since Independence, besides such research into institutional reform as detailed earlier, there has been much work concerning communal and individual mobility. In the case of the Scheduled Castes, studies on institutional reform and mobility are complementary, for unless both are considered there can be no understanding of the dynamism of social change. Studies on mobility are closely related to the theory of 'Social Stratification',[44] promoted by scholars who see the caste system as a structural rather than a cultural phenomenon.[45] Their views on mobility are, however, diverse, such as Srinivas's concept of 'Sanskritization',[46] and Damle and Lynch's 'Reference Group'.[47] Studies of mobility in the 1950s tended to be limited to rural areas, often to a single village, but in the latter half of the 1960s caste came to be analysed in terms of urban areas and wider fields of distribution. In the process, differences in mobility between rural and urban areas and limitations to the social stratification theory as applied to rural villages alone came to be recognized.

In the 1970s, there was increased reflection concerning concepts and methodology,[48] and a growing trend toward interdisciplinary study in the field of social stratification. Related to this was the popularity of research into mobility.[49] The functionalistic social stratification theory that had hitherto stood was taken up as a subject for criticism.[50] Structuralist research which placed emphasis on social change of course continued,[51] but what was notable about the 1970s was the tide of various types of historical studies. Particularly important was the work of the Cambridge School,[52] which had had as its aim since the 1960s a reconsideration of modern Indian history, and practical research into social stratification, which was connected with the theory of production modes, arising out of Marxist historiography.[53] Furthermore, from a structuralist viewpoint, Louis Dumont made an analysis of hierarchies, contributing to a deepening of the concept of social stratification and to its analytical framework.[54] Concerning the study of the Scheduled Castes, particular mention should be made of the reappraisal of the theory of history of Jotirao Phule (1827-90), a pioneer of the Dalit movement. He regarded Brahmanical ideological dominance as a special feature of the caste system,[55] and his views stimulated a new interest in how caste arose and in historical studies from a non-Brahman stance.

A characteristic of the 1980s was that interdisciplinary studies centring on historiography and historical research became the mainstream of studies of social dynamics. In particular, a series of questions arising out of Subaltern Studies,[56] which developed from criticism about elitist history, a view of history derived from the interests of the governing powers, contributed to the spread of 'history from below', focusing on the attitudes and movements of ordinary people as well as deepening criticism of sources. History from below provided a window on popular movements and rebellions and so shed new light on the dynamics of social change. Though most of the movements and rebellions did not end in success, an analysis of the group mobility that formed in their process is highly suggestive when considering the social development of the lower classes afterwards. Thus research into group and individual mobility, so very popular in the 1970s, came to occupy a central position in studies of social stratification and social change in the 1980s.[57]

### *The Bhangis*

The Sweeper or Scavenger caste, whose traditional occupation was cleaning latrines and roads, was called 'Bhangi' over a wide area of north-western India, 'Chuhra' in the Punjab, 'Dumra' or 'Domra' in Rajasthan, 'Mehtar' in Bihar, 'Bhuimalia' in West Bengal, 'Heddish' in Orissa, 'Madiga' in Andhra Pradesh, and 'Thoti' in Tamil Nadu. The Sweeper caste in one part of Uttar Pradesh claims to be called as 'Valmiki' and the Muslim Sweepers of the Punjab as 'Baleshahi' or 'Lal Begi'.[58] Given the large number of names by which the Sweeper caste is known in India, I will here refer to it as 'Bhangi'. There is no agreement about the derivation of the word 'Bhangi'. The root bhang has a wide variety of meanings, including opium addict, alcoholic, bamboo craftsman, and exile,[59] but there is no evidence to relate 'Bhangi' to any of these in particular.

The Bhangis were described in pre-Independence census reports, ethnographic surveys and gazetteers, but there was no specific research as had been made on the Chamars. The census reports contained the population distribution of each caste as well as the educational and occupational structure of the selected castes, including the Bhangis. The reports provide useful data for cross-sectional and diachronic analyses but have as yet been under-utilized.[60]

*The Tribes and Castes of Bombay* (R.E. Enthoven) is an ethnographic survey of the Bombay Presidency (including Gujarat).[61] Part of the Gazetteer of the Bombay Presidency was republished as *Hindu Castes and Tribes of Gujarat*,[62] and *History of Gujarat*[63] respectively. Individual gazetteers were also published for the five British districts of Gujarat and for a few of the princely states, and these contain much more local information about caste.

Gandhi's works about untouchability are required reading for understanding the process of the Bhangi liberation movement.[64] Gandhi placed great emphasis on the liberation of the Bhangis, who were the lowest of the Untouchables, and recommended (and practised himself) that each household should clean its own latrines. Because he wanted to do away with untouchability while preserving the *varna* framework, he found himself in sharp conflict with B.R. Ambedkar, a Mahar and leader of the Untouchables. Nevertheless his attitude towards the Bhangis had a great influence on the people concerned with the Bhangi liberation movement. The Harijan Sevak Sangh, established in 1932 (formally in 1935), included a plan of action for the Bhangis.[65] The movement was not so effective before Independence.

The mainstream of Bhangi research after Independence consisted of reports by committees investigating the sweepers set up by the central and state governments. These reports comprised both analyses of employment and working conditions of sweepers and recommendations for their improvement. I will deal with them in detail in Chapters 1 and 4.

The first general work that treated the Bhangi issue comprehensively was *Clean People and An Unclean Country*[66] (1965) by N.R. Malkani, who headed the committee set up by the central government to investigate the situation of the sweepers. The framework within which the issue was examined was the same as that in the committee's report but Malkani added personal observations not to be found in the official document. Interestingly, he described in a clear and objective way the connections between Gandhi, the Harijan Sevak Sangh and Sweeper caste.[67]

Shyamlal has conducted a sociological survey of the Bhangis in Jodhpur, Rajastan. *The Bhangis in Transition* (1984)[68] is a collection of previously published essays describing their customs, educational and occupational structures, and social changes through documentary study and field work (1971-3). Particularly important is his description of the history of the Bhangi social reform movement. A reform movement aimed at the Bhangis was initiated in 1923 by the Arya Samaj,[69] and in the following year education centres were set up in Bhangi areas of settlement. The reform movement consisted, besides the expansion of education, of forbidding the eating of beef and the drinking of alcohol, improving hygiene, and the permeation of Hinduism.[70] The Harijan Sevak Sangh also made it a platform from 1932 to abolish discrimination based on untouchability towards the Bhangis.[71] Later, in contrast to this action from 'outside', a labour union movement centred on municipal sanitary workers became active, and in 1942 a union, the Safai Mazdoor Union, was set up, followed in 1950 by the Municipal Karamchari Sangh. In addition, a reform association, the Marwar Mehtar Sudhar Sabha, began in 1945 to focus on internal reform.[72] These various organizations were concerned not only with improving employment and labour conditions, but also functioned as a pressure group on the political stage. In Gujarat, too, the labour unions became the strongest pressure groups for the Bhangis.

Shyamlal's 1992 work, *The Bhangi: A Sweeper Caste, Its Socio-Economic Portraits with Special Reference to Jodhpur City*,[73] is based on his doctoral dissertation of a field survey undertaken in 1975. While the sub-theme is a social and economic sketch, the work centres on an analysis of social structures such as caste, sect and family. Caste organization is double-layered, the Mohalla Panchayat, the local unit, and the Caste Panchayat, the ward or district unit. The Mohalla Panchayat, made up of a number of sub-castes, functions as the organ dealing with mutual aid or the settlement of conflicts on a daily basis. The Chairman (Sarpanch) and the financial officer are elected from among the standing members of the committee, comprising the most powerful people. The Caste Panchayat deals with conflicts that the Mohalla Panchayat cannot resolve and with weddings and funerals. The Chairman is called the Mehtarshah, and the position is hereditary within families who cleaned the latrines of raja families. The Caste Panchayat consists of committee members elected singly from each mohalla; from these are elected the Vice-Chairman (Chaudhari), the financial officer and the liaison officer, who assist the Mehtarshah. However, meetings of the Caste Panchayat are rare. The author witnessed only two instances, in 1954 on the occasion of a large scale funeral (Nyat Ganga) and in 1970 when there was an intra-caste conflict.[74] Since such caste organizations basically serve to preserve traditions, they tend to weaken at a time of social change. Further, a study of religion and sects showed that while Bhangi beliefs and rituals at the beginning of the twentieth century were a combination of elements from both Hinduism and Islam, the permeation of social reform movements like Arya Samaj brought the widespread introduction of Hindu rituals.[75]

Bindeshwar Pathak's *Road to Freedom: A Sociological Study on the Abolition of Scavenging in India*,[76] is a sociological study which is a direct analysis of Bhangis in Bihar. Pathak, who took part in the Bhangi liberation movement which rose to the fore around the time of the centenary of Gandhi's birth in 1969, set up an institution (Sulabh Shauchalaya Sansthan; renamed Sulabh International in 1974) in Patna in 1970 to look into improved latrines, with the intention of raising the position of the Bhangis by introducing lavatories that did not need manual cleaning. He called his academic work, linked directly to active social involvement, 'Action Sociology'.[77] *Road to Freedom* combines docu-mentary research and field work to describe skilfully the growth of the Bhangi liberation movement on a national level. It shows how in the latter half of the 1960s and throughout the 1970s the three states of Gujarat, Kerala and Orissa energetically supported the Bhangi liberation movement; how in a comparatively short space of time the effects of the movement revealed themselves in Gujarat and Kerala in particular; how, as a result of growing worldwide concern in the later 1970s about public hygiene, international bodies like WHO, UNICEF and UNDP extended monetary and technical aid to India to improve public hygiene there; and how the Indian government strengthened its financial aid commitment to the states and municipalities in the 1980s with the same purpose.[78] The book names six organizations, the Harijan Sevak Sangh, the Gandhi Smarak Nidhi,[79] the Safai Vidyalaya,[80] the Rajasthan Institute of Local Self Government, the Institute of Social Studies Trust and the Sulabh International, as having a close involvement with the Bhangi liberation movement.[81] Fieldwork was done in three local government areas in Bihar, focusing on Bhangi labourers and the possessors of latrines, among whom a socio-economic survey was conducted. Some 200,000 old style latrines needing manual cleaning by Bhangis were supposed to exist in that state.[82]

*Safai Marg-Darshika*[83] (1970) by Ishwarbhai Patel, head of the Safai Vidyalaya in Ahmedabad, is a morphology of latrines. Since Bhangi liberation is closely related to the abandonment of old-style latrines and the introduction of other types, studies on public hygiene facilities have a deep connection with raising Bhangi status. Patel is chiefly active in Gujarat, but like B. Pathak has presented a model for a substitute latrine aimed at officials in public health departments around the country and at non-governmental organizations. The Patel developed latrine and Pathak's improved latrine are morphologically the same: they use only a small amount of water (two litres), they are easy to make and are low-priced, the unit size is compact and occupies only a small space, and excrement can be converted to dry manure by rotating the use of two units, obviating the necessity to remove human waste manually. Since in India the provision of sewage was a great financial burden on local authorities, it was necessary to find other methods of abandoning the manual collection of human waste.

Autobiographies and novels are also an important means of understanding the life and ways of thinking of the Bhangis. Hazari's *I Was An Outcaste*[84] is the record of the life of the author and his family in a village in the United Provinces. The position of Bhangis in rural areas before Independence is described unemotionally and objectively, and is all the more persuasive for that.

The Indian Public Broadcasting Commission (Doordarshan) showed a thirty-minute programme in 1992 in Hindi concerning the issue of latrines (*Shauchalaya ki Samasya*) and the Safai Vidyalaya made a twenty-minute programme in 1970 named 'Curse' (*Abhishap*). The former reported on defecation in public and the attendant problems, and called for need for the wider use of improved latrines. It also touched broadly on the history of Gandhi's Bhangi liberation movement. The latter was made to further the cause of the liberation of the 'cursed' Bhangis in the following year of the Gandhi centenary. It stressed the need for Bhangi liberation by contrasting living and working conditions between the advanced and backward sections. Filming was done in several cities in the Ahmedabad District of Gujarat. It has high value as a record of manual latrine cleaning, living conditions and begging for leftover food.

## The Organization of the Study

This study combines documentary research and fieldwork. In terms of overall organization, the Introduction and Chapters 1, 2 and 4 are based on the former, and Chapters 3, 5 and 6 are the results of the latter. It is difficult to separate completely the two approaches, and even in chapters that are primarily fieldwork reports, I have used primary source material from documentary research.

Chapter 1 examines reports of committees set up by the state and central governments to improve the employment and labour conditions of scavengers and sweepers. The recommendations of these committees have exerted a great influence on the post-Independence Bhangi liberation movement and on improvements in their employment and labour conditions. The *Malkani Committee Report* of 1960 contained a detailed analysis of the labour process involved in the manual collection of human excreta and the social repercussions of the report were very great. The background and present reality of the sweeper problem and the progress of the reform initiated from 'above' are traced in this chapter through the various reports.

Chapter 2 analyses data on the Scheduled Castes contained in national census surveys. Criticism exists about the validity of this material, but I have found it to be of high merit for understanding the educational and occupational structures. The census also contains data about the various sub-castes (*jatis*) that make up the Scheduled Castes, so that comparison is made possible. The chapter traces differences in development among the Scheduled Castes in terms of the educational and occupational structures based on the censuses of 1961, 1981 and 1991.

Chapter 3 analyses public sanitation facilities and their management as a direct determinant of the labour conditions of sweepers. Manual collection of excreta remains in areas where sewage facilities are underdeveloped, while the development of mechanical means of rubbish collection has affected the work strength of sweepers and the health of their working environment. There are considerable differences among the various local authorities in the provision of public sanitation facilities. Based on a preliminary study in 1990 (documentary research and observation), the chapter analyses the present situation and looks at historical changes in the provision of public sanitation and the administration of rubbish collection, using Ahmedabad, where public sanitation facilities are well advanced in comparison to the rest of Gujarat, as an example.

Chapter 4 traces changes in employment policies within the Ahmedabad Municipal Conservancy Department. Local authorities are the principal employers of sweepers and their employment policies greatly affect the numbers employed each year and the conditions of employment. The ratio of Bhangis among the sweepers, both male and female, is high, and it is no exaggeration to say that the employment policies of local authorities actually determine the level of income and standard of living of the Bhangis as a group. In addition, labour unions where sweepers are in the majority exert a very great influence on municipal employment policies as their pressure groups. Therefore the chapter also analyses the value of the historical role the main unions have played and their present situation.

Chapter 5 analyses the employment of temporary and permanent workers as recorded in the employment lists of the Conservancy Department of the Ahmedabad Municipal Corporation. The employment list gives a detailed record of all workers employed by the Municipal Conservancy Department as of December 1991. Therefore it can be used to make a comprehensive analysis, different from a sample survey. The analysis gives information about the present age of male and female workers, their period of work, and the number of years it took to promote from temporary to permanent worker. The influence of employment policies can also be discerned to some extent in the analysis.

Chapter 6 brings together the results of a survey I undertook in 1991 among Bhangi households in eight municipalities in Ahmedabad District. Because the sample focused on Bhangi households employed by local bodies, the analysis looks at a group of middle level income. Since among the Bhangis this level is very broad, it is safe to suggest general trends among Bhangi households from it. The survey of households was a socio-economic one, focusing on the educational and occupational structures, income and expenditure, and debts of the households and their members. Analysis was made in terms of gender differences and variations among local bodies.

The final chapter clarifies the place of this work in the history of research on the subject, and discusses the prospect of the Bhangi liberation movement from my own perspective.

## NOTES

1. The Constitution of India, promulgated in January 1950, comes to of 395 clauses and 10 supplementary clauses. Those concerning groups which have been historically discriminated against are as follows: Removing discrimination - 17, 23(1), 25(2); Preferential treatment economically and in education - 15(4), 19(5), 29, 30, 46, 164, 244, 338-42); Preferential treatment in Civil Service - 16(4), 335; Reserved seats - 330, 332, 342. Based on P.M. Bakshi (comp. and ed.), *The Constitution of India with Comments*, Delhi: Universal Book Traders, 1991.
2. The ratio of reserved seats in parliament, higher education and the public service is based upon the population ratio of these groups at both the national and state levels.
3. For the Other Backward Classes, see Government of India, *Reservation for Backward Classes: Mandal Commission Report of the Backward Classes Commission, 1980*, Delhi: Akalank Publications, 1991. In this book it should be noted that I designate Scheduled Castes, Scheduled Tribes and Other Backward Classes as Backward Classes.
4. The forced resignation of the Singh government at the Centre in 1990 was triggered by the reservation policy issue, and the Solanki government in government collapsed because of anti-reservation policy riots.
5. Caste Associations were formed within the process of reconstitution of castes that took place under British rule in order to promote upward social mobility. Many of their activities focused on establishing their new group identity.
6. There are many works on the ports of Gujarat, though most of them analyse Surat. See M.N. Pearson, *Merchants and Rulers in Gujarat*, New Delhi: Munshiram Manoharlal, 1976; P. Nightingale, *Trade and Empire in Western India 1784-1806*, Cambridge: Cambridge University Press, 1970.
7. For land tax policy under British rule and its effects, see G. D. Patel, *The Land Revenue Settlements and the British Rule in India*, Ahmedabad: Gujarat University, 1969, pp. 101-12; and Hiroshi Fukazawa, 'Agrarian Relations: Western India', in Dharma Kumar (ed.), *The Cambridge Economic History of India*, Vol. 2: *c. 1757-c. 1970*, Cambridge: Cambridge University Press, 1982, pp. 188-206.
8. Materials concerning the history of Gujarat include: S. B. Rajyagor, *History of Gujarat*, New Delhi: S. Chand & Co., 1982; M.S. Commissariat, *A History of Gujarat,* Vols. I - II, Bombay: Orient Longman, 1938, 1957; Edalji Dosabhai, *A History of Gujarat: From the Earliest Period to the Present Time,* New Delhi: Asian Education Services, 1986 (1st pub. 1894); B.M. Malabari, *Gujarat and the Gujaratis*, Delhi: Mittal Publications, 1983 (1st pub. 1889); J.W. Watson, *History*

*of Gujarat*, New Delhi: Cosmo Publications, 1983 (1st pub. 1876); Vijaysingh Chavda, *Modern Gujarat: Reflections on Sources, Historiography, Society, Economy and Culture*, Ahmedabad: New Order Book Co., *c*. 1967; idem, *A Select Bibliography of Gujarat: Its History and Culture 1600-1857*, Ahmedabad: New Order Book Co., 1972; and, concerning Muslims, S.C. Misra, *Muslim Communities in Gujarat: Preliminary Studies in Their History and Social Organization*, New Delhi: Munshiram Manoharlal, 1985. The gazetteers published during colonial times have not been included here.

9. Gazetteers of each of the 19 new districts created since Independence have been published but, concerning caste, have tended to incorporate descriptions from the older works and do not show any originality. The first of the new gazetteers was issued in 1968, and the last in 1984 (Government of Gujarat, *District Gazetteer*, 19 vols., 1968-84).
10. For conditions of agricultural labour before Independence, see M.B. Desai, *The Rural Economy of Gujarat*, Bombay: Oxford University Press, 1948, pp. 155-61. For conditions of tribal agricultural workers after Independence, see J. Breman, *Of Peasants, Migrants and Paupers: Rural Labour Circulation in West India*, New Delhi: Oxford University Press, 1985, pp. 260-316.
11. For social relations among Patidars, including marriage, see D.F. Pocock, *Kanbi and Patidar: A Study of the Patidar Community of Gujarat*, Oxford: Oxford University Press, 1972, pp. 126-63; for a detailed examination of the patriotic peasants' movement, see D. Hardiman, *Peasant Nationalists of Gujarat: Kheda District 1917-1934*, New Delhi: Oxford University Press, 1981, pp. 86-113; and for a compact description of the history of the economic activities of the Patidars, see Bremen, op. cit., pp. 79-114. Bhatt has analysed the function of the Patidar Caste Association in the development of regional politics in Anil Bhatt, 'Caste and Political Mobilisation in a Gujarat District', in Rajni Kothari (ed.), *Caste in Indian Politics*, New Delhi: Orient Longman, 1986 (1st pub. 1970), pp. 299-339.
12. Concerning the formation and development of the Gujarat Kshatriya Sabha, see Ghanshyam Shah, *Caste Association and Political Process in Gujarat: A Study of Gujarat Kshatriya Sabha*, Bombay: Popular Prakashan, 1975, pp. 33-63. A detailed analysis is found in R. Kothari and Rushikesh Maru, 'Federating for Political Interests: The Kshatriya of Gujarat', in R. Kothari (ed.), op. cit., pp. 70-101.
13. Changes in the number of assembly members according to the sect and caste is analysed in Ghanshyam Shah, *Class Formation and Dominance in Gujarat*, Surat: Centre for Social Studies, 1984, pp. 49-52; and in Pravin Sheth, 'Caste, Class and Political Development,' in D. T. Lakdawala (ed.), *Gujarat Economy: Problems and Prospects*, Ahmedabad: SPIESR, 1983, pp. 196-201. It was Pravin Sheth who coined the name of the KHAM alliance that constituted the backbone of the Solanki government: Kshatriya, Harijan (Scheduled Castes), Adivasi (Scheduled Tribes), Muslims. This expression was later employed in journalism.
14. For an analysis of the background to the anti-reservation agitation in Gujarat, see I.P. Desai, 'Anti-Reservation Agitation and Structure of Gujarat Society', pp. 124-36; and P.K. Bose, 'Social Mobility and Caste Violence: A Study of the Gujarat Riots', in I.P. Desai et al., *Caste, Caste Conflict and Reservation*, Delhi: Ajanta Publications, 1985, pp. 137-47; Ghanshyam Shah, 'Middle Class Politics: Case of

Anti-Reservation Agitation in Gujarat', *Economic and Political Weekly*, 22 (19-21) (May 1987), pp. 155-72; See also Pravin Sheth and Remesh Menon, *Caste and Communal Timebomb*, Ahmedabad: Golwala Publications, 1986, which includes details of the circumstances of the anti-reservation riots of 1985.

15. The nature of the backwardness of the Scheduled Castes, Scheduled Tribes and Other Backward Classes is, at the most basic level, common among all the three groups. These include economic factors like lack of resources and low levels of income and social factors, such as a poor living environment and a low level of education.In the case of the Scheduled Castes, the various forms of discrimination suffered as a result of untouchability must be added. The Scheduled Tribes tend to be concentrated in backward areas, and are disadvantaged in economic terms. The Other Backward Classes are not considered to suffer the same degree of backwardness as the other groups, but they tend to have been less favourably treated by institutional reforms such as the reservation policy, and may be considered to comprise classes who have remained outside the economic advances and institutional reforms which have taken place since Independence. However, as the designation of these Other Backward Classes had been left to the states, there is in fact a great deal of variation in their social and economic conditions among states.
16. The term 'depressed classes' was used publicly by the authorities for the first time in the 1910s with the same meaning as 'untouchables', but there were many difficulties in determining what it meant exactly and to which groups it should be applied, so great were regional variations in caste structure and discrimination towards untouchables. The Government of India Act of 1935 employed the term 'scheduled castes' in place of 'depressed classes'. The term 'backward classes' appeared for the first time in the 1880s. At first it was a general term for the destitute classes and included the untouchables, but as the concept of depressed classes rose to the fore, it lost its general application and was applied to others than the depressed classes. Tribal people were called variously Aboriginals, Primitive Tribes or Hill and Forest Tribes, but after the Government of India Act of 1935 they were called 'scheduled tribes'.
17. The Twenty-Point Programme, which was at the centre of the campaign to eradicate poverty (*Garibi Hatao*), was instituted by Indira Gandhi (1917-84) in 1975. This programme, which focused on the lowest classes, such as the Scheduled Castes and Tribes, was part of a policy to strengthen the support base of the Congress-I, but as a result of coercive measures, such as the Emergency, Indira Gandhi fell from power in 1977. She became Prime Minister again in 1980 and issued a revised Twenty-Point Programme in 1982, which remained at the centre of the Five Year Plans of both the central and state governments. The provisions of the revised programme include: the extension of irrigation capability, re-distribution of agricultural land, enforcement of a minimum wage, rehabilitation of bonded labourers, the provision of land for dwellings and loans to build houses, the provision of potable water to villages, the electrification of villages, encouragement to plant trees and the extension of bio-gas plants, encouragement of voluntary family planning, application of welfare programmes to women, the growth of rural industries and small industries, slum improvement, and the suppression of black money. See V.R. Bhattacharya, *New Strategy of Development in Village India: Progress under Revised 20 Point-Programme*, New Delhi:

Metropolitan Book Co., 1983, pp. 3-10. The present policy to aid the poor promoted by the Gujarat state government is also based on the Twenty-Point Programme; the core schemes are the Integrated Rural Development Programme, and employment creation under the Jawahar Rozgar Yojana, which became the National Rural Employment Programme in 1989-90.

18. For its functioning and related problems, see Marc Galanter, 'Temple Entry and the Untouchability (Offences) Act, 1955', *Journal of the Indian Law Institute*, 6 (1964), pp. 185-95 and idem, 'Untouchability and the Law', *Economic and Political Weekly*, 4 (1-2) (January 1969), pp. 131-70.
19. I.P. Desai conducted a survey of 69 villages in 17 districts of Gujarat to look at specific areas of discrimination; for the results of the survey see I.P. Desai, *Untouchability in Rural Gujarat*, Bombay: Popular Prakashan, 1976. Prior to that he had published a report on one of those items, water facilities for Untouchables: *Water Facilities for the Untouchables in Rural Gujarat*, New Delhi: The Indian Council of Social Science Research (ICSSR), 1973.
20. Desai found that in 51 villages (74 per cent of the total) there was some kind of restriction on the use of the public water source by the Scheduled Castes. Before Independence, it was rare to find reserved water supplies for the Untouchables. Therefore, they had to request Caste Hindus to draw water for them, which was insulting and humiliating. After Independence, despite some restrictions on access to water sources, the Scheduled Castes in 62 villages (90 per cent) could procure own water sources. However, they were forbidden to enter Hindu temples in 61 (90 per cent) of the 66 villages in which temples existed. Desai, *Untouchability in Rural Gujarat*, pp. 51-5, 117.
21. Ibid. pp. 252-6.
22. The Gujarat State Government, through the Gujarat Agricultural Ceiling Act (1960) and its revision in 1976, designated 92,000 hectares of surplus land by 1985. Out of this, 20,000 hectares were redistributed to the Scheduled Castes, 10,000 hectares to the Scheduled Tribes, and 8,000 hectares to Other Backward Classes and cooperatives. Government of Gujarat, *Seventh Five Year Plan 1985-90*, p. 126.
23. In 1957 the National Development Council set up a Study Team under Balwantrai Mehta to investigate the reorganization of the local government structure. They recommended a three-tier system of local government: at the village (gram), block and district levels (Village Panchayat, Panchayat Samiti, and Zila Parishad). In 1958 the National Development Council endorsed the recommendations, and accordingly, the system known as Panchayati Raj has been introduced in the states and union territories. In Gujarat, the Panchayat Samiti is called the Taluka Panchayat and the Zila Parishad is called the District Panchayat. For details, see D.M. Muley, *Rural Development Administration: Problems and Prospects*, Allahabad: Chugh Publications, 1987, pp. 10, 20, 22-3; G.D. Patel, *The Land Systems of Union Territories of India*, Anand: Charotar Book Stall, 1970, pp. 520-1; Uday Mehta, 'The Impact of the Panchayati Raj on Rural India', in A.R. Desai (ed.), *Rural Sociology in India*, Bombay: Popular Prakashan, 1969, pp. 580-6.
24. Ghanshyam Shah has conducted a comparative study from a number of angles, such as voting behaviour, leadership structure, and support of the existing parties to examine how the Scheduled Castes and Tribes in Gujarat have used their

remarkably improved opportunities in the post-Independence period towards political participation, and the problems that they have faced as a result. Though the Scheduled Tribes (Adivasis) started such participation much later than the Scheduled Castes (Harijans), their political power has greatly increased in comparison to that of the Scheduled Castes, partly due to the larger size of their population and partly because they have not suffered the impediments of untouchability. Ghanshyam Shah, *Politics of Scheduled Castes and Tribes: Adivasi and Harijan Leaders of Gujarat*, Bombay: Vora & Co. Publishers, 1975, pp. 157-64.

25. For aspects of backwardness among the Scheduled Castes, see I.P. Desai, *Untouchability in Rural Gujarat*. For social and educational aspects of backwardness, see Government of Gujarat, *Report of the Socially and Educationally Backward Classes Commission*, vol. I, 1976, pp. 21-38; Government of Gujarat, *Report of the Socially and Educationally Backward Classes (Second) Commission*, vol. I, 1983, pp. 18-28, 35-6.

26. Obstacles and difficulties in achieving economic and social advancement among lower class groups, including the Scheduled Castes, have beem comparatively well studied. But little work has been done on types and extent of mutual support within high ranking castes in maintaining their preeminence. The high caste groups naturally tend to emphasize the need for the principle of competition when confronted by the reservation policy. However, their caste associations, production and distribution organizations, and chambers of commerce and industry have the character of exclusive, mutual benefit organizations. In commerce and industry in particular, their internal and inter-association ties are very strong.

27. The Vankar, most populous of the Scheduled Castes in Gujarat, gained political power through their participation in the Independence movement. The Chamar and the Garoda have also been active in forming caste associations, but most of the backward groups have not done so. The focus of internal reform in recent years has, as can be seen in the organs of caste associations and in their regulations, been on making weddings and funerals more simple and less expensive. For the Chamar, see Shalini Randeria, 'The Politics of Representation and Exchange among Untouchable Castes in Western India (Gujarat),' Ph. D. dissertation, Freien Universitat Berline, 1992, pp. 238-48. For the Shenva (same as the Senva) see Government of India, *Census of India 1961*, Vol. V, Part V-B, No. 2, *The Shenvas: A Scheduled Caste of Gujarat*, 1972, pp. 41-5.

28. G. Shah, op. cit., p. 159. Because the Scheduled Tribes in Gujarat are concentrated in the hills and mountains, they are backward in terms of education and occupation. The backwardness of the Scheduled Tribes is considerably different to that of the Scheduled Castes. Because the Scheduled Tribes are very populous, they form the core of the Backward Classes in Gujarat. The Tribal Research and Training Institute, which was associated with the Gujarat Vidyapith founded in Ahmedabad by Gandhi in 1920, and the Centre for Social Studies founded in 1970 in Surat by I.P. Desai, are the most active organs concerned with the study of the Scheduled Tribes. In terms of the amount of work done, studies on the Scheduled Tribes exceeds that of the Scheduled Castes in both quality and volume. The present analysis is confined to the Scheduled Castes, but I list here the principal studies that have been undertaken on the Scheduled Tribes in Gujarat. Ghanshyam Shah, *Economic Differentiations and Tribal Identity: A Re-study of Chaudhris*, Delhi:

Ajanta Publications, 1984 (a re-survey for comparative purposes with the socio-anthropological report made by B.H. Mehta in 1932-3 of the powerful Chaudhari tribe); Ghanshyam Shah, et al., *Tribal Education in Gujarat*, Delhi: Ajanta Publications, 1985; S.P. Punalekar and J. Ranadivi, *Tribal Education: An Inter-State Study*, Surat: Centre for Social Studies, 1984 (comparative study of Gujarat, Maharashtra and Rajastan); Jaganath Pathy, *Tribal Peasantry Dynamics of Development*, New Delhi: Inter-India Publications, 1984; Vimal Shah and Tara Patel, *Who Goes to Colleges? Scheduled Caste and Scheduled Tribe Post-Matric Scholarships in Gujarat*, Ahmedabad: Rachna Pratishthan, 1977. For a bibliography, see M.R. Mac, *Select Bibliography on Scheduled Tribes*, Surat: Centre for Social Studies, 1982.

29. For example, in the fourth century BC the Greek Megasthenes observed that occupations were hereditary and there were restrictions on marriages. In the eleventh century the Muslim scholar Biruni reported on restrictions governing occupation, marriage and communal eating. In the middle of the sixteenth century the Portuguese described restrictions regarding occupation, communal eating, etc., based on caste (bloodline) as being one feature of the local society.
30. The utility of this criterion was questioned and criticized after the 1921 census. This focused chiefly on the point that a horizontal criterion based on social and economic conditions is a more persuasive base to discuss differences in access to education and work than a vertical criterion based on religion. However, support for the utility of the vertical criterion was deep-rooted and the classification according to religion and sect remained in subsequent censuses. However, in censuses after Independence, the only caste data collected was that concerning the Scheduled Castes and Tribes.
31. With the introduction of the National Census, innumerable petitions were sent from a number of *jati* organizations voicing a concern about or seeking a new ranking for that which had appeared in the census. Some of them sought to be considered Brahman. The census committee made careful inquiry about the circumstances and when necessary carried out a change in classification.
32. The survey covered the eight provinces of Bombay, Madras, Bengal, the United Provinces, Punjab, Burma, the Central Provinces and Assam and was undertaken as a secondary task by the superintendent-in-charge of the census in each province. At first a small budget was assigned the task, but this ceased in 1909. It was based on a set of 27 ethnographic questions devised by John C. Nesfield, Denzil C.J. Ibbetson, and H.H. Risely in 1885, covering the following topics: the nomenclature of castes and sub castes; the limits within and beyond which marriage is prohibited, and prohibitions based on other factors, such as social status, occupation, religion, etc.; traditions concerning the origin of the caste; whether the caste is settled or not; whether infant marriage is practised; whether polygamy or polyandry is permitted; forms of the marriage ceremony; whether the remarriage of widows or the divorced is permitted and if so the forms of the marriage ceremony; laws of inheritance; religion and sect; gods and patron saints; whether Brahmans serve them as priests; the funeral of the dead; ceremonies performed for the propitiation of ancestors; types, forms and scope of traditional occupations; whether there is a custom of prostituting the women; and types of prohibition on sharing foods. The castes and tribes surveyed were classified into three groups: those with more than 100,000 members, those with between 5,000 and 100,000 members, and

those with fewer than 5,000 members. The survey was most detailed with regard to the first group, while bare reports were included for the third group. R.E. Enthoven, *The Tribes and Castes of Bombay*, Vol. I, Delhi: Cosmo Publications, 1975 (1st pub. 1920), pp. i-iii, 377-9.

33. The views of India held by Karl Marx (1818-83), Friedrich Engels (1820-95) and Henry Maine (1822-88) on India were formed within this interaction, and their theories concerning Asian despotism and village communities exerted an enormous influence on Western intellectual thinking on India.
34. Gen'ichi Yamazaki analyses the various hypotheses concerning the origin of caste as intermarriage among the varnas, occupational (John C. Nesfield, Denzil C.J. Ibbetson), religious (J.H. Hutton; Max Weber), Aryan family system (E. Senart), aboriginal (G. Slater), racial (H.H. Risley) and syncretic (N.K. Dutt). He also describes their various characteristics and the issues involved. Gen'ichi Yamazaki, 'Origins of Caste: A Consideration of Academic Theories', (Jap.), in *Ajia Keizai*, 14(9) (September 1973), pp. 38-57. See also Surajit Sinha, 'Caste in India: A Trend Report', pp. 233-35 and A.M. Shah, 'Historical Sociology: A Trend Report', in ICSSR, *A Survey of Research in Sociology and Social Anthropology*, Vol. I, Bombay: Popular Prakashan, 1974, pp. 434-5.
35. G.W. Briggs, *The Chamars*, Delhi: Low Price Publications, 1990 (1st pub. 1920).
36. Tracing the change in the number of articles appearing on caste in the leading journals in sociology and social anthropology, in India and abroad, S. Sinha has identified a sudden growth in their numbers after Independence: 16 through 1949, 56 between 1950 and 1959, and 168 between 1960 and 1970. He also observed changes in content. Before Independence interest was directed on the origin of caste and the historical development of the caste system. After Independence there was a great diversification in the field: caste and its connections with economics, politics, and social mobility, regional studies of caste, structural analyses of particular castes, and studies of caste ranking. S. Sinha, op. cit., p. 247. Sachchidananda has compiled a report about research on social change among the Scheduled Castes from Independence to 1970 based on the categories of social reform movements, Sanskritization and Westernization. Sachchidananda, 'Research on Scheduled Castes with Special Reference to Change: A Trend Report', ICSSR, op. cit., pp. 278-84. For a bibliography on Scheduled Caste studies, see M.R. Mac and G.V.S. Reddy, *Select Bibliography on Scheduled Castes*, Surat: Centre for Social Studies, 1983.
37. Representative studies include: M.N. Srinivas (ed.), *India's Villages*, Calcutta: West Bengal Government Press, 1955; F. G. Bailey, *Caste and the Economic Frontier*, Bombay: Oxford University Press, 1957; S.C. Dube, *Indian Village*, London: Routledge and Kegan Paul, 1955; O. Lewis, *Village Life in Northern India*, Urbana: University of Illinois Press, 1958; and M. Marriott, *Village India*, Bombay: Asia Publishing House, 1955.
38. The *jajmani* system is essentially a village system of division of labour based on client-worker relationships that entail the exchange of commodities and services among the agricultural, artisan, and service castes. Certain artisan and service castes, employed on an individual and hereditary basis by farming and land-owning families received grain after the harvest and a little money as reward for the commodities and provided services. The artisan and service castes called the farming families who were their patron 'jajman' and the farming families called

those who peformed services 'kamin'. Client relationships were also formed among artisan and service castes in other types of work. However, this did not mean that all commodities and services in the village were supplied by these relationships, and *jajmani* connections going beyond a single village also existed. The relationship between client and patron were supposed to be equal, but in reality powerful farming families in the village had the upper hand. W.H. Wiser clarified the workings of this system through the study of a North Indian village.

In this village (with a population of 754 in 161 households), Bhangis were also included in the client-patron relationship. According to Wiser, though the Bhangis had become Christians they continued to perform the role assigned to them before their conversion. This role entailed the cleaning of cesspools, latrines and roads. There were 14 latrines in the village (for women in purdah), and each family had a cesspool and a drainage ditch. Women cleaned the latrines daily and the cesspools and drains once or twice a week. Pigs were released early each morning to assist with the cleaning away of filth. Only on holidays did men clean the streets. Men also served as night watchmen, messengers and basket makers. Some worked for Europeans in the cities. They were paid twice a year by the *jajman*. W.H. Wiser, *The Hindu Jajmani System: A Socio-Economic System Inter-relating Members of a Hindu Village Community in Services*, Lucknow: Lucknow Publishing House, 1958 (1st pub. 1936), pp. 34-5. Today the patron-cleint relationships remain only among a few artisan and service castes such as carpenters and priests, due to the spread of a money economy, the institutional impact of land reform, changes in the demand structure and increased mobility, including migration. S. Commander, 'The Jajmani System in North India: An Examination of its Logic and Status across Two Centuries', *Modern Asian Studies* 17 (2), Cambridge, 1983, pp. 283-311, examines theoretically the features of the *jajmani* system and traces specific influences, such as population density, irrigation, introduction of cash payment, and technological changes.

39. Considerable differences can be seen according to population size and other local conditions, but generally bewtwen 10 and 30 castes live in a village. The class structure in rural areas is based on land holding, and there is usually considerable difference among castes in the size of land held. The dominant land owning caste in a village is generally dominant in terms of purity, education, and population and it also controls the Panchayat, the village self-governing body. Srinivas defined 'dominant caste' as the caste which actually controls the economic and social life of the village through its dominance, based on land holding, purity, economic power, education and population (all or any combination of them). M.N. Srinivas, *The Dominant Caste and Other Essays*, New Delhi: Oxford University Press, 1987, p. 97.

40. Methods of analysing general elections, as considered part of the study of politics, were refined after the fourth general election of 1967. Of particular influence were R. Kothari et al., *Context of Electoral Change in India: General Elections 1967*, Bombay: Academic Books, 1969; and A.J. Dastur et al. (eds), *Studies in the Fourth General Election*, Bombay: Allied Publishers, 1972. For Gujarat see D.N. Pathak, M.G. Parekh and K.D. Desai, *Three General Elections in Gujarat*, Ahmedabad: Gujarat University, 1966; Parvin Sheth, *Patterns of Political Behaviour in Gujarat*, Ahmedabad: Sahitya Mudranalaya, 1976.

According to Kothari, caste associations and federations seek their political and other interests, but show differing patterns of political development. Whereas caste associations are bound by endogamous ties, caste federations, made up of a number of different castes, use caste consciousness, based for example on common anti-Brahman or Kshatriya slogans, as a centripetal force, and so are free of endogamous marriage restrictions when pursuing their political and eonomic interests.In this sense the organization of caste federations is more flexible and secular. R. Kothari (ed.), *Caste in Indian Politics*, pp. 21-2. Rao also accepts this definition when analysing the Yadava organization. M.S.A. Rao, *Social Movements and Social Transformation: A Study of Two Backward Class Movements in India*, New Delhi: Manohar, 1987, p. 220.

41. With the amendment of Article 73 of the Indian Constitution in 1992, there has been a growing decentralisation of political power at the Panchayat level. In most of the states, including Gujarat, the Panchayat law has been revised and there is considerable interest in the trend the Panchayati Raj is taking. Studies of the Panchayati Raj take broadly two views, one stressing the dominance of upper, dominant castes in its working, and the other stressing the impact of institutional change. Shah holds the former view about Gujarat , while Sheth holds the latter. See their presentations at the Western Regional Workshop on Panchayats, Surat: Centre for Social Studies, 23-25 February 1994; Ghanshyam Shah, 'Decentralisation and Weaker Sections', and Pravin Sheth, 'Gujarat: Panchayati Development and Decay'.

42. Land reform was carried out under state authority. Because there were considerable variations among states in the structure of land ownership, the pattern of land management and the condition of labourers, the actual content of reform necessarily differed within each state. Research focusing on Gujarat has reported on the small land holding of the Scheduled Castes and on their lack of managerial skills (see for example, Vimal Shah and C.H. Shah, *Re-survey of Matar Taluka*, Bombay: Vora & Co., 1974, pp. 226-8 and Government of Gujarat, Directorate of Economics and Statistics, *Socio-Economic Review: Gujarat State 1993-4*, Gandhinagar, 1994, pp. 67-78 for the results of the agricultural census of 1990/1).

    Studies on land reform as one aspect of institutional reform (legal and actual) were vigorously pursued until the 1970s. Around that time, the focus of studies on agricultural economy gradually shifted to analyses of employment and class stratification corresponding to the increased population pressure on land and the permeation of the Green Revolution. In the 1980s, there was a significant growth in economic analyses that focussed on the relationship between the village and the outer world, which topics, such as migration and working in cities, and employment outside the farm and the village.

43. Galanter has constructed a balance sheet of 12 items to evaluate the reservation policy. Each item is made up of opposing concepts (the former is the positive side of the policy, the latter the negative side). (1) Redistribution, Diversion; (2) Representation, Mis-representation; (3) Integration, Alienation; (4) Acceptance, Rejection; (5) Integrity, Manipulation; (6) Incubation, Over Protection; (7) Mobilization, Enervation; (8) Stimulation, Sedation; (9) Self-Liquidation, Self-Perpetuation; (10) Fairness, Unfairness; (11) Secularism, Communalism; (12) Development, Stagnation; Marc Galanter, *Competing Equalities: Law and the Backward Classes in India*, New Delhi: Oxford University Press, 1984, pp. 81-2.

44. 'Social stratification' is a term devised by Pitirim Alexandrovich Sorokin (1889-1968) to distinguish social class. Individuals and groups hold a certain social position based on the standards of wealth, occupation and education and the possibilities they offer for social advancement. Social position is backed by ranking: social stratification is the systematization of this ranking. Social stratification theory focuses on subjects, among others, the social order, social equality and inequality, social justice, and authority. Caste is studied as a single structural unit of social stratification or as a system of social stratification itself. The advance or regression of individuals or groups within this system is related to the degree of mobility (the movement of people or resources, changing occupations, changes in attitude) achieved through the mobilization of their resources.
45. Those who see caste as a cultural phenomenon tend to see the caste system as a stagnant and exclusive system that is lacking in social mobility. Yogendra Singh divides these scholars into two groups, those who consider caste to be a phenomenon peculiar to India, and those who regard it as being universal. He includes Louis Dumont in the former group and Max Weber (1864-1920) and G.S. Ghurye in the latter. Yogendra Singh, 'Sociology of Social Stratification: A Trend Report', ICSSR, op. cit., p. 316. Among studies of the period 1950-60, the following provide on analysis of mobility. M.N. Srinivas, 'Mobility in the Caste System', in M. Singer and B.S. Cohn (eds.), *Structure and Change in Indian Society*, Chicago: Aldine Publishing Co., 1968, pp. 189-200; James Silverberg (ed.), *Social Mobility in the Caste System in India: An Interdisciplinary Symposium*, The Hague: Mouton Publishers, 1968; A. Beteille, *Caste, Class and Power*, Berkeley: University of California Press, 1965; F.G. Bailey, op. cit.
46. Sanskritization is the process by which groups from among the lower castes and tribes copy the customs, rituals, beliefs, ideology and lifestyles of the upper *varnas* (the twice-born [*dwija*]: Brahmans, Kshatriyas and Vaishyas) in order to raise their standing in local society (M.N. Srinivas, *Social Change in Modern India*, Bombay: Orient Longman, 1972 [1st pub. 1966] p. 6). Srinivas first called this concept Brahmanization, in a study of the Coorgs of south India, where he noticed the phenomenon that lower castes copied Brahman culture and rituals (M.N. Srinivas, *Religion and Society among the Coorgs of South India*, Bombay: Oxford University Press, 1952). Later sociological studies from other parts of India (for example, A.M. Shah and R.G. Shroff, 'The Vahivanca Barots of Gujarat: A Caste of Genealogists and Mythographers', in M. Singer (ed.) *Traditional India*, Philadelphia: American Folklore Society, 1959 showed the same phenomenon occurring with regard to the Kshatriyas and Vaishyas) found that *varnas* other than the Brahmans were also the objects of imitation and as a result started the use of the term Sanskritization.
47. Reference Group means some particular upper castes that provide some role models to individuals of lower castes for social development. Apart from this positive reference, there is negative reference, in which some particular castes are discriminated as a symbol of negative value. It is argued that this concept of Reference Group is useful for systematic explanation of mobility, which is built in the concepts put forward by Srinivas, such as Sanskritization or Westernization. Y.B. Damle, 'Reference Group Theory with regards to Mobility in Caste', in James Silverberg (ed.), op. cit., pp. 95-102; O.M. Lynch, 'The Politics of

Untouchability: A Case from Agra, India', in M. Singer and B.S. Cohn (eds.), op. cit., pp. 235-8.

48. In the 1970s there was a paradigm change; much discussion concerned the social background of the researcher and researchers grew more familiar with the connection between research and ideology. See, for example, S.C. Dube (ed.), *Social Sciences and Social Realities: Role of the Social Sciences in Contemporary India,* Simla: Indian Institute of Advanced Study, 1976, pp. 3-8, keynote address of the editor.

49. Regarding Gujarat, Bhatt provides an analysis of the relationship between inherent (i.e. castes), socio-economic (i.e. class) and political demensions. See, Anil Bhatt, *Caste, Class and Politics: An Empirical Profile of Social Stratification in Modern India,* New Delhi: Manohar, 1975. Apart from the study of I.P. Desai (op. cit.), a number of studies have appeared on the mobility of Scheduled Castes. These studies revealed a poor mobility of the Scheduled Castes in terms of education, occupation and land holding. See Y. Singh, 'Sociology of Social Stratification', ICSSR, *Survey of Research in Sociology and Social Anthropology 1969-1979,* Vol.2, New Delhi: Satvahan Publications, 1985, pp. 66-7.

50 Questuions concerning Srinivas' concept of Sanskritization had appeared already in the 1960s, but thc criticism intensified during the ideological debate of the 1970s for its Brahman-centrism. See, C. Parvathamma, 'The Remembered Village: A Brahmanical Odyssey', *Contributions to Indian Sociology* (New Series), 12 (1), 1978.

51 Most typical was the work of Mandelbaum, who put in order the vast amount of research that had taken place through to the 1960s. He was particularly interested in confirming groups which were the units of social relationships and studying their mutual relationships within the framework of continuity and change. In the absence of an analysis of institutional reforms, neither 'continuity' or 'change' was particularly clear. D.G. Mandelbaum, *Society in India,* Bombay: Popular Prakashan, 1987 (1st pub. 1972).

52 The research group of scholars at Cambridge University have traced the influence that the Colonial government and administrative system exerted on popular movements and the local power structure by the analysis of factions and patron-client relationships. Representative works of this period are C.J. Baker, *The Politics of South India 1920-1937,* New Delhi: Vikas Publishing House, 1976; G. Johnson, *Provincial Politics and Indian Nationalism: Bombay and the Indian National Congress 1880 to 1915,* Cambridge: Cambridge University Press, 1973; D.A. Washbrook, *The Emergence of Provincial Politics: Madras Presidency 1870-1920,* Cambridge: Cambridge University Press, 1976.

53. Representative research includes: Y. Singh, *Social Stratification and Change in India,* New Delhi: Manohar, 1977; Kathleen Gough, 'Indian Peasant Uprising', *Economic and Political Weekly,* 9 (32-34), 1974, pp. 1391-1412; idem., 'Colonial Economics in South East India', *Economic and Political Weekly,* 12 (13), 1977, pp. 541-54; Hira Singh, 'Kin, Caste and Kisan Movements: Some Questions to the Conventional Sociology of Kin and Caste', *The Journal of Peasant Studies,* 7 (1), 1979.

54. Louis Dumont, *Homo Hierarchicus: The Caste System and Its Implications,* Chicago: The University of Chicago Press, 1980 (1st pub. 1970).

55. See J.G. Phule, 'Slavery', in Y.D. Phadke (ed.), *Mahatma Phule Samagra*

*Vangmaya*, Bombay: Maharashtra Rajya Sahitya ani Sanskriti Mandal, 1980 (1st pub. 1969), pp. 71-4.

56. Subaltern is a borrowed word from Antonio Gramsci, which means the subordinate mass. Subaltern studies were organized by Ranajit Guha and several other enterprising historians to rewrite the history of India as a critique of elitist interpretation of history. This school of Historians, with sharp and critical viewpoints, influenced not only other Historians but also researchers in other related subjects. See Ranajit Guha (ed.), *Subaltern Studies 1-8*, New Delhi: Oxford University Press, 1982-94 (the editors of the seventh volume are Partha Chatterjee and Gyanendra Pandey, and those of the eighth volume are David Arnold and David Hardiman).

57. Most of the studies after the eighties analyse the impact of institutional changes and educational, occupational mobility of the Scheduled Castes. See, for example, Nandu Ram, *The Mobile Scheduled Castes: Rise of a New Middle Class*, Delhi: Hindustan Publishing Co., 1988, pp. 113-20; S.N. Chaudhary (ed.), *Changing Status of Depressed Castes in Contemporary India*, Delhi: Daya Publishing House, 1988, pp. 12-3; S.M. Dahiwale, *Emerging Entrepreneurship among Scheduled Castes of Contemporary India: A Study of Kolhapur City*, New Delhi: Concept Publishing Company, 1989, pp. 87-102; C. Parvathamma, *Scheduled Castes and Tribes: A Socio-Economic Survey*, New Delhi: Ashish Publishing House, 1984, pp. 279-82; S. Selvanathan, *Status of Scheduled Castes*, New Delhi: Ashish Publishing House, 1989, pp. 224-31; Jacob Aikara, *Scheduled Castes and Higher Education: A Study of College Students in Bombay*, Poona: Dastane Ramchandra & Co., 1980, pp. 104-5; Joseph Benjamin, *Scheduled Caste in Indian Politics and Society*, New Delhi: Ess Ess Publications, 1989, pp. 245-6; R.K. Sinha, *Alienation among Scheduled Castes*, Delhi, Manas Publications, 1986, pp. 292-5; S.K. Sharma, *The Chamar Artisans: Industrialisation, Skills and Social Mobility*, Delhi: B.R. Publishing Co., 1986, pp. 148-53.

58. The Sweeper caste is made up of a large number of sub castes. I have mentioned here the names or designations of the representative sub-castes. See P.K. Chaudhary, 'Problems of Female Scavengers of Patna', in D.N. Chaudhary (ed.), op. cit., p. 148. A list of sub castes based on the Scheduled Castes and Scheduled Tribes Orders (Amendment) Act, 1976, can be found in Government of India, *Census of India 1981*, Series 1 India, Part IX (i), Special Tables for Scheduled Castes/ Scheduled Tribes, pp. 8-75.

59. The custom of consuming bhang extracted from hemp at festivals is still prevalent in India. The interpretation connecting bhang with bamboo processing is supported by many researchers since basket making is one of the traditional economic activities of the Bhangis. While, Crook considers the origin of the word to be from the Sanskrit 'bhanga', which suggests 'a drinking habit'. See W. Crook, *The Tribes and Castes of the North Western India*, Vol.1, Delhi: Cosmo Publications, 1974 (1st pub. 1896), pp. 259-60. Ghurye connects the origin of the word with the idea of ex-communication from society. See G.S. Ghurye, *Caste, Class and Occupation*, Bombay: Popular Book Depot, 1961, p. 32. Taking into account the common usage of the word among the lower classes, Issacs insists that the original meaning was 'an isolated people'. See H.R. Issacs, *India's Ex-untouchables*, Bombay: Asia Publishing House, 1965, p. 53.

60. Though researchers have been generally keen to trace the relationship between

traditional occupations and actual occupational structure of castes (particularly of the artisan castes) and its change over time, only a very limited number of research studies are available in the field of history and economic history as Dharma Kumar lamented. See Dharma Kumar, (ed.), *The Cambridge Economic History of India*, Vol. 2: *c.1757-c.1970*, Delhi, 1982, p. xviii.

From the series of censuses conducted before Independence, we can trace the number of workers among selected castes, tribes or races who were engaged in their traditional occupations. For example, the 1931 census of the Bombay Presidency compiled the number of workers engaged in their traditional occupations among the following 22 groups, such as the Bhangi (Scavengers; the ratio of workers engaged in traditional occupations among total workers were 50 per cent among males and 43 per cent among females, respectively); the Bharwad (Shepherds and Wool Weavers; 24 per cent and 15 per cent); the Chambhar/Mochi (Shoemakers; 60 per cent and 19 per cent); the Darji (Tailors; 63 per cent and 53 per cent); the Dhobi (Washermen; 55 per cent and 50 per cent); the Hajam (Barbers; 69 per cent and 5 per cent); the Koshti (Weavers; 53 per cent and 61 per cent); the Kumbhar (Potters; 64 per cent and 50 per cent); the Lohar (Blacksmiths; 72 per cent and 20 per cent); the Mahar/Dhed (Village Servants; 15 per cent and 7 per cent); the Mang (Village Servants and Tanners; 36 per cent and 31 per cent); the Panchal (Workers in Gold, Copper, Silver and Brass; 72 per cent and 9 per cent); the Ramoshi (Watchmen; 16 per cent and 3 per cent); the Soni (Goldsmiths and Jewellers; 76 per cent and 9 per cent); the Sutar (Carpenters; 82 per cent and 10 per cent); the Teli (Oil Pressers; 31 per cent and 22 per cent); the Vaddar (Earthworkers and Masons; 61 per cent and 36 per cent); the Vanjari (Carriers; 29 per cent and 27 per cent); the Miharbahar (Indus Boatmen; 24 per cent and 11 per cent); the Europeans; the Anglo-Indians; the Zoroastrians (Traders; 15 per cent and 10 per cent). See *Census of India 1931*, Vol. 8, Bombay Presidency, Part 2, Statistical Tables, Bombay, 1933, pp. 296-7.

61. See R.E. Enthoven, *The Tribes and Castes of Bombay*, 3 vols, Delhi: Cosmo Publications, 1975 (1st pub. 1920, 1922).
62. J.M. Campbell (ed.), *Hindu Castes and Tribes of Gujarat*, 2 vols., Gurgaon: Vintage Books, 1988 (1st pub. 1901).
63. J.M. Campbell (ed.), *History of Gujarat: Ancient, Medieval, Modern*, Gurgaon: Vintage Books, 1989 (1st pub. 1896).
64. The articles on untouchability contributed by Gandhi to *The Young India* and *The Harijan* are compiled by Bharatan Kumarappa in the following book. See M.K Gandhi, *The Removal of Untouchability*, Ahmedabad: Navajivan Publishing House, 1954, pp. 193-204.
65. In 1932 Gandhi started fasting in the Yeravda Prison as a protest against the Government's move to introduce separate electoral seats for the Backward Classes. Only after the Government omitted the article providing the Untouchables separate seats in the revision of Communal Award, Gandhi stopped fasting on 26 September. This experience drove Gandhi to tackle the evil of untouchability in order to avoid the split of Hindu Society. As a result the Anti-Untouchability League was formed in October 1932, and was renamed as the Harijan Sevak Sangh in 1935.
66. N.R. Malkani, *Clean People and An Unclean Country*, Delhi: Harijan Sevak Sangh, 1971 (1st pub. 1965).

67. Ibid., pp. 40-56, 103-9.
68. Shyamlal, *The Bhangis in Transition*, New Delhi: Inter-India Publications, 1984.
69. In the nineteenth century under British rule, several religious movements were organized by Indians to counter the inflow of Western culture and thought. The Arya Samaj, one of the Hindu religious reform associations founded by Dayanand Saraswati in 1875, tried to revive the study of Vedas in India, under the slogan of 'return to Vedas', and organized several social work programmes for the lower classes. For details on this movement, see. S.K. Sharma, *Social Movements and Social Change: A Study of Arya Samaj and Untouchables in Punjab*, Delhi: B.R. Publishing Co., 1985, pp. 25-43; R.L. Raval, *Socio-Religious Reform Movements in Gujarat During the Nineteenth Century*, New Delhi: Ess Ess Publications, 1987, pp. 139-41, 173-6.
70. Shyamlal, op. cit., pp. 46-7.
71. Ibid., p. 70.
72. Ibid., p. 73.
73. Shyamlal, *The Bhangi: A Sweeper Caste Its Socio-Economic Portraits with Special Referenbe to Jodhpur City*, Bombay: Popular Prakashan, 1992.
74. Ibid., pp. 54-8.
75. Ibid., pp. 142-3.
76. Bindeshwar Pathak, *Road to Freedom: A Sociological Study on the Abolition of Scavenging in India*. Delhi: Motilal Banarsidass, 1991.
77. Ibid., p. 22.
78. Ibid., pp. 76-84.
79. Central Gandhi Smarak Nidhi was founded in Delhi by the prominent Gandhian, Appasaheb Patwardhan, in 1956. In the same year Bhangi Mukti Samiti was set up in the Smarak Nidhi for the liberation of scavengers all over India. Later in 1962, Mamasaheb Deoginkar set up the Maharashtra Gandhi Smarak Nidhi.
80. Safai Vidyalaya was founded by the Harijan Sevak Sangh in 1963 in the premises of the Sabarmati Ashram, Ahmedabad. The present director, Dr.Ishwarbhai Patel, has been in charge of the institution from the beginning, and has developed both hard and soft programmes for the liberation of the Bhangis.
81. Pathak, op. cit., p. 41.
82. Ibid. p. 93.
83. Ishwarbhai Patel, *Safai Marg-Darshika* (A Guide Book on Sanitation), Delhi: Harijan Sevak Sangh, 1970.
84. Hazari, *I Was An Outcaste: The Autobiography of An 'Untouchable' in India*, New Delhi: The Hindustan Times, 1957 (1st pub. 1951).

Chapter One

# Scavengers in Government Reports

## INTRODUCTION

In most countries sanitation work (scavenging) and cleaning (sweeping) are considered to be menial jobs and sanitary workers tend to suffer certain forms of social discrimination. In India, such social discrimination has become formalized by making cleaning the traditional occupation of a particular caste. This makes India an extreme case. The Bhangis, whose 'traditional' occupations cleaning, are regarded as the most unclean of all the *jatis* of the Scheduled Castes—the lowest strata of the caste system. They are discriminated against religiously, economically and socially not only by Caste Hindus, but by members of other *jatis* of the Scheduled Castes as well.

Cleaning may be divided broadly into road and household cleaning, drain and sewer cleaning, cleaning out latrines, cleaning hospital wards, carting away rubbish, and disposing of animal carcasses. These activities are mainly performed by a special Sweeper caste. The working environment varies widely with the type of work done. This study uses the term 'sweeper' for those involved with household and road cleaning, and rubbish disposal, whereas the term 'scavenger' is applied to labourers who remove human waste directly from dry latrines and carry it away, and to those who are involved with its final disposal.

Dry latrines were most prevalent at the time of Independence and large numbers of scavengers worked under appalling conditions. After Independence, the central and state governments set up several committees with the aim of improving their working and living conditions. This chapter studies four reports by such committees in order to trace trends in the employment and labour conditions of the scavengers, and in the public management of waste disposal.

## AN OUTLINE OF THE REPORTS

Three of the reports to be examined were made by enquiry committees of the central government and one by an enquiry committee set up by the Bombay state government. The Bombay report has been included here because it is the first report of national importance. It had considerable influence on the other three reports.

### (1) *Report of the Scavengers' Living Conditions Enquiry Committee (The Barve Committee)*[1]

#### (A) BACKGROUND

The Barve Committee was set up as a direct result of a proposal made by the state legislator V.N. Naik on the occasion of the 51st meeting of the Backward Class Board, held at Kolhapur on 10 June 1949. It suggested that the state government conduct a survey of the living conditions of scavengers, improve their working conditions and guarantee them a minimum wage, to which end a committee of five or more members should be set up. The proposal was carried unanimously. Following this, the Education and Industries Department of the Bombay state government set up the Scavengers' Living Conditions Enquiry Committee, with nine members, on 1 August 1949. One member, the Backward Class Welfare Officer, who had been put forward by the chairman of the Backward Class Board, acted as secretary.

Interest in the disposal of human waste had been rapidly growing after Independence. A number of important developments predated the setting up of the Enquiry Committee in 1949. The first was a motion brought forward by the Bombay state legislator H.I. Kalyani. He urged that state and district enquiry committees be set up to find ways of improving the working conditions of sweepers and scavengers employed by municipalities, Notified Areas and Town Areas. Furthermore, he added that two thirds of the committee members should be appointed from the sweepers and scavengers. There was lively debate over the motion, and although it was eventually withdrawn, the episode showed that the Minister of Health as well as the state government were seriously interested in the working conditions of sweepers and scavengers.

The second significant development was the meeting of the Maharashtra Provincial Harijan Sevak Sangh in August 1948. This meeting resolved to improve the working conditions of scavengers and to raise the level of the life of Bhangis, and set up a committee to move these resolutions. One of the members, V.N. Barve, was later to act as the chairman of the Scavengers' Living Conditions Enquiry Committee. Another member, Appasaheb Patwardhan, was a follower of Gandhi, who had performed satyagraha for permission to clean his own waste when he was in prison at Ratnagiri in 1933. Later he invented the Gopuri-style latrine, which could produce manure all of human waste. The conference of the Harijan Sevak Sangh in February 1949 resolved the abolition of the Bhangi monopoly on cleaning work, the compulsory education of Bhangi children to age 15, and the diffusion of the Gopuri-style latrine.

V.N. Naik, H.I. Kalyani and V.N. Barve were all appointed to the 1949 Enquiry Committee and were involved in the surveys and the compilation of reports. As was evident from the activities of the Harijan Sevak Sangh, it was the Gandhians who were at the fore-front to improve the living and working conditions of scavengers and sweepers.[2]

### (B) CONTENTS OF THE REPORT, MEMBERS OF THE COMMITTEE

The committee was initially intended to run for only two months, but it was later extended till 30 June 1951. During this time, the committee met seven times in conference and on-site inspections were also organized. Its report was published in 1958, and includes the following chapters: I Introduction, II Resume of the Committee's Work, III Historical, IV The Scope of the Committee's Work, V The Objectives, VI Elimination of the Hand Removal Method, VII Abolition of Gharaki or the Customary Rights of Scavenging, VIII Living Conditions, IX Improvement in the Condition of Scavenging Work, X Minimum Wages, XI Other Conditions of Service, XII Effect of the Proposals, XIII Some General Questions, XIV Conclusion. It thus incorporated a comprehensive range of issues concerning the living and working environment, including the minimum wage.

The chairman and the members determine the character of a committee. The state government, following the recommendations of the Backward Class Committee, appointed the following members: V.N. Barve (chairman), F.D. Ghodke (state legislator), H.I. Kalyani (state legislator), V.N. Naik (state legislator), P.L. Majmudar, B.U. Waghela, S. S. Naik, B.N. Rathod and P.H. Nanavati (the Backward Class welfare officer; secretary). The chairman and many of the members were Gandhians who, long before the committee was set up, had been concerned with the problems of sweepers and scavengers.

## (2) *Report of the Scavenging Conditions Enquiry Committee (The Malkani Committee)*[3]

### (A) BACKGROUND

Following in the footsteps of the Bombay state government, the Uttar Pradesh state government set up a committee to investigate the actual conditions of scavengers. However, it limited itself to wages, labour relations, labour conditions, educational facilities and housing problems. There was not much interest expressed in questions concerning labour tools and equipments, such as receptacles and wheelbarrows.

The Ministry of Health, investigating the reports of the various committees, decided that the recommendations of the Barve Committee would be applicable and beneficial to other states as well, and demanded their implementation in all states and union territories. The Ministry of Home Affairs also emphasized the importance of implementing the recommendations, and as a first step in improving the labour conditions of scavengers, it announced provision of wheelbarrows for scavengers and sweepers employed by municipalities, wherein 50 per cent of their purchase cost would be transferred to local bodies through the states. This plan was also broadened to include the provision of wheelbarrows by the state to privately contracted scavengers in local municipalities. In the middle of 1958, the Ministry of Home Affairs recommended providing Scheduled Caste and Scheduled Tribe colonies with the hygienic and economical Trench Latrine, which had been developed in Allahabad, and sent construction plans to all states. G.B. Pant, the Minister of Home Affairs appealed at a meeting of state Chief Ministers in April 1959 and again at a meeting of state ministers in charge of welfare in January 1960 that the carrying of human waste on the head be immediately and completely abolished. As a result, the Estimates Committee, in its 48th Report, recommended that the Ministry of Home Affairs attack the problem more directly and permit financial aid to be given to local municipalities, which wanted to improve the working conditions of scavengers.

The immediate cause for the setting up of the Malkani Committee was the conference of the Central Advisory Board for Harijan Welfare on 12 October 1957. Its chairman was G.B. Pant, the Minister of Home Affairs. During the conference, R. Bose, who later to become a member of the Malkani Committee, lodged a complaint about the transport of human waste on the head in some local bodies. In response, the chairman set up the six member Malkani Committee, for bringing about a plan to abolish that custom.[4]

## CONTENTS OF THE REPORT, MEMBERS OF THE COMMITTEE

The committee met for the first time on 3 January 1958, and decided to prepare a questionnaire. Questionnaires (2,678 in English and 320 in Hindi) were sent to all of the state governments, union territories, members of Parliament of both houses, state legislators and advisors, and to large numbers of social activists and non-government organizations. The committee also conducted inspections and surveys in the states of Andhra Pradesh, Bihar, Gujarat, Himachal Pradesh, Kerala, Madhya Pradesh, Madras, Maharashtra, Mysore, Orissa, Punjab, Rajasthan, Uttar Pradesh and West Bengal, and also in the Union Territory of Delhi. Its report was submitted in 1960.

The report includes the following chapters: I Introduction, II Cleaning of Latrines, III Transportation of Night-Soil, IV Wheelbarrows, V Implements, VI Night-Soil Depots, VII Dumping Grounds, VIII Underground Drainage, IX Design of Latrines, X Latrines on Railways, XI Customary Rights, XII Method of Scavenging in Foreign Countries, XIII Administrative Set-up, XIV Some General Aspects, XV Summary. The report presents an in-depth analysis of the structure of latrines and the labour involved in the disposal of human waste.

N.R. Malkani was elected chairman of the committee at the first meeting. A scholar strongly influenced by Gandhi, Malkani at that time was a member of the upper house of the Parliament. Other members included P. N. Rajabhoj (upper house), K.L. Balmiki (lower house), R. Bose (Orissa state legislator), N.S. Kajrolkar, and O.K. Moorthy (special official of the Ministry of Home Affairs) who was the secretary. Balmiki had been born into the sweeper caste in Uttar Pradesh.[5]

### (3) *Report of the Committee to Study the Working and Service Conditions of Sweepers and Scavengers (The Pandya Committee)*[6]

#### (A) BACKGROUND

The Government of India set up the National Commission on Labour on 24 December 1966 to survey the changes that had taken place in labour conditions since Independence and to recommend guidelines regarding wage levels, living standards, social security, industrial relations, labour legislation, and a system for labour surveys. The Commission set up a number of survey teams and committees to investigate labour issues, in detail, in a variety of industries. One of these was the Committee to Study the Working and Service Conditions of Sweepers and Scavengers; it came into being in May 1967.

The committee was entrusted with the task of examining the following issues: (1) to ascertain the accuracy of documentary surveys, (2) to assess the problems inherent in bringing about improvements in the working and living condition of sweepers and scavengers, and to suggest policy and

(3) to analyse materials collected by the previous committees, which included the Barve Committee, the Malkani Committee, the Social Welfare Team of the Planning Commission of 1958, and the Special Working Group on Cooperation for Backward Classes, set up by the Ministry of Home Affairs in 1961.

The Pandya Committee was entrusted by the National Commission on Labour to study the debate held in the lower house of Parliament on 5 July 1967 to improve the working conditions of scavengers. The first member of the lower house to raise questions about the wages and working conditions of scavengers was K.L. Balmiki. In this speeches to the lower house on 14 March 1950 and again on 18 April 1966 he reiterated those issues. On 3 April 1966 the Minister of Labour, Jagjivan Ram, himself a member of the Scheduled Castes, emphasized the need to study the conditions of scavengers. These concerns led to the debate of 5 July 1967.[7]

## CONTENTS OF THE REPORT, MEMBERS OF THE COMMITTEE

The first meeting of the committee, held in New Delhi on 6-7 October 1967, decided to compile a questionnaire and conduct an inspection. The districts that were to be investigated are listed in Table 1.1. Though the committee hoped to examine the living and working conditions of scavengers and sweepers on a nationwide basis, it was not possible due to constraints of time, staff and the necessary facilities.

The report includes the following chapters: I Preface, II General Situation, III Wages and Allowances, IV Provisions for Rest Periods, V Hours of Labour, VI Employment, VII Uniforms and Protectors, VIII Social Security, IX Labour Relations and Labour Unions, X Dwellings, XI Health Facilities, XII Abolition of Bad Customs, XIII Health Survey, XIV Education, XV Debt, XVI Customary Rights, XVII Improvement of Labour Conditions, XVIII Administration and Finance, XIX Conclusion. A special feature of this Report is its analysis of the employment and working conditions of sweepers and scavengers, an emphasis that was missing in previous reports.

The committee initially consisted of Bhanuprasad Pandya (chairman), K.L. Balmiki, N.S. Kajrolkar, B. Raut (legislator), N.R. Malkani, Dev Raj and O.K. Moorthy. Moorthy, who had acted as secretary for the Malkani Committee, did not participate due to his study-visit to the United States. K.A. Sheth, Under Secretary of Labour in the Gujarat state government, was appointed in his place. Three of the six members of the committee had previously served in the Malkani Committee.[8]

### TABLE 1.1: PLACES SURVEYED BY THE PANDYA COMMITTEE

Andhra Pradesh:
(1) Hyderabad
(2) Secunderabad
(3) Nagarjunakonda
(4) Devarkonda

Assam:
(1) Gauhati
(2) Shillong

Bihar:
(1) Patna
(2) Tatanagar
(3) Mosaboni
(4) Aditpur
(5) Gaya
(6) Bihar Sharif
(7) Rajgir
(8) Begusarai

Delhi:
(1) Delhi

Gujarat:
(1) Ahmedabad
(2) Baroda
(3) Daboi
(4) Surat

Haryana:
(1) Chandigarh
(2) Ambala

Kerala:
(1) Trivandrum
(2) Kottayam
(3) Kumuli
(4) Cochin

Madhya Pradesh:
(1) Indore
(2) Bhopal
(3) Jabalpur
(4) Satna
(5) Chhattarpur

Madras:
(1) Madras
(2) Thanjavur
(3) Tiruchirappalli
(4) Madurai

Maharashtra:
(1) Nagpur
(2) Wardha
(3) Jalgaon
(4) Bombay
(5) Poona

Mysore:
(1) Bangalore
(2) Hassan
(3) Belur
(4) Mysore
(5) Mandya

Orissa:
(1) Bhubaneswar
(2) Cuttack
(3) Puri

Punjab:
(1) Chandigarh
(2) Rajpura

Pondicherry:
(1) Pondicherry
(2) Karaikal

Rajasthan:
(1) Jaipur
(2) Amber
(3) Achrol
(4) Alwar
(5) Tijara

Uttar Pradesh:
(1) Varanasi
(2) Allahabad
(3) Kanpur
(4) Lucknow
(5) Dehradun
(6) Mussorie
(7) Hardwar
(8) Rishikesh

West Bengal:
(1) Calcutta
(2) Durgapur
(3) Bolpur

SOURCE: *The Pandya Committee Report*, p. 113.

### (4) *Report of the Task Force for Tackling the Problems of Scavengers and Suggesting Measures to Abolish Scavenging with Particular Emphasis on Their Rehabilitation (The Basu Task Force)*[9]

#### (A) BACKGROUND

Various committees had been set up after Independence to improve the working and living conditions of sweepers and scavengers. However, the manual collection of human waste continued to be practised even in the 1980s. As a result, in 1983 questions were raised in the lower house of the Parliament voicing the concerns about the delay in implementing measures to improve conditions of scavengers, with a demand that the government implement a time-bound programme to eliminate such bad practices. Indira Gandhi, the then Prime Minister, responded by saying that a programme of replacing old-style latrines and provision of an alternative occupation for scavengers would be put into action. Accordingly, the Planning Commission appointed the Task Force on 29 July 1989 to deal with the following issues: (1) to review and assess the dimension of scavenging in terms of population, families, and towns, (2) to analyse the full magnitude of the problem, (3) to examine the type of intervention including legal measures required, and (4) to identify agencies to deal with this problem in a well coordinated manner.[10]

## CONTENTS OF THE REPORT, MEMBERS OF THE COMMITTEE

The Task Force met for the first time on 18 August 1989 and, after confirming the nature of its responsibilities, organized a sub-committee to estimate the scavenger population and the number of old-style latrines. The report of the Task Force was to be presented within six months. The second meeting was held on 26 October. The report was submitted, in time, to the Planning Commission.

The report includes the following chapters: I Introduction, II Constitution of Task Force, III Review of the Programme, IV Problems of Scavengers, Their Liberation and Rehabilitation, and V Assessment. Chapter 3 reviews the reports of the Barve, Malkani and Pandya Committees, as well as that of Professor Malkani's Committee on Customary Rights to Scavenging, 1965. It also assesses the results of the various programmes for scavengers since Independence. Chapter 4 discusses in detail the plans to discontinue the manual collection of human waste in terms of technological change, legal provision, and occupational change. Since the central concern of the report was to organize the information in existing reports and to evaluate earlier programmes, inspections or systematic surveys of actual conditions were not conducted.

The Task Force included representatives from government departments concerned with the life, work and welfare of scavengers, and other advisory organizations, private and research institutions. The main government departments concerned were the Planning Commission, the Ministry of Health, the Department of Urban Development, the Department of Rural Development, and the Central Statistical Organization. Private institutions included the Harijan Sevak Sangh, Sulabh International, and Safai Vidyalaya. Twenty-six people from these organizations attended the first meeting of the Task Force; and nineteen attended the second meeting.[11]

## Evolution of Scavengers and Their Customary Rights

### *Evolution of Scavengers*

The *Barve Committee Report* provides a description of the process by which scavengers evolved – how scavenging came about and the people who became scavengers. Though the description is rather fragmentary the salient issues are outlined below.

#### BEFORE BRITISH RULE

The Artha Shastra (second century BC–second century AD) speaks of road sweepers (Pansu Dhavek) and cleaners of drains (Rajak), but dry latrines necessitating the collection of waste did not exist. Dry latrines came into existence in the Islamic period. It is mentioned in the report that the Rajputs, who were made prisoners in the course of the growing Muslim domination in India, were forced to dispose of human waste, but there is no actual proof to that affect. Words indicating latrine, such as *shet-khana* and *pakhana*, were in common use during the Mughal period. Immediately before the onset of British rule, wealthy urban classes were using cesspool privies (*soucha koop*) and well-privies (*duttans*). In addition, houses adjacent to natural drains (*nala*), had latrines which could be cleaned by domestic animals. Whatever the form, daily collection of waste by scavengers was not necessary. In both urban and rural areas, defecation was done out of doors.[12]

#### DURING AND AFTER BRITISH RULE

It is uncertain when dry latrines, which necessitated waste disposal, first appeared, but it appears they increased significantly in number with the establishment of urban municipalities under British rule.[13] The *Barve Committee Report* makes no further mention about the origin and development of dry latrines, but it is clear that scavengers emerged with the expansion of municipalities under British rule and the related increase in the number of dry latrines. It would not be incorrect to say, that they are a comparatively recent phenomenon.

Who were the scavengers? In Gujarat, the native Bhangis took on this task. However, in Maharashtra native scavenger groups were not formed, and scavenging was done by immigrant workers from Gujarat, Saurashtra, Rajsthan, Uttar Pradesh and the Punjab. In Karnataka, the disposal of human waste was carried out by immigrants from Gujarat, Saurashtra, Uttar Pradesh and particular districts of Madras like Bellary and Anantapur. These immigrants, in their places of origin, had been engaged in farming and odd jobs.[14] The *Barve Committee Report* does not mention the scale of immigration, but the fact that castes concerned with waste disposal originated from certain regions is an interesting research theme from the point of view of the dynamism of caste formation and local variation.

### *Customary Rights of Scavengers*

Will now examine issues concerning the evolution of scavengers in terms of their customary rights and the abuses to which they gave rise. Such customary rights are called *gharaki* or *gharagi* in Gujarat, and *jagirdari*, *dastoori*, and *virat* in northern India. They are hereditary rights, but can also be bought and sold or transferred. They are prevalent in Gujarat, Punjab, Rajasthan, Uttar Pradesh, Madhya Pradesh and Old Delhi.[15]

The customary rights of scavengers are of two types. The first is the right to clean dry latrines. Wages for the labour from the latrine owners are implied here. When we talk about customary rights of scavengers, the reference is usually to the first type. The second type is the right to dispose of and sell the human waste collected. It is found only in Punjab and western Uttar Pradesh, where there is a great demand for human fertilizer and where it commands a high price. Here scavengers run private waste disposal plants and distribute the income from the sale of human fertilizer among those who operate them. In other areas, human waste becomes the property of local bodies and is disposed of by them.[16]

## THE DEVELOPMENT OF CUSTOMARY RIGHTS

The *Barve Committee Report* provides on interesting excerpt, from the correspondence[17] of the Revenue Department dated 16 September 1938, setting out responsibilities of the Mahars, Dheds (also called Vankars) and the Bhangis towards the government.

> Bhangi had the duty of cleansing the courtyards and khadkis or private lanes and was entitled to receive bread, clothes and occasional gift of money from all the houses which he served. The vatandar Bhangis appear to have divided the village

or town into ward according to their shares and in each ward, the Bhangis had the customary right of cleansing street, etc. and taking the remuneration, . . . it appears that after the establishment of local bodies basket privies, i.e. privies with a receptacle came into vogue. Scavengers who had Gharaki rights of sweeping lanes and courtyards asserted their right to cleanse private latrines well, which came to be constructed in their areas. They considered the particular streets and mohallas as their private property so far as scavenging is concerned. The local bodies in these parts of Gujarat, where the customary rights prevailed allowed the latrines to by cleansed by the heriditary scavengers. In Maharashtra, Karnataka and those parts of Gujarat where the Bhangis were not indigenous the Gharaki right did not exist, the local bodies naturally assigned the work of cleansing private latrines to their own employees.[18]

Though a fragmentary description, it contains some important points about the evolution of customary rights. First, they are said to have developed from the Bhangi *vatandar* system. There were several labour division systems within and between villages during the medieval and modern periods, of which one was the *vatandar* system. A distinguishing feature of this system was that 12 types of workers (known as *varti*) at the core of the labour division, including carpenters, blacksmiths and potters, held the rights called *vatan*, which could be bought, sold, inherited or transferred. These rights were maintained by the local *vatan* farming community in the form of provision of rewards or tax exempt land, and confirmed by the rulers. Those outside these 12 specified occupations, such as oil pressers and weavers, had no *vatan*. Since the scale of *vatan* was limited by the demand for those specific services in a particular society, not all the workers in the 12 occupations held *vatan*. The *vatandar* system was the conceptualization of the form of division of labour that existed in the medieval Deccan.[19] By contrast, the *jajmani* system was the conceptualization of division of labour in northern Indian villages in the first-half of the twentieth century. In this system village craft and service castes had a specific work relationship with particular rural families through individual and hereditary ties; in formal terms this was a relationship of mutual gain but in reality the initiative was in the hands of powerful farming families. The term 'jajmani' was coined by W.H. Wiser in the 1930s as a result of his studies among rural communities in northern India.[20] Further, besides these two, there is another category of independent small producers. Very little is known about the mutual relationships among the three in terms of geography or time.

Looking at the report we find that the customary rights of scavengers have common characterstics with the *vatandar* system. First, the right to provide services is limited to the *vatan* holder. Second, the *vatan* holders alone can decide unilaterally their localities of work according to the shares they own. Third, those receiving the services cannot change the provider. Fourth, customary rights can be bought, sold, inherited or transferred. In light of this, the report's view that the customary rights of scavengers originated in Bhangi *vatan* rights is essentially valid. However, it is unclear whether this is equally applicable to areas outside western India.

The second point made in the report is that customary rights of scavengers evolved out of rights directly associated with street cleaning. The report's view that customary street-cleaning rights subsumed scavenger rights with the spread of dry latrines is very persuasive. If we accept the validity of this view, then *vatan*-holding Bhangis must have held two types of customary rights street-cleaning and scavenging in their own wards at the time when the use of dry latrines became widespread.

The report says nothing about the later development of the customary rights of scavenging or street-cleaning. However, since the rights of street cleaning did not make an issue in the report, we can surmise a process whereby street-cleaning rights disappeared at latest by the middle of the twentieth century. Local bodies incorporated the cleaning of public and some private roads and the collection of rubbish under their jurisdiction, while they did not immediately interfere with the scavenging rights regarding private latrines. As a result of this, the customary rights of scavenging remained as a major issue.

The third point put forward in the report is that in areas where there were no inherent Sweeper castes, customary scavenging rights did not develop. Since there is no further discussion on this subject, there are many questions that remain unanswered. Who cleaned the dry latrines in these areas? Did latrine cleaners possess customary sweeping rights? Did members of the sweeper caste who migrated from other areas not assert their customary sweeping and scavenging rights in the places where they settled? Why did customary scavenging rights not develop? At all events, it was easy for local bodies to undertake responsibility for the cleaning of private latrines in regions where customary scavenging rights did not exist.

## PROBLEMS ASSOCIATED WITH CUSTOMARY RIGHTS

Let us now look at some of the problems arising out of the customary scavenging rights. The first is the low quality in the service of latrine cleaning. Owners of private latrines cannot employ persons other than those who have the rights to clean them. Even if the service is not fully carried out or is substandard, latrine owners have no power of negotiation. The scavengers, for their part, have little sense of pride in their work, for it is unhygienic and poorly paid. Thus the cycle continues, the work is poorly done and the unhygienic conditions persist unchanged.

Second, in areas such as the Punjab and western Uttar Pradesh where scavengers own rights to sell and process human waste, local authorities cannot dispose of the waste that scavengers leave by the roadside and cannot intervene in the running of privately-owned waste disposal depots. As a result, towns as a whole are extremely dirty and unhygienic.

Third, the existence of customary scavenging rights has given birth to a subcontracting system. Some of those who own scavenging rights in an area, subcontract sweepers who do not have such rights to clean the dry latrines. Such people, who subcontract their rights, are called 'jagirdars' in northern India. They do not themselves perform the labour of latrine cleaning but take the full rewards from the latrine owners and only pay a nominal wage to the actual labourer. The Malkani Committee was able to contact several *jagirdars* and reported on the luxury of their houses and the rich and modern lifestyles.[21] The subcontracting system is wide spread in areas where traditional rights remain. Since labourers working under *jagirdars* are extremely dissatisfied with their wages and working conditions, they are perfunctory in the performance of their work, which results in the lowest standard of service. The system of subcontracting latrine cleaning has widened class differentials within the Sweeper caste.

## Scavenging Work

### *The Labour Process*

Scavenging involves collecting human excreta from a latrine, taking the excreta first to a temporary collection point (pail depot) and then to a disposal depot, where it is treated. Various tools and methods are used in its collection and disposal. We shall now examine the labour involved and various problems that are inherent in this work.

#### COLLECTION OF HUMAN WASTE FROM DRY LATRINES

Houses with flush lavatories connected with a sewerage system do not require the services of scavengers. Septic latrines require periodic cleaning, but do not involve scavengers. Dry latrines (also called basket latrines, service latrines) on the other hand require scavengers on a daily basis. Because dry latrines generally have a receptacle to collect excreta, they are also known as receptacle latrines.

Dry latrines comprise a squatting chamber, a receptacle chamber and an anti chamber, a small space connecting the receptacle chamber and the extraction point. The squatting chamber lies within the house and is equipped with a pedestal. Very few are built to separate faeces, urine and clean water, but some have a disposal hole for urine and clean water in the front and one for faeces at the rear, the two being separated by a higher middle section. This is to prevent the mixing of urine and faeces. The user moves to the front section after evacuating in order to clean himself. Urine and water pass from the front section through a connecting pipe to be discharged outside the house. Faeces, on the other hand, fall directly onto the floor of the receptacle chamber from the rear extraction point.

Some dry latrines have a pan at the place where the faeces drop. However, because the receptacle chamber is too large for the size of the pan, cleaning remains difficult as the faeces soil the walls and bottom of the chamber. Moreover, the pan is not standardized and it may be a bamboo basket, an oil can, broken pottery, an old wooden box, a used suitcase or tub, or a bucket with holes.[22] In other words, it is something that is worn out and cannot be used for anything else. Because labourers have to handle pans of various shapes and material, it is impossible to work without touching the excreta. The arms and legs are invariably soiled when moving the excreta from pan to carrier.

The cleaning of latrines not fitted with a pan is even more unhygienic. It is estimated that between 80 and 90 per cent of dry latrines do not have a pan.[23] In this case, the faeces fall directly onto the floor of the receptacle chamber. The chamber is cleaned out using a sheet metal or tin pot, which cause the cement or stone floor of the chamber to become pitted over time; faeces get embedded in the cavities, making thorough cleaning impossible. Further, because of deficiencies in the construction of the pedestal and the receptacle chamber, the faeces may scatter about the chamber. In this case the labourer tends to remove only what can be easily taken out. Since washing is rarely done, the receptacle chamber is always extremely dirty.

Structural deficiencies in the anti chamber too make the scavenger's task even more wretched. If it is narrow and long, the labourer must stretch his arm in through the extraction point, and at times even crawl into the anti chamber, in order to remove the faeces. If it is low in the ground, rain water will flood the receptacle chamber making the removal of faeces both unhygienic and difficult.

The main defects of existing dry latrines are: (1) the pedestals are not standardized, (2) the connecting pipe from the evacuation point of the front section is either too long or too wide, (3) the placement of the pedestal is not aligned with that of the pan, (4) because of structural defects in the pedestal, urine and water fall into the receptacle chamber, (5) because the receptacle chamber is too wide and long the faeces miss the pan, (6) because the anti chamber is narrow and low, removal of faeces is difficult, (7) many receptacle and anti chambers are constructed of absorbent material, (8) because the pipe connecting the extraction point of the front section is often linked with an open drain, the drain is dirtied, and (9) even when the extraction point of the front section is connected directly with a cesspool, it would easily overflow if the cesspool does not have a large capacity.[24]

### TRANSPORTATION OF HUMAN WASTE

Waste collected from dry latrines is transported in containers, such as a bamboo basket, a drum can or a bucket. A bamboo basket is the most widely used. Leaves, grass, paper or ashes are usually spread at the bottom of the basket to prevent leakage, and sometimes cattle dung is smeared to harden the surface. However, most labourers do not do anything to make their containers waterproof. In Orissa people carry these bamboo baskets on their hip, but in other states the general custom is to carry the baskets of waste on the head to a nearby wheelbarrow or bullock cart, or sometimes as far as the pail depot. If such facilities do not exist, labourers have to take the waste directly to the disposal depot. It is not unusual, due to inadequate waterproofing or holes in the container, for the waste to leak onto the head and body of the labourer while transporting it. Conditions are worst during the rainy season, when rain water causes the waste to liquefy and overflow. No lids or covers are used. The transportation of human waste is said to be an insult to the dignity of society and human beings.

The distance that waste has to be carried on the head, between the latrine and the bullock cart or pail depot averages between 2 fur. (402 m.) and a mile (1.6 km.). It has been found that in order to decrease the number of trips between these two points, labourers would often carry overflowing baskets or drums of waste, returning in streets marked by a trail of excrement. Many female labourers, in order to avoid the trip to the pail depot, would abandon the waste on street corners or in open drains. They would break up the faeces with a stick or their feet to prevent the drain being blocked. This is usual even in the Punjab, where human waste is considered the wealth of the scavenger and where human fertiliser fetches a high price.

The cleaning out of cesspools, where urine and water accumulate, is also the work of scavengers. The labourers take out the dirty water from the cesspool in buckets and pour it into drum cans, carrying these on their heads to the bullock cart. Both the removal of the dirty water and its transportation are unhygienic.

Scavengers use bullock carts to transport waste from the pail depots to the disposal depots. The carts filled with human waste, move very slowly; flies congregate around the open cans and the air is filled with a putrid smell. Most bullock carts are used both for transporting this waste and for collecting rubbish, and the labourer sitting in one corner of the cart gets covered with rubbish during the trip to the depot.[25]

### DISPOSAL DEPOTS FOR HUMAN WASTE

Trench depots are commonly used for this purpose. A single trench - measures on an average from 180 (12 x 5 x 3) to 315 (15 x 7 x 3) sq. ft. Local bodies run depots which are not privately owned. Most of the depots are built in the vicinity of housing areas. The processing capacity of these depots, generally very small, does not meet the needs of the local population. Barring a few municipal depots, even running costs cannot be met by the profits from the sale of human fertilizer.

Since waste and rubbish are thrown into trenches without adequate treatment, depots are plagued by flies and a bad smell. Labourers do not even have basic provisions like gloves, boots and adequate means of transportation, and so the work is made even dirtier. Handling the overflowing drum cans, they become mired with waste. Workers blackened till their knees and elbows with excreta are a common sight at all depots. They have to wear their soiled clothes all day. There are no paved pathways between trenches and no shade from the sun. Labourers have to work under precarious conditions and beneath a blazing sun. Further, even in cities with adequate water supply, there is little provision of it within the depots. In many cities there is none at all. Since water for drinking and cleaning is inadequate, labourers have to scrape away with their hands and nails the excrement that had stuck to their tools such as drum cans. Depot labour is, perhaps, the most unhygienic of all of the work associated with the cleaning of latrines. These workers are all male.[26]

*Recommendations of Government Reports*

The success of plans to abolish the disposal of human waste by hand depend on the diffusion of sewers and flush latrines. However, building a sewerage system is very costly and there is no prospect that sewers will become widespread in all cities in the short term. Provided these limitations, the various reports recommend ways to improve the working conditions of scavengers and to reduce the scale of their work.

The Barve Committee suggested a five point programme: (1) pipes from dry latrines should be connected with septic tanks, and not be permitted to flow into open drains, (2) bamboo latrine pans should be abolished and pans be standardized, being made of sheet metal and having handles, (3) the carrying of human waste on the head should be abolished, and bullock carts or wheelbarrows should be used, (4) when wheelbarrows or bullock carts are not available, buckets fitted with lids should be used and carried by hand to the pail depot, and (5) dirty water from septic tanks should not be carried on the head; as far as possible, pumps and wheelbarrows should be used.[27] The committee recommended that aqua-privies be used in large and medium-sized cities and Bhanoli type of pucca trench latrines in small cities and large villages. Neither of these requires the daily services of scavengers. The Bhanoli latrine involves the use of two concrete trenches in turn and can process faeces into fertilizer. The committee suggested the provision of government aid for converting the existing dry latrines. With regard to the existing pit-privies and well-privies, the committee recommended an inspection of the subsoil water for possible contamination. And also suggested that the construction of new latrines should require special permission from the Department of Public Health.[28] The report was essentially focused on local bodies in Bombay state, but since its recommendations were equally applicable to other states, the Ministry of Health forwarded and recommended it to local bodies in all the states and union territories. However very few states acted on the recommendations.

The Malkani Committee provided a more detailed analysis of the working conditions of scavengers and proposed a detailed plan for improvement. Recommendations included: (1) standardized pans, available at authorized outlets, should be made compulsory for all dry latrines; and those who fail to comply would be penalized by local bodies, (2) standardized scrapers should be made compulsory; they would be made available to scavengers by local bodies, (3) workers at pail and disposal depots should be encouraged to wear long boots and rubber gloves, (4) the carrying of human waste in bamboo baskets or drum cans on the head should be forbidden by law; the use of wheelbarrows, provided through aid funds, would be encouraged; and in places where wheelbarrows could not be used, covered buckets provided by the local authority should be used. (5) tractors, trailers and trucks should be used to transport human waste the state government should provide local bodies with sufficient funds to buy vehicles, (6) scavengers should be banned from cleaning out septic tanks; this should be done with a pump, (7) local bodies should put every effort into promoting the diffusion of sewerage and encouraging the adoption of flush latrines, (8) where sewerage is not available, local bodies should promote aqua-privies and septic latrines, and (9) local bodies should encourage households to convert their dry latrines by giving them financial help; the central and state governments should also encourage local bodies to do this.[29]

The central government, acting on these recommendations, provided Rs. 10.8 million during the third Five Year Plan (1961-6) to improve the working conditions of scavengers. Table 1.2 shows the amount assigned to each state and details regarding items purchased. The all India figures were as follows: 27,061 wheelbarrows, 3,025 single-wheeledbarrows, 1,122 scrapers, 1,104 buckets, 1,147 long boots and 663 pairs of rubber gloves were bought. However, the wheelbarrows were not used much at the workplace, for the following reasons: (1) there were too many designs and in most cases were unsuitable for local conditions, (2) they could not be used in narrow or unpaved lanes, (3) they were too heavy for female labourers, who comprised the majority of scavengers, and (4) the scavengers themselves were indifferent to the introduction of wheelbarrows.[30] The Malkani Committee had promoted the introduction of wheelbarrows as the key to preventing waste being carried on the head, but the plan proved to be a failure. The recommendations had in addition mentioned a number of other ways to ameliorate the situation, but because they had no legal binding on bodies, their impact was minimal. Public health authorities at the local level virtually ignored the recommendations. Though the recommendations did have a certain influence among local authorities in Gujarat, Maharashtra and Kerala.

The central government continued to provide funds to the extent of Rs. 30 million for improving the labour conditions of scavengers in the fourth Five Year Plan (1966-71). Nevertheless, the plan failed to control the carrying of human waste on the head. The main obstacles to it were: (1) opposition from the scavengers, who held customary rights, (2) insufficient funding and weak organizational powers of local bodies, and (3) lack of guidance from the state governments to local bodies.[31]

TABLE 1.2: AID MONEY AND PURCHASES ACCORDING TO STATE (DURING THE PERIOD OF THE THIRD FIVE YEAR PLAN)

| State | Allotted amount | Disburse-ments | Disposal ratio | Purchases |
|---|---|---|---|---|
| Andhra Pradesh | 2274 | 2354 | 103.5 | N.A. |
| Assam | 100 | 100 | 100.0 | N.A. |
| Bihar | 1108 | 1103 | 99.5 | (1)1240 |
| Gujarat | 324 | 279 | 86.1 | N.A. |
| Jammu & Kashmir | 19 | 19 | 100.0 | (1)836 |
| Kerala | 474 | 422 | 89.0 | (1)182 (2)636 (3)192 (4)1048 (5)133 |
| Madhya Pradesh | 694 | 250 | 36.0 | N.A. |
| Madras | 954 | 1245 | 130.5 | (1)11619 |
| Maharashtra | 954 | 518 | 54.3 | (1)553 (3)930 (4)56 (5)1014 (6)660 |
| Mysore | 632 | 440 | 69.6 | (1)3071 (2)2389 |
| Orissa | 470 | 434 | 92.3 | N.A. |
| Punjab | 1610 | 1334 | 82.8 | (1)9560 |
| Rajasthan | 950 | 697 | 73.4 | N.A. |
| Uttar Pradesh | 2799 | 1022 | 36.5 | N.A. |
| West Bengal | 1057 | 579 | 54.8 | N.A. |
| Total | 14419 | 10796 | 74.9 | (1)27061 (2)3025 (3)1122 (4)1104 (5)1147 (6)663 |

NOTE: The figures in brackets are as follows: (1) wheelbarrow (2) one-wheeledbarrow (3) scrapers (4) buckets (5) long boots (6) rubber gloves.

SOURCE: Same as Table 1.1.

In 1980/1, the Home Ministry devised a central government funded plan to convert dry latrines into flush privies, and to encourage scavengers to undertake other forms of employment. By 1987/8 it had disbursed a total of Rs. 335 million for this purpose. In addition, low cost sanitation schemes were launched by various state organs to assist the building of cheap flush latrines. For example, the Ministry of Urban Development up till March 1989 had distributed loans worthy Rs. 100 million to convert 641 public latrines and 43,450 private latrines in 149 cities in 12 states. The Housing and Urban Development Corporation disbursed Rs. 639 million till March 1990 to construct 66,486 private latrines in 272 cities in 13 states. The Department of Environment and Forests, as part of the Ganga Action Plan, gave Rs. 123 million as aid to convert 25,000 private latrines and 10,760 public latrines in 36 cities in 3 states. State governments spent Rs. 400 million to convert 40,298 latrines.[32]

The Basu Task Force pointed out that a lack of coordination among the various plans, and the absence of a supervisory system after the construction of latrines in the 1980s reduced the efficiency of mobilized resources.[33] Thirty per cent of the converted latrines were in fact not used because of blocked pipes, overflows, seepage from septic tanks and non-construction of the upper section (the lower section of the latrine was funded by aid money, while the upper section was the responsibility of the latrine owner). Further, the lack of cooperation between the central and state governments, and between the state governments and local bodies, and inadequate financial support by state governments led to delays in the execution of the plans, thus reducing the level of results.

Taking these points into consideration, the Basu Task Force proposed the following recommendations: (1) the Ministry of Health should set up a Project Management Unit to coordinate and supervise the plans, (2) State Level Coordinating Committees should be established as the state unit, (3) Local Coordinating Committees consisting of the District Magistrate, officials from the Ministry of Health, and representatives from public organizations should be set up to report periodically to the State Level Coordinating Committee on problems in the implementation of the plan, and that (4) the carrying of human waste on the head and the building of dry latrines should be forbidden by law.[34] It stressed that the various plans should not be concerned solely with the conversion of existing dry latrines, but should provide financial aid to the poorer classes for the construction of their private latrines, and towards the construction of new public latrines in stations, markets and slum areas. The Task Force also proposed the need for implementing a time-bound programme to convert all dry latrines to flush ones by the end of the eighth Five-Year Plan (1992-7) and estimated that the required amount of financial assistance by the central government would be Rs. 5,500 million.[35]

## Employment Conditions and Trade Unions

Those involved with the disposal of human waste can be divided into two broad groups: scavengers with customary rights over private latrines and those employed by governmental organizations and large-scale facilities. The chief employers of the latter are the various local bodies (Corporations, Municipalities, Nagar Panchayats and Gram Panchayats), Cantonment Boards, hospitals, port authorities, railways, factories, and the central and state governments.[36] Since the analyses appearing in the various reports centre on local bodies, which are the major employers of scavenger labour,

I will limit my discussion of employment conditions here to such labourers. Employment conditions will be examined in terms of wages, type of employment, working hours and holiday provisions, and recruitment and promotion. I will also examine the functioning of the scavenger trade unions and the issues involved, which have influenced to no small extent the determination of employment conditions.

### *Wages*

Before World War II, there was no comprehensive examination of issues related to the employment conditions of the lower echelon employees in local government or of employees in the sanitation department. Basic provisions such as recruitment, promotion, penalties, dismissal, wages, allowances, pensions, provident fund, working hours and holiday provision, were entrusted to local bodies through the District Municipal Act, the Municipal Boroughs Act, etc. Regulations made by local bodies needed the approval of the state government, but since the state government rarely intervened in the decisions of local bodies, there were enormous discrepancies among the local bodies in terms of the employment conditions of employees. With the steep rise in prices that occurred during World War II, local bodies distributed an Interim Relief Allowance or a Local Allowance to their employees, but this was a provisional arrangement and was not satisfactory. Lower ranking employees in the central and state governments were treated likewise.[37]

As a result, the government set up the Central Pay Committee in May 1946. The purpose of this committee was to make a detailed investigation of the wage structure and holiday provisions of civil service employees in the central government and to make comprehensive recommendations.[38] Sweepers and scavengers employed by the central government were categorised as Class 4 civil servants, and the recommendations of this committee regarding Class 4 employees exerted an influence on the Barve, Malkani and Pandya Committees.

In 1948, during the Central Pay Committee's period of investigation, the Central Legislature passed the Minimum Wage Act (1948). The minimum wage was determined as the wage that could maintain the worker's life and efficiency. The Act listed those agricultural and non-agricultural occupations to which the minimum wage should apply, and it included the lower level employees of local governments. The state governments set up small committees for each designated occupation and gave them the task of determining the minimum wage, within three years of the passing of the Act, for agricultural occupations and within two years for non-agricultural occupations. The minimum wages determined by the state governments were also to be applicable to local bodies. However, the state governments did not act in concert and there were considerable differences in basic wages, allowances, and holiday provision both between states and among the local bodies within states. There were also many local bodies which did not honour the Minimum Wage Act.[39]

It was under these conditions that the Barve and Malkani Committees strongly asserted that all state governments should promptly appoint small committees to investigate the wages and other allowances accruing to scavengers. Both committees stressed that all local bodies should honour the Minimum Wage Act under the guidance of the state government.[40]

Later some improvement was seen in the wage levels of local bodies, and according to the survey conducted by the Pandya Committee, the wage paid to scavengers by most local bodies exceeded the minimum wage. However, a considerable wage differential existed when compared with the Class 4 employees of the central government. Thus the Pandya Committee stressed that all local bodies should accept the wage provisions of Class 4 employees of the central government.[41]

Let us examine the wages and other allowances offered by local bodies in the latter half of the 1960s, based on materials collected by the Pandya Committee. Table 1.3 shows the wage structure provided by local bodies for scavengers by state. The total wage is composed of basic pay plus dearness pay and dearness allowance; this is regulated by the Minimum Wage Act. Other allowances include house rent and a special compensatory allowance, made up of an unclean allowance, a washing allowance and a local allowance.

Wage differentials between states and local bodies were shrinking during this period, but differences in the wage structures remained considerable. The Punjab and Haryana state governments determine wages for scavengers and sweepers employed by local bodies, but in other states it is left to the local bodies. As a result, in the states of Gujarat and Maharashtra, with a well-developed trade union movement, wage levels were comparatively high, while in other states wages were kept low. Local bodies in small cities and in rural areas, where labour is unorganized, had extremely low wages, some even below the minimum wage. In the states of Madras, Bihar, and Madhya Pradesh, there were wage differentials for the same work according to gender. There were in addition, a few local bodies where children under 15 were employed.

TABLE 1.3: WAGE STRUCTURE FOR SCAVENGERS ACCORDING TO STATE AND LOCAL BODY (SECOND HALF OF THE 1960s)

(*Rupees*)

| State | Local body | Wage | | | | Other benefits | |
|---|---|---|---|---|---|---|---|
| | | Basic pay | Dear-ness pay | Dearness allowance | Total | House rent allowance | Special compensatory allowance* |
| Andhra Pradesh | Hyderabad | 50.00 | – | 47.00 | 97.00 | – | (4)6.00 |
| Bihar | Gaya | 17.50 | – | 70.50 | 88.00 | 1.00 | – |
| | Patna | – | – | – | 82.00 | – | – |
| Gujarat | Ahmedabad | 70.00 | 13.00 | 59.00 | 142.00 | 9.00 | (1)5.00<br>(2)1.50<br>(3)6.00 |
| | Baroda | 62.50 | – | 59.00 | 121.50 | 5.00 | (1)4.00 |
| Kerala | Cochin | 65.00 | – | 40.00 | 105.00 | 7.00 | (1)10.00<br>(4)5.00 |
| | Trivandrum | 65.00 | – | 40.00 | 105.00 | 7.00 | (1)5.00<br>(4)10.00 |
| Madras | Tiruchi-rappali | 17.50(male) | – | 89.00 | 106.50 | 3.00 | – |
| | | 15.50(female) | – | 89.00 | 104.50 | 3.00 | – |
| | Madurai | 17.50(male) | – | 77.00 | 94.50 | 5.00 | – |
| | | 14.00(female) | – | 77.00 | 91.00 | 5.00 | – |
| Mysore | Mysore | 50.00 | – | 47.00 | 97.00 | 7.00 | – |
| | Hassan | 50.00 | – | 47.00 | 97.00 | 2.00 | – |
| Madhya Pradesh | Indore | 55.00 | – | 47.00 | 102.00 | 7.00 | – |
| | Bhopal | 55.00 | – | 47.00 | 102.00 | 7.00 | (1)1.00 |
| Maha-rashtra | Bombay | 45.00 | – | 115.00 | 160.00 | 6.00 | (1)7.00<br>(2)2.00 |
| | Poona | 30.00 | – | 89.00 | 119.00 | 7.00 | (1)2.00<br>(4)8.00 |
| Orissa | Cuttack | 42.00 | 3.00 | 52.00 | 97.00 | – | – |
| | Puri | 42.00 | – | 50.00 | 92.00 | – | – |
| Uttar Pradesh | Allahabad | 27.00 | – | 63.00 | 90.00 | – | (1)1.00 |
| | Lucknow | 25.00 | – | 58.00 | 83.00 | 0.50 | (4)2.00 |
| West Bengal | Calcutta Port | 70.00 | 11.80 | 65.00 | 146.80 | 15.00 | (1)3.50<br>(4)7.50 |
| | Durgapur | 35.00 | – | 78.00 | 113.00 | 5.00 | – |

NOTE: * The figures in brackets indicate (1) unclean allowance (2) washing allowance (3) local allowance (4) other allowances. In both wages and allowances the lowest scale is given.

SOURCE: *The Pandya Committee Report*, pp. 114-24.

According to the Central Pay Committee recommendations the ratio of basic pay should be higher than that of the dearness allowance. However, as it is obvious in Table 1.3, among many local bodies the dearness allowance exceeds the basic pay. The negative effect of this extends to pensions, which are calculated on the basic pay.

A rent allowance is generally paid, though this is not so in the states of Bihar, Orissa, Rajasthan and Uttar Pradesh. The unclean allowance is paid by many local bodies, the Barve Committee recommended that this be institutionalised, the Malkani and Pandya Committees recommended that payment be made in kind, like soap, oil, gloves and long boots.[42] The Pandya Committee stressed that not only wages but the various allowances should be put at the level of Class 4 employees in the central government and recommended that the Parliament enact a law to this effect.[43]

### *Terms of Employment*

Local bodies employ scavenger labour in a variety of forms: as permanent employees, or on a daily, temporary or part-time basis. The scale of non-permanent employment is not clear, but wages and living conditions are certainly worse than that of permanent employees.

Local bodies tend to employ large numbers of scavengers on a temporary basis. The advantage of such an arrengement is that the basic pay scale can be lowered and there is no need to pay any dearness allowance. Furthermore, the payment of benefits, such as paid holidays, maternity leave and the provident fund can be avoided. Part-time employment is widely practised in municipalities and rural authorities where customary rights remain in force. Part-time labourers receive only nominal wages.

In response, the Barve Committee recommended the following: (1) full-time labourers should be promoted to permanent employee status after one year when there is a vacancy, (2) cases of temporary and part-time employment should be reported to the Director of Local Authorities, the organ coordinating between local bodies and state government, (3) such workers should not be employed for more than three months without permission from the Director of Local Authorities, (4) part-time labourers should not be put to work more than twice a day, and (5) the permission of the Director of Local Authorities must be obtained for the wages of temporary and part-time labourers.[44] The Malkani Committee also endorsed these recommendations.[45] The Pandya Committee went further and recommended that part-time work, which had not been authorised by the appropriate Director of Local Authorities should be banned by law.[46]

*Working Hours and Holiday Provisions*

The working hours of scavengers and sweepers employed by local bodies are determined by the Minimum Wage Act to be nine hours a day and up to 48 hours a week. Confrontation between labourers and the local bodies over working hours were deep-rooted. The labourers were dissatisfied over the heavy work-load, the long hours, the numerous checks, and the forced substitutional work on behalf of absentees. The local bodies were equally critical of the performance of workers: slow irregular working hours, unnotified absenteeism and slipshod work. Such a situation led to a vicious cycle of low wages, bad working conditions and inefficient labour.

In order to resolve the issue of working hours, the Barve Committee recommended that all local bodies adopt the following working hours: (1) keeping in view the unsanitary working conditions of scavenging, a workman should work no more than five hours a day, (2) if the same workman is required to scavenge and also to sweep the streets, four hours of scavenging and two hours of sweeping should be maximum, and (3) a workman should not be made to work for more than seven hours a day for sweeping work.[47] Successive committees also followed this standard.[48] The Pandya Committee also estimated that on average 40 latrines are serviced by each scavenger.[49] Table 1.4 shows that the working hours of scavengers range widely between five and eight hours. There are little instances among the local bodies that working hours of scavengers are shorter than those of sweepers. This indicates that the working conditions of scavengers are more severe than those of sweepers.

The number and place of checks affect working conditions greatly. Table 1.4 shows that checks usually occur at the workplace. When the head quarter or ward offices are near the workplace there is no problem, but when they are not, and checks are carried out somewhere other than the workplace, then the actual working hours of labourers get lengthened. Two checks a day are usual, but there are some cases where there are three or four checks. The working hours are usually divided into two, and the various committees have recommended that checks should be made twice a day to correspond with the beginning of work in the morning and in the afternoon.[50]

With regard to provision of holidays, the only local bodies to be in line with those of Class 4 government workers are the states of Punjab and Haryana. Only around one half of the local bodies grant a full day at the weekend; the rest offer a half-day once or twice a week. Paid holidays are made up of casual, privileged and sick leave, but there are large variations

TABLE 1.4: WORKING HOURS AND EMPLOYMENT METHODS ACCORDING TO STATE AND LOCAL BODY (SECOND HALF OF THE 1960s)

| State | Local body | Method of employment | | | Hours worked per day | | Checks | |
|---|---|---|---|---|---|---|---|---|
| | | Waiting list | Direct employment | Compensatory* | Scavengers | Sweepers | Times | Place** |
| Andhra Pradesh | Hyderabad | 0 | x | 0 | 8 | 7.5 | 4 | (1) |
| Bihar | Gaya | 0 | x | 0 | N.A. | N.A. | N.A. | N.A. |
| | Patna | 0 | x | 0 | N.A. | N.A. | N.A. | N.A. |
| Gujarat | Ahmedabad | 0 | x | 0 | 8 | 8 | 2 | (1) |
| | Baroda | 0 | x | 0 | 7 | 7 | 2 | (1) |
| Kerala | Cochin | 0 | x | 0 | 5.5 | 5.5 | 1 | (4) |
| | Trivandrum | x | 0 | 0 | 6 | 6 | 2 | (1) |
| Madras | Tiruchirappalli | x | x | 0 | 7 | 7 | 2 | (2) |
| | Madurai | 0 | x | 0 | 7.5 | 7.5 | 2 | (1) |
| Mysore | Mysore | x | x | x | 8 | 8 | 4 | (2) |
| | Hassan | x | x | x | 8 | 8 | 3 | (3) |
| Madhya Pradesh | Indore | 0 | x | 0 | N.A. | N.A. | N.A. | N.A. |
| | Bhopal | 0 | x | 0 | N.A. | N.A. | N.A. | N.A. |
| Maharashtra | Bombay | 0 | x | 0 | 8 | 8 | 2 | (1) |
| | Poona | 0 | x | 0 | 6.5 | 6.5 | 4 | (1) |
| Orissa | Cuttack | x | 0 | x | 6 | 6 | 1 | (1) |
| | Puri | x | x | 0 | 6 | 8 | 1 | (3) |
| Uttar Pradesh | Allahabad | 0 | x | 0 | 8 | 8 | 2 | (1) |
| | Lucknow | 0 | x | 0 | 7 | 7 | 4 | (1) |
| West Bengal | Calcutta Port | N.A. | N.A. | N.A. | 6 | 6 | N.A. | N.A. |
| | Durgapur | x | 0 | 0 | 6.5 | 6.5 | 2 | (1) |

NOTES: * Compensatory employment means that the position of a retiree is filled by a member of his family.

** The figures in brackets refer to: (1) workplace (2) local office (3) head office of local body (4) other.

SOURCE: *The Pandya Committee Report*, pp. 132-8.

between states and local bodies. There is also great variation in maternity leave. Some local bodies have no provision at all, while others grant three months. The majority of scavengers and sweepers are women and so maternity leave has an importance no less than the other forms of paid leave. Concerning provision of holidays, the Pandya Committee recommended that those of Class 4 government employees should be followed.[51]

*Recruitment and Promotion*

Most local bodies recruit replacements in full time work from a waiting list, which lists names of job applicants in order of their registration. Some local bodies require that a certain period of work, such as temporary work, is a necessary condition for full-time employment, while others do not. In any case, the rule is that applicants move up the list in order of their registration. In addition, a large number of local bodies, when a full-time employee dies, becomes incapacitated or retires, hire a family member in his or her place as a measure of compensation, if the successor fulfils the conditions of employment, such as age, and resides in the family of the original worker. When no such successor exists, the position is filled from the waiting list.

The process by which a full time worker is employed is not transparent, and the Pandya Committee received many complaints from labourers, including the following: (1) peons and jamadars (also called mukadams: supervisors at workplace), who deliver notices of appointment, often failed to deliver them, (2) the person delivering the notice levied a fee for the delivery, (3) people low on the waiting list received priority through bribes, (4) raising the bribe money, labourers fell into the shackles of moneylenders and their high interest rates, (5) the moneylenders were often supervisors or low ranking officials in the Sanitation Department, and (6) though the conditions of employment were met, employment was not offered.[52] It is apparent from these complaints that corruption has been systematized and that many officials in the Sanitation Department are involved in it. The Pandya Committee observed that opportunities for promotion to other jobs, such as peon, jamadar or driver, were restricted because of their caste, and that local bodies avoided employing women as it entailed the burden of female-specific costs, such as maternity leave.[53] The committee recommended that to eliminate corruption, notification of employment should be sent by registered mail, employment procedures should be supervised by appropriately ranked officials, and that the employment of women should not be avoided.[54]

### *Trade Unions*

The legal base for an organized trade union movement in India is the Trade Union Act of 1926. This Act determines the registration procedure for unions and the nature of their activities, and guarantees protection for legal union activities. The majority of labourers in scavenging in urban areas belong to a trade union, and have a certain negotiating power with the local bodies employing them. The Industrial Disputes Act of 1947 provides the necessary structure to resolve industrial disputes between employers and workers through conciliation, arbitration and awards. Disputes that are not resolved through conciliation or arbitration are passed on to an Industrial Tribunal. Many of the awards by this tribunal have served as incentives in the improvement in term of employment and labour conditions, and welfare of workers. The negotiating power of scavengers with the local bodies has been strengthened through the decisions of the tribunal.[55]

Scavenger and sweeper trade unions flourished in the western states that have had a strong trade union movement. However, a few state governments have in real terms forbidden the application of the Industrial Disputes Act to scavengers and sweepers,[56] with the result their capacity for negotiating with local bodies has been weak.

Trade unions formed by scavengers and sweepers, despite the problem of leadership and corruption, have made an important contribution in improving the employment conditions of workers, particularly in terms of wages. However, there have hardly been any specific movements to improve their working conditions. Their demands for the improvement of their living conditions are virtually limited to the construction of more quarters. Issues related to their internal reform, such as drunkenness and gambling, debts and lack of education, are hardly touched upon. A conflict over wages and the absence of an internal reform are the main features of these trade unions.[57]

## Development of Sanitary Administration and Abolition of Customary Rights

### *Sanitary Administration System*

Scavengers employed by the central and state governments are ranked as Class 4 government employees. Their terms of employment are fairly stable and their working conditions have improved. By comparison, the employment and labour conditions of scavengers employed by local bodies are generally poor, and vary a great deal. Since most scavengers work for local bodies, the improvement of their employment and working conditions is an important issue for the sanitary administration system.

Scavengers employed by local bodies are attached to the sanitation or health departments. Lower ranking officials in these departments are defacto supervisors in charge of problems relating to their employment and work conditions. However, in most cases, these officials have no powers to improve the conditions of the workers, and few even have the desire to do so. Since they have had no suitable training in sanitation they have little interest in trying to better the conditions of scavengers.

The Pandya Committee was the only one to offer specific proposals about the sanitary administration system. Broadly these were as follows: (1) that local bodies employing more than 500 scavengers and sweepers should bear complete responsibility for their working conditions, and that a Welfare Officer be appointed to guarantee that the local body carries out directives from higher authorities, and (2) that bodies with fewer than 500 such workers should appoint a lower ranking official as special inspector in charge, who should receive short-term training in a social welfare facility.[58] It also recommended that an ad hoc committee of prominent social activists and state government officials, be set up by local bodies, in order to raise the awareness of workers on the need to improve their work environment and of people in general to the situation of the scavengers. This, it was felt, would bring about better understanding between the scavengers, the general public, and local bodies.[59]

The performance of connective organs between the local bodies and the state government was crucial for the reform of sanitary administration system.

The Barve Committee recommended the appointment of special officers attached to the district officer liaise between the local bodies and the state government. The Bombay government had already created such a post to deal with all questions relating to local bodies. However, since the district officer was pressed for time, it recommended the appointments a special officer to deal with the problems of sweepers and scavengers.[60] Accordingly in 1966 the central government recommended to the various states that officials be placed in local self-government departments to deal with local issues, and announced that it would finance 75 per cent of the cost.[61] The Pandya Committee proposed the setting up of standing committees at the state level parallel with the special committees of local bodies. These were recommend to the state government ways to improve rapidly the living and working conditions of scavengers.[62]

The Pandya Committee pointed out that the division of responsibility between ministries and departments was inadequate and imprecise. It recommended that problems relating to scavengers be divided into three distinct areas. (1) living conditions and welfare, (2) working conditions, and (3) employment conditions. The first are, it said should be the responsibility of the Social Welfare Ministry of the central government and the Departments of Harijan Welfare of the state governments, the second should be undertaken by the Ministry of Health of the central government and the Departments of Urban Development of state governments, and, the third area, particularly wage issues, should be dealt with by the Ministry of Labour of the central government and the Departments of Labour of the state governments. Questions regarding municipal sanitary administration should be handed by the Ministry of Health of the central government and the Departments of Urban Development of state governments.[63] The committee also recommended that the Social Welfare Ministry, which dealt with general matters relating to the welfare of Scheduled Castes and Tribes, should take the responsibility for liaising between the central and state governments and the municipalities.[64]

According to the above-mentioned demarcation, the central and state governments were expected to extend subsidies and loans to local bodies. It was recommended that local bodies need to prepare own action plan with the detail of capital requirement. And that they should raise funds as a measure of self help through the imposition of scavenging cess and sewage rates, and also by marketing processed human waste and rubbish.[65]

### *The Abolition of Customary Rights*

Besides labour management, the abolition of the customary rights of privately employed scavengers constituted a major issue of sanitary administration of local bodies. These rights emerged in areas where sweeper castes were indigenous and became a hindrance in the systemetic sanitary management by the local bodies. It is not possible to assess fully the regional distribution of these customary rights or the extent to which they exist within the local bodies, nor their exact nature. The various committees sent questionnaires to a large number of local bodies in which questions about customary rights were also included, but the response was poor and its accuracy was generally low. Among the 63 local bodies in Gujarat, which the Barve Committee contacted, only 30 admitted the existence of customary rights. According to committee member, B.U. Waghela, who was knowledgeable about customary rights, these rights were distributed widely in many cities in Gujarat excluding Surat.[66]

The connecting of dry latrines to underground drains is the most critical factor in the abolition of customary rights of scavengers. However, the central and state governments and the local bodies were unable to undertake the construction and extension of the high-cost sewerage system on a priority basis due to budgetary constraints. As a result, attention was focused on connecting the remaining dry latrines to the sewerage system in areas where it already existed, and converting dry latrines to septic latrines in areas, which did not have the system. Septic tanks need periodic cleaning, and this work could be taken over by municipal vacuum trucks and pumps. The conversion of dry latrines to flush or septic privies had progressed steadily following the submission of the *Malkani Committee Report*, and in the nine years between 1973/4 and 1983, it is stimated that dry latrines in India had decreased by 40 per cent in urban areas and by 12 per cent in rural areas.[67] However, a large number of dry latrines still remain all over India, especially in urban areas.

Legislation is also important in the policy to abolish customary rights. Legal restrictions however can be of little use unless they are well coordinated among all levels of administration, central, state and local. The task of direct negotiations with the holders of customary rights is that of the local bodies, and it is in their bye-laws that the most direct and concrete controls are to be found. However, the power of these bye-laws is limited by the state laws regulating the local self government. It is obvious that unless there is some improvement in the concerned state laws, effective bye-laws cannot be made. Unless there is a pressure by the central government, the state governments generally show little concern about abolishing the customary rights of scavengers.

Given the situation, local bodies which were eager to improve the situation, first banned the new construction of dry latrines. This was a measure to restrain the increase in the number of dry latrines. It was difficult to frame regulations to abolish or convert already existing dry latrines or to discontinue the use of customary rights because of the loopholes in state laws which regulated the bye-laws, and the strong opposition from the *jagirdars* who held the rights.[68]

Under the lack of legal pressure, the local bodies had to begin negotiations on the abolition of customary rights with *vatandar* scavengers. The focus of the negotiations has always been on the issues of employment and compensation. The holders of customary rights have the following demands for giving up their rights: (1) all scavengers who lose their customary rights should be employed full-time by the local body, (2) they should be paid the minimum wage and be provided with uniforms and other benefits, (3) their hours of work should be restricted, amenities like proper housing be provided, and (4) there should be adequate compensation to scavengers not employed by the local body.[69] On the contrary, the local bodies were often half-hearted about municipalisation of scavenging work because of the possibility of strikes by workers if scavenger labour was absorbed by the local bodies, the impossibility of paying compensation from limited financial resources, and that customary rights holders outnumbered the workers the local bodies could absorb.[70] A single example of the municipalization of scavenging work from Baroda (now Vadodara) was reported in the *Barve Committee Report*. In 1941, a total of Rs. 32,000 as compensation was paid to 300 holders of customary rights, and, furthermore, the majority were employed. At Rs. 4 per dry latrine,[71] each holder cleaned on an average 27 latrines, and their compensation worked out Rs. 108.

The Malkani Committee felt that the arguments presented by local bodies against the abolition of customary rights were not convincing enough. It recommended that (1) the local bodies make *jagirdars* site supervisors and employ as many holders of customary rights as possible, (2) the finance for this should be obtained by imposing or increasing scavenging cess, (3) local bodies that are unable to offer employment in their sanitary department should absorb scavengers into their water, electricity, drainage and security departments, and (4) local bodies that are unable to offer compensation or employment be offered financial help by the central and state governments.[72] The Barve, Malkani and Pandya Committees argued that holders of customary rights should be absorbed by the local bodies. The *Basu Task Force Report*, on the other hand, pointed out that as long as the sweepers and scavengers employed by local bodies remained in the cleaning services they would be denied the opportunity to advance socially, and stressed the need for them to be transferred to other departments. To this end, it recommended the implementation of a rehabilitation programme involving occupational training and financial support.[73]

*Dry Latrines and the Scavenger Population*

A number of approaches are needed to abolish the customary right of scavengers, but only concerted action can bring about the necessary results. The committees have made several recommendations concerning its abolition, but their influence at the local level has been severely circumscribed. As a result, the number of dry latrines has not decreased to the extent expected. As Table 1.5 shows, in 1983, 18.08 per cent of households in urban areas throughout India were using dry latrines. Since about 30 per cent of urban dwellers are estimated to be without latrines, the ratio of dry latrine owning households to the total number of latrine owners in urban areas is closer to 25 per cent.

Dry latrines are generally concentrated in the older parts of a city. Where the buildings are congested and space to build septic tanks is severely limited. Even in cities like Bhubaneswar and Chandigarh where sewage systems have been developed, it had proven difficult to connect latrines in the old parts of the cities to the system because of their placement and construction. Connecting latrines to the sewage system is a financial burden on latrine owners, since it involves the dismantling of the dry latrine and undertaking major household repairs in order to build a flush privy. As a result, though aware of the shortcomings of dry latrines, owners are not too eager to convert them. Furthermore, as seen in the case of Old Delhi, increase in the population of this part of the city after Independence led to a rise in the number of dry latrines.

Among states there is a great variation in the ratio of households owning dry latrines. In Jammu & Kashmir the proportion is as high as 65 per cent. Among the states which have been listed in the reports as areas with high concentration of customary rights, Uttar Pradesh and Punjab show a high ratio of households owning dry latrines, while Rajasthan and Madhya Pradesh show average. Gujarat, with its diffusion of sewage and septic systems, has a proportionally low figure. The northern states have a proportionally high rate of dry latrine ownership, which contrasts strongly with that of the relatively low ratio of southern states. The states of Kerala and Karnataka in southern India have the lowest ratios. Since these two states do not have indigenous sweeper caste, the customary rights did not pose a great problem for local governments.

However, when the distribution of the total number of dry latrines is considered, we find that the north-south distinction seen in the distribution of the ratio of dry latinre owning households has not been maintained. Uttar Pradesh has the largest number of dry latrines, constituting over

TABLE 1.5: RATIO OF HOUSEHOLDS WITH DRY LATRINES IN URBAN AREAS BY STATE

*(%, 100 households)*

| State, Territory | 1983 | 1989 | | |
|---|---|---|---|---|
| | Proportion of households with dry latrines (%) | Estimated households with dry latrines (100 households) | Ratio to the total number of households in India with dry latrines (%) | State ranking in numbers of households with dry latrines |
| Andhra Pradesh | 12.45 | 4,163 | 5.78 | 6 |
| Bihar | 13.39 | 2,672 | 3.71 | 9 |
| Gujarat | 8.15 | 1,951 | 2.71 | 10 |
| Himachal Pradesh | 24.74 | 237 | 0.33 | 15 |
| Jammu & Kashmir | 65.36 | 1,695 | 2.35 | 11 |
| Karnataka | 5.55 | 1,395 | 1.94 | 12 |
| Kerala | 2.59 | 267 | 0.37 | 14 |
| Madhya Pradesh | 22.45 | 6,119 | 8.49 | 4 |
| Maharashtra | 13.97 | 7,401 | 10.27 | 2 |
| Orissa | 12.31 | 1,155 | 1.60 | 13 |
| Punjab | 28.18 | 3,023 | 4.20 | 8 |
| Rajasthan | 18.89 | 3,430 | 4.76 | 7 |
| Tamil Nadu | 15.55 | 6,135 | 8.51 | 3 |
| Uttar Pradesh | 39.31 | 19,311 | 26.80 | 1 |
| West Benngal | 16.51 | 5,576 | 7.74 | 5 |
| Delhi | 14.07 | 2,241 | 3.11 | – |
| Pondicherry | 4.47 | 36 | 0.05 | – |
| All India | 18.08 | 72,057 | 100.00 | – |

NOTES: The 1983 figures are based on the 38th National Sample Survey (January-December 1983).
The 1989 estimate is extracted from the 1983 ratio and does not consider fluctuations in the period 1983-9.

SOURCE: *The Basu Task Force Report*, pp. 58-61.

25 per cent of the total number in urban India. The five states of Maharashtra, Tamil Nadu, Madhya Pradesh, West Bengal and Uttar Pradesh possess 62 per cent of the total number of dry latrines.

Table 1.6 shows the ratio of households owning dry latrines among rural households. In India as a whole, 2.29 per cent of rural households own dry latrines. Because the majority of rural households defecate outdoors, the ratio of latrine owning households is small. Still, there are as

TABLE 1.6: RATIO OF HOUSEHOLDS WITH DRY LATRINES IN RURAL AREAS BY STATE

*(%, 100 households)*

| State, Territory | 1983 | 1989 | | |
|---|---|---|---|---|
| | Proportion of households with dry latrines (%) | Estimated households with dry latrines (100 households) | Ratio to the total number of households in India with dry latrines (%) | State ranking in numbers of households with dry latrines |
| Andhra Pradesh | 1.81 | 1,676 | 6.79 | 4 |
| Bihar | 1.67 | 1,932 | 7.79 | 3 |
| Gujarat | 1.79 | 795 | 3.21 | 10 |
| Himachal Pradesh | 0.29 | 24 | 0.10 | 15 |
| Jammu & Kashmir | 7.53 | 645 | 2.60 | 7 |
| Karnataka | 0.76 | 383 | 1.54 | 12 |
| Kerala | 1.37 | 554 | 2.23 | 8 |
| Madhya Pradesh | 1.20 | 1,004 | 4.05 | 6 |
| Maharashtra | 1.39 | 1,160 | 4.68 | 5 |
| Orissa | 0.60 | 291 | 1.17 | 13 |
| Punjab | 1.26 | 264 | 1.06 | 14 |
| Rajasthan | 0.90 | 489 | 1.97 | 11 |
| Tamil Nadu | 1.03 | 797 | 3.21 | 9 |
| Uttar Pradesh | 4.49 | 8,032 | 32.38 | 1 |
| West Bengal | 2.91 | 2,338 | 9.43 | 2 |
| Delhi | 2.17 | 16 | 0.06 | – |
| Pondicherry | – | – | – | – |
| All India | 2.29 | 24,803 | 100.00 | – |

NOTES: The 1983 figures are based on the 38th National Sample Survey (January-December 1983).

The 1989 estimate is extracted from the 1983 ratio and does not consider fluctuations in the period 1983-9.

SOURCE: Same as Table 1.5.

many as 2.4 million households with dry latrines in rural areas. This is not a particularly small figure compared with that of the 7.2 million households with dry latrines in urban areas. With the increasing impact of urban lifestyle on the rural areas, the number of latrines is steadily increasing, and there is a concern that this may give rise to a renewed growth in customary rights.

In Uttar Pradesh, which has the highest proportion of latrine ownership after Jammu & Kashmir, almost one-third of all dry latrines in rural India are concentrated. The three states of Uttar Pradesh, Bihar and West Bengal possess 50 per cent of all dry latrines in rural areas.

The number of sweepers (defined broadly, including scavengers), increased from 802,000 in 1961 to 855,000 in 1981, an increase of 50,000 in 20 years.[74] The Census compiles the numbers of broadly defined sweepers, but without a distinction between sweepers and scavengers. So, it is not possible to trace the exact number of scavengers. Still, we may safely infer that the number of scavengers has decreased gradually due to a nationwide movement since the 1960s to abolish dry latrines, while, the number employed as sweepers has increased with urbanization.

A useful source of information to estimate the scale of scavenging is the number of dry latrines. Scavenging is divided into three processes: collection, transportation and disposal. The number of labourers needed to clean a certain number of dry latrines may, despite some regional differences, be considered fairly constant and so the number of dry latrines would indicate the relative strengths of scavengers in each state. Unfortunately, regular surveys on dry latrines have not been conducted and as a result it is not possible to trace changes over time. As of 1983, Uttar Pradesh had the largest number of dry latrines in India, in both urban and rural areas. There is an urgent need to create an awareness regarding the ills of dry latrines and to develop organized efforts to abolish them, especially in states with large numbers of them as shown in Tables 1.5 and 1.6.

## Conclusion

Since the 1980s there has been a definite growth in the provision of septic tanks for dry latrines and the conversion of dry latrines into flush privies, changes that are essential for the management of public hygiene and sanitation. Due to the paucity of data, changes in the number of dry latrines remain open to conjecture, there is every possibility that they would increase in rural areas. Developing efficient sanitary management, which involves coordination among central and state governments and local bodies, and strengthening of popular involvement through the mediation of social activists, is an essential requirements in the eradication of dry latrines. The reduction in the number of dry latrines will depend on whether or not controls will be placed on dry latrines in rural areas, where sanitary management is least developed.

The Barve, Malkani and Pandya Reports have been emphatic on the need for providing employment to holders of customary rights in the sewage and cleaning departments of the municipalities, and on the improvement of the employment and working conditions of these employees. This view is based on the premise that the sweeper caste would remain in their monopolised labour market, and that the government and local bodies would continue to absorb them in sufficient numbers. The proposals in these reports aim at normalizing the unstable and severe employment and working conditions of the most backward community among the Scheduled Castes.

*The Basu Task Force Report*, on the other hand, recognized that the employment generation capacity of the government and local bodies to be limited, and suggested a social rehabilitation programme that would provide scavengers with alternative job opportunities. The principal targets of this programme would be the children of households who had lost their customary rights. Through the implementation of a scholarship system, occupational training, and the reservation policy it was intended that they would raise the level of education and find profitable occupations. The Report does not discuss about breaking the monopolised labour market, but its vision of raising the socio-economic standing of sweepers and scavengers through social rehabilitation is clearly more advanced than those of the other committees. The differences in vision reflect changes in the times. When the former three committees were in session, the most pressing and important problem was to secure the socio-economic development of scavengers by absorbing them as municipal labourers and improving their employment and working conditions. However, by the time of the Basu Task Force, while there were still large variations in the condition of sweepers among states and local bodies, general improvement in these areas had been secured. The remaining pressing problem was to raise their educational and occupational mobility so that they could have a firm standing in the society.Its recommendations therefore reflect this change.

## NOTES

1. Government of Bombay, 1958. Also called the *Barve Committee Report* after its chairman, V.N. Barve. This usage will be adopted hereafter. Haryana and Karnataka states have also published reports on sweepers: (1) Government of Haryana, *Report of the Commission to Enquire into the Living Conditions of Safai Mazdoors Employed by Local Bodies and Private Scavengers Working in Haryana State,*

*1969-72*; (2) Government of Karnataka, *Report of the Committee on Improvement of Living and Working Conditions of Sweepers and Scavengers,* 1976.

2. This description of the setting up of the committee relies on Chapters 1 and 2 of the *Barve Committee Report.*
3. Ministry of Home Affairs, 1960. Also called the *Malkani Committee Report* after its chairman, N.R. Malkani.
4. This description of the setting up of the committee relies on Chapter 1 of the *Malkani Committee Report.*
5. The composition of the committee appears in Chapter 1 of the *Malkani Committee Report.*
6. National Commission on Labour, 1969. Also called the *Pandya Committee Report* after its chairman, Bhanuprasad Pandya.
7. This description of the setting up of the committee relies on Chapter 1 of the *Pandya Committee Report.*
8. The composition of the committee appears in Chapter 1 of the *Pandya Committee Report.*
9. Government of India, Planning Commission, 1990-1. Also called the *Basu Task Force Report* after its chairman, S.K. Basu.
10. This description of the setting up of the task force and its programme is from Chapters 1 and 2 of the *Basu Task Force Report.*
11. Lists of participants at the first and second meetings are given in the appendices of the *Basu Task Force Report.*
12. The description of the pre-British situation is compiled from points raised in the *Barve Committee Report*, p. 21.
13. *Barve Committee Report*, p. 21.
14. Ibid.
15. *Malkani Committee Report*, p. 79.
16. This description is based upon of the *Malkani Committee Report*, pp. 79-80. Of the four reports, the *Barve* and *Malkani Committee Reports* include a detailed study of the customary rights of scavengers.
17. Unfortunately, no reference was made to the contents of the correspondence itself.
18. *Barve Committee Report*, p. 32.
19. For *vatan* and *vatandar* system, see Hiroyuki Kotani, *Medieval Indian Society* (Jap.), Tokyo: Iwanami Shoten, 1989; and Hiroshi Fukazawa, *A Study of the Socio-Economic History of Rural India* (Jap.), Tokyo: Toyo Keizai Shinposha, 1972.
20. Wiser discovered 24 types of traditional occupations connected with caste in the village where he stayed. See W.H. Wiser, *The Hindu Jajmani System: A Socio-Economic System Inter-Relating Members of a Hindu Village Community in Service*. Lucknow: Lucknow Publishing House, 1958, pp. xviii-xxiii.
21. *Malkani Committee Report*, p. 80.
22. Ibid., p. 9.
23. Ibid., p. 8.
24. *Barve Committee Report*, pp. 61-2.
25. Based on the description in the *Malkani Committee Report*, pp. 19-33.
26. Ibid., pp. 57-62.
27. *Barve Committee Report*, pp. 63-4.
28. Compiled from the *Barve Committee Report*, pp. 29-31.

29. Summarized from the *Malkani Committee Report*, pp. 109-25.
30. *Pandya Committee Report*, p. 55.
31. *Basu Task Force Report*, p. 5.
32. Based on the details of the various expenditures in the *Basu Task Force Report*, pp. 14-15.
33. Ibid., p. 17.
34. Ibid., pp. 17, 51.
35. Ibid., p. 18.
36. *Pandya Committee Report*, p. 9.
37. Based on the *Barve Committee Report*, p. 70.
38. Ibid.
39. Based on the information about minimum wages in the *Barve Committee Report*, pp. 74-5.
40. Ibid., p. 101; *Malkani Committee Report*, p. 134.
41. *Pandya Committee Report*, pp. 17-8.
42. *Barve Committee Report*, p. 102; *Malkani Committee Report*, p. 134; *Pandya Committee Report*, p. 18.
43. *Pandya Committee Report*, pp. 17-18.
44. *Barve Committee Report*, p. 80.
45. *Malkani Committee Report*, p. 135.
46. *Pandya Committee Report*, p. 72.
47. *Barve Committee Report*, p. 68.
48. *Malkani Committee Report*, p. 103; *Pandya Committee Report*, pp. 73-4.
49. *Pandya Committee Report*, p. 23.
50. *Malkani Committee Report*, p. 135; *Pandya Committee Report*, p. 74.
51. *Pandya Committee Report*, p. 73.
52. Ibid. pp. 25-6.
53. Ibid. pp. 26-7.
54. Ibid.
55. *Pandya Committee Report*, p. 33.
56. Ibid. No mention is made of the states concerned.
57. The Bhave, Malkani and Pandya Committees all point this out.
58. *Pandya Committee Report*, p. 62.
59. Ibid., pp. 65-6.
60. *Barve Committee Report*, p. 90.
61. *Pandya Committee Report*, pp. 62-3.
62. Ibid., p. 66.
63. Ibid., p. 64.
64. Ibid., p. 65.
65. Ibid., p. 68.
66. *Barve Committee Report*, p. 33.
67. *Basu Task Force Report*, p. 56.
68. Some conflicts regarding the customary rights of scavengers were brought to district courts in Punjab, Uttar Pradesh, and Gujarat. Their customary rights were mostly approved by the courts. See *Malkani Committee Report*, p. 82. In 1945 the Bombay High Court also confirmed the order of the district court, which approved the customary rights of scavengers in the premises of the Srinagar Weaving Mills, Ahmedabad. See *Barve Committee Report*, p. 34. No other legal cases on customary rights are mentioned in these reports.

69. *Malkani Committe Report*, p. 81.
70. Ibid.
71. *Barve Committee Report*, p. 33.
72. *Malkani Committee Report*, pp. 81-4.
73. *Basu Task Force Report*, pp. 13-14.
74. Ibid., p. 3.

Chapter Two

# Differentials in Socio-economic Development Among the Scheduled Castes

## SCHEDULED CASTES IN GUJARAT

In Gujarat the Scheduled Castes comprise 7 per cent of the total population, which is one of the lowest proportions among the major states (Table 2.1). On the contrary, the percentage for the Scheduled Tribes is fairly high among the major states. The combined population ratio of Scheduled Castes and Scheduled Tribes shows 22 per cent, ranking around the middle among the states. The Scheduled Tribes are concentrated in the south and hilly area, whereas the Scheduled Castes are comparatively evenly distributed in Gujarat. The pattern of their regional distribution has been working as one of the important factors in determining the regional level of rural wages and the form of agricultural management.[1]

The urban proportion ratio of the Scheduled Castes in Gujarat is extremely high among the major states, showing 38 per cent. Interestingly, this ratio is almost same with the state average. Incidence of social and educational backwardness in rural areas is thought to be higher than in urban areas.[2] In this regard the high urban population ratio of the Scheduled Castes may be taken as one of the indicators to explain that incidence of their backwardness is lower than their counterparts in other states. On the other hand, the urban population ratio of Scheduled Tribes is just slightly above the national average. There is a tremendous gap in urban population ratio between the Scheduled Castes and Scheduled Tribes in Gujarat. .

The literacy rate of the Scheduled Castes in Gujarat is not only the third highest in India, but also hardly different from the overall state literacy rate. Notably, the male literacy rate of the Scheduled Castes is two points higher than the state average male literacy rate. The literacy level is generally reflected by the social and economic situation of the targeted group including the urban population ratio. In this sense, the Scheduled

TABLE 2.1 SCHEDULED CASTES AND SCHEDULED TRIBES BY STATE (1991)

*(per 10,000, %)*

| State | Population (10,000) | Population Ratio | | Urban Population Ratio | | Literacy Rate | | |
|---|---|---|---|---|---|---|---|---|
| | | SCs | STs | SCs | STs | State | SCs | STs |
| Andhra Pradesh | 6,650 | 15.93 | 6.31 | 17.31 | 7.60 | 44.09 | 31.59 | 17.16 |
| ArunachalPradesh | 87 | 0.47 | 63.66 | 29.47 | 5.84 | 41.59 | 57.27 | 34.45 |
| Assam | 2,241 | 7.40 | 12.82 | 13.82 | 3.38 | 52.89 | 53.94 | 49.16 |
| Bihar | 8,637 | 14.55 | 7.66 | 9.02 | 7.00 | 38.48 | 19.49 | 26.78 |
| Goa | 117 | 2.08 | 0.03 | 47.68 | 76.33 | 75.51 | 58.73 | 42.91 |
| Gujarat | 4,131 | 7.41 | 14.92 | 37.94 | 8.09 | 61.29 | 61.07 | 36.45 |
| Haryana | 1,646 | 19.75 | – | 17.71 | – | 55.85 | 39.22 | – |
| Himachal Pradesh | 517 | 25.34 | 4.22 | 6.33 | 2.48 | 63.86 | 53.20 | 47.09 |
| Karnataka | 4,498 | 16.38 | 4.26 | 23.40 | 14.94 | 56.04 | 38.06 | 36.01 |
| Kerala | 2,910 | 9.92 | 1.10 | 18.52 | 3.49 | 89.81 | 79.66 | 57.22 |
| Madhya Pradesh | 6,618 | 14.55 | 23.27 | 21.86 | 4.85 | 44.20 | 35.08 | 21.54 |
| Maharashtra | 7,894 | 11.09 | 9.27 | 36.61 | 12.47 | 64.87 | 56.46 | 36.79 |
| Manipur | 184 | 2.02 | 34.41 | 52.28 | 8.42 | 59.89 | 56.44 | 53.63 |
| Meghalaya | 178 | 0.51 | 85.53 | 45.19 | 13.56 | 49.10 | 44.27 | 46.71 |
| Mizoram | 69 | 0.10 | 94.75 | 34.01 | 45.21 | 82.27 | 77.92 | 82.73 |
| Nagaland | 121 | – | 87.70 | – | 12.04 | 61.65 | – | 60.59 |
| Orissa | 3,166 | 16.20 | 22.21 | 10.74 | 5.14 | 49.09 | 36.78 | 22.31 |
| Punjab | 2,028 | 28.31 | – | 20.55 | – | 58.51 | 41.09 | – |
| Rajasthan | 4,401 | 17.29 | 12.44 | 19.79 | 4.65 | 38.55 | 26.29 | 19.44 |
| Sikkim | 41 | 5.93 | 22.36 | 11.42 | 8.16 | 56.94 | 51.03 | 59.01 |
| Tamil Nadu | 5,586 | 19.18 | 1.03 | 21.32 | 12.01 | 62.66 | 46.74 | 27.89 |
| Tripura | 276 | 16.36 | 30.95 | 15.84 | 1.65 | 60.44 | 56.66 | 40.37 |
| Uttar Pradesh | 13,911 | 21.05 | 0.21 | 11.79 | 5.86 | 41.60 | 26.85 | 35.70 |
| West Bengal | 6,808 | 23.62 | 5.9 | 15.39 | 5.15 | 57.70 | 42.21 | 27.78 |
| India (total) | 83,858 | 16.48 | 8.08 | 18.72 | 7.39 | 52.21 | 37.41 | 29.60 |

NOTES: SCs = Scheduled Castes; STs = Schedule Tribes.
Jammu & Kashmir are not included in the table (the 1991 Census was not conducted there). Figures for the Union Territories (Andaman and Nicobar Islands, Chandigarh, Dadra and Nagar Haveli, Daman and Diu, Delhi, Lakshadweep, Pondicherry) are not listed individually but included in the India's total.

SOURCE: Govemment of India, Census of India 1991, Series-1 India, Paper of 1993, *Union Primary Census Abstract for Scheduled Castes and Scheduled Tribes*, Delhi, 1992, pp. 11, 13-14.

Castes in Gujarat are supposed to be less backward socially and economically compared with those of other states.[3]

The pattern of production and the per capita GDP of Gujarat are also indices that show indirectly the relative superiority of the social and economic base of the Scheduled Castes in the state. Gujarat is one of the leading states in industrial development. The Scheduled Castes of Gujarat have entered industry, especially the organized sector, in large numbers and are in receipt of a comparatively stable income, and public health and welfare facilities.[4] Historically, they also formed an important source of labour when the cotton industry developed in the last quarter of the nineteenth century.[5]

### *Geographical Distribution of the Major Scheduled Castes*

The geographical distribution of the Scheduled Castes of Gujarat is fairly even, especially in comparison to the high concentration of Scheduled Tribes in the south and hilly zone of the state. The Scheduled Castes comprise more than 10 per cent of the population of four districts; and between 5 per cent and 10 per cent in ten districts (Map 2.1). The population ratio is relatively small in the south and hilly zone. The urban population ratio of the Scheduled Castes is high in advanced districts where manufacturing has developed. The three districts with the highest urban population ratios are Ahmedabad (72 per cent), Surat (55 per cent) and Vadodara (40 per cent). Those with the lowest urban population ratios are backward districts: Dangs (0 per cent), Sabarkantha (8 per cent) and Banaskantha (9 per cent).

The Scheduled Castes in Gujarat are divided into 30 groups in the 1991 Census.[6] Table 2.2 shows the population and urban population ratio of the main *jatis* studied in this chapter. Table 2.3 shows the population ratios of the main *jatis* as a proportion of the Scheduled Castes in the five geographical and cultural regions of Gujarat.

In general, the Scheduled Castes in rural areas are a source for agricultural labour and are also required to undertake unclean work, such as disposing of fallen animals.[7] Besides, the majority of these *jatis* were expected or forced to follow 'particular' 'hereditary' or 'traditional' occupations,[8] though the links between caste and traditional occupation have now loosened considerably.

The *jati* with the largest population among the Scheduled Castes in Gujarat is the Vankars.[9] Their traditional occupation is weaving, but they have largely abandoned this occupation in the course of their efforts in

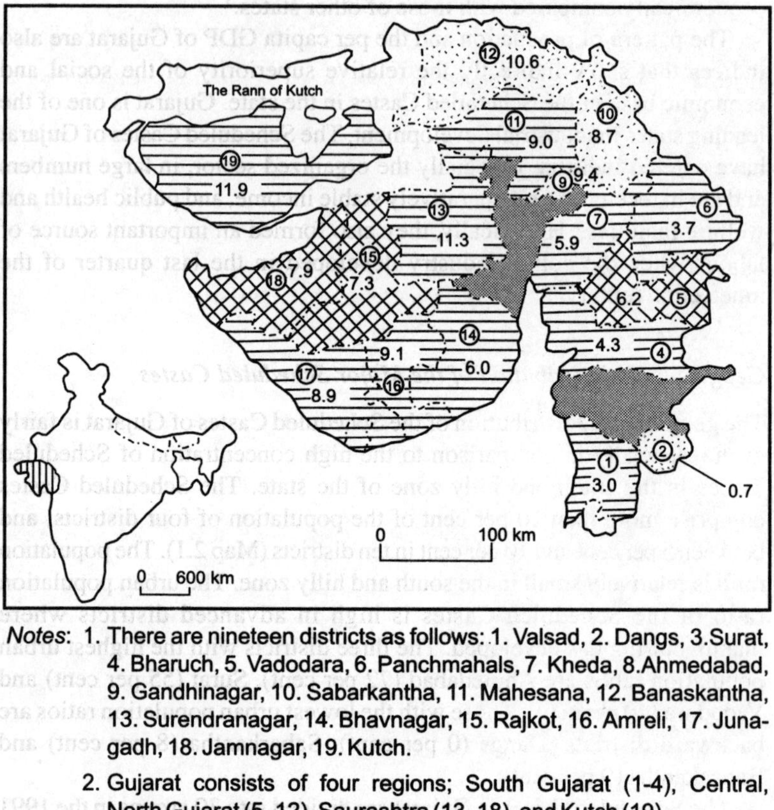


*Notes*: 1. There are nineteen districts as follows: 1. Valsad, 2. Dangs, 3.Surat, 4. Bharuch, 5. Vadodara, 6. Panchmahals, 7. Kheda, 8.Ahmedabad, 9. Gandhinagar, 10. Sabarkantha, 11. Mahesana, 12. Banaskantha, 13. Surendranagar, 14. Bhavnagar, 15. Rajkot, 16. Amreli, 17. Junagadh, 18. Jamnagar, 19. Kutch.

2. Gujarat consists of four regions; South Gujarat (1-4), Central, North Gujarat (5-12), Saurashtra (13-18), and Kutch (19).

3. Figures in the map show the distribution of SC population by distinct (%).

4. Urban population ratio of SCs is indicated in the map as follows:

40% and above — 10-24%

25-39% — below 10%

*Source*: Compiled from CD ROM Data: Government of India, *Census of Gujarat: A Kaleidscope (1961-2001)*, 2002.

MAP 2.1: DISTRIBUTION OF SC POPULATION BY DISTRICT (1991)

TABLE 2.2 POPULATION AND URBAN POPULATION RATIO OF THE MAIN JATIS OF THE SCHEDULED CASTES (1991)

(*thousand persons, %*)

| Caste | Population | | Urban population ratio (%) |
|---|---|---|---|
| | thousand | Proportion within SC (%) | |
| Chamar | 831 | 27.15 | 32.57 |
| Bhangi | 359 | 11.73 | 51.57 |
| Garoda | 63 | 2.06 | 38.89 |
| Vankar | 1,269 | 41.47 | 37.29 |
| Meghval | 145 | 4.74 | 33.17 |
| Senva | 82 | 2.68 | 14.85 |
| Others | 310 | 10.17 | 47.24 |
| SCs (total) | 3,060 | 100.00 | 37.94 |

SOURCE: Compiled from CD ROM Data: Government of India, *Census of Gujarat: A Kaleidscope (1961-2001)*, 2002.

TABLE 2.3 POPULATION DISTRIBUTION OF THE SCHEDULED CASTES BY *JATI* AND REGION (1991)

(%)

| Region | Chamar | Bhangi | Garoda | Vankar | Meghval | Senva | Others | Total |
|---|---|---|---|---|---|---|---|---|
| Kutch | 6.81 | 4.52 | 2.28 | 7.82 | 71.38 | 0.08 | 7.11 | 100.00 |
| Peninsular region | 23.64 | 8.96 | 1.01 | 53.86 | 2.41 | 0.54 | 9.58 | 100.00 |
| Central, North Gujarat | 31.74 | 14.14 | 2.78 | 35.96 | 0.43 | 4.39 | 10.56 | 100.00 |
| South Gujarat | 20.39 | 9.40 | 0.75 | 54.61 | 3.22 | 0.14 | 11.49 | 100.00 |
| Gujarat (total) | 27.15 | 11.73 | 2.06 | 41.47 | 4.74 | 2.68 | 10.17 | 100.00 |

NOTE: The figures show the row percentages. The column of 'Others' includes both the other SC *jatis* and unclassified SC members.

SOURCE: Same as Table 2.2.

changing their occupational structure since the beginning of the twentieth century. They are distributed broadly over the state and comprise more than half the population of Scheduled Castes in southern and peninsular Gujarat. In urban population ratio they are on an average with the Scheduled Castes as a whole.

The traditional occupation of the Chamars[10] is tanning. The national census groups the Chamars with *jatis* like the Mochi, whose traditional occupation is leatherwork. The present study considers them to represent *jatis* that are involved with tanning and leatherwork. They are distributed broadly throughout the state, and are the second populous Scheduled Castes in all the regions but Kutch. Their urban population ratio is a little lower than that of the Scheduled Caste average.

The traditional occupation of the Bhangis[11] is scavenging and sweeping. Like the Vankars and the Chamars, they are distributed widely over the state. They differ in many respects from the other *jatis* of the Scheduled Castes, and, unlike them, have an extremely high urban population ratio.

The total population of the above three *jatis* constitutes 80 per cent of the population of the Scheduled Castes.

The traditional occupation of the Garodas[12] is the performing of rituals for the Scheduled Castes. Since Caste Hindu priests have not provided services to the Scheduled Castes, the Garodas have taken on this role of performing rituals for the Scheduled Castes. They are concentrated in central and northern Gujarat, and Kutch. Their urban population ratio is much the same as for the Scheduled Castes as a whole.

The traditional occupation of the Senvas[13] is drumming and rope-making. They play the drum generally at festivals and wedding ceremonies. Their distribution is limited to central and northern Gujarat and their urban population ratio is extremely low. Like the Senvas, the Meghvals[14] are also a local *jati*, concentrated in Kutch.

While socially and economically the Chamars and Vankars are extremely advanced within the Scheduled Castes, the Bhangis, Garodas, Senvas and Meghvals have remained backward. The Bhangis constitutes the most backward community among them.

## Differentials in Socio-economic Development among the Scheduled Castes

Land holding patterns and occupational and educational structures have been closely associated with the level of socio-economic development. The indices for the Scheduled Castes show their backwardness as a whole. Still, there are considerable differentials between the advanced and backward *jatis* among the Scheduled Castes.

### *Land Holding*

The main land holding groups in Gujarat are certain farming castes, such as the Patidars and the Kolis, and some upper castes like the Rajputs and the Brahmans. A large number of surveys have reported that these castes were dominant in land holding, while the Scheduled Castes fell behind both in the proportion of land-holding households and the area of land held per household.[15]

Table 2.4 presents the land holding patterns among the Scheduled Castes in Gujarat based on the large-scale survey conducted in 1980 covering 6,044 sample households. Their land holding patterns vary with the regions in correspond to the intensity of agriculture. For example, the average size of holding is large in Kutch where extensive cultivation is practiced, while it is small in central, northern and southern Gujarat, where intensive cultivation is comparatively well developed. Overall, 48 per cent of households possess less than 2 acre (0.81 ha.) and 92 per cent own less than 10 acre (4.05 ha.). Thus, the table indicates clearly that land holding among the Scheduled Castes is on a very small scale.

Though data is not available to indicate differentials in land holding among the various *jatis* of the Scheduled Castes, the Census data

TABLE 2.4: DISTRIBUTION OF LAND HOLDING AMONG THE SCHEDULED CASTES BY SIZE-GROUP AND REGION (1980)

*(Households, %)*

| Region | Less than 1 acre | 1-2 acres | 2-4 acres | 4-6 acres | 6-8 acres | 8-10 acres | More than 10 acres | Total |
|---|---|---|---|---|---|---|---|---|
| Kutch | 11 | 16 | 59 | 69 | 66 | 55 | 83 | 359 |
| | (3.06) | (4.46) | (16.43) | (19.22) | (18.39) | (15.32) | (23.12) | (100,00) |
| Peninsular | 228 | 378 | 467 | 241 | 88 | 70 | 86 | 1,558 |
| region | (14.63) | (24.26) | (29.98) | (15.47) | (5.65) | 44.49) | (5.52) | (100.00) |
| Central, North | 946 | 890 | 731 | 345 | 152 | 81 | 193 | 3,338 |
| Gujarat | (28.34) | (26.66) | (21.90) | (10.34) | (4.55) | (2.43) | (5.78) | (100.00) |
| South | 237 | 193 | 162 | 54 | 22 | 20 | 101 | 789 |
| Gujarat | (30.04) | (24.46) | (20.53) | (6.84) | (2.79) | (2.54) | (12.80) | (100.00) |
| Gujarat | 1,422 | 1,477 | 1,419 | 709 | 328 | 226 | 463 | 6,044 |
| (total) | (23.53) | (24.44) | (23.48) | (11.73) | (5.43) | (3.74) | (7.65) | (100.00) |

NOTES: The figures in the upper line show the distribution of households according to the size of holding held per surveyed household in each region.
The figures in the bottom line show the percentage (%) of the households.

SOURCE: Compiled from M. Masvi, *Gujaratna Harijano* (in Gujarati), Ahmedabad, Tribal Research and Training Institute, 1982, pp. 132-3.

concerning the distribution of workers by industrial category provides material to infer such differentials.

*Occupational Structure*

Tables 2.5 and 2.6 show per thousand distributions of male main workers among the Scheduled Castes by industrial category in 1991 in rural and urban areas respectively. The data in these tables refer to main workers who work for more than half-a-year (183 days). Those workers who work for less than half-a-year are defined as 'marginal workers' in the Census. Since the proportion of male marginal workers is very small, 11 per 1,000 persons in rural areas and 4 per 1,000 persons in urban areas in 1991, we mainly deal with main workers.

In rural areas, it seems that the ratio of male cultivators out of the total male main workers has a positive association with the proportion of land holding, because the cultivators are considered to own their land though the size of land holding is unknown. The number of cultivators per 1,000 rural male main workers is relatively large among the advanced group; 260 for the Chamars and 214 for the Vankars in 1991. While, the number appears small among the backward group; 96 for the Bhangis, and 150 for the Senvas.[16] On the contrary, the ratio of male agricultural labourers tends to appear large among the backward group because agricultural labour constitutes a major economic activity for the landless in rural areas. It is 684 for the Senvas and 580 for the Bhangis. Thus, agriculture is a major industry absorbing a vast majority of main workers, and the ratio between cultivators and agricultural labourers is inter-related based on the availability of land in rural areas.

The next important industry after agriculture is manufacturing, processing, servicing and repairs, which is divided into two; (a) household industry, [17] and (b) other than household industry. The former includes various 'traditional' occupations of the Scheduled Castes, such as leather works of the Chamars, weaving of the Vankars, basket making of the Bhangis, etc. The latter includes employment in Small Scale Industries[18] and factories,[19] which is generally more rewarding than that of household industry. Household industry has been loosing its economic base over time due to competition with modern sectors. Accordingly, its ratio of the Scheduled Castes has declined drastically, showing 46 per 1,000 main workers in 1991. Still, as many as 76 per 1,000 Bhangi main workers are engaged in household industry. In other than household industry, the ratios of the Chamars and the Vankars are higher than those of backward group.

TABLE 2.5: PER THOUSAND DISTRIBUTION OF MALE MAIN WORKERS BY *JATI* AND INDUSTRIAL CATEGORY IN RURAL AREAS (1991)

*(numbers per 1,000 main workers)*

| Industrial Category | Chamars | Bhangis | Garodas | Vankars | Meghvals | Senvas | SCs |
|---|---|---|---|---|---|---|---|
| I. Cultivators | 260 | 96 | 97 | 214 | 241 | 150 | 211 |
| II. Agr. Labourers | 487 | 580 | 422 | 499 | 516 | 684 | 512 |
| III. Livestock, etc | 6 | 16 | 13 | 8 | 12 | 11 | 9 |
| IV. Mining, etc | 5 | 4 | 3 | 9 | 18 | 3 | 7 |
| V. Manufacturing, etc | | | | | | | |
| (a) Household | 33 | 76 | 23 | 50 | 36 | 19 | 46 |
| Industry | 86 | 55 | 52 | 79 | 53 | 39 | 75 |
| (b) Other than (a) | 18 | 11 | 28 | 25 | 48 | 14 | 22 |
| VI. Construction | 18 | 13 | 25 | 19 | 9 | 9 | 17 |
| VII. Trade and | 21 | 29 | 49 | 26 | 28 | 43 | 26 |
| Commerce | 66 | 120 | 288 | 71 | 39 | 28 | 75 |
| VIII. Transport, etc | | | | | | | |
| IX. Other Services | | | | | | | |
| Total | 1,000 | 1,000 | 1,000 | 1,000 | 1,000 | 1,000 | 1,000 |
| Main workers per 1,000 persons | 495 | 509 | 426 | 506 | 498 | 518 | 501 |
| Marginal workers per 1,000 persons | 6 | 8 | 7 | 5 | 6 | 6 | 6 |

NOTES: (1) The figures show numbers of workers in each category per 1,000 main workers except for the two columns, which show numbers of main workers and marginal workers respectively per 1,000 persons.

(2) Categories as listed in the 1991 Census are following. I. Cultivators, II. Agricultural Labourers, III. Livestock, Forestry, Fishing, Hunting and Plantations, Orchards and Allied Activities, IV. Mining and Quarrying, V. Manufacturing, Processing, Servicing and Repairs (a) Household Industry (b) Other than Household Industry, VI. Construction, VII. Trade and Commerce, VIII. Transport, Storage and Communications, IX. Other Services,

SOURCE: Same as Table 2.2

The other important industry in which the ratios are diversified among the Scheduled Castes is 'Other Services'. In this industry, the proportion of Garodas and Bhangis surpasses the other *jatis*. The Garodas are employed chiefly as priests and office workers, while the Bhangis work as sweepers.

In urban areas, the major industries are manufacturing and other services. The combined ratio of the two industries for the Scheduled Castes shows 628 per 1,000 male main workers in 1991. The most crucial indicator

TABLE 2.6: PER THOUSAND DISTRIBUTION OF MALE MAIN WORKERS BY *JATI* AND INDUSTRIAL CATEGORY IN URBAN AREAS (1991)

(*numbers per 1,000 main workers*)

| Industrial Category | Chamars | Bhangis | Garodas | Vankars | Meghvals | Senvas | SCs |
|---|---|---|---|---|---|---|---|
| I. Cultivators | 9 | 3 | 5 | 7 | 13 | 7 | 7 |
| II. Agr. Labourers | 68 | 38 | 78 | 65 | 64 | 101 | 61 |
| III. Livestock, etc | 7 | 7 | 10 | 8 | 8 | 9 | 8 |
| IV. Mining, etc | 7 | 5 | 10 | 19 | 4 | 10 | 12 |
| V. Manufacturing, etc | | | | | | | |
| (a) Household | 27 | 2 | 8 | 14 | 5 | 15 | 15 |
| Industry | 378 | 94 | 181 | 321 | 231 | 346 | 289 |
| (b) Other than (a) | 79 | 29 | 74 | 111 | 137 | 115 | 89 |
| VI. Construction | 105 | 53 | 89 | 94 | 83 | 85 | 90 |
| VII. Trade and | 84 | 106 | 95 | 102 | 185 | 103 | 105 |
| Commerce | 236 | 663 | 450 | 259 | 270 | 209 | 324 |
| VIII. Transport, etc | | | | | | | |
| IX. Other Services | | | | | | | |
| Total | 1,000 | 1,000 | 1,000 | 1,000 | 1,000 | 1,000 | 1,000 |
| Main workers per 1,000 persons | 458 | 412 | 404 | 442 | 456 | 452 | 442 |
| Marginal workers per 1,000 persons | 4 | 4 | 3 | 4 | 3 | 12 | 4 |

NOTES: (1) The figures show numbers of workers in each category per 1,000 main workers except for the bottom two columns, which show workers and marginal workers respectively per 1,000 persons.

(2) Categories as listed in the 1991 Census are same as Table 2.5.

SOURCE: Same as Table 2.2

to show the socio-economic differentials among the *jatis* of the Scheduled Castes is the number per 1,000 main workers who are engaged in other than household industry in urban areas. The Vankars and the Chamars show high numbers, 321 and 378 respectively. This may be attributed to the strength of their socio-economic base. The fact that the Senvas also have the high ratio can be attributed to their high level of concentration in Ahmedabad City, which makes an exceptional case. On the contrary, the ratios for the Meghvals, the Garodas and the Bhangis are low. Particularly, the ratio for the Bhangis is as low as 94 per 1,000.

There are also large differences among the Scheduled Castes in the ratio of other services, the category under which most Bhangis and Garodas in urban areas are employed. It is well known to us that the majority of Bhangis work as sweepers, while most Garodas seem to work as office workers or priests under this category. Adherence to these traditional occupations, particularly by the Bhangis, inhibits any dynamism for social and economic development by the community, and actually pegs its socio-economic standing to a low level.

The preceding examination confirms the inter-links between rural and urban distributions of male main workers by the *jatis* of Scheduled Castes. The key factor that mediates the inter-links is land holding patterns in rural areas, which directly regulate the rural occupational structure of each *jati*, and indirectly influence the urban occupational structure through utilization of rural based resources in the course of settlement in urban areas.

The differentials identified among the *jatis* of the Scheduled Castes regarding male main workers also apply to female main workers. Tables 2.7

TABLE 2.7: PER THOUSAND DISTRIBUTION OF FEMALE MAIN WORKERS BY *JATI* AND INDUSTRIAL CATEGORY IN RURAL AREAS (1991)

*(numbers per 1,000 main workers)*

| Industrial Category | Chamars | Bhangis | Garodas | Vankars | Meghvals | Senvas | SCs |
|---|---|---|---|---|---|---|---|
| I. Cultivators | 128 | 41 | 53 | 110 | 121 | 46 | 106 |
| II. Agr. Labourers | 770 | 750 | 750 | 746 | 772 | 863 | 759 |
| III. Livestock, etc | 26 | 12 | 11 | 21 | 3 | 35 | 21 |
| IV. Mining, etc | 3 | 1 | 1 | 4 | 15 | 0 | 4 |
| V. Manufacturing, etc | | | | | | | |
| (a) Household | 13 | 77 | 19 | 43 | 26 | 22 | 37 |
| Industry | 15 | 19 | 12 | 28 | 32 | 19 | 23 |
| (b) Other than (a) | 5 | 3 | 8 | 5 | 14 | 3 | 5 |
| VI. Construction | 3 | 3 | 4 | 4 | 1 | 2 | 3 |
| VII. Trade and | 1 | 4 | 2 | 1 | 1 | 1 | 1 |
| Commerce | 36 | 90 | 140 | 38 | 15 | 9 | 41 |
| VIII. Transport, etc | | | | | | | |
| IX. Other Services | | | | | | | |
| Total | 1,000 | 1,000 | 1,000 | 1,000 | 1,000 | 1,000 | 1,000 |
| Main workers per 1,000 perons | 188 | 179 | 130 | 214 | 202 | 227 | 220 |
| Marginal workers per 1,000 persons | 156 | 153 | 119 | 146 | 104 | 191 | 148 |

NOTES: (1) The figures show numbers of workers in each category per 1,000 main workers except for the bottom two columns, which show numbers of main workers and marginal workers respectively per 1,000 persons.

(2) Categories as listed in the 1991 Census are same as Table 2.5.

SOURCE: Same as Table 2.2

and 2.8 show per thousand distributions of female main workers among the Scheduled Castes by industrial category in 1991 in rural and urban areas respectively. Two important distinguishing features emerge when female main workers are compared with their male counterparts. (1) the female main workers of the Scheduled Castes comprise an average of 200 per 1,000 rural population and 101 per 1,000 urban population, which is an extremely low level, and (2) the female marginal workers per 1,000 rural population appear very high. The overall trend among female main workers is that in rural areas they are overwhelmingly involved in agricultural labour, and that in urban areas their main occupation is under the category of other services. And even in urban areas, agricultural labour is the third

TABLE 2.8: PER THOUSAND DISTRIBUTION OF FEMALE MAIN WORKERS BY *JATI* AND INDUSTRIAL CATEGORY IN URBAN AREAS (1991)

*(numbers per 1,000 main workers)*

| Industrial Category | Chamars | Bhangis | Garodas | Vankars | Meghvals | Senvas | SCs |
|---|---|---|---|---|---|---|---|
| I. Cultivators | 12 | 1 | 4 | 6 | 11 | 5 | 7 |
| II. Agr. Labourers | 229 | 24 | 255 | 168 | 148 | 293 | 133 |
| III. Livestock, etc | 3 | 1 | 0 | 3 | 3 | 7 | 2 |
| IV. Mining, etc | 4 | 1 | 0 | 13 | 5 | 2 | 7 |
| V. Manufacturing, etc | | | | | | | |
| (a) Household | 31 | 6 | 25 | 51 | 6 | 68 | 30 |
| Industry | 202 | 18 | 143 | 225 | 215 | 211 | 151 |
| (b) Other than (a) | 105 | 12 | 41 | 98 | 116 | 82 | 72 |
| VI. Construction | 50 | 11 | 39 | 48 | 35 | 50 | 37 |
| VII. Trade and | 22 | 30 | 20 | 23 | 64 | 11 | 28 |
| Commerce | 342 | 896 | 473 | 365 | 397 | 271 | 533 |
| VIII. Transport, etc | | | | | | | |
| IX. Other Services | | | | | | | |
| Total | 1,000 | 1,000 | 1,000 | 1,000 | 1,000 | 1,000 | 1,000 |
| Main workers per 1,000 persons | 77 | 176 | 69 | 91 | 114 | 78 | 101 |
| Marginal workers per 1,000 persons | 13 | 10 | 11 | 12 | 6 | 11 | 12 |

NOTES: (1) The figures show numbers of workers in each category per 1,000 main workers except for the bottom two columns, which show numbers of main workers and marginal workers respectively per 1,000 persons.

(2) Categories as listed in the 1991 Census are same as Table 2.5.

SOURCE: Same as Table 2.2

most numerous industrial category after other-than-household industry.

Differentials in the distribution of female main workers among the *jatis* of the Scheduled Castes are not as clear-cut as for male main workers. Still, some differentials are identified in the proportion of cultivators in rural areas (which reflects differing scales of land holding) and in the proportion of workers who are engaged in the other-than-household industries in urban areas. Here too, the comparatively strong economic base of the Vankars and the Chamars can be discerned. Another conspicuous feature is that the ratio of female main workers among the Bhangis who are categorized under other services is extremely high in urban areas. While, the proportion of female main workers among the Garodas who work in other services is relatively low compared to their male counterparts, partly because females do not usually function as priests. Further, the numbers of female main workers per 1,000 population among the Garodas are smaller than other *jatis* both in rural and urban areas.

Per thousand distribution of female marginal workers by industrial category shows a similar pattern with that of female main workers. In rural areas, the ratio of female marginal workers under the category of agricultural labourers averages 720 per 1,000 for the Scheduled Castes, followed by 153 per 1,000 for cultivators in 1991. Disparity in the occupational structure of female marginal workers among the *jatis* of the Scheduled Castes is very small.

The occupational structure has changed considerably over the thirty years between 1961 and 1991. Tables 2.9 and 2.10 present per thousand distribution of male workers among the Scheduled Castes by industrial category in 1961 in rural and urban areas respectively. In the 1961 Census, there was no distinction between main and marginal workers. Therefore, it is not possible to make direct comparison with the data provided for main workers in the 1991 census. The worker category defined by the 1961 Census can be regarded as roughly corresponding to the combined main and marginal worker category of the 1991 Census, and comparison between 1961 and 1991 Census results is useful, at least, for analyzing the trend of differentials among the Scheduled Castes.

In rural areas, a basic characteristic of the distribution of male workers by industrial category in 1961 was that the ratio of cultivators was higher than that of agricultural labourers, and that the ratio for household industry was much higher than that of manufacturing other than household industry. After the 1960s, we observe a tremendously increasing population pressure on rural land, resulting in a significant decrease in the ratio of cultivators

TABLEL.2.9: PER THOUSAND DISTRIBUTION OF MALE WORKERS BY *JATI* AND INDUSTRIAL CATEGORY IN RURAL AREAS (1961)

(*numbers per 1,000 workers*)

| Industrial Category | Chamars | Bhangis | Garodas | Vankars | Meghvals | Senvas | SCs |
|---|---|---|---|---|---|---|---|
| I. Cultivators | 378 | 242 | 204 | 360 | 227 | 350 | 335 |
| II. Agr. Labourers | 292 | 323 | 168 | 301 | 320 | 401 | 302 |
| III. Mining, etc | 6 | 10 | 7 | 12 | 29 | 8 | 13 |
| IV. Household Industry | 174 | 152 | 108 | 120 | 207 | 59 | 144 |
| V. Manufacturing other than Household Industry | 23 | 12 | 41 | 43 | 16 | 9 | 28 |
| VI. Construction | 11 | 4 | 8 | 26 | 51 | 3 | 21 |
| VII. Trade and Commerce | 3 | 3 | 5 | 5 | 3 | 2 | 4 |
| VIII. Transport, etc | 4 | 22 | 41 | 10 | 5 | 11 | 9 |
| IX. Other Services | 109 | 232 | 418 | 123 | 142 | 157 | 144 |
| Total | 1,000 | 1,000 | 1,000 | 1,000 | 1,000 | 1,000 | 1,000 |
| Workers per 1,000 persons | 528 | 534 | 380 | 536 | 560 | 540 | 532 |

NOTES: (1) The figures show numbers of workers in each category per 1,000 workers except for the bottom column, which shows a number of workers per 1,000 persons.

(2) Categories as listed in the 1961 Census are following. I. Cultivators, Agricultural Labourers, III. Mining, Quarrying, Livestock, Forestry, Fishing, Hunting, Plantations, Orchards and Allied Activities, IV. Household Industry, V. Manufacturing other than Household Industry, VI. Construction, VII. Trade and Commerce, VIII. Transport, Storage and Communications, IX. Other Services.

SOURCE: Compiled from Government of India, Census of India 1961, Vol. V Gujarat, Part V-A, *Tables on Scheduled Castes and Scheduled Tribes*, 1964.

and a rapid increase in the ratio of agricultural labourers. In addition, differences in the ratio of cultivators among the various *jatis* of the Scheduled Castes suggest that in 1961 the Chamars and the Vankars were relatively superior in terms of land holding. And even thirty years later, by 1991, the relative differential in land holding among these *jatis* has changed little.

Vital changes took place in manufacturing. The household industry that had absorbed a large number of workers[20] in rural areas in 1961 shrank dramatically by 1991, while the ratio of workers in other-than-household

TABLE 2.10: PER THOUSAND DISTRIBUTION OF MALE WORKERS BY *JATI* AND INDUSTRIAL CATEGORY IN URBAN AREAS (1961)

*(numbers per 1,000 workers)*

| Industrial Category | Chamars | Bhangis | Garodas | Vankars | Meghvals | Senvas | SCs |
|---|---|---|---|---|---|---|---|
| I. Cultivators | 37 | 4 | 23 | 14 | 15 | 8 | 17 |
| II. Agr. Labourers | 35 | 4 | 16 | 18 | 19 | 16 | 20 |
| III. Mining, etc | 4 | 10 | 1 | 1 | 16 | 4 | 11 |
| IV. Household Industry | 55 | 9 | 32 | 29 | 38 | 35 | 40 |
| V. Manufacturing other than Household Industry | 581 | 44 | 391 | 593 | 283 | 644 | 420 |
| VI. Construction | 27 | 16 | 13 | 48 | 79 | 28 | 38 |
| VII. Trade and Commerce | 20 | 5 | 15 | 21 | 23 | 11 | 17 |
| VIII. Transport, etc | 41 | 153 | 34 | 69 | 45 | 37 | 69 |
| IX. Other Services | 200 | 755 | 475 | 207 | 482 | 197 | 368 |
| Total | 1,000 | 1,000 | 1,000 | 1,000 | 1,000 | 1,000 | 1,000 |
| Workers per 1,000 persons | 476 | 442 | 405 | 452 | 499 | 498 | 456 |

NOTES: (1) The figures show numbers of workers in each category per 1,000 workers except for the bottom column, which shows a number of workers per 1,000 persons.

(2) Categories as listed in the 1961 Census are same as Table 2.9.

SOURCE: Same as Table 2.9

industry rose.[21] In this process, various traditional crafts and services providers, such as carpenters, blacksmiths, weavers and potters, lost their economic base in rural areas.

In urban areas, changes during this period in the occupational structure of male workers include: a decrease in the relative importance of manufacturing in other-than-household industry, and a gradual diversification of occupational structure toward the construction, trade and commerce, and transport and communication industries. The number of per thousand workers in manufacturing other-than-household industry in 1961 appears to be larger than that in 1991. This is partly because the leading cotton textiles and related industries, flourishing and absorbing a vast number of workers in 1961, declined sharply by 1980s, and partly because newly emerging manufacturing units became more capital intensive. As urbanization increased, the ratio of the construction, trade and commerce, and transport and communication industries increased while the relative importance of manufacturing in absorbing workers further decreased. There was, however, no erosion of the predominance of manufacturing in the GDP and its superiority in employment conditions. Even in 1961, the proportion of Vankar and Chamar workers in manufacturing other-than-household industry was fairly high, as was that of Bhangi and Garoda workers in other services. The superiority of advanced groups such as the Vankars and Chamars in the urban occupational structure over the backward group has not basically changed in the three decades under study.

### *Educational Structure*

There was a small increase in the literacy rate in the first half of the twentieth century under British rule (Table 2.11). Since the Brahmans and the Baniyas already had a high literacy rate, this increase can be attributed to the gradual entry of powerful farming castes, and certain artisan and service castes into primary education. The literacy rate increased rapidly only after Independence due to the establishment of educational facilities, increasing aspiration for education, and gradual decrease in the economic value of child labour. Immediately after Independence education became a priority for the state government (then Bombay State) and provisions

TABLE 2.11: TRENDS IN LITERACY IN GUJARAT (1901-91)

| Census Year | Numbers literate (100,000) | | | Sex ratio of literate* | Literacy rate (%) | | |
|---|---|---|---|---|---|---|---|
| | Male | Female | Total | | Male | Female | Total |
| 1901 | 6.76 | 0.45 | 7.21 | 67 | 14.52 | 1.01 | 7.93 |
| 1911 | 8.05 | 0.85 | 8.94 | 111 | 15.98 | 1.88 | 9.12 |
| 1921 | 9.42 | 1.62 | 11.04 | 172 | 18.00 | 3.28 | 10.85 |
| 1931 | 11.56 | 2.21 | 13.77 | 191 | 18.89 | 3.96 | 11.98 |
| 1941 | N.A. | N.A. | N.A. | N.A. | N.A. | N.A. | N.A. |
| 1951 | 25.13 | 10.14 | 35.27 | 404 | 30.17 | 12.79 | 21.69 |
| 1961 | 43.73 | 19.10 | 62.83 | 437 | 41.13 | 19.10 | 30.45 |
| 1971 | 63.64 | 31.91 | 95.55 | 501 | 46.11 | 24.75 | 35.79 |
| 1981 | 95.55 | 53.41 | 148.96 | 641 | 54.44 | 32.30 | 43.70 |
| 1991 | 130.81 | 81.96 | 212.77 | 627 | 61.50 | 41.18 | 51.67 |

NOTE: *The number of literate females per 1000 literate males.
SOURCE: Government of Gujarat, *The Bulletin of Economics and Statistics*, Vol. XXV No. 2, April-June 1985, p. 7, Table 2. Also, Government of India, Census of India 1991, Series-7 Gujarat, Supplement of Paper 1 of 1991, *Provisional Population Totals*, 1993, p. 33.

were made for the free distribution of textbooks, uniforms and meals for school children. At present, there is a campaign to encourage more girls to complete middle school education, and to raise the school attendance rate of the Scheduled Tribes, educationally the most backward of all the groups. In 1981, the literacy rate of the Scheduled Castes was 35 per cent, the Scheduled Tribes 20 per cent and other groups 40 per cent. The literacy rate improved dramatically by 1991, especially among the Scheduled Castes. The differential between male and female literacy rates decreased considerably.

Now we examine the differentials in the distribution of literate by educational level among the main *jatis* of the Scheduled Castes. Firstly, we deal with the case of males in rural areas. There are considerable differentials in the literacy rate and the level of education between the advanced and backward groups in 1991 (Table 2.12). The Vankars and Chamars are better in both the indices, while the Meghvals, Senvas and Bhangis are educationally backward. Differentials between the advanced and backward groups are larger at the higher educational level. The Meghval population is concentrated in Kutch, a socio-economically-backward district. The

TABLE 2.12: DISTRIBUTION OF MALE LITERATE BY *JATI* AND EDUCATIONAL LEVEL IN RURAL AREAS (1991)

(%)

| Caste | Literacy Rate | Literate without Schooling | Primary | Middle | Higher Secondary etc. | Under-graduate & above |
|---|---|---|---|---|---|---|
| Chamars | 70.33 | 27.15 | 19.33 | 9.71 | 11.49 | 2.64 |
| Bhangis | 63.07 | 29.84 | 18.77 | 7.90 | 5.56 | 0.98 |
| Garodas | 89.58 | 26.17 | 23.42 | 14.94 | 19.09 | 5.97 |
| Vankars | 75.61 | 26.81 | 20.13 | 11.42 | 13.81 | 3.43 |
| Meghvals | 57.63 | 31.58 | 16.07 | 5.60 | 3.85 | 0.53 |
| Senvas | 66.24 | 29.42 | 20.14 | 8.60 | 7.25 | 0.83 |
| SCs | 71.21 | 27.58 | 19.50 | 10.06 | 11.41 | 2.67 |

NOTES: (1) 'Literate without schooling' shows the ratio of literate who have had no formal education or who did not complete their primary education. 'Primary' is Years 1-5, 'Middle' is Years 6-8.

(2) The column of 'Higher Secondary' includes Matriculation, Secondary, Higher Secondary, Intermediate and Pre-University.

(3) The column of 'Undergraduate and above' includes undergraduates, post-graduates, and graduates of specialist courses.

SOURCE: Same as Table 2.2

Bhangis and Senvas have an extremely weak land-holding base, which is directly connected with their low literacy rates. Interestingly, the literacy rate of the Garodas is exceptionally high. Their inclination towards their traditional occupation, which prerequisites literacy, is much to do with their high literacy rate. In this aspect the Garodas resemble the Brahmans, the priests for the Caste Hindus. The Garodas also exhibit superiority over the other *jatis* in the level of education. They are particularly well-represented at the higher level. The proportion of graduates among the Garodas is more than double the average of other *jatis*.

The urban-rural differentials in the literacy rate of males have been shrinking rapidly due to the spread of primary, middle and higher secondary education in rural areas, though the proportion of graduates is half as much as that of urban areas. In urban area, the differentials in the literacy rate among the *jatis* are relatively small (Table 2.13). The disparities among the *jatis* appear in the ratio of those completing higher secondary and graduates. The Garodas, the Vankars and the Chamars constitute the most advanced groups in urban area, while the Meghvals, the Bhangis and the Senvas are educationally backward.

Tables 2.14 and 2.15 present the distribution of female literate by educational level in rural and urban areas respectively. In rural areas, the literacy rate of females is still very low, 39 per cent only. What is more, the proportion of lower educational level, particularly, that of 'literate without

TABLE 2.13: DISTRIBUTION OF MALE LITERATE BY *JATI* AND EDUCATIONAL LEVEL IN URBAN AREAS (1991)

(%)

| Caste | Literacy Rate | Literate without Schooling | Primary | Middle | Higher Secondary etc. | Under-graduate & above |
|---|---|---|---|---|---|---|
| Chamars | 84.39 | 22.94 | 22.41 | 15.58 | 17.57 | 5.89 |
| Bhangis | 76.59 | 29.64 | 24.35 | 12.64 | 8.71 | 1.25 |
| Garodas | 92.72 | 21.36 | 22.00 | 17.41 | 23.33 | 8.61 |
| Vankars | 85.71 | 21.82 | 20.85 | 15.72 | 20.01 | 7.35 |
| Megbvals | 69.71 | 24.98 | 21.83 | 11.72 | 9.23 | 1.96 |
| Senvas | 79.33 | 26.58 | 23.23 | 14.75 | 12.54 | 2.22 |
| SCs | 82.35 | 23.69 | 21.86 | 14.77 | 16.63 | 5.39 |

NOTE: For description of the educational levels, see Table 2.12.
SOURCE: Same as Table 2.2

TABLE 2.14: DISTRIBUTION OF FEMALE LITERATE BY *JATI* AND EDUCATIONAL LEVEL IN RURAL AREAS (1991)

(%)

| Caste | Literacy Rate | Literate without Schooling | Primary | Middle | Higher Secondary etc. | Under-graduate & above |
|---|---|---|---|---|---|---|
| Chamars | 37.40 | 17.78 | 11.24 | 4.23 | 3.61 | 0.54 |
| Bhangis | 34.30 | 20.08 | 10.56 | 2.32 | 1.09 | 0.25 |
| Garodas | 53.71 | 22.32 | 17.27 | 6.80 | 6.37 | 0.95 |
| Vankars | 43.72 | 19.71 | 13.46 | 5.14 | 4.69 | 0.72 |
| Moghvals | 21.13 | 14.96 | 5.32 | 0.57 | 0.25 | 0.03 |
| Senvas | 35.57 | 21.18 | 10.84 | 2.25 | 1.23 | 0.07 |
| SCs | 38.96 | 18.90 | 11.85 | 4.12 | 3.54 | 0.55 |

NOTES: For description of the educational levels, see Table 2.12.
SOURCE: Same as Table 2.2

TABLEL.2.15: DISTRIBUTION OF FEMALE LITERATE BY *JATI* AND EDUCATIONAL LEVEL IN URBAN AREAS (1991)

(%)

| Caste | Literacy Rate | Literate without Schooling | Primary | Middle | Higher Secondary etc. | Under-graduate & above |
|---|---|---|---|---|---|---|
| Chamars | 60.13 | 20.07 | 18.49 | 9.56 | 9.79 | 2.22 |
| Bhangis | 46.56 | 22.78 | 16.07 | 4.81 | 2.44 | 0.47 |
| Garodas | 68.87 | 21.68 | 21.01 | 11.68 | 11.96 | 2.54 |
| Vankars | 62.05 | 20.14 | 18.19 | 9.99 | 10.77 | 2.96 |
| Meghvals | 33.60 | 16.11 | 11.16 | 3.36 | 2.65 | 0.32 |
| Senvas | 55.25 | 23.96 | 18.92 | 6.89 | 4.96 | 0.52 |
| SCs | 56.53 | 20.39 | 17.48 | 8.37 | 8.25 | 2.05 |

NOTES: For description of the educational levels, see Table 2.12.
SOURCE: Same as Table 2.2.

schooling' is relatively large. Also, differentials in the literacy rate among the main *jatis* are large. The Megvals, the Bhangis and the Senvas lag behind the Garodas and the Vankars. In urban areas, the proportion of middle educational level is larger, and differentials in the literacy rate among the main *jatis* are smaller than those of rural areas.

From the above four tables, the gender differential among the *jatis* can be ascertained as follows: (i) there is a larger gender differential regarding literacy and formal education in rural over urban areas; (ii) the gender differential widens in the higher reaches of education in both rural and urban areas; (iii) the gender differential among the *jatis* in higher secondary and graduate levels is lesser in urban areas than in rural areas; and (iv) the gender differential within the same *jati* is smaller among the advanced group in both rural and urban areas. Overall, the differential among the *jatis* tends to appear larger in the female literacy rate and their educational levels than that of males. In this regard, the gender differentials are effective indices to measure the actual disparities among the *jatis* in terms of resource availability and its mobilization for education.

The educational structure of the Scheduled Castes has changed considerably over the thirty years between 1961 and 1991. For the year 1961, Tables 2.16 and 2.17 show the distribution of male literate by educational level in urban and rural areas respectively. Between 1951 and 1961, the literacy rate rose in higher rate than before due to the rigorous provision of the government to promote primary education. As a result, the male literacy rate for the Scheduled Castes increased to 45 per cent in urban areas and 30 per cent in rural areas in 1961. Though primary education got some momentum, the proportion of higher secondary and above level among male literate was still very low in both rural and urban areas.

Among the *jatis* of the Scheduled Castes, the Garoda males were markedly ahead of the other *jatis* not only in the literacy rate but also in the

TABLE 2.16: DISTRIBUTION OF MALE LITERATE BY *JATI* AND EDUCATIONAL LEVEL IN URBAN AREAS (1961)

(%)

| Caste | Literacy Rate | Literate without Schooling | Primary & Middle | Higher Secondary etc. | Under-graduate & above |
|---|---|---|---|---|---|
| Chamars | 44.55 | 17.46 | 25.74 | 1.23 | 0.12 |
| Bhangis | 37.80 | 13.09 | 24.20 | 0.37 | 0.14 |
| Garodas | 62.81 | 20.67 | 39.64 | 2.42 | 0.08 |
| Vankars | 49.96 | 16.70 | 30.99 | 2.08 | 0.19 |
| Meghvals | 30.38 | 13.42 | 16.49 | 0.44 | 0.03 |
| Senvas | 38.77 | 12.92 | 24.96 | 0.89 | – |
| SCs | 44.88 | 16.01 | 27.33 | 1.40 | 0.14 |

NOTE: Primary and Middle schooling was not differentiated in the 1961 Census.
SOURCE: Same as Table 2.9

TABLE 2.17: DISTRIBUTION OF MALE LITERATE BY *JATI* AND EDUCATIONAL LEVEL IN RURAL AREAS (1961)

(%)

| Caste | Literacy Rate | Literate without Schooling | Primary & Middle | Higher Secondary & above |
|---|---|---|---|---|
| Chamars | 30.17 | 14.00 | 15.92 | 0.25 |
| Bhangis | 23.29 | 10.60 | 12.63 | 0.06 |
| Garodas | 58.94 | 26.51 | 31.69 | 0.74 |
| Vankars | 36.27 | 14.70 | 21.17 | 0.40 |
| Meghvals | 13.93 | 7.57 | 6.34 | 0.02 |
| Senvas | 20.73 | 12.60 | 8.10 | 0.03 |
| SCs | 30.13 | 13.36 | 16.51 | 0.26 |

NOTE: Primary and Middle schooling, as well as Higher Secondary and Undergraduate education were not differentiated in the 1961 census data for rural areas.

SOURCE: Same as Table 2.9.

proportion of higher secondary level. The Vankars and the Chamars followed the Garodas, but their superiority had been derived mainly from differentials in literacy rates because there was a general lack of participation at the higher secondary and above levels among all *jatis*. The number of graduates has a special implication for socio-economic development of graduates themselves as well as community as a whole to which they belong. Table 2.18 presents the comparative figures of graduates by sex among the Scheduled Castes for the years 1961 and 1991. The data for rural areas in 1961 does not distinguish between upper secondary and graduate levels and so has been omitted. Figures for male graduates in urban areas in 1961 reveal a strong presence by the Vankars of more than half the total number; followed by the Bhangis and the Chamars. It is notable that the Bhangis had as many male graduates as the Chamars in 1961, though its reason is unknown. It is also interesting to note that the Garodas had very less number of male graduates irrespective of their supremacy in literacy rate over the other *jatis*. Female graduates were mostly from the Vankars in 1961. By 1991, the number of graduates had increased considerably. The Vankars and the Chamars, the most populous *jatis*, were the leading contributors. The combined figures for the two *jatis* represent 83 per cent of the male graduates and 84 per cent of the female graduates of the Scheduled Castes in the rural areas; and 82 per cent of the male graduates and 85 per cent of the female graduates in urban areas in

TABLE 2.18: DISTRIBUTION OF NUMBERS COMPLETING UNDERGRADUATE EDUCATION BY *JATI* AND SEX IN RURAL AND URBAN AREAS (1961, 1991)

(*persons*)

| Caste | 1961 | | 1991 | | | |
|---|---|---|---|---|---|---|
| | Urban areas | | Urban areas | | Rural areas | |
| | Male | Female | Male | Female | Male | Female |
| Chamars | 42 | 1 | 6,933 | 2,350 | 6,240 | 1,203 |
| Bhangis | 46 | 0 | 963 | 339 | 713 | 169 |
| Garodas | 4 | 0 | 926 | 247 | 990 | 150 |
| Vankars | 149 | 10 | 15,276 | 5,560 | 11,836 | 2,334 |
| Meghvals | 3 | 0 | 392 | 59 | 211 | 13 |
| Senvas | 0 | 0 | 119 | 24 | 247 | 20 |
| SCs | 246 | 11 | 27,088 | 9,338 | 21,666 | 4,210 |

SOURCES: Same as Tables 2.2 and 2.9.

1991. Though we do not have data on *jati*-wise beneficiaries of reservation system for higher education, we may surmise that the Vankars and the Chamars have been the main beneficiaries of the system taking into consideration their population size and resource availability.

Variations in the levels of education among the *jatis* in rural areas are basically related to those in urban areas. In rural areas, land holding patterns directly regulate resource availability of individuals as well as community. A fragile rural economic base causes a similar fragility in the economic base of migrants to urban areas. A weak economic base reduces their opportunities to pursue higher education, which is necessary for acquiring a profitable job, and there is a tendency for this cycle to continue in successive generations of migrants. The industrial structure of Gujarat is more diversified with the development of manufacturing and service industries than other states. Still, in the present setting of Gujarat, where the rural population ratio is 70 per cent and the proportion held by agriculture in the state GDP is 35 per cent, the regulatory power of land holding still remains strong.

### THE BHANGIS AND TRADITIONAL OCCUPATIONS

The type of occupations available in rural areas is far more limited than in urban areas. In rural areas, those who are engaged in agriculture among the Scheduled Castes either as cultivators or as agricultural labourers constitute 72 per cent of male main workers in 1991, while the figure for male workers was 64 per cent in 1961. Though the ratio of cultivators decreased drastically between 1961 and 1991, the ratio of agricultural labourers increased tremendously, making it the most important industry in terms of the number of workers in rural areas. Further more, many of the traditional occupations that make up the bulk of household industry and other service industries disappeared or declined during that period, making the ratio of the agricultural sector even higher. For the powerful agricultural castes in rural areas, this was a favourable condition for their agricultural management.

In rural areas, occupational restrictions against the Scheduled Castes are still observed with some kind of coercion with regard to the performance of economic activities that are considered dirty. These include the disposal of dead cows, bullocks, buffaloes, dogs and cats, and anything that deals with cleaning. Specific jobs are assigned to the Scheduled Castes as a whole, but within the various *jatis* of the Scheduled Castes there is a ranking based on the concept of cleanliness and social and economic differences. It is the Bhangis who have to undertake the disposal of the bodies of cats and dogs, work considered to be the most filthy and other cleaning tasks. Such occupational restrictions against the Scheduled Castes are built in the rural economy as one of the means of dominance by the upper castes.

In urban areas, occupational restrictions against the Scheduled Castes have almost disappeared in recent years. What regulate the occupational structure of the Scheduled Castes are their network, available resources and educational structure. Naturally, the ratios of workers among the advanced groups of the Scheduled Castes who are employed in rewarding jobs or white collar jobs are relatively high. By contrast, the backward groups have a narrow range of job options, as they are bound to their traditional occupations. A typical example of this is the Bhangis.

It would be useful to examine trends in the number of workers among the Scheduled Castes who are engaged in tanning and scavenging/sweeping based on the 1961 and 1981 Censuses.[22] These works are typical unclean occupations specific to the Scheduled Castes. Tables 2.19 and 2.20 clearly show that the *jatis* associated with these occupations traditionally, the Chamars for tanning and the Bhangis for sweeping, share the majority of workers in each occupation. However, we observe a keen contrast in the trends in their association with tanning and sweeping during the 20 years between 1961 and 1981.

Tanning had 14,622 and 2,081 workers among the Scheduled Castes in

TABLE 2.19: DISTRIBUTION OF WORKERS IN TANNING AND SWEEPING BY *JATI* AND SEX IN RURAL AND URBAN AREAS (1961)

*(persons %)*

| Caste | Tanning | | | | Sweeping | | | |
|---|---|---|---|---|---|---|---|---|
| | Numbers of workers | | Ratio among workers (%) | | Numbers of workers | | Ratio among workers (%) | |
| | male | female | male | female | male | female | male | female |
| SCs | | | | | | | | |
| rural | 10,843 | 3,779 | 3.94 | 1.93 | 2,826 | 1,154 | 1.03 | 0.59 |
| urban | 1,779 | 302 | 2.22 | 0.99 | 8,813 | 6,548 | 11.01 | 21.49 |
| Chamars | | | | | | | | |
| rural | 8,098 | 2,868 | 12.80 | 6.52 | 148 | 78 | 0.23 | 0.18 |
| urban | 1,337 | 225 | 8.04 | 4.29 | 138 | 38 | 0.83 | 0.72 |
| Bhangis | | | | | | | | |
| rural | 108 | 38 | 0.32 | 0.20 | 2,501 | 1,017 | 7.50 | 5.47 |
| urban | 75 | 23 | 0.51 | 0.30 | 8,318 | 6,140 | 56.61 | 81.12 |
| Vankars | | | | | | | | |
| rural | 464 | 153 | 0.40 | 0.17 | 52 | 27 | 0.05 | 0.03 |
| urban | 215 | 29 | 0.59 | 0.22 | 106 | 114 | 0.29 | 0.87 |
| Meghvals | | | | | | | | |
| rural | 1,501 | 520 | 4.75 | 2.44 | 11 | 9 | 0.03 | 0.04 |
| urban | 95 | 8 | 2.14 | 0.35 | 19 | 41 | 0.43 | 1.79 |

SOURCE: Same as Table 2.9.

rural and urban areas respectively in 1961. These numbers had decreased dramatically to 809 in rural areas and 227 in urban areas by 1981. The decrease is particularly marked in rural areas. The tanning sector had been virtually eliminated in rural Gujarat. The same trend can also be seen in urban areas. As a result of the changes over the 20 years, the linkage between the Chamars and tanning had been almost completely severed. The main reason for this was that traditional tanning method had lost its economic value due to changes in technology, communication and consumer structures in Gujarat. At the same time, we have to see the Chamars' positive achievements in widening occupational choices made available to them.

Scavenging and sweeping however presents an entirely different 0picture. In 1961, there were 15,361 sweepers among the Scheduled Castes in urban areas, and by 1981 the number increased to 34,322, more than doubled. In rural areas, there was also an increase in the number of sweepers,

TABLE 2.20: DISTRIBUTION OF MAIN WORKERS IN TANNING AND SWEEPING BY *JATI* AND SEX IN RURAL AND URBAN AREAS (1981)

(*persons %*)

| Caste | Tanning | | | | Sweeping | | | |
|---|---|---|---|---|---|---|---|---|
| | Numbers of workers | | Ratio among workers (%) | | Numbers of workers | | Ratio among workers (%) | |
| | male | female | male | female | male | female | male | female |
| SCs | | | | | | | | |
| rural | 763 | 46 | 0.19 | 0.03 | 4,859 | 1,254 | 1.19 | 0.92 |
| urban | 212 | 15 | 0.12 | 0.04 | 21,445 | 12,877 | 11.83 | 31.75 |
| Chamars | | | | | | | | |
| rural | 701 | 44 | 0.60 | 0.12 | 89 | 14 | 0.08 | 0.04 |
| urban | 190 | 10 | 0.41 | 0.14 | 238 | 99 | 0.51 | 1.39 |
| Bhangis | | | | | | | | |
| rural | 6 | – | 0.01 | – | 4,269 | 1,136 | 9.96 | 8.84 |
| urban | 1 | – | 0.00 | – | 18,441 | 11,215 | 64.35 | 89.47 |
| Vankars | | | | | | | | |
| rural | 29 | 1 | 0.02 | 0.00 | 117 | 43 | 0.07 | 0.07 |
| urban | 13 | 5 | 0.02 | 0.03 | 488 | 261 | 0.63 | 1.71 |
| Meghvals | | | | | | | | |
| rural | 6 | 1 | 0.02 | 0.01 | 7 | 3 | 0.03 | 0.03 |
| urban | 1 | – | 0.01 | – | 148 | 163 | 1.70 | 7.94 |

SOURCE: Compiled from Government of India, Census of India 1981, Series 5, Gujarat, Part IX(i), *Special Tables for Scheduled Castes*, 1988.

from 3,980 to 6,113. The great majority of sweepers were the Bhangis, whether in terms of urban or rural area, or sex. During this period, the Bhangis accelerated their entry into sweeping both in urban and rural areas. Accordingly, the ratio of male sweepers among the Bhangi male workers increased from 57 per cent in 1961 to 64 per cent in 1981 in urban areas. Though the number of Bhangi female sweepers was short of that of Bhangi male sweepers in urban areas, the ratio of female sweepers among the Bhangi female workers showed an exceptionally high level. It shifted from 81 per cent to 90 per cent in urban areas between 1961 and 1981.

Despite the concentration of Bhangi workers in sweeping, the proportion of Bhangi sweepers among the Scheduled Caste sweepers in urban areas actually fell from 94 per cent in 1961 to 86 per cent in 1981. This reflects the rapid growth in demand for sweepers and scavengers. Though the number of Bhangi sweepers has increased, it was not sufficient to meet the demand. Demand for sweepers has been increasing in rural areas, too. In response to it, there has been a gradual increase in the number of Bhangi sweepers as well as the ratio of sweepers among the Bhangi workers for both the sexes. The need for collecting rubbish and night soil has been increasing in rural areas under the influence of urbanization.

Sweepers in urban areas are engaged in various activities, the most important of which are the cleaning of drains, the disposal of human waste, the collection of rubbish, and street cleaning. The increase in demand for their services has been especially marked with the development of sanitary facilities for sewage treatment, night soil disposal and the rubbish management system. Since the collection of rubbish will be discussed in Chapter Three, a brief discussion on sewage treatment and night soil disposal is presented here.

Table 2.21 gives the distribution of towns by most common type of sewerage and population size of towns (1991). Only 31 per cent of the towns in Gujarat have a modern sewer system as most common type of sewerage. The ratio is 61 per cent only even among the towns with more than 50,000 population. Most towns have open surface drains and cesspools, and sweepers are indispensable for the maintenance and cleaning of these facilities. Table 2.22 shows the distribution of towns by

TABLE 2.21: DISTRIBUTION OF TOWNS AND CITIES BY POPULATION SIZE AND MOST COMMON TYPE OF SEWERAGE (1991)

(*numbers of towns and cities*)

| Most common type of sewerage/drainage | Population size of towns/cities | | | | | | |
|---|---|---|---|---|---|---|---|
| | over 100,000 | 50,000-100,000 | 20,000-50,000 | 10,000-20,000 | 5,000 10,000 | under 5,000 | Total |
| Sewer | 10 | 21 | 19 | 21 | 9 | 2 | 82 |
| Open surface drains | 8 | 9 | 28 | 53 | 24 | 5 | 127 |
| Box surface drains | – | 1 | 1 | 1 | – | – | 3 |
| Sylk drains | – | – | 1 | 1 | – | – | 2 |
| Cesspool method | 1 | 1 | 8 | 12 | 16 | 4 | 42 |
| Pit system | – | – | 1 | 3 | 2 | – | 6 |
| Total | 19 | 32 | 58 | 91 | 51 | 11 | 262 |

NOTES: (1) Towns and cities are divided into five groups based on population.
(2) A joint Municipality for Patan and Veraval towns is included in the group of 50,000-100,000 persons, and a joint Nagar Panchayat for Sikka and Digvijaygram is included in the group of 10,000-20,000 persons.

SOURCE: Compiled from Government of India, Census of India 1991, Series 7 Gujarat, Part IX-A, *Town Directory*, pp. 28-9, Table 16 (A).

TABLE 2.22: DISTRIBUTION OF TOWNS AND CITIES BY POPULATION SIZE AND MOST COMMON METHOD OF DISPOSAL OF NIGHT SOIL (1991)

(*numbers of towns and cities*)

| Most common method of disposal of night soil | Poppulation size of towns/cities | | | | | | |
|---|---|---|---|---|---|---|---|
| | over 100,000 | 50,000-100,000 | 20,000-50,000 | 10,000-20,000 | 5,000 10,000 | under 5,000 | Total |
| Wheel barrow | 1 | 4 | 8 | 17 | 8 | 2 | 40 |
| Septic tank | 10 | 18 | 36 | 61 | 38 | 7 | 170 |
| Sewerage plant | 8 | 10 | 14 | 13 | 5 | 2 | 52 |
| Total | 19 | 32 | 58 | 91 | 51 | 11 | 262 |

NOTES: For description of the population size of towns and cities, see Table 2.21.
SOURCE: Compiled from Government of India, Census of India 1991, Series 7 Gujarat, Part IX-A, *Town Directory*, pp. 30-1, Table 16(C).

most common method of disposal of night soil and population size of towns (1991). Only 20 per cent of towns have modern treatment plants as most common method, and 65 per cent of towns rely on septic tanks. Periodic removal of waste from these is essential. In 15 per cent of towns night soil is carried by wheelbarrow, and even in large towns this method partially remains. Hindu society views human excreta as the most polluted of all things, and the manual disposal of night soil is considered as the dirtiest type of economic activity. A variety of methods are used, but overall, there is little difference in the method of collection whatever the population size of the town. The cleaning out of septic tanks and the collection of human waste from latrines is carried out almost exclusively by the Bhangis.

Sewage, night-soil disposal and rubbish collection are basically the responsibility of local bodies. The workers they employ carry out these tasks. As statewide data about the sweepers employed by local bodies are not available, we examine here the case of the Ahmedabad Municipal Corporation (AMC: population 2.96 million in 1991). Table 2.23 gives the distribution of employees of the AMC by class and community in 1987. The permanent employees of the AMC are divided into four classes. Sweepers and other sanitary workers belong to the fourth class. They number around 9,500 out of the 15,948 permanent employees in this class. Their basic wage, for both male and female workers, is between Rs. 750

TABLE 2.23: DISTRIBUTION OF PERMANENT EMPLOYEES OF AHMEDABAD MUNICIPAL CORPORATION BY CLASS AND COMMUNITY (1987)

*(numbers of workers)*

| Class | Basic wage (Rs.) | SCs | STs | OBCs | P.H.* | Others | Total |
|---|---|---|---|---|---|---|---|
| I | 2,200-4,200 | 6 | 2 | 3 | 1 | 111 | 123 |
| II | 2,000-3,200 | 36 | 4 | 10 | 4 | 298 | 352 |
| III | 950-1,500 | 701 | 85 | 466 | 22 | 4,095 | 5,369 |
| IV | 750-940 | 10,790 | 987 | 1,134 | 29 | 3,008 | 15,948 |
| Total | | 11,533 | 1,078 | 1,613 | 56 | 7,512 | 21,792 |

NOTE: *P.H. means physically handicapped.
SOURCE: Information from the Roster Branch of the Ahmedabad Municipal Corporation (December 1989).

and Rs. 940 a month, on the same scale as that of gardeners, machine fitters and general manual workers. Even so, there is little participation by members of other *jatis* of the Scheduled Castes, who regard sweeping and other sanitary works as an unclean work.

The progress of urbanization and industrialization generally brings about the decline of traditional occupations that are mostly not competitive with a new technology backed by mass production. Also, it loosens the occupational restrictions against the Scheduled Castes, and provides wider choice of occupations to those who are resourceful. The Vankars and the Chamars are almost completely free of their traditional occupations and their socio-economic progress has been remarkable among the Scheduled Castes. On the other hand, urbanization has made the Bhangis even more closely identified with their traditional occupation. Demand for sweepers has been ever increasing. There is no indication at the present time that there will be any change in the way society regards this work, and there will probably be no rapid modernization of facilities or methods for the disposal of waste products. For the Bhangis, caught up in a mesh of backwardness, any autonomy in the power to widen their choice of better occupations remains remote. As a result, for the time being, the utilization of reservations for the Scheduled Castes and other policy packages targeted the landless and backward classes makes a very important issue for the development of the Bhangis.

## NOTES

1. For levels of wages in the agricultural sector and regional differences, see Government of Gujarat, *Report of the Gujarat State Land Commission*, 1979, Chap. 8, and B.B. Patel, *The Structure of Inter-District Inter-Sector and Inter-Industry Wage Differentials in Gujarat*, Baroda: M.S. University, 1976.
2. Government of Gujarat, *Report of the Socially and Educationally Backward Classes (Second) Commission*, Vol. 1, p. 35. The Gujarat State Government has convened three commissions to date to determine a standard for defining socially and educationally backward classes and for deciding a framework for reservation. The first was in 1976, the second in 1983 and the third in 1986. Reports of the first two commissions have been published.
3. It has been proven that even in 1961, school attendance by the Scheduled Castes in Gujarat was higher than in other states. That year the literacy rate of the Scheduled Castes was 22.5 per cent, compared with 10.3 per cent for the Scheduled Castes of India as a whole. Moreover, among states Gujarat has the smallest difference between the literacy rate of Scheduled Castes and that of Non-Scheduled Castes. V.N. Kothari, *A Study of Economic Profiles of the Scheduled Castes in Gujarat*, Baroda: M.S. University, 1976, pp. 23-5.
4. For the growth of manufacturing in Gujarat since Independence, performance records, the labour environment and changes in productivity, see D.T. Lakdawala (ed.), *Gujarat Economy: Problems and Prospects*, Ahmedabad: SPIESR, 1983, in particular the eight essays in Section V, Industrial Structure and Industrial Relations.
5. The first cotton factory in Gujarat was set up in Ahmedabad in 1858 (production began in 1861) by Ranchhodlal Chhotalal (1823-98), a man of Brahman extraction. Ahmedabad subsequently became, with Bombay, the centre of the Indian cotton industry. The Untouchables entered the cotton industry in Gujarat in great numbers. Particularly in the early period, Caste Hindus avoided factory work, which made the proportion of Untouchable labourers in the industry especially high.
6. The six groups studied in this work are:
   1. Bhambi, Bhambhi, Asadaru, Asadi, Chamadia, Chamar, Chambhar, Chamgar, Haralayya, Harali, Khalpa, Machigar, Madar, Madig, Mochi, Nalia, Telugu Mochi, Kamati Mochi, Ranigar, Rohidas, Rohit, Samgar (called here Chamar).
   2. Bhangi, Mehtar, Olgana, Rukhi, Malkana, Halalknor, Lalbegi, Balmiki, Korar, Zadmalli (called here Bhangi).
   3. Garoda, Garo (called here Garoda).
   4. Mahyavansi, Dhed, Dhedh, Vankar, Maru Vankar, Antyaj (called here Vankar).
   5. Meghval, Meghwal, Menghvar (called here Meghval).
   6. Senva, Shenva, Chenva, Sedma, Rawat (called here Senva).

   Each group includes *jatis* with different regional names, variant names of the same *jati*, and *jatis* with the same or similar traditional occupations, though they do not intermarry. The representative name of each group is the name of the *jati*, which previous research had identified as the most powerful in the group. Social and economic differentials between *jatis* of the same group cannot be dealt with because data is not available for the individual *jatis*.

   The group divisions of the Scheduled Castes in the 1961 Census differ from those of the 1991 Census, as they have been divided into four regions.

However, it is possible to compare these figures with the 1991 groupings through the table for the state as a whole. The 1961 Census data given in this study has been made to correspond with the 1991 group divisions, and the representative group names have also been unified.

The list of Scheduled Castes in the 1961 Census is found in Government of India, Census of India 1961, Vol. V Gujarat, Part V-A, *Tables on Scheduled Castes and Scheduled Tribes*, 1964, p. 385. The same list for the 1991 Census is in Government of India, *Census of Gujarat: A Kaleidscope (1961-2001)*, 2002.

7. For details about the occupational regulations and the actual economic activities of the Scheduled Castes in rural areas, see I.P. Desai, *Untouchability in Rural Gujarat*, Bombay: Popular Prakashan, 1976. Also, the Gujarat Vidyapith has published four volumes of reports on the Scheduled Castes, which deal with distribution of persons and households by sex, age, school attendance, occupation and landholding, as well as debt, housing environment, illness, farming tools, domestic animals, etc. Since the main purpose of the surveys was to analyse differences among the Scheduled Castes by district, very little of the data has been organized by *jati*. Also, no division was made between rural and urban areas. The reports are listed below. Figures in brackets indicate the number of households surveyed.
    1. M. Masvi, *Gujaratna Harijano* (in Gujarati), Ahmedabad: Tribal Research and Training Institute, 1982 (34,118).
    2. M. Masvi and C. Upadhyay, *Gujaratna Harijano-2* (in Gujarati), Ahmedabad: Tribal Research and Training Institute, 1983 (49,154).
    3. M. Masvi and C. Upadhyay, *Gujaratna Harijano-3* (in Gujarati), Ahmedabad: Tribal Research and Training Institute, 1984 (45,425).
    4. C. Upadhyay and D. Parmar, *Gujaratna Harijano-4* (in Gujarati), Ahmedabad: Tribal Research and Training Institute, 1985 (61,595).
8. How particular, hereditary or traditional occupations are connected with *jati* formation or growth, to what extent members of a particular *jati* follow traditional occupations, and the nature of historical change in the reproduction structure of traditional occupations are questions which still need to be clarified. We have several research works on the traditional occupations of individual *jatis* conducted in the post-Independence period, but they are limited to a few occupations such as pottery-making, tanning and sweeping. We still have to draw basic information about traditional occupations from the Censuses, survey and settlement reports, ethnological survey reports, and gazetteers in the pre-Independence period.
9. For the Vankars, see J.M. Campbell (ed.), *Hindu Castes and Tribes of Gujarat*, Vol. 2, Gurgaon: Vintage Books, 1988 (1st pub. 1901), pp. 338-43; and R.E. Enthoven, *The Tribes and Castes of Bombay*, Vol. 1, Delhi: Cosmo Publications, 1975, pp. 322-8.
10. For the Chamars, see Campbell, op. cit., Vol. 2, pp. 345-6 and Enthoven, op. cit., Vol. 2, pp. 190-3.
11. For the Bhangis, see Campbell, op. cit., Vol. 2, pp. 334-8 and Enthoven, op. cit., Vol. 1, pp. 104-12.
12. For the Garodas, see Campbell, op. cit., Vol. 2, pp. 344-5 and Enthoven, op. cit., Vol. 1, pp. 230-1.

13. For the Senvas, see Campbell, op. cit., Vol. 2, pp. 346-7 and Enthoven, op. cit., Vol. 3, pp. 336-8. A monograph on the Senva as a whole appeared as part of the report in the Census of 1961. Government of India, Census of India 1961, Vol. V, Part V-B, No. 2, *The Shenvas: A Scheduled Caste of Gujarat*, 1972.
14. For the Meghvals, see ibid. pp. 43-52.
15. Reports about surveys of large numbers of villages include V. Shah and C.H. Shah, *Resurvey of Matar Taluka*, Bombay: Vora Publications, 1974; C.H. Shah et al., *Second Resurvey of Matar Taluka*, Ahmedabad: The Gujarat Institute of Area Planning, 1987; M.B. Desai, *Tenancy Abolition and the Emerging Pattern in Gujarat*, Baroda: M.S. University, 1971; Government of Gujarat, *Report of the Socially and Educationally Backward Classes Commission*, Vol. 2, 1976.
16. Although the number of cultivators per 1,000 rural male main workers for the Meghvals is 241, they are backward because they concentrate in Kutch and are engaged in extensive agriculture. While, the Garodas are not considered to be backward though the number of cultivators per 1,000 rural male main workers is 97 only. They enjoy better social status than other backward *jatis* among the Scheduled Castes.
17. Household industry is defined as a manufacturing unit where the main work force comes from the household, whose scale is smaller than a Factory, and where the work site is the home (in urban areas) or within the village of residence (in rural areas). Household industry covers not only manufacturing but also processing and repairs.
18. The State government encourages the development of small scale industries, in order to expand employment and reduce wage and local development differentials. The small scale industries, exempted from the industrial licensing system, are provided special concessions in terms of financing, taxation and the purchase of goods, and are sanctioned on the basis of fixed capital alone. The amount of fixed capital permitted has changed over the years; in 1992 it was Rs.6 million (Rs.7.5 million in the case of related industries). The number of units in this category in Gujarat grew rapidly from 5,127 in 1964 to 115,384 in 1990. The average number of workers employed daily in small scale industries was 276,955 in 1987/8.
19. Factory is such an enterprise that is defined and regulated by the Factory Act of 1947. According to the Act, it has more than 20 workers (where there is no motive power) and more than 10 workers (where there is motive power). It is compulsory for factories to register with the Commissioner of Factories. Since the Act stipulates both working and employment conditions, there are considerable differences between factories and other manufacturing units in wages and employment conditions. The number of factories increased from 3,649 in 1960 to 14,513 in 1990. The average number of workers employed daily in factories was 729,696 in 1986.
20. Workers in household manufacturing in the state in 1961 (both sexes) numbered 555,606. Of these, 49.60 per cent were employed in processing products from husbandry, 20.68 per cent in textiles, 9.79 per cent in the processing of mineral products, 9.62 per cent in processing forest products, and 4.51 per cent in processing agricultural products (Others, 5.80 per cent). Government of India, Census of India 1961, Vol. V Gujarat, Part IX, *Census Atlas*, 1965, p. 94.

21. The number of workers (both sexes) of the Scheduled Castes in the Household Industry (A) and Other-than-Household Industry (B) in 1961 were: (A) 34,164 and (B) 28,892 in rural areas and (A) 6,152 and (B) 74,182 in urban areas. The ratio of workers between (A) and (B), combining rural and urban areas was (A) 56.52 per cent and (B) 43.48 per cent in 1961 and (A) 28.12 per cent and (B) 71.88 per cent in 1981, this has been a significant change. (From Government of India, Census of India 1961, *Tables on Scheduled Castes and Scheduled Tribes*, pp. 8, 38 and Government of India, Census of India 1981, *Special Tables for Scheduled Castes*, p. 12.)
22. Data on workers engaged in tanning and scavenging/sweeping is not available in the 1991 Census, the 1881 Census results were taken for comparison.

Chapter Three

# Sanitary Facilities and Sweepers

## Introduction

As a result of the rapid and large scale population influx large cities in India share certain common urban problems. This rapid increase in population has not only led to increased population density in the cities but has also contributed to the growing proportion of slum dwellers and worsening of urban hygiene. The system of public health facilities and administration has not been able to respond effectively to the speed and scale of urbanization. Thus there is a critical need for a reorganization of public health services, such as drains and sewage, sanitation and rubbish collection.

This chapter will examine the reorganization of public health services in Ahmedabad, India's seventh largest city.[1] Having expanded as an industrial centre from the latter half of the nineteenth century, its population has increased very rapidly since 1940. The city has expanded as Ahmedabad absorbed its neighbouring areas, resulting in further increases in population. Since the tempo of expansion has been greater than other large cities the need to reorganize public health services has been all the move greater. This chapter will also examine the organization of labour and the nature of the work of the municipal departments in charge of sanitation, which have the main responsibility for public health services in the city. The disposal of human waste and polluted water is the responsibility of the sewage disposal office, the collection of rubbish, and its transportation and disposal are undertaken by the Conservancy Department, and the Refuse Department respectively.

## Development of the Municipal Administration System and Urban Sanitary Conditions

### *Municipal Administration System and Expansion of the City*

Ahmedabad was founded in 1411 by Sultan Ahmad Shah I. Since that time it has experienced a large number of political upheavals, but it still retains considerable influence as the political, cultural an economic centre of

Gujarat. From ancient times it has been a vital strategic centre, standing at the core of a number of important routes: the northern route that joins Gujarat and Delhi, the western route to Sind, and the southern route to the key maritime cities of Surat and Khambhat and on to Vadodara. Between 1411 and 1947, Ahmedabad saw four changes in the governing power. Between 1411 and 1573 it was ruled by an independent Islamic dynasty, before becoming a part of the Mughal Empire (1573-1753). With the disintegration of the Empire it was ruled by the Marathas from 1753 to 1817. Following its annexation by the East India Company in 1817, it remained under British rule until 1947. In 1950 Ahmedabad was incorporated into Bombay state (previously Bombay Province). Following the reorganization of the state along linguistic lines in 1956, it became the temporary capital of the new state of Gujarat in 1960. In 1970 the state capital was moved to Gandhinagar, specially built for the purpose.[2]

## DEVELOPMENT OF THE MUNICIPAL ADMINISTRATIVE SYSTEM

During the rule of the British East India Company (1817-57), a Non-Statutory Committee administered the city. The city was ruled by the Collector, the highest official, in collaboration with an urban elite comprising leading citizens, merchant gilds and government servants. An urgent issue for the city administration of the time was the reconstruction of the town wall, which had been damaged and lay in ruins under the Mughals and the Marathas. The repair of the wall was intended to protect the city and its commerce and industry, and to aid the collection of Town Duties.[3] The Town Wall Committee was constituted in 1831 and the rebuilding of the wall was completed in 1842.[4]

In 1850 the British East India Company decided that municipal charges should not be drawn out of the general revenue. In addition, Bombay government determined that no assistance will be provided for town improvements unless the townspeople made adequate contributions (Act XXVI of 1850). This act allowed the establishment of municipal institutions which involved the public, if the townspeople were ready for taking initiatives to improve the city. As a result of a petition by leading townspeople, a statutory municipal committee with 30 commissioners was set up in 1858. Among the commissioners, 16 were non-officials and 14 were officials, both English and Indian. They were appointed on behalf of the government, by the Collector, who was the president of the committee. The collector was usually the dominant voice, but occasionally his proposals were refused.[5]

The British government, after 1858 took over from the East India Company and directly ruled over Ahmedabad. In 1873 the Ahmedabad municipality was reconstituted as the city municipality according to the Bombay District Municipal Act (VI of 1873). This reconstitution, however, was a mere formality. The act empowered the Governor of Bombay to permit the election of non-official members, to the municipality, but when the Nagarseth (the city head) and a large number of citizens signed a petition seeking elections in Ahmedabad, they were refused.[6]

A major change in the municipal government occurred as a result of an initiative by the Viceroy in 1882 to expand local self government. The provincial governments were urged to extend more autonomy to local bodies and have popular elections. As a result, 12 commissioners were elected in 1883, in the first municipal elections in Ahmedabad. Ranchhodlal Chhotalal was appointed the first non-official chairman of the Managing Committee (the nucleus of municipal government). He had founded Ahmedabad's first textile mill in 1858 and had contributed greatly to the betterment of urban hygiene.

In the second decade of the twentieth century there was a heightening of a mass political consciousness, with the emergence of a peasant movement in Kheda District[7] and a trade union movement of textile mill workers in Ahmedabad.[8] Gandhi and his supporters guided these movements. A change occurred in the Ahmedabad municipal government at this time. V.J. Patel, the leader of the Kheda peasant movement, was elected to the municipal commission in 1917. He was severely critical of the inefficient water supply system and the evasion of taxes. Since he had support within the commission, he was elected president of the municipality in 1924. During his period in office (until 1928) he worked towards the extension of water supply and drainage facilities, the provision of a green belt of parks and gardens, and to initiate suburban planning schemes.[9] In 1926 the municipality became the Borough municipality.

Following Independence, in 1949, the Bombay Municipal Corporation Act was enacted. As a result the Borough municipality was reconstituted as the Municipal Corporation, which continues to exist. Today the Ahmedabad Municipal Corporation is one of the administrative bodies of the Ahmedabad City Taluka, one of the seven Talukas of Ahmedabad District. It forms, with surrounding villages and towns, the Ahmedabad Urban Agglomeration. Each of these villages and towns have their own self governing structure, but is due for absorption into Ahmedabad with the further development of the city. There are great variations between the Ahmedabad Municipal Corporation and the neighbouring villages and towns in terms of provision of sanitation and its management.

## EXPANSION OF THE MUNICIPAL AREA AND POPULATION GROWTH

The historical development of the city of Ahmedabad is shown in Map 3.1. Built on the east bank of the Sabarmati river in 1411, Ahmedabad developed as an important political and economic centre of Gujarat. During the Maratha rule it covered an area that is currently known as the Old Town (also called the Walled City). In 1857 Ahmedabad consisted of the area surrounded by the wall, the same as it had been under Maratha rule. When a railway was built between Ahmedabad and Surat in 1864, the station was constructed to the east of the city, where, in the last quarter of the nineteenth century, many textile mills were constructed. The city also developed in the direction of the Cantonment, on the east bank of the Sabarmati, north of Ahmedabad. By the beginning of the twentieth century, the area to the east and north had been absorbed into the city. The Ellis Bridge, the first to link the east and west banks of the Sabarmati, was built in 1892. Two more bridges were built before Independence, and two were built later, all contributing to the growth of the west bank, which developed in the first half of the twentieth century as a residential area with educational and cultural facilities. The east bank too had continued to grow as the textile industry expanded. Both areas were incorporated into the municipal administration. The same pattern of development on the east and west banks continued after Independence as more land was taken over by the administration. After the 1960s, the machinery, chemical and metal industries showed rapid growth on the east side of the city, and this area was brought into the city in 1986.

Table 3.1 shows changes in Ahmedabad's city area and population. As the figure shows clearly, population increased constantly between 1872 and 1931. During this time Gujarat suffered from large-scale famines and plagues (1876, 1899/1900, 1900/1, 1901/2, 1911/12, 1918/19), and the population of Vadodara and Surat either remained stagnant or decreased, while the population of Ahmedabad increased constantly during these years depending on the growing textile industry. There were 9 textile mills in Ahmedabad in 1891; by 1931 these had increased to 76. In 1891 the mills employed 7,451 workers, and in 1931 the number had risen to 69,562.[10] If we consider family dependents and workers in associated industries, the number of people the mills supported would be considerably higher. After 1931 the rate of population increase in the city averaged around 40 per

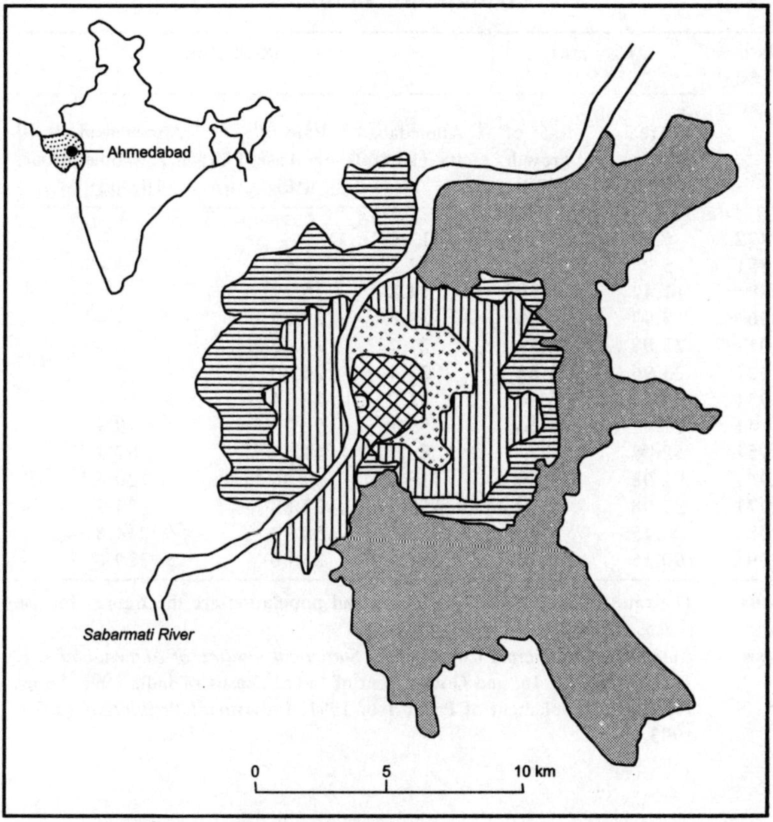


*Note*: Expansion of City Area by Year.

1411 | 1857 | 1901
1939 | 1960 | 1986

*Source*: K.C. Jain, 'Ahmedabad: An Expanding Metropolis', in R.P. Misra (ed.), *Million Cities of India*, New Delhi: Vikas Publishing House, 1978, p. 214, Fig. 21 and information from Refuse Department, Ahmedabad Municipal Corporation.

MAP 3.1: CHANGES IN AHMEDABAD'S CITY AREA

TABLE 3.1: CHANGES IN AREA AND POPULATION OF THE AHMEDABAD MUNICIPALITY

| National Census Year | City area | | Population | | |
|---|---|---|---|---|---|
| | Area (sq. km.) | Rate of growth (%) | Ahmedabad city (10,000) | Rate of increase (%) | Ahmedabad Urban Agglomeration (10,000) |
| 1872 | 5.72 | – | 12.0 | – | – |
| 1881 | 5.95 | 3.96 | 12.8 | 6.64 | – |
| 1891 | 11.42 | 95.69 | 14.8 | 16.29 | – |
| 1901 | 14.93 | 30.68 | 18.6 | 25.25 | – |
| 1911 | 23.08 | 54.59 | 21.7 | 16.62 | – |
| 1921 | 23.96 | 3.82 | 27.4 | 26.40 | – |
| 1931 | 25.29 | 5.54 | 31.0 | 13.14 | – |
| 1941 | 52.47 | 105.86 | 59.1 | 90.73 | 59.1 |
| 1951 | 52.47 | – | 83.7 | 41.59 | 87.7 |
| 1961 | 92.98 | 77.30 | 115.0 | 37.36 | 120.6 |
| 1971 | 92.98 | – | 158.7 | 37.88 | 174.2 |
| 1981 | 98.15 | 5.56 | 238.2 | 50.12 | 254.8 |
| 1991 | 190.15 | 93.73 | 294.9 | 23.80 | 329.8 |

NOTE: The rates of increase for both area and population are the figures for the census period.

SOURCES: Ahmedabad Municipal Corporation, *Statistical Outline of Ahmedabad City 1988-89*, pp. 11, 16; and Government of India, Census of India 1991, Series 7 Gujarat, Supplement of Paper 1 of 1991, *Provisional Population Tables*, 1993, p. 53.

cent per decade. Though there was a gradual decline in the number of textile workers, the population increase was maintained by the rapid growth of other industries.

### *Sanitary Facilities: Historical Development*

#### BEFORE BRITISH RULE

During Mughal times water was supplied to the city by aqueducts and wells, including attractive step-wells. However, the aqueducts later fell into disrepair and people obtained drinking water from wells, rivers, and cisterns that contained rainwater collected from roofs.[11]

There was no system of drainage, and this was a setback to public health. Further, streets were dirty—there was mud during the rainy season, and dust and rampant weeds during the dry season. The Mughal Emperor Jahangir (reigned 1605-28) called Ahmedabad the 'city of mud' (Gardabad). Deficiencies in the water supply and in the provision of drainage threatened the health of the city.

## DURING AND AFTER BRITISH RULE

When the British East India Company began to govern Ahmedabad, sanitation in the city was the same as it had been under the Mughals. A pressing problem that faced early British administrators was the repair of the town wall. It was after the completion of the wall that specific efforts were directed to the provision of a water supply, drainage, and the disposal of rubbish and human waste.

The first attempt to improve the water supply was made in 1849. Water pumped from the Sabarmati river by Persian wheels turned by bullocks was filtered through vegetable charcoal and gravel and taken to the Manek Chowk (part of the city centre) by an 8 inch earthen pipe. However, the supply was insufficient.[12]

Later, a pumping station was erected on the east bank of the Sabarmati and water was supplied to part of the city. However, in 1885, a systematic investigation showed that the pumped water was far more contaminated than had been thought. The station was located in the south-western part of the city, directly below the city's main drainage outlet into the Sabarmati. Inadequate filtering resulted in cholera, which first broke out among users of the city water supply. Well water was too dangerous, as the subsoil water had been contaminated by the seepage from drains, particularly from cesspools. Even water from the upper reaches of the river was contaminated due to the washing clothes, bathing of animals, and dispose of half burnt dead bodies in its water. The least impure water was that taken from the 8,000 to 9,000 household cisterns that provided drinking water from rainwater collected from roofs and courtyards. This method dates back to the Mughal period.[13] All in all, the problem of drinking water was critical in Ahmedabad at this time. In 1891, the efforts of Ranchhodlal Chhotalal, the chairman of the Managing Committee, brought about an improved water supply scheme whereby filtered water was supplied to the city through pipes. This ameliorated the problem of drinking water.[14] Further, V.J. Patel, for whom supply of water was a priority issue, made great improvements during his term of office, in the 1920s.

Some of the drainage and sewage functions were provided by traditional cesspools, the *khalkuva*. Made of brick and about 25 ft. deep, they were built out on the street that was close to the house. But these were not used during the rainy season because of the fear of overflow. Jains did not use cesspools as insects breed and get killed in them. Many Muslims had *khalkuva* latrines inside their houses for their women in purdah. The traditional cisterns not only contaminated the subsoil water but the water of the Sabarmati too. However, the majority of households had no cisterns. Dirty water and human waste was supposed to be put into large iron pans provided on the streets or the courtyards. The only drains at that time were storm water gutters along the main roads. They were not paved and as a result got flooded during the rainy season. The iron pans, like most latrines, had to be emptied daily by Bhangis. Where such facilities were not available, dirty water was just left outdoors.[15]

Improvements in sanitation began in 1870. That year the Collector imposed a *khalkuva* cess tax throughout the walled city, to enable the municipality to provide regular and systematic latrine cleaning. Owners of cesspools, at first, preferred to have their latrines cleaned by the Bhangis working on private contract, but gradually they started using the services of municipal servants. In 1884, the area covered was extended to Saraspur, and by 1890, to the whole city. After 1884 the night-soil was carried by a tramway outside the city to a depot two and a half miles away, where it was processed and sold to cultivators. The problem of subsoil contamination by cesspools was addressed in 1877 when the construction of deep cesspools was forbidden, and in 1879 when all existing deep cesspools were closed.[16] By the 1970s most municipal latrines were directly connected to a sewer.

A drainage scheme was begun in the 1880s. When the British East India Company began its rule, there existed the storm water gutters. But, they were extremely defective. Some of the dirty water drained into cesspools but most of it was tipped into the storm water gutters. Inadequate drainage and seepage from cesspools, contaminated the ground and subsoil water. Since 1883, Ranchhodlal Chhotalal had been stressing the need to build an underground drainage system as an urgent target in his public health policy. The costs involved, however, brought strong opposition from some of his fellow Commissioners and no progress was made. Finally, the government ordered the municipality to act on the question, and in 1888 an underground drainage system was built, as an experiment, in Khadia ward. When the work was completed in 1895, its efficiency was recognized and from 1903 onwards the scheme was extended to the rest of the city.[17]

Improved public health measures, in the form of a drinking water supply and a drainage system, had been taken in hand by the end of the nineteenth century. Their provision occurred together with the progress of the city plan by the second decade of the twentieth century. With the development of drainage facilities, a greater proportion of human waste disposal was handled by the sewage system. Since Ahmedabad in nineteenth century had been regarded as the one of the worst instances of sanitary neglect among Indian cities, its inhabitants were all the more committed to improvement in hygiene and sanitation. With increased influence of public representatives on local bodies, the provision of public health services progressed energetically and systematically. The underground drainage system was made available throughout the city centre, earlier than in other major Indian cities.

An inhibiting in the improvement of urban sanitation in Ahmedabad was the rapid increase in its population. This resulted in a higher population density, deterioration in the collection and disposal of rubbish and night-soil, and, especially after Independence, the growth of a large number of slums. A greater proportion of the population found itself excluded from municipal sanitation services. The provision of water supply, and removal of night-soil and rubbish collection in slum areas are gaining more importance in proportion to the increase of slum population.

A second factor was the expansion of city area. Though other cities have also experienced such expansion, Ahmedabad poses a special problem because of the size and rapidity of its growth. The large-scale expansion made it necessary to reorganize sanitation facilities and its management, particularly for the newly absorbed areas where sanitation facilities were poor. In February 1986, surrounding countryside with an area of 92 sq. km. was absorbed into the Ahmedabad city. The next section discusses the impact of this expansion on the sanitation managment system

## Sanitation Facilities and their Management

I shall now examine the urban hygiene situation in Ahmedabad in the 1980s, focusing on sanitation facilities and their management. The main sanitation facilities provided by the city authorities are: sewage, rubbish collection and night-soil disposal.

### *The Sewage System: An Outline*

The flowchart in Figure 3.1 shows how sewage is processed. In 1981 the population of Ahmedabad city was 2.4 million and by 1991 it had increased

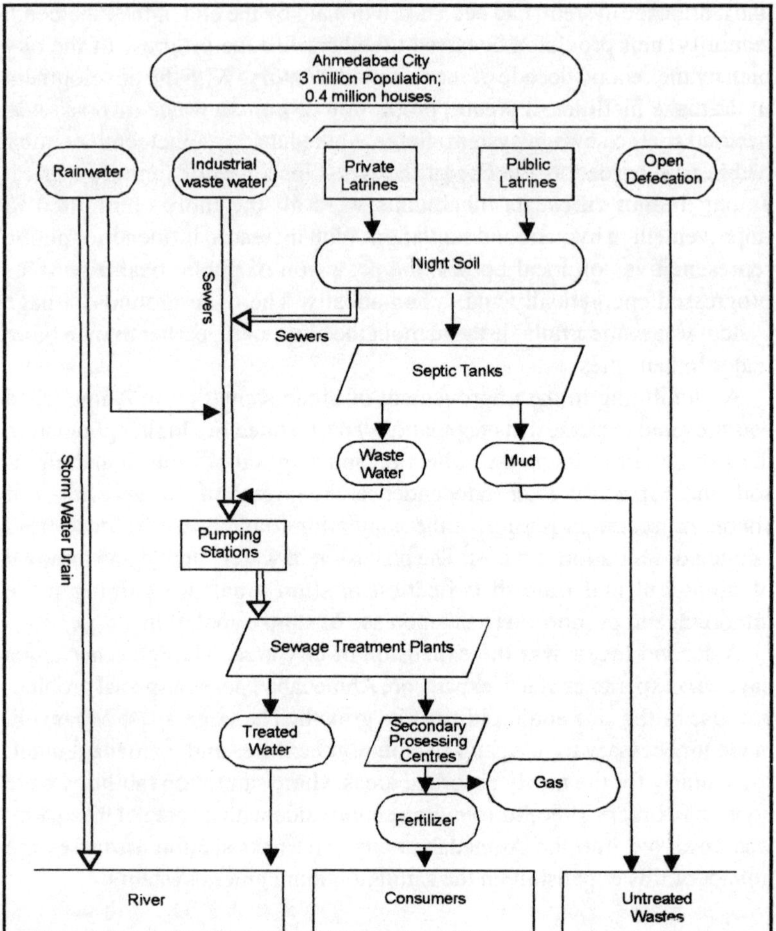


*Note*: Signs mean as follows:

Route; Night Soil, Waste Water, and Other Products;

Sewers, Storm Water Drains; Treatment Facilities;

Other Facilities

*Source*: Original Chart by Author.

FIG. 3.1: FLOW CHART OF DRAINAGE (1991)

to 3 million. According to the 1981 census, there were 391,000 houses in the city; of these 370,000 were occupied, and the total number of households was 372,000. As a result of a slum survey by the city authorities conducted in 1976, 420,000 people were found to be living in 81,000 hutments.[18] Later the slum population grew particularly in the eastrn part of the city, and in 1988 it was estimated to be 625,000.[19]

At present, a sewage network extends throughout most of the pre-1986 city area (98.15 sq. km.), and the waste water and night soil from each household is collected by drains and sent to two sewage plants via a number of pumping stations. The chief network has 4 main pumping stations and 16 minor pumping stations. In 1960/1 the city had only 380 km. of pipes; this had grown to 930 km. in 1980/1 and to 1,008 km. in 1986/7.[20] Buildings which have received planning permission from the city authorities are all connected to the sewage system.

Since there is no sewage network in the newly incorporated (post 1986) area (92 sq. km.), waste water and night soil are collected in cesspools or septic tanks. Cesspools are cleaned out periodically, and the waste is dumped directly into the sewerage system at two points in the city. It is estimated that there are about 25,000 cesspools and septic tanks.[21] Because these are concentrated in the newly incorporated area of the city, the city has no accurate information regarding their numbers, sizes and construction material.

In 1986 there were 15,000 public latrines.[22] These were connected to the sewage network and waste was processed in sewage treatment plants.

Factories in Ahmedabad are concentrated in the area east of the Sabarmati river. Industrial waste water, which flows through the sewers, is processed at the Pirana sewage treatment plant. This plant was built in 1975 to deal with the increasing amount of industrial and domestic waste water, and has a capacity of 72 million gallons a day. The Vasna plant on the west bank of the Sabarmati was constructed in 1970 to treat waste water from that area with a capacity of 12 million gallons a day. Primary treatment is given at the sewage plants, though some waste is processed at secondary processing centres to extract fuel gas and fertilizer. In 1989, gas and fertilizer produced was worth Rs.2 million and Rs.0.5 million respectively.[23] Two more plants are being built, which would have a daily capacity of 34 million gallons and 16 million gallons a day.

The average rainfall in Ahmedabad is 739 mm per annum. The rain flows via storm water drains on the sides of roads directly to the Sabarmati river, though some of it is taken through the sewers to the treatment plants.

TABLE 3.2: SEWERS AND STORM WATER DRAINS IN AHMEDABAD

(*in km.*)

| Year | Sewer | | Storm water drain | |
|---|---|---|---|---|
| | Length laid in the period | Total length | Length laid in the period | Total length |
| 1961/2 | 37.4 | 417.7 | 8.1 | 113.0 |
| 1966/7 | 33.2 | 602.7 | 2.1 | 143.8 |
| 1971/2 | 30.5 | 756.8 | 2.8 | 158.1 |
| 1976/7 | 15.4 | 850.5 | 7.2 | 171.1 |
| 1981/2 | 11.8 | 932.5 | 10.2 | 229.0 |
| 1985/6 | 9.3 | 978.3 | 3.4 | 255.6 |
| 1986/7 | 29.2 | 1,007.5 | 0.4 | 256.0 |
| 1987/8 | 14.1 | 1,021.6 | – | 256.0 |
| 1988/9 | 25.2 | 1,036.8 | – | 256.0 |

SOURCE: Ahmedabad Municipal Corporation, *Statistical Outline of Ahmedabad City 1988-89*, Ahmedabad, 1990, p. 169.

### *Disposal of Human Waste and Sewage System*

The Ahmedabad Municipal Corporation was set up in 1950 and since its inception has been greatly concerned about extending the sewage network. Table 3.2 shows that work had progressed speedily in the period 1960s to the early 1970s, and in 1976/7 the total length of sewage pipes that had been laid was 850 km. At this time many houses in the city were connected to the system. However, with the incorporation of the new area in 1986, the diffusion ratio of sewage in the city fell dramatically. Extending the sewage system to the new area was of great urgencies for the city authorities. Accordingly the annual construction rate again picked up speed. The project of connecting houses in the new area to the sewage system was to be completed in 1992/3.[24] However, the target has not been achieved yet.

#### CESSPOOLS, SEPTIC TANKS AND SEWAGE REMOVAL

In 1986 there were about 500 cesspools in the old city and about 25,000 in the newly incorporated area. There are two types of construction: the pukka type, built of brick and cement and the kachha type, which is merely a hole in the ground. The pukka type that is generally used in households is 10 ft. in diameter and 15 ft. deep; access is by an iron manhole that is 1.5 ft. in diameter. The type of cesspool used by multiple families is usually

20 ft. in diameter and 50 ft. deep. It is estimated that 60 per cent of the city's cesspools are of the pukka type and 40 per cent of the kachha type.[25]

According to ownership, cesspools can be divided into three types: those managed and owned by (1) the city, (2) enterprises, and (3) individual residents. The first type is provided for buildings occupied by local bodies, the second type is for industrial and commercial use and built on land designated for business use, while the third type is located in residential areas. The capacity of cesspools in residential areas varies according to the number of households using them. In slum areas cesspools are of the kachha type, but in other areas they are mostly of the pukka type.[26]

The sewage disposal management is controlled by two offices located in Saijpur Bogha and Behrampur. The method of removal varies in the capacity of the cesspool and its location. Tankers equipped with pumps have a weak sucking power and the hose length is no more than 20 ft. They are used when access to the cesspool is easy. Tankers come in two types, with capacities of 3,000 and 6,000 l. respectively. Vacuum trucks have strong sucking power and employ 60ft. long hoses. However, they cost about Rs. 300,000, which is twice the price of the tankers. They have a capacity of 5,000 l. At places where these vehicles cannot gain access, tractor drawn pumps with a capacity of 3,000 l. are used. If tractors are unable to enter, the sewage is removed by using a Honda motor. Hoses can be extended upto 70 to 80 ft. but their sucking power is weak. The life of a motor, which costs Rs. 15,000, is between two and four years. At present the Saijpur Bogha Zonal Office has seven tankers with a capacity of 6,000 l., seven tankers with a capacity of 3,000 l., five vacuum trucks with a capacity of 5,000 l., and a few tractors and motors. Ideally, there should be 40 tankers and 40 vacuum trucks.[27]

The disposal of sewage is managed in two shifts. The first shift is from 7 a.m. to 1 p.m. and the second is from 2 p.m. to 8 p.m. At the Saijpur Bogha Zonal Office, 23 trucks are used for the first shift and 12 for the second shift. Each truck has one driver and three labourers. For this purpose 35 drivers and 104 labourers are employed each day. Generally, one vehicle travels to the disposal site four times during a shift. These disposal sites, which are linked directly to the sewers, are at Naroda and Behrampur. A tanker with a capacity of 6,000 l. disposes of about 24,000 l. of waste water and excreta per shift.[28]

For the use of the tanker for sewage disposal, a formal request has to be registered in the appropriate Zonal Office. Upon receiving the request the office is supposed to send a tanker, but generally with much delay for a

TABLE 3.3: SEWAGE REMOVED IN AHMEDABAD (No. of Times)

| Period | Number of registrations | Times removed | Carried forward |
|---|---|---|---|
| Sep. 1986-March 1987 | 4,885<br>(698) | 4,409<br>(630) | 476 |
| April 1987-March 1988 | 14,918<br>(1,243) | 14,738<br>(1,228) | 180 |
| April 1988-March 1989 | 23,391<br>(1,949) | 22,420<br>(1,868) | 971 |
| April 1989-Dec. 1989 | 15,127<br>(1,681) | 14,186<br>(1,576) | 941 |

NOTE: Figures in brackets are the monthly average.
SOURCE: Saijpur Bogha Zonal Office, Ahmedabad Municipal Corporation (20 July 1990).

variety of reasons. This service is free of cost for individually owned cesspools. The office charges Rs. 50 for the cleaning of cesspools for commercial or industrial use per trip. Community cesspools and those at public latrines are periodically cleaned on a rotation basis by the city authorities without any charges. The tanker service is also available to residents outside the city. Besides a basic fee of Rs. 200 per vehicle per trip, they are charged with a surcharge of Rs. 10 per km. calculated from the Zonal Office.[29]

Table 3.3 shows the number of registrations, the number of sewage disposals carried out and the number of disposals carried forward between 1986 and 1989. The number of registrations increased remarkably from April 1987, one year after the new area was incorporated into the city. This lag of one year is due to the fact that most people in that area did not know that sewage disposal was free.[30] Disposals carried forward refers to the number of unfinished works carried forward to the following period. Excepting the period April 1987 to March 1988, delayed disposals made up more than half of the monthly average of disposals.

The large number of delays indicates indirectly the length of time between registration and sewage disposal. Due to such inordinate delays many cesspools could not be used. The extreme shortage of equipment and the difficulties in labour management appear to be the major reasons for it. Table 3.4 indicates these problems clearly. Tankers are the main equipment used for disposal; there is a large differential between the number of tankers and those actually in operation. Some of the tankers at the Zonal Office were not operational, either because they were broken down

Plate 1: Removing night soil from dry latrines with improved implements (Viramgam, 1969, courtesy of Safai Vidyalaya).

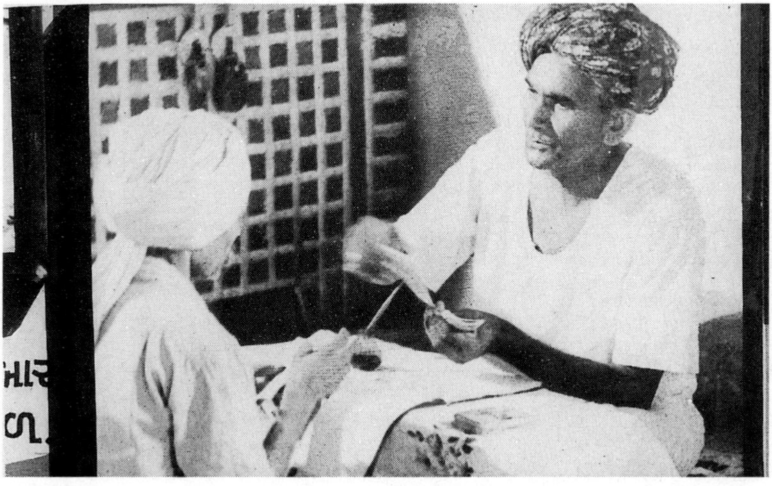

Plate 2: Borrowing money from Mahajan (moneylender) (Viramgam, 1969, courtesy of Safai Vidyalaya).

Plate 3: Sweeping with a long broom (Ahmedabad, 1991).

Plate 4: Improved wheelbarrow in use (Ahmedabad, 1991).

Plate 5: A sweeper with an old type of wheelbarrow
(Ahmedabad, 1991).

Plate 6: Spreading lime after cleaning public toilets
(Ahmedabad, 1991).

Plate 19: A filthy public toilet (Ahmedabad, 1990).

Plate 20: A sweeper making a broom at his leisure (Ahmedabad: 1991).

Plate 21: A tractor being used to transport human waste (a suburb of Ahmedabad, 1991).

Plate 22: Sweepers on the way to their beats after roll call (Dholka, 1991).

Plate 23: Demonstration by sweepers in celebration of a successful strike (Ahmedabad, 1991, courtesy of the Nokar Mandal).

TABLE 3.4: ACTIVITIES OF THE SAIJPUR BOGHA ZONAL OFFICE (20 MAY 1990)

| Shift | Tankers Reque-sted | Autho-rized tankers | Tankers broken down | Tankers not despat-ched | Unavail-abiliy of driver | Late-ness of tanker | Tankers in operat-ion | Cess pool according to type | | | | | | | | |
|---|---|---|---|---|---|---|---|---|---|---|---|---|---|---|---|---|
| | | | | | | | | private | | community | | commercial | | municipal | | sum total of times |
| | | | | | | | | No. of tankers | times | No. of tankers | times | No. of tankers | times | No. of tankers | times | |
| First | 23 | 18 | 5 | 5 | – | 4 | 8 | 8 | 34 | 8 | 28 | – | – | 2 | 9 | 71 |
| Second | 12 | 12 | 4 | – | – | 1 | 8 | 7 | 25 | 4 | 18 | – | – | 1 | 3 | 46 |
| Total | 35 | 30 | 9 | 5 | – | 5 | 16 | 15 | 59 | 12 | 46 | – | – | 3 | 12 | 117 |

NOTE: The figures are those of the movements on one day, 20 May 1990. The total is the sum total of the combined figures of the first and second shifts. Times refers to the number of return journeys to the sewer inlet.

SOURCE: Saijpur Bogha Zonal Office, Ahmedabad Municipal Corporation (20 July 1990).

or because they had not been despatched from the vehicle repair section. Other organizational difficulties, such as late arrival of the tanker or the unavailability of a driver (though this does not appear in the table), can also be added. Among the number of return trips tankers in operation made to the disposal sites, more than half were from private cesspools, followed by those from community and city cesspools. This ratio may roughly reflect the ratio of the total capacity of cesspools by ownership type.

## PROVISION OF LATRINES AND THEIR MAINTENANCE

It is not clear as to how many private houses have latrines nor the total number of such latrines. Domestic latrines in the newly incorporated area are connected to cesspools or septic tanks, while most in the old city are directly connected to sewers. The city authorities are also responsible for latrines other than those used in individual houses. These include community latrines in slum areas, municipal chawl latrines built under Article 188 of the Bombay Municipal Corporation Act of 1949, private chawl latrines built by landowners in chawls, and urinals built by municipal authorities throughout the city.[31] The present situation regarding these latrines is set out in Table 3.5. 'Latrine blocks' refer to buildings with multiple latrines, connected by common pipes to a common drain inlet. Municipal chawl latrines comprise more than half the total available laterines. The average number of latrines in a latrine block is 8.2 for municipal chawl latrines, 6.8 for community latrines, 6.1 for private chawl latrines and 2.6 for urinals.[32] The increase in the city's population density has led to a severe shortage of laterines. For example, there are only 2,661 community latrines in the slum areas, which must be shared among 600,000 slum dwellers. There is thus roughly one latrine to every 250 people. Since the maximum number of users per latrine is supposed to be 25 people,[33] at least ten times the present number of latrines will be required to meet the needs of the slum population.

Further, many of the existing latrines are broken or defective, which lowers their use ratio even further. Drain blockage, cistern malfunction and an insufficient supply of water to clean the pans are among the major problems. The main reason for blockages is that sanitary napkins and other unsuitable materials are flushed down drains. This reflects the lack of concern for communal property. The necessary repair of damaged doors, floors, and pedestals is rarely undertaken. The maintenance of these latrines is generally poor. In this situation about 80 per cent of the slum population,

TABLE 3.5: LATRINES OF VARIOUS TYPES (1987)

(*Numbers*)

| Type | Latrine blocks | Latrines | Unusable latrines | Latrines broken and needing repair | | | | | | |
|---|---|---|---|---|---|---|---|---|---|---|
| | | | | Drain | Cistern | Not enough water | Door | Floor | Unit | Wall-roof |
| Community | 392 | 2,661 | 107 | 346 | 181 | 246 | 776 | 622 | 450 | 547 |
| Municipal chawl | 1,088 | 8,794 | 424 | 779 | 333 | 485 | 2,058 | 1,894 | 1,247 | 2,111 |
| Private chawl | 692 | 4,209 | 279 | 379 | 405 | 450 | 1,871 | 1,112 | 636 | 1,286 |
| Urinal | 617 | 1,629 | 45 | 62 | 117 | 351 | 220 | 314 | 53 | 245 |
| Total | 2,789 | 17,293 | 855 | 1,566 | 1,036 | 1,532 | 4,925 | 3,942 | 2,386 | 4,189 |

SOURCE: P.U. Asnani, 'Maintenance of Health: Imperative Now The 2001 AD Context,' The Times Research Foundation, Seminar in Ahmedabad, 2001: *Imperative Now Towards A New Metropolitan Management Strategy*, Vol. 10, Calcutta, 1988, Appendix.

that is, 500,000 people, are supposed to defecate outdoors.[34]

To ameliorate the situation of insufficient latrines, the city authorities introduced a scheme of subsidising upto 80 per cent of construction costs of building privately owned latrines in slum and chawl areas. Further, the cost of connecting these latrines to the sewers was virtually borne by the city, with the latrine owner only required to pass a nominal sum of Rs.10. In the period 1978 to 1990, 13,000 private domestic latrines were built with municipal subsidies.[35] It was planned that a further 21,000 private latrines would be built in the period 1990 to 1993. In addition, it is estimated that 79,000 community and chawl latrines would be required by the end of the twentieth century to meet the needs of the growing population.[36]

The cleaning and maintenance of all but private latrines are the responsibility of the city authorities. However, upkeep of public latrines is poor due to the shortage and inefficient work of the cleaners.

### *Rubbish Collection and Disposal*

With the recent rise in the living standards of people, and changes in consumer goods, the average amount of rubbish thrown out per person per day has risen to 400-500 gm., and this is expected to rise to 700 gm by the end of the twentieth century. In addition, with the sharp rise in the population of Ahmedabad, the 1,400 ton. of rubbish collected daily by the municipality in 1988/9 is projected to rise up to 3,500 ton. by the year 2000.[37] Recent trends in the volume of rubbish shown in Table 3.6 indicate

TABLE 3.6: TRENDS IN THE VOLUME OF RUBBISH IN AHMEDABAD

| Year | Amout of rubbish | |
|---|---|---|
| | Year (10,000 ton.) | Day (ton.) |
| 1961/2 | 16.5 | 452 |
| 1966/7 | 18.7 | 512 |
| 1973/4 | 20.1 | 550 |
| 1976/7 | 24.2 | 662 |
| 1981/2 | 31.6 | 867 |
| 1985/6 | 37.2 | 1,019 |
| 1986/7 | 47.6 | 1,304 |
| 1987/8 | 51.1 | 1,399 |
| 1988/9 | 50.4 | 1,380 |

SOURCE: Ahmedabad Municipal Corporation, *Statistical Outline of Ahmedabad City 1988-89*, Ahmedabad, 1990, p. 168.

that between 1961 and 1988 there was a threefold increase in the volume of rubbish. Let us now examine how the city authorities have reacted to this increasing volume, brought on by rapid urbanization and the rise in living standards.[38]

A new method of rubbish collection was introduced in 1987. In the earlier system, there was no designated place or day for putting out household rubbish, and so it tended to be left on the roadside. As a result, rubbish was always piled high along the roads, causing serious health risks and damaging the landscape. Nor was there any restriction on rubbish disposal in public areas, such as markets, and so rubbish was put out at any time. Sweepers employed by the city authorities collected the rubbish in their designated areas at specified times using brooms and dustpans, and took it by wheelbarrows to one of the 400 rubbish collection points in the city. They invariably came into direct contact with the rubbish while unloading it. Since the collection points were not covered, the rotting rubbish led to deterioration in terms of health and hygiene in the surrounding areas. There were few collection points, and sweepers often had to travel very long distances. It was virtually impossible to designate new points because of strong local opposition. Six ton trucks, with one driver and six workers, came periodically to the collection points for loading the rubbish into the 7ft.-high bed of the truck using baskets. In this process, they were covered with rubbish and ran a high risk of disease (especially of the eyes and breathing). Workers also came into direct contact with the rubbish while unloading the trucks at the dump. There was little concern about hygiene in this method of rubbish collection and disposal. Further, no rubbish disposal programme had been planned to take into account future population increases.[39]

The World Bank provided Rs. 38 million to improve this unhygienic arrangement and in 1987 the Solid Waste Management Programme was introduced. The purpose of this project was to introduce hygienic methods of garbage collection and disposal by economizing on labour through the introduction of mechanization and by improving the working conditions of sweepers. The main points of difference with the old system were as follows: (1) the introduction of a house to house collection system, (2) the provision of a community bin (capacity 80 l.) for every 25 households in residential areas, including slums and chawls, (3) discontinuing open collection points and substituting closed rubbish containers with a capacity of between 3 and 6 ton, (4) the introduction of mechanical road sweepers, (5) the introduction of container bins and collection vehicles for commercial rubbish, (6) the placing of rubbish bins on streets and public facilities, and

(7) the introduction of small-sized collection vehicles for congested areas of within the walled city.[40]

With the introduction of the new system, house to house collection of rubbish was begun on an experimental basis in some residential areas. Community bins have been placed in a large number of residential areas, and has been made compulsory that rubbish be dumped in them. This checks the depositing of household rubbish on the roadside. For a designated area, sweepers are responsible for cleaning roads and public areas, and collect and transport the rubbish from there. The area covered by an individual sweeper is based on its population density, and varies from 3,000 sq. m. where the density is high to 10,000 sq. m. where it is low.

Sweepers are required to complete their work in the stipulated time with the minimum equipment and wheelbarrows. The wheelbarrows have been redesigned and have the capacity for transporting six small rubbish containers. In this system the sweeper comes into direct contact with rubbish only while transferring it from the community bins into the small containers. Using the old-style wheelbarrows, which were designed to meet the needs of the open disposal points, the sweeper inevitably had to touch the rubbish when loading and unloading it. Under the new system, rubbish is taken by wheelbarrows to the nearest covered rubbish container. Based on the population density, covered containers are placed approximately 500 m. apart. Because they are covered, they are far more hygienic than the former type of open disposal. Of the 461 containers placed at different points in the city, 205 have a capacity of 6 ton. and the rest have a capacity of 3 ton. Rubbish can be deposited directly into them from the small containers. Large container trucks make periodic rounds and take the filled containers away to designated dumps, where the rubbish is emptied out.

At present there are 16 dumps in the city.[41] Periodic disinfecting takes place, and the rubbish is piled up to make roads and residential land. Rubbish is not dumped into the sea, burned or converted as fertilizer because it is not economically viable.

The growing degree of mechanization is evident from the planned placement of rubbish trucks shown in Table 3.7. The figures indicate the gross number of trucks to be used over three shifts. Their schedule is as follows: Shift 1 runs from 7 a.m. to 3 p.m., Shift 2 from 2.30 p.m. to 10.30 p.m. and Shift 3 from 10 p.m. to 6 a.m. The largest numbers of trucks and workers are employed in the first shift, and very few are used in the third shift. The first shift uses 79 trucks and 378 workers, the second, 71 trucks and 92 workers, and the third, 15 trucks and only a few workers. These

TABLE 3.7: PLANNED DISPOSITION OF RUBBISH COLLECTION VEHICLES (31 AUGUST 1990)

| Zone | Vehicles | | | | | | Labourers |
|---|---|---|---|---|---|---|---|
| | Large trucks | Large container trucks | Small trucks | Vehicles Auto 3-wheeled | Small container vehicles | Others | |
| Western | 8 | 3 | 4 | 0 | 5 | 10 | 100 |
| Central | 26 | 9 | 1 | 11 | 8 | 5 | 160 |
| Northern | 10 | 4 | 3 | 1 | 3 | 5 | 60 |
| Eastern | 8 | 3 | 1 | 3 | 4 | 8 | 80 |
| Southern | 8 | 3 | 4 | 0 | 4 | 5 | 70 |
| Total | 60<br>(28) | 22<br>(11) | 13<br>(10) | 15<br>(13) | 24<br>(10) | 33<br>(29) | 470 |

NOTE: The number of vehicles represents the gross number of vehicles planned over three shifts as of 31 August 1990. The figures in the brackets show the net number of vehicles.

SOURCE: Refuse Department, Ahmedabad Municipal Corporation (20 July 1990).

workers assist in the loading and unloading of rubbish. The high number of workers in the first shift reflect the amount of rubbish collected as well as the extra number of workers required for the larger trucks.

The large trucks and the large container trucks are most widely used for rubbish collection. These trucks transport rubbish directly in containers, or remove and place it in the bed of the truck, from the container points to the dump. There are 461 container points in the city.

The western part of the Ahmedabad city is well-planned, consisting of new and quality housing. The central part consists chiefly of the old walled city, where roads are narrow and buildings crowded together. It is also the traditional commercial centre. In this area there is great scope for the use of the automatic three-wheeled vehicles, which can turn in a small space. The northern part, with a concentration of slumns, is comparatively under-developed, and has the second largest garbage dump. The eastern and southern parts include the industrial area incorporated into the city in 1986. This part of the city too has large slum dwellings.

Mechanization, which is at the centre of the new project, is progressing steadily, but this does not necessarily mean that the efficiency of rubbish collection has risen. Mechanization has advanced in terms of the change over to closed container bins and the removal of rubbish from them to the dumps. However, there has been no progress in the process of collecting rubbish from residential and public areas to the container bins which still remains to be labour intensive. The introduction of community bins has been more effective from the point of view of hygiene than economizing on labour. There are indications that the rubbish collection situation between the house and the closed container is actually worsening.

The municipal sweepers are responsible for cleaning public spaces, including roads, and public facilities. It is estimated that 1,100 more municipal sweepers are necessary to handle the given work load.[42] In addition the city has more than 2,500 slum and chawl areas, where there is little awareness of hygiene among the inhabitants. The city authorities charge a nominal fee for cleaning these areas. So far 750 additionally-employed sweepers have been sent to the 1,450 areas which had contracted for cleaning services. However, due to financial constraints the municipality cannot undertake any further contracts. More than half of the slum areas are excluded from the municipal cleaning services.

The proportion of municipal expenditure assigned to street-cleaning and rubbish collection has shown a constant rise: it was 5.90 per cent in 1971/2, 6.89 per cent in 1977/8, 7.54 per cent in 1982/3, and 8.20 per cent in 1986/7.[43] Among items of expenditure, it placed fifth in 1986/7, that is after repayment of loans (20.42 per cent), education (16.98 per cent), medical assistance (10.43 per cent), and water provision (8.25 per cent).[44]

Table 3.8 details expenditure trends in the Refuse Department. The table shows clearly that a great proportion of the expenditure is towards

TABLE 3.8: TRENDS IN EXPENDITURE IN THE REFUSE DEPARTMENT (1985/6-1990/1)

(*Rs. 100,000, %*)

| Budgeted item | 1985/6 | 1986/7 | 1987/8 | 1988/9 | 1989/90 | 1990/1 |
|---|---|---|---|---|---|---|
| Hygiene facilities | 40 | 50 | 59 | 67 | 75 | 82 |
| | (0.50) | (0.56) | (0.60) | (0.54) | (0.39) | (0.42) |
| Street cleaning | 463 | 498 | 571 | 712 | 1,042 | 1,091 |
| | (5.74) | (5.59) | (5.51) | (5.73) | (5.38) | (5.62) |
| Transportation and disposal of waste | 142 | 171 | 191 | 119 | 230 | 236 |
| | (1.76) | (1.92) | (1.84) | (0.96) | (1.19) | (1.21) |
| Slum and chawl cleaning | 57 | 58 | 69 | 68 | 144 | 153 |
| | (0.71) | (0.65) | (0.67) | (0.55) | (0.74) | (0.78) |
| Total | 702 | 777 | 890 | 966 | 1,491 | 1,562 |
| | (8.70) | (8.71) | (8.59) | (7.77) | (7.69) | (8.05) |

NOTE: The figure in brackets is the ratio of each budgeted item in the total expenditure of the AMC.

SOURCE: Refuse Department, Ahmedabad Municipal Corporation.

wages to sweepers. The mere introduction of community bins and the mechanization of rubbish disposal is of little help in economizing on labour. Unless there is mechanization of the process of rubbish collection from the house to the closed container bins or a radical reform of the rubbish management system, no reduction in the number of sweepers is possible. Rather, the existing system demands more workforce of sweepers to cope with ever increasing rubbish. The introduction of mechanisation at this stage needs the concensus and cooperation of the users of the new system. Also, it would pose a severe financial burden on the municipality. Municipal sanitation management stands at a crossroads between mechanization and economizing on the labour force. In other words, given the financial pressures on the system, how can high level of expenditure on labour be sustained with the expenditure involved in the purchase and upkeep of necessary technology?

## THE MUNICIPAL SANITATION SECTION

### *Its Labour Organization*

The labour organization of the sanitation section is divided into two broad streams, the Refuse Department and the Conservancy Department. The Refuse Department transports and disposes of household waste, building waste, hospital waste, and carcasses of dead animals. It employs 170 drivers and 300 labourers. The drivers of small vehicles, such as three-wheeled vehicles, also help to load and unload rubbish. Large vehicles have one driver and two to three labourers. All employees of the Refuse Department are male. Table 3.9 gives the higher and lower basic pay levels

TABLE 3.9: STAFF ORGANISATION OF THE REFUSE DEPARTMENT (1990)

| Occupation title | No. | Basic pay (Rs.) low/high |
|---|---|---|
| Deputy Director of the Refuse Dept. | 1 | 3,000/4,500 |
| Manager for Solid Waste | 1 | 2,200/4,000 |
| Superintendent for Waste Disposal | 1 | 1,640/2,900 |
| Public Hygiene Superintendent | 1 | 1,640/2,900 |
| Public Hygiene Inspectors | 12 | 1,350/2,200 |
| Public Hygiene Sub-Inspectors | 12 | 1,200/1,800 |
| Labourers | 480 | 750/940 |

NOTE: The basic pay in monthly.
SOURCE: Refuse Department, Ahmedabad Municipal Corporation.

for each post. When allowances such as rent and travel expenses are added, the amount a labourer actually receives is around double the basic pay.

The staffing pattern of the Conservancy Department is given in Table 3.10. This department is much larger than the Refuse Department, and it employs one-third of all Class 4 workers in the municipality and about one quarter of the total work force. Sweepers are employed either permanently or as day or casual labour. Table 3.10 only provides figures for permanent labourers. The wages of permanent labourers are at the same level as of those in the Refuse Department, and including allowances, are around Rs. 1,200-2,000 a month. Besides the weekly holiday, an additional holiday is permitted to make a five day working week. The working day is seven hours, from 7 a.m. to 11 a.m. and 3 p.m. to 6 p.m. More than half of the permanent employees are women. Permanent employees are eligible for municipal housing for sweepers, built at ten sites around the city. The rule is one family per room; there are 2,500 rooms provided for permanent workers in the city.[45] The areas assigned to the permanent staff are generally in the vicinity of their place of residence.

Day-labourers are used as substitutes for absentee employees and paid a wage of Rs. 45 per day. The municipality maintains a list of day-labourers based on the list of applicants, and work is offered under a priority system (in terms of date of registeration, and experience). When there is a vacant permanent position, a replacement is chosen from those at the top of the day-labourer list.

TABLE 3.10: STAFF ORGANIZATION OF THE CONSERVANCY DEPARTMENT (1990)

| Occupation title | No. | Basic pay (Rs.) low/high |
|---|---|---|
| Director of the Conservancy Department | 1 | 4,100/5,300 |
| Deputy Medical Officers | 2 | 3,500/5,000 |
| Deputy Hygiene Officers | 3 | 3,000/4,500 |
| Assistant Hygiene Officers | 5 | 2,200/4,000 |
| Hygiene Managers | 5 | 2,000/3,200 |
| Public Hygiene Superintendents | 46 | 1,640/2,900 |
| Hygiene Inspectors | 113 | 1,350/2,200 |
| Hygiene Sub-Inspectors | 236 | 1,200/1,800 |
| *Mukadams* (site foremen) | 114 | 800/1,150 |
| Labourers | 5,117 | 750/940 |

NOTE: The basic pay in monthly.
SOURCE: Conservancy Department, Ahmedabad Municipal Corporation.

Casual work is of an entirely different nature. It consists of cleaning jobs that are not assigned to permanent or day-labourers. Casual workers are employed only before (March-May) and during the monsoon season (June-September). During the former period, sewers are cleaned, public latrines and drains are repaired, and rubbish from slum areas and illegally dumped rubbish are collected and disposed of. During the Monsoon season, roads and the slum areas are cleared of mud and dirty water.[46] As many as 500 people a day are employed as casual workers. At a daily wage of Rs. 25, the remuneration is considerably below the day-labourer rate. Casual employees are all male. The special cleaning appropriation for the pre-monsoon and monsoon seasons in 1989/90 was Rs. 10 million.[47]

The *mukadam* is the group leader, with around 50 employees under him. Though he is no more than a local supervisor, his powers of control over permanent and day employees are great. The lower-ranking officials in the Conservancy Department too have a great deal of influence over these employees, since they are in charge of maintaining the list of day-labourers and finding replacements for permanent positions.

### *Problems Relating to Labour Management*

The *mukadam* is in charge of on-site work supervision. He checks the presence and work standards of workers, and finds replacements for absentees. Since his reports affect work and pay assessment of sweepers, the *mukadam* has enormous influence over them. Poor work habits among sweepers, such as not being puntual, absenteeism and poor work standards, make it easy for the *mukadam* to exploit them. It is believed that the *mukadam* collects a sum of money (now Rs. 50 ) from each sweeper every month to overlook their poor work habits.[48] Some female sweepers have also suffered sexual harassment.[49] Exploitation by the *mukadam* in its various forms has been an issue of concern both within the Conservancy Department and the sweepers' unions.

Besides the *mukadam*, some permanent sweepers too exploit sweepers working on a temporary basis. Permanent employees receive maximum benefit in terms of wages and social benefits. Below them are ranked day-labourers, casual workers and privately contracted sweepers. Social and occupational restrictions continue to affect the Bhangis, who are mostly sweepers as it is difficult for them to do any other kind of work. Given this situation, some of the permanently employed sweepers subcontract their work to other sweepers at a low rate of remuneration. Even if the work is fully subcontracted, the labourer is supposed to receive not more than Rs.150 to 200 a month.[50] The *mukadam* who is well aware of the going-on would collect a fee from the permanent employee to overlook the fact.

The relationship between the *mukadam* and the permanent and day employees is complicated. Despite the exploitation which occurs, it is essentially one of protector and protected. The *mukadam's* closeness to the lower-ranking officials makes him even more powerful. It must be pointed out that the higher-ranking officials in the Conservancy Department have been trying to modernize labour management and improve its efficiency. Their efforts at breaking the unholy alliance among the *mukadam*, the permanent employees and the lower-ranking officials have so far met with little success.

## Conclusion

The most important question facing the Conservancy Department is the setting up of a modern system of waste management that is able to respond effectively to the rapidly increasing volume of garbage and waste. The modernization of the system must respond to the twin demands of making the urban environment clean and healthy, and of improving the work environment of the sweepers. At the same time, it is necessary to evolve strategies to economize on labour costs, which constitutes a considerable financial burden to the municipality. However, mechanization of waste management involves purchasing new machinery, which would add to the financial burden. In the absence of comparative data on the costs of rubbish disposal per unit weight, calculated as a sum of labour, machinery maintenance, and depreciation costs, it would not be possible to assess the effectiveness of reducing labour costs.[51] However, the introduction of mechanization has been piecemeal and its effect on labour reduction has so far been minimal. Nevertheless, the modernization of the system should be evaluated in terms of its long term development rather than its immediate impact.

The majority of Bhangis who work as sweepers are employed by the municipality. Their average household income, which is in the range of Rs.1,500 to 3,000 per month,[52] is not inferior to other *jatis* of the Scheduled Castes. However, their educational backwardness deprives them of any upward mobility in the workplace. The fact that the Bhangis are mostly concentrated in municipal occupation makes them utterly dependent on the employment policies of the municipality for the very existence of their community.

Until now, in response to growing urbanization, there has been a steady increase in the number of sweepers employed by the municipality. Recently though, as seen in the Ahmedabad Municipal Corporation, there has been a movement to restrict expenditure on labour costs. The massive expenditure on labour is not a unique feature of Ahmedabad alone, but continues to be a major financial burden for other local bodies as well. In this situation, confrontation between the municipality and the Bhangi community over the number of employees and employment conditions has currently become more acute. Both the municipality and the Bhangi community now stand at a crossroads.

## NOTES

1. Greater Ahmedabad had a population of 3,300,000 in 1991, after Bombay (12,570,000), Calcutta (10,920,000), Delhi (8,380,000), Madras (5,360,000), Hydrabad (4,280,000) and Bangalore (4,090,000).
2. A compact history of Ahmedabad is given in Government of Gujarat, *Ahmedabad District Gazetteer,* Ahmedabad, 1984, pp. 61-170.
3. K.L. Gillion, *Ahmedabad: A Study in Indian Urban History*, Berkeley and Los Angeles: University of California Press, 1968, p. 110.
4. The cost of the repairs was met by a small increase in the town duties, a decision agreed to jointly by leading citizens and the government. The increase was to be reduced once the work was completed to a level sufficient to provide upkeep and maintenance for the wall. However, the Acting Judicial Commissioner for Gujarat, Giberne, suggested that the increased duties be continued in order to provide for other city improvements. This was accepted by the townspeople. The improvements included the watering of main roads (to lay the dust and harden the surface), a dharmshala (charity rest house for travellers), and a grain market. Finance was also made available to remove excreta from the vicinity of the city gates, to provide lighting in some streets, to maintain fire engines, to provide and clean a small number of public latrines, to remove rubbish, and to construct police posts.
5. Gillion, op. cit, p. 117.
6. Ibid., p. 121.
7. For a detailed study of the peasant movement, see D. Hardiman, *Peasant Nationalists of Gujarat: Kheda District 1917-1934,* New Delhi: Oxford University Press, 1981.
8. For the course of the labour union movement, see M.H. Desai, *A Righteous Struggle: A Chronicle of the Ahmedabad Textile Labourers' Fight for Justice*, Ahmedabad: Navajivan Publishing House, 1968; and S. Patel, *The Making of Industrial Relations: The Ahmedabad Textile Industry 1918-1939*, New Delhi: Oxford University Press, 1987.
9. Gillion, op. cit., p. 170. For a detailed study, see D. Pathak and P. Sheth, *Sardar Vallabhbhai Patel: From Civic to National Leadership*, Ahmedabad: Navajivan Publishing House, 1980, Chapter 10.

10. Based on documents belonging to the Ahmedabad Textile Mills' Association.
11. Gillion, op. cit., p. 129.
12. Ibid.
13. Ibid., p. 131.
14. Ibid., p. 139.
15. Ibid., p. 132.
16. Ibid., p. 133.
17. Ibid., p. 140.
18. Ahmedabad Municipal Corporation, *Report on Census of Slums in Ahmedabad 1976*, Ahmedabad, 1977, p. 49.
19. P.U. Asnani, 'Maintenance of Health: Imperative Now The 2001 AD Context', The Times Research Foundation, Seminar in Ahmedabad, 2001: *Imperative Now Towards A New Metropolitan Management Strategy,* Vol. 10, Calcutta, 1988, p. 3.
20. Ibid., p. 11.
21. Oral information from the Saijpur Bogha Zonal Office (July 1990).
22. Asnani, op. cit., Appendix E.
23. Oral information from the Pirana plant (July 1990).
24. Oral information from the Refuse Department, Ahmedabad Municipal Corporation (July 1990).
25. Oral information from the Saijpur Bogha Zonal Office (July 1990).
26. Ibid.
27. Ibid.
28. There are two disposal sites at Behrampur and three at Naroda. They are about 50 sq. cm. in size.
29. Oral information from the Saijpur Bogha Zonal Office (July 1990).
30. Ibid.
31. Asnani, op. cit., p. 12.
32. Ibid. Calculated from Appendix E.
33. Ibid. p. 29.
34. Health and Hospitals Department, Ahmedabad Municipal Corporation, internal materials (Civic Amenities, p. 9).
35. Ibid., p. 8.
36. Asnani, op. cit., p. 30.
37. Ibid., p. 32.
38. Other than ordinary rubbish the city also collects building waste, hospital waste and the bodies of dead animals. Collection methods are as follows:

    *Building waste*: Of the 1,400 tons of solid waste collected daily in Ahmedabad, 200 tons (15 per cent of the total) is building waste. The city charges a nominal rate of Rs.150 per truck/outing to remove and dispose of up to 7 tons of waste. Container trucks are used. In actuality, though, most building waste is dumped illegally on roadsides. The city collects this and uses it to strengthen the ground at rubbish dumps, or layers it among domestic and commercial rubbish. With the population increase and the resultant building boom, the amount of building waste to be disposed is increasing yearly. There is, at present, no effective legislation to contend with illegal dumping.

    *Hospital waste*: Hospital waste is taken away in special three-wheeled vehicles and incinerated at 900 degrees. Other solid waste is buried; only hospital waste is burned.

*Dead animals*: The city has at present three vehicles to deal with animal carcasses and they are dispatched when requested by a citizen. Most of the carcasses are small animals like dogs and cats. The same vehicles are used for catching wild dogs. It is impossible to know the exact number, but it appears that larger animals like cows and buffaloes count for only a small proportion of the carcasses dealt with. The carcasses are buried in a designated place at the rubbish dump.

The above information was conveyed orally by the Refuse Department, Ahmedabad Municipal Corporation (July 1990).

39. Oral information from P.U. Asnani, Health and Hospitals Department, Ahmedabad Municipal Corporation (July 1990).
40. Asnani, op. cit., p. 18.
41. These 16 places are distributed around the city. The biggest has been built on the river plain of the Sabarmati. The rubbish is compressed and made into paths.
42. Asnani, op. cit., pp. 14-15.
43. Ahmedabad Municipal Corporation, *Statistical Outline of Ahmedabad City 1988-89,* Ahmedabad, 1990, pp. 96-7.
44. Ibid.
45. Oral information from the Refuse Department (July 1990).
46. Internal materials of the Refuse Department.
47. Oral information from the Refuse Department (July 1990).
48. Ibid.
49. This problem is of great concern to the sweepers' union.
50. Oral information from the Refuse Department (July 1990).
51. Asnani calculates that the cost of collection and disposal of 1 ton of rubbish was Rs. 59 under the old system and Rs.23 under the new system (oral communication from Asnani, July 1990). However, he did not consider the maintenance and management costs of the machinery used for disposal, nor the cost of depreciation.
52. C. Upadhyay and D. Parmar, *Gujaratna Harijano-4* (in Gujarati), Ahmedabad: Tribal Research and Training Institute, 1985, p. 246.

Chapter Four

# Employment Policies of the Conservancy Department

## INTRODUCTION

Sweepers and scavengers employed by the central and state governments, ranked as Class 4 employees, are assured of stable conditions of employment and labour. Their numbers are, however, small. On the other hand, the service and working conditions of the scavengers and sweepers employed by local bodies are generally poor and vary considerably. Since the majority of sweepers and scavengers work for local bodies, the improvement of their service and working conditions has become the focus of reform.

This chapter examines in detail the changes that have occurred in the service, working and living conditions of sweepers and scavengers employed by the Ahmedabad Municipal Corporation (AMC). Ahmedabad is more advanced than the other local bodies in the degree to which its workers have organized their trade unions, and in its legal and institutional structure.

## SWEEPERS AND AWARDS

The Industrial Disputes Act of 1947 regulates the means of settling industrial disputes between workers and employers in terms of conciliation, arbitration and awards. The Act consists of seven chapters: (1) introduction (title and definition), (2) power-holding organs, (3) commission of the dispute, (4) authority and responsibilities of power-holding organs, (5) strikes and lockouts, (6) penalties, and (7) other regulations. It applies to industrial disputes between employers and workers, between employers, and between workers in the private, cooperative, government and semi-government sectors. According to the Act, an apparatus has been set up keeping in view the type and scale of industrial disputes to make settlements, awards and judgements, such as works committees, boards of conciliation, courts of enquiry, labour courts, tribunals and national tribunals.Their limitations and responsibilities are all defined by the Act.[1]

Since the Act is also applicable to local bodies, disputes between labour and the management within them are subject to its framework. Personal and individual disputes that cannot be solved by conciliation or arbitration are dealt with by labour courts or industrial courts, where an award is granted. Disputes which are collective or related to the legal system are examined by tribunals. The state government appoints arbitrators when employers and workers both agree to entrust the solution of the dispute to a tribunal. The arbitrator has the responsibility to grant an award within a specified length of time agreed to by both parties. The tribunal award is a means of resolving industrial disputes and its decision is final and mandatory. However, disputes involving Class 1 and Class 2 staff in local bodies are not included in the scope of the Act because according to its terms of reference they are not considered 'workmen'.[2] The Act is only applicable to disputes involving Class 3 and Class 4 workers, that is, lower managerial staff, office workers and manual labourers.

Since Independence in 1947, four individual arbitrators have been appointed to resolve industrial disputes at the AMC. Their awards have extended to many areas of service, working and living conditions, including employment, promotion, wages, holidays, days and hours of work, uniforms, and housing. Most of them have dealt with common problems of Class 3 and Class 4 workers, though some have been related to a particular group, such as transport workers and sweepers. The AMC has occasionally had arbitrators act as a one-man wage committee, as in the case of recommendations revising wages of all workers, including Class 1 and Class 2 employees. Though, unlike an award, an arbitrator's recommendations have in this case no legal power of compulsion, they are generally held in high regard by both parties. In order to understand the changes in the service, working and living conditions of sweepers and scavengers, we shall now examine four awards that are representative of the various awards and wage committee decisions.

### *The Shah Award, 1948*

Little is known about how dispute between employers and workers in local bodies were resolved before Independence, owing to a lack of relevant material. While even in the post-Independence period there is a paucity of materials for the earlier years, the content of awards can be traced through the government gazettes. The first award after Independence was given by Mr Justice M.C. Shah in 1948. Just before Independence, the government had appointed Harshadbhai V. Divatia, in accordance with the requirements of the Defence of India Rule, as arbitrator to resolve a dispute among sweepers, *mukadams* and the Ahmedabad Borough Municipality (ABM). Justice Shah later took over, and was entrusted with the task of setting wage disputes between workers other than the *mukadams* and sweepers, and the Municipality. In February 1948 he announced the awards concerning these disputes.[3]

The sweepers and *mukadams* made six demands: The first was a revision of their pay scales. In 1939 monthly wages of male sweepers by the municipality were fixed at Rs. 17, Rs. 15 for women and Rs. 19 for *mukadams*. The fixed wage system was replaced in 1945 by a new pay scale; for male sweepers Rs. 17-0.5-22 (a minimum of Rs. 17 and a maximum of Rs. 22, with an annual increase of Re. 0.5), for female sweepers Rs. 15-0.5-22, amd for *makadams* Rs. 19-1-25. The new pay scales were well received, though the minimum wage was the same as that of the pre-1945 fixed wage, and it was hoped that the scales would be upgraded. In 1946 the wage for male sweepers was revised to Rs. 20-1-25, for female sweepers to Rs. 18-1-25 and for *mukadams* Rs. 25-1-30. However, the pay scale of sweepers employed by the Bombay state government was revised soon after and sweepers and *mukadams* employed by the municipality demanded a further revision in order to maintain a parity in wages: Rs. 25-1-40 for male and female sweepers and Rs. 30-1-50 for *mukadams*. The arbitrator revised the pay scale to Rs. 25-1-30 for male sweepers and Rs. 30-1-35 for *mukadams*. However, since female sweepers were required to cover only half of the area covered by male sweeper, their scale was set at Rs. 23-1-30. Explaining the rationale behind the award, Justice Shah pointed out that it was based on the following three points: that municipal workers were receiving a Re. 1 annual wage increase in contrast to the Re. 0.5 of state government sweepers, that the dearness allowance of Rs. 24 was the same as that given by the state government, and that the Rs. 5 special allowance for scavengers would continue.[4]

The second demand was that the temporary additional pay be raised to the level of state employed sweepers. In September 1946 the state government had made a temporary additional allowance of Rs. 5 for employees earning up to Rs. 40 a month, and Rs. 10 for those earning between Rs. 40 and Rs. 250. The arbitrator refused this demand, on the ground that the grain allowance, provided independently by the municipality since 1942, served the same function. The grain allowance of

Rs. 4 was considered to be equivalent to 25 per cent of the monthly expenditure on grain. It was raised to Rs. 5 in June 1946.[5]

The third concerned the payment of an annual bonus of Rs. 60 to workers receiving a monthly wage of up to Rs. 40, and of Rs. 120 to those receiving between Rs. 40 and 250 a month. This demand was also rejected on the ground that the grain allowance fully substituted for a bonus.[6]

The fourth demand sought that uniforms be periodically supplied to sweepers, and umbrellas to *mukadams*. The fifth asked that 'Harijan cleaners', recruited as substitute labour during the sweepers' strike of June 1946, be employed as drivers. Both demands were rejected as they had not been given much importance by the workers.[7]

The final demand was that rent free quarters to all sweepers and *mukadams* be provided or that a house rent allowance of Rs. 10 a month be paid to them. As of August 1947, 2,703 sweepers and 65 *mukadams* were employed. The arbitrator, estimating the number of families (households) to be around 1,600, pointed out that 360 families had already been accommodated at a nominal rent of Rs. 2 per month, that a further 439 had benefited by the deduction of sanitary cess tax, and that the municipality had a scheme to build 772 quarters for workers including sweepers. He commended the efforts of the municipality in providing housing for sweepers and rejected the union's demands.[8]

The general award (the Shah Adjudication) was intended for workers other than sweepers, primary school teachers and employees of the Department of Transport. The award was in five clauses: (1) revision of pay scales, (2) an increase in the dearness allowance, (3) an increase in the housing allowance, (4) an increase in the overtime allowance, and (5) the payment of an interim allowance.[9] I will not discuss these in detail, but mention just one point which relates to the sweepers. The arbitrator revised the pay scale of unskilled and illiterate workers, classified as Class 4 employees by the Central Pay Commission, from Rs. 20-1-30 to Rs. 30-0.5-35.[10] This widened the differential in the minimum wage between sweepers and other Class 4 workers.

### *The Jeejeebhoy Award, 1958*

After the handing down of the Shah Award, a dispute over wages broke out between the Department of Transport, AMC and its workers. Though both parties reached an agreement in August 1956, the dispute flared up again and an award was sought through F. Jeejeebhoy, chairman of the Labour Appellate Tribunal of India, to settle this and other unresolved disputes. The award was declared in February 1958,[11] which included a separate award for scavengers and sweepers as well as a general award for all permanent employees of the AMC. Let us look at the former first.

The first demand was for an increase in the number of permanent employees. The arbitrator rejected it, pointing out the fact that in 1957-8 there had been an increase of 300 permanent sweepers, despite the slackening of demand for road sweepers as a result of the growing construction of paved roads. Further, he quoted a statement by the commissioner in charge that the existing number of permanent employees was sufficient.[12]

The second concerned the employment of female sweepers. The unions accused the AMC of avoiding employing female sweepers. The arbitrator recommended that there should be no gender discrimination in employment if the worker was appropriate for the position, and that if there was no difference in the work done by male and female sweepers, the pay scale should be the same.[13] This award eliminated discrimination against female sweepers in employment and wages.

The third concerned the tenure of employees in the Night Soil Department. The unions demanded that jobs in the department be made permanent. The arbitrator rejected the demand for the following reasons: that the necessity of such labour would decrease as the sewer system developed, that of the 429 workers employed as casual labour in the department, 161 had already been promoted to permanent employment, that another 140 workers had been absorbed as permanent employees in other departments, and that the remaining 128 workers too were scheduled to be placed in other departments.[14]

The fourth, regarding the promotion of workers in the Malaria Department to permanent positions, was rejected on the ground that the department itself was of a temporary nature and that its employees would remain casual workers for as long as the AMC maintained its policy in that regard.[15]

The fifth concerned a cycle allowance for *mukadams*. The provision of a cycle allowance for some *mukadams* was at the Commissioner's discretion. The arbitrator recommended that a cycle allowance be paid when *mukadams* needed to accompany inspectors around work areas by cycle.[16]

The sixth related to the provision of sufficient tools to sweepers for cleaning purpose. Because enough brooms and baskets were not provided, cleaning was made very difficult. The arbitrator upheld the union claim and recommended that the AMC make adequate supplies available to sweepers.[17]

The seventh concerned the cleaning of storm water drains. Clearing away of mud and slush during the rainy season was the responsibility of the Engineering Department, while cleaning the storm water drains was the job of the sweepers. The arbitrator rejected the demand of sweepers that the cleaning of the drains should also come under the jurisdiction of the Engineering Department.[18]

The eighth demand related to the checking and reporting system. The AMC insisted that workers should report at the beginning and the end of the morning and afternoon shifts, that is, four times a day, at the main office, while the unions argued that they should only have to report twice a day, at their work site. The arbitrator recommended that workers should report twice a day, at the beginning of each shift, at the nearest muster station where tools and equipment were kept, taking into consideration the travelling time and distance to be covered by the worker.[19]

Let us now examine the general recommendations that were made for all workers. The main issues of concern were wages and treatment of temporary workers. The unions asked for increased house rent and compensatory city allowances, and a revision of the pay scale. The arbitrator allowed increases in the rent and compensatory city allowances to be in line with those of the Bombay state government. However, due to financial constraints faced by the AMC, the increase in the pay scale was only Rs. 5.[20] As a result, the minimum wage for sweepers in the Conservancy Department just rose from Rs. 70 to 75 a month. In response to the demand that temporary workers be promoted to permanent status, the arbitrator advised the promotion of as many employees as feasible. He rejected the demand for provident fund and various allowances to casual workers. However, the daily wage of casual labourers was raised from Rs. 2 and 8 annas a day to Rs. 2 and 13 annas.[21]

### *The Thakore Award, 1976-1980*

Following the Jeejeebhoy Award, wage disputes rose again between the AMC and its workers during the 1960s. The focus of the disputes was a revision of the pay scales and allowances, with retrospective effect, for workers other than sweepers and employees of the Department of Transport, who had not been the recipients of the Jeejeebhoy Award. In March 1964 the arbitrator Indrajit G. Thakore presented an award that was favorable to the workers, and as a result wage disputes did not flare up again for a considerable period of time, and for the decade after 1964 there was no revision of pay scales. During this period, however, real wages declined sharply due to inflation, and increase in the dearness allowance was not enough of a compensation. Though the central and state governments, and the major private enterprises, revised their wages at the time, the AMC failed to follow suit. I.G. Thakore was reappointed as arbitrator, with the agreement of both the employer and the workers. In the period 1976-80, acting as both arbitrator and a one-man pay commission, he presented the award which focuses on the revision of wages.

His award and recommendations were six fold and came into effect during 1976-80. They included: (1) a révision of pay scales, (2) an award for workers in the Department of Transport, (3) an award for other municipal workers, (4) an award for sweepers, (5) a revision of allowances, and (6) other issues. The award concerning the sweepers had 16 clauses, and since they cover a number of significant issues, I will examine them in detail.[22]

The first demand concerned the working hours and shifts. At the time, the duration of the first shift was 6 a.m. to 11 a.m. and that of the second, 3 p.m. to 6 p.m., making it an 8-hour working day. The unions asserted that in actual fact its duration was 12 hours, because workers, on an average had to travel an hour to work, and that they were in effect on the job from 5 a.m. to 7 p.m., excepting the 2-hour break from 12 a.m. to 2 p.m. This meant that they spent little time with their children and had no opportunities for a cultural or social life. In view of this, the unions demanded a working day of 7 hours and one shift. The AMC, however, opposed this demand on the grounds that any cut in working hours would necessitate the employment of additional sweepers, which would be a financial burden on them. Further, it pointed out that the proposed cut in working hours would be unfair to other municipal labourers, who had an 8 hours day, and that an 8-hour-workday was prevalent in private enterprises, including the textile industry, which follows the regulations of the Factory Act. After a careful examination of the Malkani, Barve, Pandya and other committee reports about sweepers and scavengers, the arbitrator confirmed that each committee had recommended a working day of not more than seven hours, though no particular mention had been made of shifts. He also ordered the AMC to organize and finance a delegation of representatives from the sweepers' trade unions to investigate the situation in other municipalities like Delhi, Bombay, Pune and Nagpur. The delegation found that Bombay and Pune had a working day of 7 hours in two shifts, and that Delhi and Nagpur had one of 7.5 hours in one shift. The arbitrator subsequently argued that the experience of other municipalities and the recommendations of the reports were against an 8-hours day, and that it would not be necessary to employ additional workers since sweepers would work more efficiently. On this basis he announced an award shortening the work day to 7.5 hours with the proviso that it would eventually become 7 hours. He rejected the union's demand for one shift, saying it would be impossible and impractical under the existing system, but as a compromise determined that the first shift would start at 6.30 a.m. in the four winter months, and at 6 a.m. for the remainder of the year. The AMC had argued for starting the first shift at 6 a.m. so that street cleaning could be finished before the volume of traffic grew, while the unions had demanded a 7 a.m. start to make it convenient for workers to travel.[23]

The second demand was for opening of creches. The unions pointed out that as there were no creches female workers had to take their babies and young children to the worksite, and asked that creches be provided by the AMC at muster stations. The AMC refused on the grounds that the sweepers had not used the creche set up earlier on an experimental basis at a hospital, that there was no space available at the muster stations, and that the small numbers involved did not warrant the expense of setting up creches. The arbitrator recommended that the AMC, as an experiment should try setting up a creche near the worksite rather than in a hospital far from it. And that creches should be increased in number if they proved effective. He added that effective welfare could not improve as long as the sweepers did not limit their families.[24]

The third was regarding the provision of uniforms. The existing system was to provide five sets of uniform every two years. Male workers got a set of long pant and a long-sleeved shirt, and four sets of short pants and short-sleeved shirts. Female workers received five saris, petticoats and blouses. They were all made of home-spun cotton (*khadi*).[25] The unions, on the other hand, demanded that three sets of uniform be supplied each year, for men, three pairs of long pants and long-sleeved shirts, and for women, three saris, petticoats and blouses. Because home-spun cotton was not durable they asked for machine-woven clothes. The arbitrator, noting that a distinction should be made between work and home wear, made an award that uniforms for workers should be issued annually: one set of long pant and long-sleeved shirt and two sets of short pants and short-sleeved shirts for men, and three sets of clothes to women.[26] He made no reference to the use of home-spun cotton.

The fourth demand, for a laundry allowance of Rs. 5, was not considered because the same demand had already been met in Part One of the award. The fifth demand that *mukadams* receive a woolen coat and trousers annually, was also approved.[27]

The sixth demand related to medical care for sweepers. The unions pointed out that it was difficult for sweepers to visit municipal hospitals and pharmacies because they were closed by the time they finished work, and also testified that sweepers had received discriminatory treatment at hospitals. They therefore demanded that medical care be improved for sweepers and their children, who were at high risk from diseases like tuberculosis and cancer. The arbitrator dismissed the claim for medical services for sweepers' children, but recommended that prosecutions be made in case of discrimination and that medical care be made available to sweepers at a time and place convenient for them.[28]

The seventh demand was that *umedvars* (casual labourers on the waiting list) of with more than one-year's experience should be employed as permanent workers (*kaymi*). The AMC, however, insisted that it could only make such promotions when vacancies arose. The arbitrator stated that it was regrettable that large numbers of *umedvars* were being employed on what was virtually a permanent basis, and this indicated that in fact permanent work was available. He therefore ordered the AMC to increase the number of *kaymis*, taking into consideration its financial situation. It was decided that *umedvars* who had worked constantly for more than 240 days a year over five years as of 1 January 1978 would be made permanent employees in three phases. The eligible *umedvars* were divided into three groups according to the date of their registration on the waiting list; the first group was to be promoted on 1 April 1978, the second in April 1979, and the third in April 1980. The arbitrator suggested that this award be not confined to sweepers alone, and recommended that the qualifications and conditions that he set out for promotion be not regarded as inflexible.[29]

The eighth demand was that sweepers working in the chawls (workers' residential areas) be absorbed into the municipality. The AMC had yearly contracts with some of the residents in the chawls. These sweeping services were provided by temporary workers not on the waiting list (*hangamis*). Unlike the *umedvars* there was no provision for their jobs permanent. The arbitrator found no reason to distinguish chawl sweepers from those working in other areas, and based on his ruling in Clause 7, ordered that additional quotas be set for permanent employees and that qualified *hangamis* be absorbed into the permanent work force.[30]

The ninth demand related to the provision of living quarters to sweepers in their designated wards. Of the 3,200 permanent workers and the approximately 600-700 day workers none of the latter and between 900 and 1,000 of the former had been allocated quarters. The unions also criticized the AMC for having suspended its building plan. The arbitrator pointed out that the AMC had lost its former momentum in constructing quarters for Harijans and ordered it to prepare a new building scheme, taking its financial situation into consideration. He specified that the quarters should be built in the ward where the sweepers worked and urged the establishment of a subsidy and loan system to help sweepers construct their own houses.[31]

The tenth demand was that preference in employment be given to the children of sweepers employed by the AMC, as it was difficult for them to gain employment in any other occupation. The arbitrator referred to the compensatory employment scheme in the Jeejeebhoy Award regarding the provision of a job to members of the family in case of the death of a permanent employee. But this was limited to the Scheduled Castes and Backward Classes under the reservation scheme. He suggested that members of the sweeper community should not restrict themselves to cleaning work but seek employment in other departments of the municipality. He added that the special quota should be reserved for qualified children (who had completed secondary education) of sweepers so that they could seek more lucrative employment elsewhere.[32]

The eleventh demand concerned the pay day. The sweepers were paid between the 7th and the 10th of each month. They demanded that they should also be paid on the 5th like the other workers of the municipality. The arbitrator refused the demand, stating that sweepers were paid later than other workers because of the clerical work involved in processing the wages of so many sweepers and that as far as the pay day itself, there was no problem since it was fixed on a particular day.[33]

The union's twelfth demand was that an unclean allowance of Rs. 10, already being paid to 1,200 sweepers (of the total number of 3,500) be given to all sweepers. While the unions emphasized the fact that sweeping work necessarily involved removing animal dung and human excreta from the streets. The arbitrator was of the opinion that the removal of animal dung had nothing to do with the allowance, and it should be restricted to sweepers working in places where public defecation was widespread.[34]

The thirteenth was a demand for the establishment of a Grievance Committee to deal with routine problem at the workplace. The AMC responded by saying that since the Ahmedabad City Sweepers' Association had been deputed to deal with workers' complaints there was no need to create a special committee. The arbitrator pointed out that problems dealt with by the union and the Grievance Committee were different and that trifling routine problems often caused the greatest disruption. He ordered that a Grievance Committee of three representatives each from the municipality and the unions be set up on four different zones.[35]

The fourteenth demand was that free milk be distributed to the children of sweepers. The unions asserted that sweepers constituted the poorest group in the community and suffered due to mal nutrition. The arbitrator refused the demand on the grounds that the sweepers were by no means the poorest group employed by the AMC and that they were, in fact, better off in many ways than other manual labourers.[36]

The fifteenth demand dealt with holidays. Sweepers received one full day holiday a week, but only a half-day on public holidays. The unions appealed that the 14 designated public holidays observed by the AMC annually be made full day holidays and if this was not possible, wages for a half-day's work should be calculated as two full days' work. Based on the examination of the reports of the Second and Third Central Pay Commissions and the Second Gujarat State Pay Commission, the arbitrator concluded that national holidays could not be made full holidays for sweepers because of the public nature of their work. However, because the public holidays recognized by the AMC were comparatively few compared with those of other municipalities, he instructed that all national and state holidays should be regarded as half-day holidays. He also awarded five additional days as paid holiday for sweepers.[37]

### *The Barot Award, 1984-1992*

By the line the Thakore Award was presented, the unions again demanded a revision of pay scales and allowances. They argued that the award had not been able to revise all the minute details in the pay scales of a variety of jobs and that there had been a considerable rise in prices by the time the award was announced. In 1980 the AMC agreed to appoint G.S. Barot as an arbitrator, to revise pay scales and allowances of municipal workers.

Between 1984 and 1992, Barot presented the following 17 awards concerning a variety of these issues: (1) interim relief and medical allowances, (2) revision of the interim relief allowance, (3) revision of pay scales, (4) compensatory allowance for firemen, (5) pay revision for primary school teachers, (6) pay revision for duplicating technicians, (7) revision of housing allowances and rents, (8) cycle and two-wheeler allowances, (9) revision of general allowances, (10) revision of special wages for special work, (11) overtime and heavy labour allowances, (12) revision of rankings for biochemical workers, (13) special wages and allowances for transportation workers, (14) claims by pensioners, (15) promotion policy, (16) promotion policy for transportation workers, and (17) special wages and allowances for other labourers. Barot's Award was two-pronged, covering a general revision of wages and allowances and individual provision for workers in areas not covered by the Thakore Award. Since the demands of sweepers had already been dealt with in detail in that award, they were not examined individually by Barot. Let us, therefore, look at the Barot Award in terms of the revision of pay scales and allowances, and promotion policy, as they affected sweepers.[38]

Thakore had tried to revise the pay scales of the AMC workers to the level recommended by the Second Gujarat State Pay Commission report of January 1973, but since all the necessary documents had not been submitted by the unions, some departments had been left out. Barot examined the documents now submitted by the employer and the unions and undertook a revision of pay scales on the pattern of the Thakore Award. While he was examining these issues, the Third Gujarat State Pay Commission, convened in October 1982, submitted its report (June 1985). This was still being considered by the state government when the report of the Fourth Central Pay Commission was issued in June 1986. In contrast to the report of the Third Gujarat State Pay Commission, which was based on the average consumer price index of 500 (100 in 1960) as on 1 July 1983, that of the Fourth Central Pay Commission was based on the index of 608 (31 December 1985). The revised pay scale of the former came into effect on 1 July 1983 and the latter on 1 January 1986. Employees of the state government and unions pressured the state government to revise the pay scales in accordance with the recommendations of the Fourth Central Pay Commission. Following a discreet investigation, the government acceded. The Barot Award, to keep pace with the state government, followed the pay scale revisions of the Fourth Central Pay Commission. The unions demanded that the revisions be made with retrospective effect (prior to 1 January 1986), on the grounds that the agreement with the AMC to appoint an arbitrator was in 1980, and that the revisions of the Third Gujarat State Pay Commission came into effect on 1 July 1983. The arbitrator rejected this demand, because the new scales for state employees went into effect on 1 January 1986. The pay scale for sweepers was revised from Rs. 196-3-220-EB (Efficiency Bar)-3-232 to Rs. 750-12-870-EB-14-940.[39]

The minimum wage in the new pay scale was Rs. 750 per month, with an annual increment of Rs. 12 with a maximum of Rs. 870 in ten years. At this time an aptitude check (EB) is carried out. This was a mere formality for sweepers, whereby the public sanitary inspector of sweepers had to communicate to the central office that there were no physical or mental abnormalities in the workers. After that the sweeper would receive an annual increment of Rs. 14 rising to a maximum of Rs. 940 after five years. The outstanding characteristic of the revision was the enormous rise in the basic wage. Pensions, also rose as they were based on the basic wage, and the welfare of sweepers improved.

Barot investigated more than 30 kinds of allowances. Of those, the most important, from the point of view of sweepers, were the interim relief, and the dearness, housing and compensatory city allowances, and these were paid to all employees. Special allowances that applied to the sweepers included the washing, unclean (*gandgi*), night soil, bad climate, and *silai* (stitching) allowances. The interim relief allowance was given for the period leading up to the pay scale revision and was of a temporary nature. In May 1980, after the Thakore Award, the AMC had decided to make a voluntary across-the-board payment of Rs. 25 per month, which was revised to Rs. 50 in April 1982. In March 1985, Barot added to this a further 10 per cent of the basic wage. Class 4 employees of the state government received Rs. 35 between April 1982 and March 1985; the amount less than that AMC employees received. There were strong representations from the AMC for the need to adjust the pay differentials with the former state government scales during the period. In view of this, Barot ordered that the payment of Rs. 50 only be made with retrospective effect from June 1983, bringing it in alignment with the state government employees.[40]

The dearness allowance was calculated as a certain proportion of the basic wage, taking into consideration trends in the consumer price index. It constituted a great proportion of the wage received. Following the revision in wages, its proportion decreased though it still remained the largest among the allowances. The arbitrator ordered that in calculating the dearness allowance, the state government method should be followed.[41]

As a result of the revisions in the housing and rent allowance, sweepers who owned or rented houses were given an across-the-board payment of Rs. 150 a month.[42] Sweepers living in municipal housing paid rents depending on when they took position of the accommodation. Some received a housing allowance equivalent to 15 per cent of their basic pay in exchange for a nominal rent. The AMC wanted to discontinue payment of housing allowance to those who lived in municipal housing. In order to simplify the complicated situation, the arbitrator awarded a housing allowance to those who lived in accommodation with a fixed rent but ruled that no allowance be paid to those who did not pay rent or only paid a nominal or proportional rent.[43]

The compensatory city allowance corresponded to the state government's compensatory local allowance. It was revised and introduced by the central government on 1 October 1986 and by the state government on June 1 1987. The unions wanted the date of the revision to be backdated to the former, but the arbitrator made the award according to the date on which the state government's revision came into effect. The allowance for sweepers was revised to Rs. 30 a month.[44]

The washing allowance applied to 12,000 workers who wore uniforms, including sweepers, firemen and nurses. The payment differed with each department. Considering of the high cost of washing, a 50 per cent rise was sought, with Rs. 10 to be the minimum monthly payment. The sweepers' award was revised from Rs. 5 to 10. The unclean allowance applied to more than 3,500 sweepers, who cleaned public latrines or drains or had to remove human excreta from the streets. The night-soil allowance was paid to 60 workers who were involved with removing animal carcasses and emptying and cleaning the traditional cesspool (*khalkuva*) that remained in the city. These two allowances were revised from Rs. 8 to 18 per month. The bad climate allowance was paid to those who worked at water treatment plants or pumping stations. The purpose of this allowance was to keep provide a nutritional diet to the worker, an incentive to work in an unpleasant environment. It was originally a proportion of the basic wage (Rs. 9 to 15 a month) but was revised to an across-the-board payment of Rs. 30. The stitching allowance was given to employees who has to wear a uniform at the workplace. Ready made clothing in standard sizes had been supplied, but there was dissatisfaction because they were ill-fitting. Accordingly, the AMC distributed material and paid an annual allowance for stitching. After the revision, the sweepers' allowance was raised from Rs. 10 to 20. Through all of these allowances to sweepers were finalized in October 1989, the payments were backdated to 1 July 1988.[45]

One of the focal points of the award was the promotion policy for Classes 3 and 4 workers. Promotion opportunities were closed to the 17,000 Class 4 workers, consisting of sweepers, watchmen, miscellaneous workers, gardeners and general manual labourers, and to Class 3 workers, like firemen, tailors, telephone operators, blacksmiths and carpenters. Since the great majority of these workers performed the same job under the same pay scale as when had first joined work, there was deep dissatisfaction, which discouraged their motivation to work. The unions demanded that higher pay scales should be given to them after a certain number of years of service. Soon after the arbitrator started studying the promotion policy, on 20 February 1991, the state government announced a promotion scheme for its workers.[46] Under this scheme, promotion was assured for workers who received less than Rs. 3,500 a month (most Classes 3 and 4 workers). After the first twelve years of service their pay scale would be raised by one rank, and subsequently after 24 years of service, by another rank.

TABLE 4.1: WAGE CALCULATION

(*in Rs.*)

| Base wage | Allowances | | | | | | Total |
|---|---|---|---|---|---|---|---|
| | Dearness | House and rent | City | Medical | Washing | Unclean | |
| 750 | 533 | 150 | 30 | 75 | 10 | 18 | 1,566 |
| 940 | 668 | 150 | 30 | 75 | 10 | 18 | 1,891 |
| 1,400 | 994 | 250 | 45 | 75 | 10 | 18 | 2,792 |

NOTE: The dearness allowance is 71 per cent of the base wage as of July 1992.
SOURCE: Calculated from Barot Award, Part 3, pp. 5, 15, 18.

Accordingly, the arbitrator ordered in May 1991 that the same scheme should be applied to the AMC workers.[47] Two months later, on 5 July 1991, the state government revised this plan further, increasing the pay scale by one rank after 9, 18 and 27 years of service.[48] This revision was applied automatically to the AMC scheme. As a result, the pay scale of sweepers earning a starting wage between Rs. 750 and going upto a maximum of Rs. 940 (Scale 1) increased to Rs. 775-1,025 (Scale 2) in the tenth year of service, to Rs. 800-1,150 (Scale 3) in the nineteenth year, and to Rs. 950-1,400 (Scale 4) in the twenty-eighth year.

A sweeper who started work at the lowest rate on Scale 1 of Rs. 750 would earn Rs. 859 (Scale 2) in the tenth year, Rs. 980 (Scale 3) in the nineteenth year, and Rs. 1,150 (Scale 4) in the twenty-eighth year, and would earn a maximum base wage of Rs. 1,400 in the thirty-eighth year. Since several important allowances such as the dearness, the house and rent, and the compensatory city allowances, are based on the base wage, the impact of the increased basic wage is shown in Table 4.1. Before the revision of the promotion policy, the wages of sweepers remained at Scale 1 through their entire careers. A worker who began with a monthly wage of Rs. 1,566 would earn a maximum wage of Rs. 1,891 after 15 years, with no change thereafter. The differential between the highest and lowest in the wage scale was merely Rs. 325. After the implementation of the promotion scheme, the wage increase for a sweeper after 38 years of service would show a differential of Rs. 1,226.

## SWEEPERS AND EMPLOYMENT POLICY

An examination of the various awards indicates that the demands of the unions were centred on the revision of pay scales and allowances, and on the improvement of employment and service conditions. The enlargement of the quota of permanent workers and the improvement in their service conditions were benefits for the good of the Bhangi community as a whole. However, the Awards constitute only one part of the AMC's employment policy. Let us now examine the other aspects of its employment policy and their impact on the sweeper community.

### *The Waiting List*

The Pandya Committee of 1969 reported that most local bodies filled vacancies in the permanent quota through the waiting list, and the system of compensatory employment. A small number of them reported that they used labour exchanges, but this method was not actually followed.

Up till 1972 the AMC maintained two types of waiting lists, though the origin of such list is unknown. Workers with acting status were put onto List A, while substitute workers were put onto List B. The latter filled in for permanent employees and acting status workers (during their absence). When a vacancy for a permanent provision was created by death, retirement or resignation, a new permanent worker was appointed from List A, according to seniority in terms of the registration date and the number of years worked. Vacancies in List A were likewise filled from List B, again according to seniority. Workers with acting status received virtually the same pay, holidays and working conditions as permanent workers, except that they were not eligible for benefits such as the provident fund or house building loan.

Workers in List B were casual labourers called *umedvars* (candidates). Their daily wage was calculated by dividing the total amount received in terms of the base wage, dearness allowance and compensatory city allowance of a permanent employee by 26 workdays (the maximum number of work days in a month). They received no benefits, such as paid holidays. There were large differences in the number of days the *umedvars* worked in a month. Since the number of absentees was always lower than the number of *umedvar* substitutes on any given day they were selected in terms of their registration seniority. As a result, those senior on the list worked almost the same number of days as the permanent employees, while those lower down could work only a few days in a month. The *umedvars*, for daily recruitment, would gather at the nearest muster station before the beginning of the first shift and wait for allotment of work.

The *hangamis* were another group of sweepers who worked under an annual contract for the AMC to clean chawls, and under a monthly contract during the monsoon season to clean roads and drains. They were casual workers not on any waiting list. *Hangamis* were given a minimum daily wage, though it was often revised by pay commissions and awards, it always remained below that of *umedvars*.

Lists A and B were revised annually based on the applications received from sweepers. At that time promotions from List A to permanent employees status and from List B to List A , as well as newly registered names on List B, were verified. Since the actual promotions had stuck by the early 1970s, the AMC decided to suspend the revision of Lists A and B in 1973. The unions reacted quickly and an agreement was reached with the AMC to allow fresh recruitment of *umedvars*. The suspended A and B lists were frozen, and new applicants were registered on a separate C list. Casual workers on List C were also called *umedvars* and had the same employment and service conditions as workers on List B. However, with the creation of the new list, it was inevitable that List B had absolute priority over List C in terms of promotion.

Thakore, who handed down his award for sweepers on 21 January 1978, had to cope with this complex situation. He ordered that all those who had worked for more than 240 days a year for a period of five years as of 1 January 1978 were to be made permanent employees by 1980. As a result virtually all workers on the A and B lists were promoted, so there was no purpose in retaining these lists. Thus after the Award, only List C was maintained and all those who fulfilled the conditions were made permanent. During the year, the criteria for permanent employment were revised. The AMC decided to apply Barot's Award of 30 June 1978 on the promotion of workers in the Engineering Department to the sweepers.[49] As a result, the criterion for promotion from List C to permanent employment was relaxed to a total of 5 years with 900 days experience. This criterion is still in use. The relaxation of the comparatively strict regulations of the Thakore Award of 240 days a year to a total of 900 days (in 5 years) was advantageous to the sweepers. Furthermore the total number of working days that were required decreased to 900, from the 1,200 days under the Thakore Award. The number of applicants registered on List C, determined by the AMC, were based on information from the muster stations. The muster stations reported to the AMC as to the number of *umedvars* they would need annually, and the number to be registered. At the time of selection being organized by the muster stations, the applicant's suitability (in terms of age and strength) and his/her experience as a *hangami* were mainly considered.

### *Compensatory Appointment*

Compensatory appointment system allows a suitable member of the family of a permanent worker of the AMC, who has died or become disabled in service to be the worker's successor and be given priority in permanent employment. Its purpose is to prevent economic hardship in a family as a result of the death or disability of the main worker. The system was already institutionalized in many municipalities all over India in the late 1960s. There were considerable differences between local bodies in terms of rules and regulations of the system. The system also changed depending on the relative strengths of the management and labour, and consequently did not remain the same over time even in the same municipality. Since compensatory appointment is as important as the waiting list in the employment of sweepers, we will trace the changes in the system as they occurred in the AMC.

The first regulation on compensatory appointment in the case of sweepers emerged from the Jeejeebhoy Award of 1958. The unions had urged that on the death of a permanent worker, his/her spouse or a family member should be employed on a permanent basis. The arbitrator ordered the AMC to give priority in permanent employment to a suitable family member of a deceased worker, since sweepers and scavengers could not easily get other jobs and also because the bereaved family would face added difficulties if they were evicted from municipal housing.[50] However, as Jeejeebhoy had not specified the conditions of employment, such as the age of the dead worker and whether or not the family of the deceased had other sources of income, the AMC decided to extend compensatory employment only to a family which had been left without any source of income as a result of the death of a worker while in service. Such families were termed *niradhar*, and the recipient of compensatory employment was called *warasdar* (successor or heir).

The system of compensatory employment set up by the Jeejeebhoy Award was amended initially in 1972. That year both the AMC and the unions agreed to add disability (medically unfit) alongwith death as conditions for compensatory employment. Disability was defined as a condition, caused by illness or injury, which prevented the worker permanently from performing his duties. This has to be authorized by the municipal hospital in the form of a certificate of disability. Again, the recipients of compensatory employment due to disability were confined to *niradhars*. This agreement was not written down but has remained a customary practice.[51]

In May 1977 Gujarat state revised its compensatory employment (called compassionate appointment) system, which it had begun in 1975, with the purpose of tightening the system against abuse.[52] As a result of the revision, beneficiaries were confined to the families of Class 4 workers and manual workers in Class 3 who had died in service. Restrictions were also put on the age of beneficiaries: they were to be not less than one year below the lower age limit, and not more than twenty years above the upper age limit, stated in the Recruitment Rules. Beneficiaries were to be employed, except in special cases, within five years of the death of the worker. The system was to apply only to families whose monthly income was less than Rs. 400, though this limit was revised several times in later years because of the raise in the cost of living; in 1991 it was set at Rs. 1,000. Compassionate appointment was limited to death of a worker in service, and not applied to disabilities.

The revision of compassionate appointment had an indirect impact on AMC's compensatory employment policy. During the period of the Thakore Award (1976-80), large number of applications for compensatory employment were received as a result of the broadening of the permanent worker quota. As Table 4.2 shows, as many as 310 applications were authorized in 1981 and 1982. After 1983, the AMC began tightening its overall employment policy and the numbers of authorizations declined sharply. The AMC's reaction to the Thakore Award and the trade union split in 1983 were major factors behind the cuts in employment.

In March 1984, the Deputy Commissioner in charge of public sanitation issued a circular[53] directing that compensatory employment be applied only in the case of workers who died or were disabled at least five years before the retirement age of 60. The circular had been issued to curb the number of applications by removing the high risk age group from consideration. The unions vigorously opposed this reversal, with the result that the AMC had no course but to revise the age restriction.

In January 1987, the Commissioner instructed that the departments concerned raise the age limit for compensatory employment from age 55 to 58.[54] In the same circular he cautioned that in cases where the remarried widow of an employee was employed or where the family received financial support from a source outside the immediate family, they could not be classified as *niradhars*. This suggests that there were a number of such cases among applicants for compensatory employment. As a result of these developments, instead of placing *niradhars* at the top of a special waiting list for permanent employment vacancies, they were employed temporarily with acting status, under which permanent employment after

TABLE 4.2: NUMBER OF APPLICATIONS FOR COMPENSATORY APPOINTMENT (BY REASON)

(*no. of applications/authorizations*)

| Year | Applications according to reason | | | | No. of authorizations |
|---|---|---|---|---|---|
| | Death | Disability | Retirement | Total | |
| 1980/1 | 1 | – | – | 1 | N.A. |
| 1981/2 | 1 | – | 1 | 2 | 153 |
| 1982/3 | 3 | 1 | – | 4 | 157 |
| 1983/4 | 21 | 14 | 1 | 36 | – |
| 1984/5 | 37 | 19 | 1 | 57 | 8 |
| 1985/6 | 13 | 3 | 8 | 24 | 7 |
| 1986/7 | 19 | 2 | 1 | 22 | 16 |
| 1987/8 | 10 | 4 | 3 | 17 | 27 |
| 1988/9 | 3 | 2 | – | 5 | 32 |
| 1989/90 | 5 | 1 | – | 6 | 39 |
| 1990/1 | 4 | 1 | 1 | 6 | 24 |
| 1991/2 | N.A. | N.A. | N.A. | N.A. | 35 |
| Total | 117 | 47 | 16 | 180 | 498 |

NOTES: (1) The financial year of the AMC begins on 1 April.
(2) Figures for authorizations in 1991/2 are based on records through to August.
(3) All applications on the grounds of retirement were refused.

SOURCE: The Ahmedabad Municipal Corporation.

one year was guaranteed. Thus though the age limit was relaxed, the standards by which *niradhars* were certified became far stricter, and the number of authorization for compensatory employment remained at a low level. The unions put forward their claims at tribunals for further relaxation of the standards.

In May 1991, agreement was reached between the AMC and the Ahmedabad Municipal Servants' Association and the age limit was revised to within six months of retirement.[55] The sons, unmarried or divorced daughters, spouses, sons' wives and adopted children all became eligible as beneficiaries. Of great importance was the fact that restrictions on *niradhar* were abolished so that any person from the above category in the family of the deceased worker could become a permanent sweeper of the AMC irrespective of family income. These regulations were backdated to January 1987. As a result, most of the cases of death or disability that had occurred since the previous revision were redressed, while older cases were placed out of consideration. The revision caused a split in the unions.

While the new system was favourable for the beneficiaries, there was a danger that municipal employment would become hereditary. Because it raised the ratio of compensatory employees in the employment quota, it was an obstacle in the promotion of *umedvars* and indirectly restricted the movement of *hangamis* to the status of *umedvars*.

The application process for compensatory employment begins with the submission of a number of documents at the muster station where the deceased or disabled worker was based: birth certificate, ration card, letter of assent from family, certificate of residence, death or disability certificate, and a school certificate. The official in charge at the muster station would check these and send them over to the Welfare Labour Officer at the Central Office of the AMC. The documents are checked in light of the compensatory employment regulations. Prior to 1986, to check the veracity of the documents, a visit to the home of the applicant would have been essential to question the family and neighbours about the relationship between the dead or disabled worker and the applicant. After receiving a report from the Welfare Labour Officer, the Deputy Commissioner for Public Sanitation was authorized to arrive at the final decision regarding employment of a candidate. Between 1986 and 1990, the Conservancy Department actually reviewed the applications. The Sanitary Inspector and the Public Sanitation Inspector visited the applicant's home for enquiry. In November 1990, this task reverted to the Welfare Labour Officer. After the revision of the regulations for *warasdars* in May 1991, document inspection was deemed sufficient in all but suspect cases.[56]

## Sweepers and Trade Unions

The collective action of registered trade unions was guaranteed under the Trade Union Act of 1926, and the Industrial Disputes Act of 1947 further strengthened the importance of trade unions in industrial disputes between the management and labour. The trade union movement was particularly strong in the states of Gujarat and Maharashtra in western India, encompassing a broad stratum of workers, the unions contributed greatly to the improvement of their employment and working conditions. Most Class 4 municipal workers belonged to a union, and the sweepers, a powerful pressure group, alongwith the transport workers and primary school teachers' unions, became the nucleus of the union movement within the AMC. This section moves on from the discussion of industrial disputes and awards to an examination of the history and present status of trade unions that had functioned as pressure groups for labour in those disputes.

*Awards and Trade Unions*

An award implies agreement and compliance by both the management and labour on its procedure and the final decision of an arbitrator. When a dispute emerges, the AMC commissions a professional consultant to refute and provide counter evidence against the claims of the unions. The unions, on the other hand, acts as the representative of workers in disputes with the help of lawyers. The identity of the unions concerned with the dispute and their demands can be ascertained through the contents of the award. The various unions mentioned in the awards that we have examined in this study are as follows.

The sole union cited in the Shah Award of 1948 was the Ahmedabad Municipal Servants' Association.[57] Its main demand was the revision of pay scales and allowances, and submitted a list of beneficiaries comprising employee groups A to D.[58] A and B groups corresponded to the current Classes 1 and 2 respectively. The Industrial Disputes Act of 1947 was promulgated in April; the request to Shah for an award was made by the government on 12 August 1947. For both the management and labour this was the first dispute to be settled within the provisions of the Act. The union included groups A and B in its list because it was not clear that the Act applied only to labourers (workmen). The arbitrator naturally excluded these groups from his award. Groups C and D that the union had submitted were equivalent to Classes 3 and 4, which included lower ranking inspectors and clerical workers, but the lowly ranked sweepers and transport workers were excluded form the union's list of manual workers. As a result, a special award was handed down regarding the workers who comprised the majority of Class 4. This shows that the Ahmedabad Municipal Servants' Association at that time had centred around members in administrative and clerical positions.

The spokesman for the sweepers was Shantilal H. Shah. The Shah Award makes no mention of his background or of his connections with the sweepers, but there is oral evidence that he put together the demands of sweepers on behalf of the Ahmedabad City Sweepers' Association,[59] which had grown out of the Textile Labour Association, Ahmedabad, in 1930. The Textile Labour Association, Ahmedabad, was founded in 1920 by Ansuyaben Sarabhai, a scion of the Sarabhai family, under the guidance of M.K. Gandhi, and, as Gujarat's largest trade union, developed its collective action based on the principle of non-violence. Both associations were at the same site and the Sweepers' Association also adopted the principle of non-violence.

The Jeejeebhoy Award of 1958 mentioned the Indian National Trade Union Congress (Gujarat Branch), the Ahmedabad Municipal Engineering Department Workers' Union, the Ahmedabad City Sweepers' Association, the Ahmedabad Corporation Employees' Union, the Ahmedabad Municipal Servants' Association, the Ahmedabad Municipal Kamdar Sangh, and the Motor Drivers and Motor Workers' Association, Ahmedabad.[60] The vigorous growth of the union movement in the decade between the two awards is striking.

The Ahmedabad City Sweepers' Association represented the demands of sweepers. M.T. Shukla, the union spokesman at the time of the Jeejeebhoy Award , still plays a central role in it, and has provided valuable historical introduction for this study. He stated that besides the issues mentioned in the Jeejeebhoy Award, the union worked to get rid of bad customs among sweepers, such as drinking, extravagance and begging for leftover food.[61]

Fifteen unions and associations were cited in the Thakore Award of 1976.[62] The main ones were the Ahmedabad Municipal Servants' Association, the Ahmedabad Municipal Mazdoor Association, the Ahmedabad City Sweepers' Association, the Motor Drivers and Motor Workers' Association, the Ahmedabad General Mazdoor Union, the Ahmedabad Municipal Teachers' Mandal, the Ahmedabad Municipal Officers' Association and the Ahmedabad Municipal Supervisory Staff Association. Unlike the previous practice, unions seeking awards currently no longer based only on a department, but also on rank. The Ahmedabad Municipal Servants' Association still remained the largest union in terms of membership, but its relative importance has lessened with the emergence of new unions.

The Ahmedabad City Sweepers' Association coordinated the demands of sweepers as it had done earlier. The Thakore Award brought about a drastic change in the employment, working, and living conditions of AMC sweepers. The award reflected the arbitrator's learning and passion for research, and also the excellent spadework done by the union. The union well examined the documents concerning the sweepers and produced a relatively consistent list of demands.

The post-1984 Barot Award covered 26 unions.[63] Most of these unions were concerned with awards about pay scales and allowances, which was of great importance to the majority of their members; only a few received an award about particular departments or workers. Representatives of the unions were the Ahmedabad Municipal Nokar Mandal (formerly the Ahmedabad Municipal Servants' Association) and the Ahmedabad Municipal Mazdoor Association, both superior to other unions in membership and support base. The increase in the number of unions after the Thakore Award was particularly remarkable among teachers and hospital workers. The following unions specializing in legal disputes emerged during this period: the Gujarat Municipal and Panchayat Kamdar Association and the CPIM affiliated Ahmedabad Municipal Kamdar Karamchari Union. Also, the Dalit, Adivasi, Baxi Panch Municipal Kamdar Karamchari Mandal emerged with main focus on issues affecting workers belonging to the Scheduled Castes, Scheduled Tribes and Backward Classes.

Since issues concerning sweepers had been fully dealt with in the Thakore Award, they were not taken up individually in the Barot Award. Like other workers, the sweepers demanded a revision of pay scales and allowances, and the establishment of a promotion scheme. The unions which dealt with awards concerning sweepers were: the Ahmedabad Municipal Nokar Mandal, the Ahmedabad City Sweepers' Association, the Gujarat Municipal and Panchayat Kamdar Association, and the Ahmedabad Municipal Kamdar Karamchari Union. After the Thakore Award the power equation between the unions concerned with the sweepers underwent a great change. The influential Ahmedabad City Sweepers' Association, which had long dealt exclusively with issues affecting sweepers, lost its power to influence, while the Ahmedabad Municipal Nokar Mandal, which had succeeded in organizing sweepers, took over the leadership. Other unions too began looking at issues concerning sweepers as the diversification of the union movement proceeded. Let us now examine the process of this change and the status of some of the major unions.

### *Trade Unions in the Early 1990s*

In 1991, 64 registered trade unions were functioing in the AMC.[64] Among them five have been particularly concerned with improving the employment, working and living conditions of sweepers: These include The Ahmedabad Municipal Nokar Mandal, the Ahmedabad City Sweepers' Association, the Gujarat Municipal and Panchayat Kamdar Association, the Ahmedabad Municipal Kamdar Karamchari Union, and the All India Safai Mazdoor Congress (which is attempting to strengthen its connection with municipal sweepers).

### THE AHMEDABAD MUNICIPAL NOKAR MANDAL (FORMERLY AHMEDABAD MUNICIPAL SERVANTS' ASSOCIATION)

The popularly known Nokar Mandal is supported by Classes 3 and 4 workers. Established in 1930, it was the general union for all municipal workers, but with the promulgation of the Industrial Disputes Act of 1947, workers not classified as 'workmen' by the Act lost interest in staying in the union. As is clear form the Shah Award, 1948, it did not include sweepers. With the growth in the number of unions and their diversification of interests in the early 1970s, this union began losing its former superiority. The necessity of bringing in the very large group of sweepers, who had so far been excluded, seemed to be a means of preventing erosion of its sphere of influence. A dispute about its future direction grew within the union around the time of the Thakore Award. Disaffected officials had joined other unions and were beginning to concern themselves with sweeper issues. By the end of the decade the union still had little influence among sweepers.

However, in the early 1980s the Ahmedabad City Sweepers' Association, which had until now the greatest power in terms of organizing sweepers, split as a result of internal dissension. In 1983 the original director, having been expelled from the management committee, moved over to the Nokar Mandal, taking with him a large number of *mukadams* and sweepers. The Nokar Mandal set up a division called the Safai Kamdar Nokar Mandal under its umbrella to absorb the sweepers who had moved with him[65] As a result of this mass move, the negotiating power of the Nokar Mandal became stronger. In 1991 about 20,000 of the 35,000 municipal employees were members of the union. About 8,000 of this number were sweepers, which represents 40 per cent of the membership of the Nokar Mandal. About 7,000 sweepers were permanent employees, and the rest 1,000 were day workers. Of these, female workers comprised 60 per cent and 35 per cent respectively.[66] The total strength of AMC sweepers, including both permanant and day workers, was about 11,000 in 1991. Thus the majority of sweepers belonged to the Nokar Mandal.

In August 1991, the union demanded permanent employment for the *warasdars*, promotion to permanent employment for the *umedvars*, periodic supply of work tools, prompt payment of pensions, provident fund, and insurance, increase in construction of municipal housing, and abolition of illegal work inspection.[67]

The permanent employment of *warasdars* went along according to plan during the period of the Thakore Award, but between 1982 and 1991 the number employed was sharply restricted. According to the Commissioner's circular of May 1991, 42 *warasdars* had been made permanent employees backdating to 1987. Of the pre-1987 *warasdars*, 185 were in the middle of a dispute at the industrial court as of August 1991.[68]

The promotion of *umedvars* to permanent employment had two problems. In many cases, *umedvars* had not been permanently employed even though they had worked for 5 years or 900 days. By May 1991 there were 500 such *umedvars*. According to the Commissioner's circular issued that month, most of them had been absorbed as permanent employees, but the 95 *umedvars* who had not been taken as there were no vacancies in the quota took the case to the industrial court. The second problem was that when the AMC expanded the urban area in February 1986, the work of cleaning the merged area was entrusted to the *umedvars* only. The Nokar Mandal demanded that the new quota be created in the merged area, and such *umedvars* be given permanent employment.[69]

The periodic distribution of tools, such as wheelbarrows, brooms and dustpans, increase in municipal housing, the issue of *warasdars*, and the promotion of temporary workers, were common demands taken up by other unions, too. The AMC's 200 warnings and 11 suspensions issued to sweepers were declared unfair by the Nokar Mandal.[70]

There were a number of reasons why the Nokar Mandal was able to organize such a large number of sweepers. First, the protector-protectee relationship between the *mukadams* (site supervisors) and sweepers was used to draw them into the union. The union preserved that traditional relationship by treating the *mukadams* with great warmth. What made the massive transfer of sweepers to the Nokar Mandal possible was the close connection that the original director had with the *mukadams*. Second, the Nokar Mandal was active in pursuing disputes through the courts, although not quite to the same degree as the Gujarat Municipal and Panchayat Kamdar Association. It attended to the problems of its individual members, and, when it considered it necessary, took them to the industrial court with the aid of the union lawyer. A member's appreciation of his union is greatly influenced by the degree to which he feels the union is responsive to his problems. Third, the union controlled the Board of Directors of the Ahmedabad Municipal Cooperative Bank and the Ahmedabad Municipal Servants' Consumers Cooperative Society, the most important institutional and financial facilities for sweepers. The bank had been set up in 1973 by municipal employees, and as of August 1991 it had a stock capital of Rs. 10 million and an operating capital of Rs. 150 million, and a clear profit of Rs. 3.2 million. In 1991, 24,000 municipal workers, including the 7,000 permanently employed sweepers, were members of this bank. Around 65 per cent of the total finance was furnished to workers from the Scheduled Castes or Backward Classes. Sweepers could receive a loan of up to Rs. 10,000 per transaction; this was deducted from their monthly wage at the rate of Rs. 250 over a period of 60 months or 5 years. Thus the amount repaid was 50 per cent greater than the amount borrowed.[71] In those years the rate of increase in consumer prices has been more than 10 per cent, and a private moneylender would charge a monthly rate of between 10 per cent and 15 per cent. Therefore, the interest rates on loans offered by the Cooperative Bank were attractive to the sweepers. Though financing was limited to purchase or repair of houses, wedding ceremonies, or adulthood ceremonies, the final sanctioning of loans rested with the Finance Committee of the Board of Directors, and the operation was very flexible for union members. The Ahmedabad Municipal Servants' Consumers Cooperative Society, which had been formed in 1975, provided its members with electrical goods such as televisions, fans, and mixers, as well as grain, at low cost. Repayment was made by deductions from wages over a certain period of time. As a result, televisions and fans prevailed among municipal sweepers. Like the Cooperative Bank, the conditions for purchasing these goods for union members were very flexible. Since 1985 when the Nokar Mandal took over control of the Board of Directors of the Cooperative Bank and Society, sweepers have entered the union in large numbers.[72]

Demonstrations were held by union workers to resolve particularly urgent problems. They were regulated by the Industrial Disputes Act, and penal regulations were applicable on illegal actions.[73] When negotiations between the management and labour broke down, the unions could decide to hold a strike. However, strikes by sweepers occurred very rarely since they would jeopardize public health.[74]

## THE AHMEDABAD CITY SWEEPERS' ASSOCIATION

The Sweepers' Association is also called the Majoor Mahajan (labourers' cooperative). Established in 1930, as the only union of sweepers, it was connected with the Shah, Jeejeebhoy and Thakore Awards. Before the 1980s it played a main role in improving employment, working, and living conditions of sweepers. An exceptional feature of this union was its concern with the abolition of their bad customs, such as drinking, extravagance and begging for food. Such concern for internal reform was not found among the other unions. Another important concern was the establishment of a Credit Cooperative Society. In 1954, 20 years before the

Ahmedabad Municipal Cooperative Bank was set up (1973), the Sweepers' Association formed the Ahmedabad City Sweepers' Credit Cooperative Society to provide finance to sweepers. It attracted large numbers of sweepers until the 1970s, but as a result of the 1983 split in the union, the Cooperative Society also became factionalized. Subsequently, the union lost control over the management of the Cooperative Society in 1985. Amidst the growth and diversification of unions in the late 1970s, the Majoor Mahajan, content in its existing role, did not develop in response to the new conditions. As a result, it lagged behind the Nokar Mandal. The membership as of 1991 consisted of 400 permanently employed sweepers and 150 *umedvars.*[75]

Demands of the union in 1991 included the permanent employment of *warasdars*, replacing vacancies among *mukadams*, improvement of wheelbarrows, periodic provision of tools and materials, increase in municipal housing, permanent employment of *umedvars, and* the promotion of *hangamis* to *umedvars.*[76]

Unique to the Majoor Mahajan was the demand to promote *hangamis* (annually and seasonally contracted day workers) to *umedvar* status (List C). The focus of the demand was on an increase in the daily wage and employment security. Workers on List C had a higher daily wage (Rs. 45 for *umedvars* as opposed to Rs. 25 for *hangamis*, April 1991). Also, they could be promoted as permanent workers after 5 years or 900 days service. The AMC had restricted the numbers entering List C in the latter half of the 1980s, but as a result of the 1986 enlargement of the city's boundaries, large numbers of *hangamis* in the area were promoted as *umedvars*. However after 1987, when the consequent reorganization of the Conservancy Department was completed, new applications to List C were completely suspended. To have it reopened was one of the most important demands of the Majoor Mahajan.

New *mukadams* were not appointed after 1983 and by 1991 the quota of 250 had shrunk by 100. The concern of the Majoor Mahajan in the appointment of replacements at the earliest was due to its interest in having the newly appointed *mukadams* join their union, which would encourage other sweepers to do so.

## THE GUJARAT MUNICIPAL AND PANCHAYAT KAMDAR ASSOCIATION

This union was established in June 1986 to give legal support to municipal labourers in local bodies throughout Gujarat, including the AMC. It was set up by a person who had worked as the secretary of the Ahmedabad

Municipal Servants' Association (Nokar Mandal) between 1966 and 1977 and was expelled from its management committee during the period of the Thakore Award. He later worked as a sanitation superintendent in the western zone of the Conservancy Department and was also involved in tribunal disputes. He dealt with the administrative work of the union at his apartment every Sunday.

The Association regularly sent a union official to the industrial court held at the AMC central office on Mondays, Wednesdays and Thursdays. Broad questions concerning the employment, working conditions and pay scales of unionists were brought to the court. The cases frequently related to allowances, the permanent employment of day labourers, and promotion orders. Of the 1,000 or so cases deliberated in the court each year, about 400 cases were brought up by the Kamdar Association and 200 by the Nokar Mandal. The Association dealt with only ten cases concerning sweepers by 1991, because sweeper unionists were few. All these cases were related to housing allowance payments on purchase of a municipal dwelling.

The Association also extended legal aid to employees of other local bodies in the state, outside of Ahmedabad. Besides appearing in the industrial court, the Association made a great contribution in the submission of documents during the time an award was worked out. It had about 5,000 members—both permanent and daily employees.[77]

### THE AHMEDABAD MUNICIPAL KAMDAR KARAMCHARI UNION

The Ahmedabad Municipal Kamdar Karamchari Union is also known as the Lal Jhanda or Red Flag Union. It was established in 1977 as a federated union of the Centre of Indian Trade Unions, affiliated with the left wing of the Indian Communist Party. The present secretary had worked as a secretary in the Nokar Mandal between 1972 and 1980. But he moved to the Kamdar Karamchari Union in 1980 when it allied with the Congress-I party.

The Kamdar Karamchari Union had a membership of 1,200 sweepers in 1980, but its membership declined sharply as a result of the increasing influence of the Nokar Mandal. And in 1991 it could count no more than 200 members, especially sweepers who worked under particularly bad conditions: rubbish collectors, disposers of carcasses, and cleaners of the old-fashioned cesspools.

Activities of the Union were limited to demands for increasing municipal housing and in improving the health condition of sweepers. According to the Union, the great majority of sweepers who were engaged in rubbish collection or the disposal of carcasses died before retirement as a result of tuberculosis and cancer. Since the working conditions could not be changed immediately, the Union had been demanding a provision of 0.5 l. of milk and 100 g. of butter a day in order to increase the physical resistance of labours working under such poor conditions.[78] It represented its members during the settlement of awards but did not conduct disputes at tribunals on behalf of them. The union had little influence among sweepers, and there was small likelihood of it being able to reorganize itself.

### ALL INDIA SAFAI MAZDOOR CONGRESS (GUJARAT BRANCH)

The All India Safai Mazdoor Congress was established in 1964 as a nationwide union by the sweepers and for the sweepers. Buta Singh, a Rasjasthan-born member of the Lok Sabha (Lower House of Parliament) and a former Minister of Home Affairs is the central figure of this Congress. Its central office is located in the grounds of his official residence in New Delhi. He was born into the Sweeper caste. The Congress had 700,000 members when it was founded, which increased to 900,000 by 1991, with branches in the major states. The Gujarat Branch was founded in Ahmedabad in 1969. In 1991, there were sub-branches in 30 local bodies in 12 Districts, with the membership of 12,000. Of which 2,500 belonged to the Ahmedabad Branch.[79]

Its policy was very different to that of the Nokar Mandal and the Majoor Mahajan,which worked under conditions operating in the AMC. There were a lot of variations among states, local bodies, urban and rural areas in terms of the employment, and working and living conditions of sweepers. The chief concern of the Congress was to diminish these differences and to raise the overall status of the Sweeper caste. Its all-India demands included national administration of sweeper services, rating sweepers as technicians, promoting education for sweeper children, banning by law the handling and carrying of human waste on the head by scavengers, provision of a special medical service, provision of transportation between the home and the workplace, establishing a quota of sweepers based on ward population, banning the sweeper contract system, provision of free accommodation, compensatory employment instances of death, disability and retirement, and the guarantee of a minimum wage to sweepers of private dwellings.[80] The most important of these was the national administration of sweeper services. If this could be accomplished, sweepers employed by local bodies, ports, and factories would become public servants of the central government and virtually almost all differences in employment and labour conditions between states, local bodies, urban areas and rural areas would disappear. Further, by regarding sweepers as technicians, not unskilled labour, the possibility of better pay and promotion opportunities would open up. The Congress anticipated that a special medical system for sweepers, the provision of transportation between the home and the workplace, the provision of free accommodation and compensatory employment could be achieved in the case of the central government workers. Besides sweepers who could be absorbed by the central government, there were labourers performing sweeping and scavenging work for contractors or under private contract with individual households. The ban on carrying human waste on the head, the ban on the private contract system, and the guarantee of a minimum wage would give legal protection to these workers. To accomplish these objectives on a national scale seems difficult at the present moment due to the tremendous financial and political obstacles in the way of introducing a national administration of sweepers.

In Gujarat, the carrying of human waste on the head has been banned, and the employment and working conditions of sweepers in the large municipalities has vastly improved. As a result, the Gujarat Branch of the Congress concentrated its attention on the betterment of employment and working conditions in small to middle scale local bodies (Municipalities, Nagar Panchayats, Gram Panchayats). They pursued disputes over the observance of minimum wage, delays in the payment of wages in arrears by many months, the setting of the quota of permanent employees, the provision of uniforms and tools, and suspensions of employees. Because small and medium scale local bodies were short of funds, sweepers tended to be employed part-time, and many of these bodies did not observe the minimum wage regulation.[81] There were frequent delays in the payment of wages which caused sweepers severe financial problems. The objective of the Congress was to resolve these issues and bring them on par with these in the urban areas.[82] The association of the Congress with the AMC was confined to the issues of promotion for a few unionist *warasdars*.

## Conclusion

By analysing the tribunal awards, it has been possible to trace changes in the pay scales of sweepers in the ABM/AMC since the 1940s. After the introduction of pay scales in 1945, the rates received by municipal sweepers were revised to match, after a certain lapse in time, those of Class 4 employees in the state government. However, a gap in allowances persisted through the Thakore Award. During the deliberations over the Barot Award, the state wage system had been brought in line with that of the central government. And Barot was eager to bring the AMC wage system, including allowances, align with that of the state government. Following the adjustment of AMC pay scales as a result of the Barot Award, the AMC workers were paid the same scales as central government labourers. The conditions of the compensatory employment system introduced by the Jeejeebhoy Award were relaxed in the 1970s to include disability acquired during service. The AMC, forced to enlarge the quota of permanently employed sweepers by the Thakore Award, began tightening permanent recruitment in the early 1980s. Besides, it set strict conditions for authorizing compensatory employment. The unions reacted strongly to the AMC's reversion of policy with strikes and legal disputes. A compromise was reached between the Commissioner and the unions in May 1991 in which the AMC agreed to promote the majority of eligible *umedvars* to permanent status and to give all post-January 1987 *warasdars* acting status, through a new successor's employment system. However, because the pre-1987 *warasdars* were not cared at all, it remained a point of contention with the unions.

Another major institutional reform of the 1990s was the introduction of a promotion scheme for Classes 3 and 4 workers. The Barot Award ordered that the state government's revised promotion scheme of May 1991 be applied directly to the AMC workers. This was designed to improve wages without necessarily changing posts or work, which brought in considerable economic benefits to workers. Before the promotion scheme was introduced, sweepers had worked on a single pay scale and increments ceased after 15 years of service. The new promotion scheme ensured annual increments for 38 years, and this pushed up the lifetime wage as well.

These reforms have made permanent work at the AMC far more attractive to sweepers than before. This may reduce their incentive to move into other occupations, and enhance a tendency among them to adhere to sweeping, over which they have a monopoly in the workplace. However, with the establishment of the successor's employment system there is a strong possibility that a considerable proportion of the permanent workforce will become hereditary and this will constitute an obstacle in the promotion of newly employed sweepers. The introduction of mechanization by the AMC will also work to limit the number of sweepers employed in the future, and this will probably ensure that the expansion of the sweeper quota will remain below the rate of city expansion or population growth.

The improvement in the working conditions of sweepers has lagged behind significantly despite the many favourable changes in their employment conditions. The introduction of vehicular rubbish collection has improved the work process, but the majority of sweepers still have to work under the old conditions of cleaning roads, public latrines and gutters. Sweepers still have to come into direct contact with rubbish, human waste, dirty water and decomposed materials. As a result, even today large numbers have to be treated for respiratory and stomach diseases. It is clear from an analysis of the various awards that the demands of the unions have centred on the improvement of employment conditions, and that those concerning working conditions have been mostly limited to demands for periodic provision of uniforms and tools. The unions believe that the enlargement of the quota and a rise in wages are of utmost importance to workers, and have focused on working conditions only to the extent that they do not become obstacles towards this aim. A drastic reform in working conditions and environment through mechanization may result in lessening of the demands for the traditional sweeper.

The unions have concentrated their demands, for improvement in the living conditions of sweepers, on an increase in municipal housing. The construction of quarters for municipal workers was a prime concern of the AMC until the 1960s, but the municipality lost interest in this after the 1970s. Increasing municipal housing to meet the demands of a growing work force was a serious financial burden on the AMC, and the management of municipal housing also became more difficult due to the emergence of complicated vested interests. Since 1991 the AMC has pushed ahead the sale of its accommodation to dwellers (Rs. 5,000-8,000) to extricate itself from these problems. Since sweepers usually find it difficult to rent private apartments, they either opt for municipal housing or slums.

The unions function as the most important pressure group for sweepers, partly because the majority of the community work in the sanitation section of local bodies where the unions play a decisive role in bringing about an improvement in the employment, working and living conditions of sweepers, and partly because the community lacks the other political and administrative ties that play a part in facilitating their social advancement. The Vankars and the Chamars, though part of the Scheduled Castes, have shown surprising social advancement in recent years. The fact that they even send representatives to the local bodies and the state legislature sets them apart from the Sweeper caste, which is still a political voice.

The municipal trade union movement set its course with the enactment of the Trade Union Act in 1926 and was greatly strengthened by the Industrial Disputes Act of 1947. The Sweepers' Association, which was set up before the promulgation of the latter, drew sweepers into the trade union movement until the beginning of the 1980s. As the only union, specifically for sweepers, it is unsurpassed in its long history and breadth of activity. However, with the trend towards diversification in the union movement that gained impetus from the late 1970s, its influence declined as a result of its failure in reorganizing the union, and the resultant internal divisions. The Nokar Mandal, on the other hand, was successful in its restructuring by using its credit society as a method of attracting members and strengthening its role in tribunals for resolving labour problems. The membership has been on the increase due to the supportive policies.

Sweepers working for the AMC can by no means be considered economically weak. The chief problems facing them are the lack of internal reform, and competitive power. Their adherence to sweeping as an occupation, over which they have a monopoly, chains them to a low level of education and poor skills, while their inability to undertake internal reform brings about a wasteful and fragile disposition. It is, of course, a fact that social and occupational restraints and discrimination make it difficult in bringing about improvements. However, unless sweepers launch a mass movement to overcome their internal weakness, social development seems to be difficult.

## NOTES

1. Enterprises that employ more than 100 workers are responsible for setting up of works committee made up of the representatives of both employers and employees to resolve labour-management problems. The state government can set up boards of conciliation for particular areas and industries to resolve industrial disputes which cannot be solved by works committees. Labour courts and tribunals, appointed by the state government, are expected to handle complicated industrial disputes. National and intra-state disputes are examined by national tribunals. See *The Industrial Disputes Act, 1947*, Lucknow: Eastern Book Company, 1992, pp. 22-35.
2. The Industrial Disputes Act is applicable only to such workers who are under the supervision and control of employers in the master-servant relationship. Upper and middle administrative officers employed by local bodies are beyond the purview of the Act. See *The Industrial Disputes Act*, op. cit., pp. 26-8.
3. 'Award in the matter of The Industrial Disputes between The Ahmedabad Municipality and The Sweepers & Mukadams Employed under it before Mr. M.C. Shah', *The Bombay Government Extra-ordinary Gazette*, 26 February 1948 (hereafter, Shah Award).

4. Ibid., pp. 46-9.
5. Ibid., pp. 49-50.
6. Ibid., p. 50.
7. Ibid.
8. Ibid.
9. 'Adjudication between The Ahmedabad Municipality & Its Workmen before Shri M.C. Shah', *The Bombay Government Extra-ordinary Gazette*, 9 August 1948 (hereafter, Shah Adjudication), pp. 5-44.
10. Ibid., p. 17.
11. 'Arbitrator's Award between (1) Municipal Corporation of The City of Ahmedabad and (2) The Ahmedabad Transport Service, and Their Employees before Shri F. Jeejeebhoy', *The Bombay Government Extra-ordinary Gazette*, 6 March 1958 (hereafter, Jeejeebhoy Award).
12. Ibid., p. 15.
13. Ibid., p. 16.
14. Ibid.
15. Ibid.
16. Ibid.
17. Ibid.
18. Ibid.
19. Ibid.
20. Ibid., pp. 6-7.
21. Ibid., pp. 7-8. An anna is a sub-division of a rupee. Sixteen annas make one rupee.
22. See Award & Recommendations of Shri Indrajit G. Thakore, Arbitrator and One Man Pay Commission for Revision of Wage Scales, H.R.A., C.R.A. and Other Allowances, etc. of The Employees including Officers of The Ahmedabad Municipal Corporation, Part 4, 1978 (hereafter, Thakore Award, Part 4).
23. Reconstructed from Thakore Award Part 4, pp. 6-12.
24. Ibid., pp. 12-14.
25. Gandhi stressed the importance of using home-made products, such as *khadi* during the independence movement. *Charkha*, the Indian spinning wheel, had a central place among rural industries in the blueprint of Gandhi's independence struggle.
26. Thakore Award, Part 4, pp. 15-16.
27. Ibid., p. 16.
28. Ibid., pp. 16-18.
29. Ibid., pp. 18-19.
30. Ibid., pp. 19-21.
31. Ibid., pp. 21-3.
32. Ibid., pp. 23-5.
33. Ibid., p. 25.
34. Ibid., pp. 25-6.
35. Ibid., pp. 26-7.
36. Ibid., pp. 27-9.
37. Ibid., pp. 29-48.
38. The documents on which I depend are typed materials of Barot Award prepared by the Municipal Corporation. For the revision of pay scales, I refered to Award Part 3 of Shri G.S. Barot, July 1987 (hereafter, Barot Award, Part 3). Also, Award

Part 9 of Shri G.S. Barot, October 1989 (hereafter, Barot Award, Part 9) and Award Part 15 of Shri G.S. Barot, May 1991(hereafter, Barot Award, Part 15) were refered to for allowances and promotion respectively.

39. Barot Award, Part 3, pp. 2-10.
40. Ibid., pp. 10-13.
41. Ibid., p. 14.
42. Ibid., p. 15.
43. Rajput, K.C. (comp.), *Award, Judgement, Pay Commission Report & Important Circulars by Shri G.S. Barot*, Ahmedabad, The Gujarat Municipal & Panchayat Kamdar Association, 1992, pp. 226-34.
44. Barot Award, Part 3, pp. 17-18.
45. Barot Award, Part 9, pp. 9-11, 16, 23-4, 26.
46. Government of Gujarat, Finance Department, Government Resolution No. AOP-1019/3/M, Gandhinagar, 20 February 1991.
47. Barot Award, Part 15, p. 3.
48. Government of Gujarat, Finance Department, Government Resolution No. AOP-1091/3/M, Gandhinagar, 5 July 1991.
49. Adjudication between The Ahmedabad Municipal Corporation and the Workmen Employed under it in the matter of Permanency of Daily Rated Workmen of the Engineering Department before Shri G.S. Barot, 30 June 1978.
50. Jeejeebhoy Award, p. 15.
51. Oral information from Shri D.J. Patel, Labour Officer of the Municipal Corporation (August 1991).
52. Government of Gujarat, General Administration Department, D.O. No. 1076/408/K, Gandhinagar, 12 May 1977.
53. The Ahmedabad Municipal Corporation, Central Office, Circular No.151, 7 March 1984.
54. The Ahmedabad Municipal Corporation, Central Office, Circular No. 3843, January 1984.
55. The Ahmedabad Municipal Corporation, Central Office, The Formula of Settlement between The Ahmedabad Municipal Servants' Association and The Ahmedabad Municipal Corporation, 7 May 1991.
56. Oral information from Shri D.J. Patel, Labour Officer of the Municipal Corporation (August 1991).
57. Shah Award, p. 4.
58. Ibid., pp. 8-9.
59. Oral information from Shri D.J. Patel, Labour Officer of the Municipal Corporation (August 1991).
60. Jeejeebhoy Award, pp. 1-2.
61. Oral information from Shri M.T. Shukla, the president, The Ahmedabad City Sweepers' Association (August 1991).
62. Thakore Award, Part 1, pp. 1-3.
63. Barot Award, Part 3, p. 1.
64. The total number of registered trade unions in August 1991, was provided by D.J. Patel.
65. Oral information from Shri Harish Makvana, the Secretary, The Ahmedabad Municipal Servants' Association (August 1991).
66. Ibid.

67. From a letter of The Ahmedabad Municipal Servants' Association addressed to the Commissioner, 7 November 1990.
68. Oral information from Shri Harish Makvana, the Secretary, The Ahmedabad Municipal Servants' Association (August 1991).
69. Ibid.
70. From a letter of The Ahmedabad Municipal Servants' Association addressed to the Commissioner, 7 November 1990.
71. Oral information from Shri P.B.Patel, the Manager, The Ahmedabad Municipal Co-operative Bank (August 1991).
72. The availability and the function of formal financial institutions affects the socio-economic conditions of sweepers to a great extent. Sweepers employed by small or medium local bodies, tend to depend upon private money lenders with high interest rates, because of the non-availability of formal financial institutions. In this regard, sweepers employed by the Ahmedabad Municipal Corporation have an advantage, however, there are serious problems in the management of its financial institutions.
73. Workers in public service are not allowed to go on strike within six months of the declaration of strike toward employers, or within fourteen days after the re-declaration, or during conciliation period. Illegal strikers are punishable with imprisonment for a maximum of one month or/and the penalty of Rs. 50. See *The Industrial Disputes Act, 1947*, op. cit., pp. 71, 101.
74. Sweepers employed by the ABM/AMC have gone on strike five times after Independence. The half-day strikes in 1948 and 1954 were organized by The Ahmedabad City Sweepers' Association. We do not know the demand of sweepers in these strikes. One-day strike in 1977 was organized by the Ahmedabad City Sweepers' Association and The Ahmedabad Municipal Servants' Association for the revision of dearness allowance. Again, the Ahmedabad Municipal Servants' Association organized a strike for the promotion of *warasdars* in May 1991, which succeeded in drawing a concession from the Commissoner. However, the two-day strike in August 1991, organized by the same union for the payment of arrears, was a failure.
75. Oral information from Shri P. Solanki, the Secretary, The Gujarat Municipal and Panchayat Kamdar Association (August 1991).
76. From a pamphlet of The Gujarat Municipal and Panchayat Kamdar Association (29 April 1991).
77. Oral information from Shri Rajendra Shah, the Secretary, The Gujarat Municipal and Panchayat Kamdar Association (July 1991).
78. Oral information from Shri Anand Parmar, the Secretary, The Ahmedabad Municipal Kamdar Karamchari Union (August 1991).
79. Oral information from Shri Chimanlal Bhutadia, the vice-president, All India Safai Mazdoor Congress (August 1991).
80. From a resolution of All India Safai Mazdoor Congress (21 September 1991).
81. For details on minimum wages, see B.B. Patel, *Report on The Implementation of Minimum Wages for Sweepers in Village Panchayats in Saurashtra*, Ahmedabad: Gandhi Labour Institute, 1990.
82. Oral information from Shri Chimanlal Bhutadia, the vice-president, All India Safai Mazdoor Congress (August 1991).

Chapter Five

# Mobility of Sweepers Employed by the Ahmedabad Municipal Corporation

## INTRODUCTION

This chapter examines the occupational mobility of sweepers employed by the Ahmedabad Municipal Corporation, based on the following materials: the list of permanent and casual employees of the Conservancy Department of the AMC compiled in 1991, and the list of permanent employees of the Refuse Department. The former list records the following details about the permanent employees of the Conservancy Department; name, date of birth, date of permanent employment, and caste name. The latter list of permanent employees of the Refuse Department also includes the date of registration of the labourer on the waiting list. The sex of the employee can be ascertained from the name. The age of the labourer at the time of the registration on the waiting list is calculated from the date of birth and the date of entry on the waiting list. The age when the labourer became permanently employed is calculated from the date of birth and the date of permanent employment, and finally the duration of waiting period is calculated from the date of entry on the waiting list and the date of permanent employment. These figures can be used as data for a cross-sectional analysis. The data can also be arranged for a time series analysis to trace changes over time. The list of casual labourers of the Conservancy Department contains details, such as: name, date of entry on the waiting list, and the days worked each year. Since the date of birth is not known, age analysis is not possible. However, the distribution of working days and the working years of day labourers of each sex can be calculated. Except the names of the workers, these lists are incomplete in terms of other details. However, the number of workers about whom full information is available is sufficient enough and does not pose any problem in the employment analysis of the Conservancy and Refuse Department labourers.

### *Sweepers and Other Related Workers in the Municipal Corporation*

The term 'Sweepers' usually denotes labourers employed by the Conservancy Department, but they are also employed in other departments of the AMC as shown in Table 5.1. Most sweepers in the Conservancy Department clean roads and public latrines. Only a small number of sweepers are engaged in cleaning out septic tanks and the old-fashioned cesspools which remain in the city. Workers in the Refuse Department dispose of the rubbish that the Conservancy Department sweepers have picked up and deposited in bins at designated collection sites. These workers load rubbish into trucks and unload it at dumps. Most sweepers in the Sewage Department work at water treatment plants and pump stations. A number of them clean the main and branch sewers. Sweepers in hospitals and clinics clean buildings and grounds, and also dispose off medical waste and patients' waste. The proportion of sweepers exposed to diseases is high, and those working in hospitals and clinics are certainly at risk. The Sewage Department does not employ casual labour; the other departments use both casual and permanent workers. Besides these there are 570 drivers who are attached to the Vehicle Division to transport rubbish, other solid wastes and carcasses. It would be incorrect to describe them as sweepers and hence they have not been included in the table.

As Table 5.2 shows, the number of municipal workers increased by 1.75 times between 1966/7 and 1988/9; and the city population also doubled in the same period. The rate of increase of municipal workers has therefore been a little slower than that of the city population. During that period, the proportion of permanent workers in the AMC work force fairly increased due to the improvement in employment conditions of municipal workers

TABLE 5.1: DISTRIBUTION OF AMC SWEEPERS BY DEPARTMENT AND TYPE OF EMPLOYMENT (1991)

*(persons)*

| Type of employment | Department | | | | | Total |
|---|---|---|---|---|---|---|
| | Conservancy | Refuse | Sewage | Hospitals | Clinics | |
| Permanent | 5,800 | 500 | 1,000 | 2,000 | 200 | 9,500 |
| Temporary | 1,200 | 250 | – | N.A. | N.A. | 1,450 |
| Total | 7,000 | 750 | 1,000 | 2,000 | 200 | 10,950 |

NOTE: Worker numbers are approximate.

SOURCE: Information from Conservancy Department, Ahmedabad Municipal Corporation (August 1991).

TABLE 5.2: CHANGES IN NUMBERS OF WORKERS OF THE AMC AND THE CONSERVANCY DEPARTMENT

(*persons, %*)

| Year | AMC workers | | | Conservancy Department workers | |
|---|---|---|---|---|---|
| | permanent | temporary | total | workers | ratio of workers (%) |
| 1960/1 | N.A. | N.A. | N.A. | 2,349 | N.A. |
| 1966/7 | 11,158 | 3,826 | 14,984 | N.A. | N.A. |
| 1977/8 | 14,443 | 4,492 | 18,935 | 4,812 | 25.41 |
| 1984/5 | 22,042 | 2,233 | 24,275 | 6,032 | 24.85 |
| 1988/9 | 22,531 | 3,579 | 26,128 | 6,837 | 26.17 |

NOTES: (1) The AMC works to a financial year of 1 April to 31 March.
(2) AMC employed municipal school teachers, employees of the Department of transportation, and workers in hospitals and libraries are not included in the table.
(3) The Conservancy Department figures include both permanent and temporary workers.
(4) The ratio of workers is the percentage of Conservancy Department workers out of the total AMC workers.

SOURCE: Compiled from Ahmedabad Municipal Corporation, *Statistical Outline of Ahmedabad City*, Ahmedabad, 1977/8, 1984/5 and 1988/9.

as a whole. The ratio of Conservancy Department workers among AMC workers has been somewhat constant at around 25 per cent since 1977/8. Sweepers (in the widest definition of the term) were posted in various departments, and they constituted about 40 per cent of the AMC work force.

Table 5.3 examines changes in the number of beneficiaries and rubbish collected per worker of the Conservancy Department. Permanent sweepers

TABLE 5.3: CHANGES IN THE NUMBERS OF BENEFICIARIES AND THE AMOUNT OF RUBBISH COLLECTED PER WORKER OF CONSERVANCY DEPARTMENT

(*persons, kg.*)

| Year | Number of beneficiaries per worker (persons) | Rubbish collected per worker per day (kg.) |
|---|---|---|
| 1960/1 | 490 | 192 |
| 1977/8 | 407 | 184 |
| 1988/9 | 425 | 202 |

NOTE: These figures have been calculated by dividing the city population and amount of rubbish for each year by the number of workers in the Conservancy Department

SOURCE: Same as Table 5.2

of the Conservancy Department all have their own daily beat, the area for which they are responsible. In order to create uniform working conditions for sweepers, beats with dense population or in shopping streets are set smaller in area, while those with sparse population are larger. They range from 3,000 sq. m. to 10,000 sq. m. Since the working conditions and tools of sweepers have hardly changed between 1960/1 and 1988/9, little change has been seen either in the beneficiary worker ratio, and in the amount of rubbish collected per worker.

## An Analysis of Mobility

### *Distribution of Workers by Zone, Sex and Age Group*

The AMC grew from 93 sq. km. in 1960 to 98 sq. km. in 1980 and then underwent a great expansion in 1986 when it absorbed surrounding areas bringing its total areas to 190 sq. km. Until 1986, the cleaning and waste services had been divided into four zones (north, south, east and west), each supervised by a Deputy Sanitary Officer. After 1986 it was divided into five zones (north, south, east, west and central). Each zone varies in area, population and socio-economic character. In 1817, when Ahmedabad was occupied by the British East India Company, the city was limited to the settlement within the walls. Later there was growth of commercial areas to the north in the direction of the cantonment, while industrial areas expanded to the eastern and southern parts. The western side of the Sabarmati river observed a growth in residential, educational and cultural facilities. The city area gradually increased in the wake of this development. As a result, each zone has specific sanitary problems. For example, the central zone has huge quantities of commercial and market waste, compounded with the problems of collecting rubbish from a congested area, while the eastern and southern areas are facing sanitation problems due to the concentration of slums, and the large area that has been absorbed into the municipality comparatively recently.

The city is divided into 53 wards. The average population of a ward is about 40,000; figures range from 20,000 to 60,000. One third of the wards (18) are in the central zone. As Table 5.4 shows, the number of permanent sweepers of the Conservancy Department in each zone largely corresponds to the population for whom cleaning services are performed. Thus, one third of the sweepers are concentrated in the central zone. The ratio between male and female permanent workers does not vary among the zones; overall, males comprise 42 per cent and females 58 per cent.

TABLE 5.4: DISTRIBUTION OF WORKERS BY ZONE AND SEX (1991)

*(persons, %)*

| Zone | permanent workers | | | | day workers | | |
|---|---|---|---|---|---|---|---|
| | Conservancy Dept. | | | Refuse Dept. | Conservancy Dept. | | |
| | male | female | total | male/total | male | female | total |
| Northern | 372 | 512 | 884 | 54 | 78 | 123 | 201 |
| | (15.5) | (15.8) | (15.7) | (11.2) | (24.5) | (17.4) | (19.6) |
| Western | 279 | 401 | 680 | 100 | 56 | 122 | 177 |
| | (11.7) | (12.3) | (12.1) | (20.7) | (17.2) | (17.3) | (17.3) |
| Eastern | 555 | 654 | 1,209 | 80 | 87 | 161 | 248 |
| | (23.2) | (20.2) | (21.4) | (16.5) | (27.3) | (22.8) | (24.2) |
| Southern | 361 | 581 | 942 | 83 | 31 | 87 | 118 |
| | (15.1) | (17.9) | (16.7) | (17.1) | (9.7) | (12.4) | (11.5) |
| Central | 826 | 1,097 | 1,923 | 167 | 68 | 212 | 280 |
| | (34.5) | (33.8) | (34.1) | (34.5) | (21.3) | (30.1) | (27.4) |
| Total | 2,393 | 3,245 | 5,638 | 484 | 319 | 705 | 1,024 |
| | (100.0) | (100.0) | (100.0) | (100.0) | (100.0) | (100.0) | (100.0) |

NOTE: The figures in brackets show the column percentages.

SOURCE: Compiled from the permanent and temporary workers' lists of the Conservancy and Refuse Departments of the Ahmedabad Municipal Corporation.

The ratio of the number of Conservancy Department day workers among zones does not necessarily correspond to that of permanent workers. Further there are large variations among zones in the ratio of day workers according to sex. Such differences arise because each muster station is in charge of employing and selecting day workers.

The duties of the Refuse Department are complementary to those of the Conservancy Department, but the chain of command is different. Since the large offices of the Refuse Department are situated in the central and western zones, many permanent workers of the department are posted there.

### *An Analysis of Permanent Workers by Sex and Age Group*

The following analysis deals with the distribution of permanent workers in the Conservancy and Refuse Departments by age, age at the time of permanent employment, and the duration of waiting period for permanent employment in due consideration of differences sex.

## CONSERVANCY DEPARTMENT

Table 5.5 shows the distribution of permanent workers in the Conservancy Department by age and sex. The minimum age of employment in the department is 18, and the age of retirement is 58 for *mukadams* and 60 for workers. Five males and two females appear to be younger than the minimum age, and 23 males and 18 females older than the retirement age. There might have been an error in recording or the workers might have been employed despite the regulations.

A general feature is that the bulk of workers fall into the 30s-50s age range while the proportion of workers in their twenties is low. While 40 per cent of workers are in their thirties, 28 per cent in their forties and 20 per cent in their fifties. Proportion of workers in their twenties is below 10 per cent. The changes brought about in the AMC employment policy have exerted a two-fold influence on the age and sex distribution of workers. First, as a result of tightening its employment policy in the 1980s, the requisite number of years for a *umedvar* to become a permanent worker increased considerably. Particularly, promotions among workers in their twenties were adversely affected. Second, though it is not possible to verify the number of workers who left because of death or injury by age, the AMC compensatory employment system probably caused a considerable variation in the ratio of workers in their early and late fifties.

The first characteristic concerning the sex differential is that the number of female workers exceeds male. The second difference lies in age structure between male and female workers. The ratio of workers below 29 is relatively large among male workers while the share of age group between 35 and 49 is large among female workers. This is probably due to the fact that females generally enter employment later than males and their age range is broader.

Table 5.6 examines the distribution of workers by the age they were made permanent. Promotion to permanent employment is either by the waiting list or by compensatory employment. In the former case, the period for promotion from *umedvar* to permanent employee is comparatively short when the labour demand-supply relation is favorable to the labourers. In the latter case, the application procedure takes a certain number of years. But once the approval is granted, the worker is registered as a permanent employee immediately or after serving as *umedvar* or an apprentice for a short period.

A general characteristic is that the peak age group for gaining permanent employment is 20-34, with the number of permanent appointments being 77 per cent of the whole. Besides the condition of "minimum age for

TABLE 5.5: DISTRIBUTION OF WORKERS BY PRESENT AGE AND SEX (1991)

*(persons, %)*

| Present age<br>Sex | 15-19 | 20-4 | 25-9 | 30-4 | 35-9 | 40-4 | 45-9 | 50-4 | 55-9 | 60+ | Total |
|---|---|---|---|---|---|---|---|---|---|---|---|
| Male | 2 | 31 | 282 | 490 | 401 | 289 | 329 | 335 | 176 | 46 | 2,387 |
| | (0.1) | (1.6) | (11.8) | (20.5) | (16.8) | (12.1) | (13.8) | (14.0) | (7.4) | (1.9) | (100.0) |
| Female | 1 | 28 | 216 | 664 | 680 | 463 | 512 | 415 | 218 | 37 | 3,234 |
| | (0.0) | (0.9) | (6.7) | (20.5) | (21.0) | (14.3) | (15.8) | (12.8) | (6.8) | (1.2) | (100.0) |
| Total | 3 | 65 | 498 | 1,154 | 1,081 | 752 | 841 | 750 | 394 | 83 | 5,621 |
| | (0.1) | (1.2) | (8.8) | (20.5) | (19.2) | (13.4) | (15.0) | (13.3) | (7.0) | (1.5) | (100-0) |

NOTE: The figures in brackets show the row percentages. Of the 5,638 workers registered on the list, the records of 17 are missing.

SOURCE: Compiled from the permanent workers' list of the Conservancy Department of the Ahmedabad Municipal Corporation.

TABLE 5.6: DISTRIBUTION OF WORKERS BY AGE WHEN THEY GAINED PERMANENT EMPLOYMENT AND SEX (1991)

(*persons, %*)

| Age of permanent employment / Sex | 10-14 | 15-19 | 20-4 | 25-9 | 30-4 | 35-9 | 40-4 | 45-9 | 50-4 | 55-9 | Total |
|---|---|---|---|---|---|---|---|---|---|---|---|
| Male | 8 | 113 | 676 | 738 | 375 | 147 | 62 | 34 | 5 | 1 | 2,159 |
| | (0.4) | (5.2) | (31.3) | (34.2) | (17.4) | (6.8) | (2.9) | (1.6) | (0.2) | (0.0) | (100.0) |
| Female | 6 | 49 | 435 | 862 | 802 | 440 | 218 | 65 | 7 | 3 | 2,887 |
| | (0.2) | (1.7) | (15.1) | (29.9) | (27.8) | (15.2) | (7.6) | (2.2) | (0.2) | (0.1) | (100.0) |
| Total | 14 | 162 | 1,111 | 1,600 | 1,177 | 587 | 280 | 99 | 12 | 4 | 5,046 |
| | (0.3) | (3.2) | (22.0) | (31.7) | (23.3) | (11.6) | (5.6) | (2.0) | (0.2) | (0.1) | (100.0) |

NOTE: The figures in brackets show the row percentages. Of the 5,638 workers registered on the list, the records of 592 are missing.

SOURCE: Same as Table 5.5

employment", the time consuming procedure of waiting list system makes it difficult for teenagers to move up the waiting list during a given period. This is why there are very few appointments from this age group. Out of the total number of promotions in the 40-plus range, 8 per cent have been probably due to the system of compensatory employment.

Differences between the sexes are apparent in the distribution of workers' ages at the time of permanent employment. Females tend to obtain permanent employment later than males and their age range is broader. Particulary, there is a remarkable difference between male and female workers below 24 age group. Females in this age group, if unmarried, have household duties, including the care of younger siblings, and if married, they are occupied with pregnancy, child birth and child-raising. This is probably one of the major reasons for their late entry into employment. Further, it is believed that males in the under 34 age group have been the chief beneficiaries of the compensatory employment scheme. Women beneficiaries, on the other hand, are concentrated in the 30-plus age group.

The correlation between the present age and the age when permanently employed is shown in Table 5.7 for males and Table 5.8 for females. These statistics reinforce the fact that there is a clear age differential between the sexes regarding the age of permanent employment and that the AMC employment policies have influenced the age structure of male and female workers considerably.

Sex variation in age at the beginning of employment is clearly shown in the ratio of workers whose age at the time of permanent employment was below 29 among those presently aged over 30. Whereas the ratio for males is 96 per cent of those aged 30-4, that for females is 85 per cent. In the age group of 40-4, the ratios are 42 per cent for males and 22 per cent for females. In the range 50-4, it is 68 per cent for males and 30 per cent for females, and in the range 60-plus, it is 54 per cent and 17 per cent respectively. Thus in terms of a 30-plus present age range, the average age at which males gain permanent employment appears lower than that of females. Even among males, the ratio for those now in the 50-plus is higher than for the 30-plus and 40-plus age groups; this indicates that until about 25 to 30 years ago, it was comparatively easy for the under-29 age group to be promoted to permanent employment. The ratio for females of 50-plus, however, is extremely small, which shows that until 25 to 30 years ago there was discrimination in giving permanent employment status to females.

To verify this point, Table 5.9 gives the distribution of permanently employed workers by period and sex. Until 1964, the number of male permanent workers appears to be significantly higher than that of females.

TABLE 5.7: CORRELATION BETWEEN PRESENT AGE AND AGE OF PERMANENT EMPLOYMENT OF MALE WORKERS (1991)

(*% persons*)

| Age of permanent Employment / Present age | 10-19 | 20-4 | 25-9 | 30-4 | 35-9 | 40-4 | 45-9 | 50-4 | 55-9 | Total |
|---|---|---|---|---|---|---|---|---|---|---|
| 10-19 | 100.0 | – | – | – | – | – | – | – | – | (1) |
| | 0.8 | – | – | – | – | – | – | – | – | 0.0 |
| 20-4 | 26.9 | 73.1 | – | – | – | – | – | – | – | (26) |
| | 5.8 | 2.8 | – | – | – | – | – | – | – | 1.2 |
| 25-9 | 16.8 | 59.1 | 24.1 | – | – | – | – | – | – | (232) |
| | 32.2 | 20.3 | 7.6 | – | – | – | – | – | – | 10.7 |
| 30-4 | 4.7 | 45.3 | 45.6 | 4.4 | – | – | – | – | – | (430) |
| | 16.5 | 28.8 | 26.2 | 5.1 | – | – | – | – | – | 19.9 |
| 35-9 | 1.4 | 15.4 | 57.5 | 23.6 | 2.1 | – | – | – | – | (369) |
| | 4.1 | 8.4 | 28.7 | 23.2 | 5.4 | – | – | – | – | 17.1 |
| 40-4 | 1.9 | 7.4 | 33.1 | 43.9 | 12.6 | 1.1 | – | – | – | (269) |
| | 4.1 | 3.0 | 12.1 | 31.4 | 23.1 | 4.8 | – | – | – | 12.5 |
| 45-9 | 4 .2 | 27.7 | 16.5 | 30.3 | 17.1 | 3.9 | 0.3 | – | – | (310) |
| | 10.7 | 12.7 | 6.9 | 25.0 | 36.1 | 19.4 | 2.9 | – | – | 14.4 |
| 50-4 | 3.5 | 34.0 | 30.2 | 7.9 | 12.6 | 8.2 | 3.1 | 0.5 | – | (318) |
| | 9.2 | 16.0 | 13.0 | 6.7 | 27.2 | 41.9 | 29.4 | 40.0 | – | 14.7 |
| 55-9 | 7.3 | 27.6 | 20.3 | 14.7 | 6.7 | 11.7 | 10.4 | 1.3 | – | (163) |
| | 9.9 | 6.6 | 4.9 | 6.4 | 7.5 | 30.6 | 50.0 | 40.0 | – | 7.6 |
| 60+ | 19.5 | 22.0 | 12.2 | 19.5 | 2.4 | 4.9 | 14.6 | 2.4 | 2.5 | (41) |
| | 6.7 | 1.4 | 0.6 | 2.2 | 0.7 | 3.3 | 17.7 | 20.0 | 100.0 | 1.9 |
| Total | (121) | (676) | (738) | (375) | (147) | (62) | (34) | (5) | (1) | (2,159) |
| | 5.6 | 31.3 | 34.2 | 17.4 | 6.8 | 2.9 | 1.6 | 0.2 | 0.0 | 100.0 |

NOTE: The figures in the upper line show the row percentages (the distribution of present age group workers by the age group of permanent employment), while the figures in the lower line present the column percentages (the distribution of age group workers of permanent employment by the present age group). The figures in brackets in the row Total show the number of workers by age of permanent employment, while the figures in brackets in the column Total show the number of workers by present age. Of the 2,393 workers registered on the list, the records of 234 are missing.

SOURCE: Same as Table 5.5.

TABLE 5.8: CORRELATION BETWEEN PRESENT AGE AND AGE OF PERMANENT EMPLOYMENT OF FEMALE WORKERS (1991)

(*% persons*)

| Age of permanent employment<br>Present age | 10-19 | 20-4 | 25-9 | 30-4 | 35-9 | 40-4 | 45-9 | 50-4 | 55-9 | Total |
|---|---|---|---|---|---|---|---|---|---|---|
| 10-9 | 100.0 | – | – | – | – | – | – | – | – | (1) |
| | 1.8 | – | – | – | – | – | – | – | – | 0.0 |
| 20-4 | 57.9 | 42.1 | – | – | – | – | – | – | – | (19) |
| | 20.0 | 1.8 | – | – | – | – | – | – | – | 0.7 |
| 25-9 | 11.0 | 51.7 | 37.3 | – | – | – | – | – | – | (145) |
| | 29.1 | 17.2 | 6.3 | – | – | – | – | – | – | 5.0 |
| 30-4 | 2.1 | 29.6 | 52.9 | 15.4 | – | – | – | – | – | (565) |
| | 21.8 | 38.4 | 34.7 | 10.7 | – | – | – | – | – | 19.6 |
| 35-9 | 0.3 | 6.8 | 42.0 | 46.3 | 4.6 | – | – | – | – | (607) |
| | 3.6 | 9.4 | 29.6 | 34.7 | 6.7 | – | – | – | – | 21.0 |
| 40-4 | 2.1 | 2.3 | 17.6 | 48.5 | 25.3 | 4.2 | – | – | – | (427) |
| | 16.4 | 2.3 | 8.7 | 25.6 | 24.5 | 8.2 | – | – | – | 14.8 |
| 45-9 | 0.6 | 20.1 | 15.4 | 23.6 | 31.6 | 7.6 | 1.1 | – | – | (488) |
| | 5.5 | 22.5 | 8.7 | 14.2 | 35.0 | 17.0 | 9.2 | – | – | 16.9 |
| 50-4 | – | 7.4 | 22.6 | 17.3 | 25.9 | 22.3 | 4.1 | 0.4 | – | (394) |
| | – | 6.7 | 10.3 | 8.4 | 23.2 | 40.4 | 24.6 | 28.6 | – | 13.6 |
| 55-9 | – | 2.0 | 6.3 | 19.5 | 19.5 | 33.2 | 17.5 | 1.5 | 0.5 | (205) |
| | – | 0.9 | 1.5 | 4.9 | 9.1 | 31.2 | 55.4 | 42.9 | 33.3 | 7.1 |
| 60+ | 2.8 | 8.3 | 5.6 | 11.1 | 22.2 | 19.4 | 19.4 | 5.6 | 5.6 | (36) |
| | 1.8 | 0.8 | 0.2 | 1.5 | 1.5 | 3.2 | 10.8 | 28.5 | 66.7 | 1.3 |
| Total | (55) | (435) | (862) | (802) | (440) | (218) | (65) | ( 7) | (3) | (2,887) |
| | 1.9 | 15.1 | 29.9 | 27.8 | 15.2 | 7.6 | 2.2 | 0.2 | 0.1 | 100.0 |

NOTE: For description of the row and column percentage, see Table 5.7. Of the 2,393 workers registered on the list, the records of 234 are missing.

SOURCE: Same as Table 5.5

TABLE 5.9: DISTRIBUTION OF PERMANENT WORKERS BY SEX AND PERIOD

*(persons, %)*

| Period<br>Sex | 1945-9 | 1950-4 | 1955-9 | 1960-4 | 1965-9 | 1970-4 | 1975-9 | 1980-4 | 1985-9 | 1990-1 | Total |
|---|---|---|---|---|---|---|---|---|---|---|---|
| Male | 6 | 37 | 54 | 215 | 157 | 174 | 391 | 745 | 366 | 15 | 2,160 |
| | (100.0) | (92.5) | (85.7) | (81.7) | (35.8) | (43.3) | (41.4) | (41.7) | (34.6) | (36.6) | (42.8) |
| Female | 0 | 3 | 9 | 48 | 281 | 228 | 553 | 1,042 | 692 | 26 | 2,882 |
| | – | (7.5) | (14.3) | (18.3) | (64.2) | (56.7) | (58.6) | (58.3) | (65.4) | (63.4) | (57.2) |
| Total | 6 | 40 | 63 | 263 | 438 | 402 | 944 | 1,787 | 1,058 | 41 | 5,042 |
| | (100.0) | (100.0) | (100.0) | (100.0) | (100.0) | (100.0) | (100.0) | (100.0) | (100.0) | (100.0) | (100.0) |

NOTE: The figures in brackets show the column percentages. Of the 5,638 workers registered on the list, the records of 596 are missing.

SOURCE: Same as Table 5.5

The male-female differential among permanent employees of this time is too great to be seen as anything other than a function of discrimination in employment against females. Since 1965, the number of female permanent workers has surpassed that of male at any given point of time. The table also allows us to conjecture fluctuation in the scale of employment during the period. For example, the number of permanent employees recruited in 1970-4 is below that of 1965-9. It can be assumed that the scale of permanent employment has shrunk in the period 1970-4. The suspension of new additions to the A and B lists can be understood in this context. Similarly, the impact of the Thakore Award can be seen in the number of permanent employees in 1975-9. The figures confirm that the *umedvars* on Lists A and B were given permanent employment in great numbers in the first part of the 1980s as a result of the Award. The AMC, which felt a sense of crisis as a result of this trend toward enlarging the permanent quota, adopted a policy of restricting employment in the latter half of the 1980s. The impact of this policy on the number of permanent employees in the period 1985-9 is very clear.

Since it is not possible to know from the permanent employees' list any details about how many *umedvars* or *warasdars* were promoted in each year, this information has to be traced through other data. Table 5.10 shows changes in the number of promoted *umedvars* and *warasdars* by year. Only the number of *umedvars* permanently employed from List C is recorded here. As a result of the Thakore Award of 1978, most of the A and B list *umedvars* were promoted to permanent employment between that year and 1983/4. The AMC, following the abolition of Lists A and B, began making permanent appointments from List C from the middle of the 1980s.

Table 5.11 compares the sex ratio of those who were promoted from *umedvar* and examines the distribution of workers by the year they completed the stipulations for permanent employment (more than five years and more than 900 days). These figures are based on the number of *umedvars* given in Table 5.10 which have been rearranged by sex and the year in which the stipulated period of work was accomplished. The reason that the figures vary greatly from those in Table 5.10 is due to the time lag between qualification and actual promotion. The ratio of permanent employees by sex is 42 per cent for males and 58 per cent for females during the reference period, and this is close to the ratio of the permanent workers in the conservancy department as a whole. There is a large variation in the number of workers who completed the conditions for permanent appointment from year to year.

TABLE 5.10: CHANGES IN THE NUMBER OF PROMOTED *UMEDVARS* AND *WARASDARS* BY YEAR

(*persons*)

| Year | 1981/2 | 1982/3 | 1983/4 | 1984/5 | 1985/6 | 1986/7 | 1987/8 | 1988/9 | 1989/90 | 1990/1 | 1991/2 | Total |
|---|---|---|---|---|---|---|---|---|---|---|---|---|
| Warasdars | 153 | 157 | – | 8 | 7 | 16 | 27 | 32 | 39 | 24 | 35 | 498 |
| Umedvars | N.A. | N.A. | 538 | – | 276 | 87 | 247 | 110 | 70 | 110 | 251 | 1,689 |
| Total | 153 | 157 | 538 | 8 | 283 | 103 | 274 | 142 | 109 | 134 | 286 | 2,187 |

NOTE: The period here runs from 1 April to 31 March.

SOURCE: Same as Table 5.1

TABLE 5.11: DISTRIBUTION OF PERMANENT WORKERS BY SEX AND YEAR OF COMPLETION OF CRITERIA FOR PROMOTION

*(persons, %)*

| Year / Sex | 1980 | 1981 | 1982 | 1983 | 1984 | 1985 | 1986 | 1987 | 1988 | 1989 | Total |
|---|---|---|---|---|---|---|---|---|---|---|---|
| Male | 6 | 89 | 182 | 40 | 51 | 54 | 54 | 62 | 29 | 8 | 575 |
| | (42.9) | (53.9) | (58.9) | (50.0) | (32.7) | (29.8) | (39.7) | (33.9) | (25.9) | (22.9) | (41.9) |
| Female | 8 | 76 | 127 | 40 | 105 | 127 | 82 | 121 | 83 | 27 | 796 |
| | (57.1) | (46.1) | (41.1) | (50.0) | (67.3) | (70.2) | (60.3) | (66.1) | (74.1) | (77.1) | (58.1) |
| Total | 14 | 165 | 309 | 80 | 156 | 181 | 136 | 183 | 112 | 35 | 1,371 |
| | (100.0) | (100.0) | (100.0) | (100.0) | (100.0) | (100.0) | (100.0) | (100.0) | (100.0) | (100.0) | (100.0) |

NOTE: The figures in brackets show the column percentages. The period here runs from 1 January to 31 December.
SOURCE: Same as Table 5.1

TABLE 5.12: DISTRIBUTION OF *UMEDVARS* BY THE YEAR THEY CLEARED PROMOTION CITERIA AND BY THE NUMBER OF WORKING YEARS UNTIL THEIR CLEARANCE

(*person*, %)

| Year | No. of *umedvars* by the number of working years | | | | | | | | | | Total | Average no. of working years |
|---|---|---|---|---|---|---|---|---|---|---|---|---|
| | 5 | 6 | 7 | 8 | 9 | 10 | 11 | 12 | 13 | 14 | | |
| 1982 Male | 1 | 0 | 0 | 0 | 0 | 0 | 0 | 0 | 0 | 0 | 1 | 5.00 |
| Female | 4 | 1 | 0 | 0 | 0 | 0 | 0 | 0 | 0 | 0 | 5 | 5.20 |
| 1983 Male | 1 | 2 | 5 | 0 | 0 | 0 | 0 | 0 | 0 | 0 | 8 | 6.50 |
| Female | 0 | 4 | 9 | 0 | 0 | 0 | 0 | 0 | 0 | 0 | 13 | 6.69 |
| 1984 Male | 25 | 6 | 11 | 7 | 0 | 0 | 0 | 0 | 0 | 0 | 49 | 6.00 |
| Female | 36 | 10 | 23 | 33 | 0 | 0 | 0 | 0 | 0 | 0 | 102 | 6.52 |
| 1985 Male | 5 | 8 | 2 | 6 | 4 | 0 | 0 | 0 | 0 | 0 | 25 | 6.84 |
| Female | 5 | 19 | 17 | 21 | 11 | 0 | 0 | 0 | 0 | 0 | 73 | 7.19 |
| 1987 Male | 11 | 2 | 6 | 4 | 1 | 0 | 1 | 0 | 0 | 0 | 25 | 6.44 |
| Female | 9 | 1 | 5 | 6 | 9 | 10 | 3 | 0 | 0 | 0 | 43 | 8.09 |
| 1988 Male | 8 | 5 | 4 | 4 | 4 | 3 | 4 | 0 | 0 | 0 | 32 | 7.50 |
| Female | 6 | 10 | 10 | 11 | 18 | 7 | 13 | 8 | 0 | 0 | 83 | 8.66 |
| 1989 Male | 4 | 8 | 10 | 8 | 9 | 8 | 2 | 1 | 1 | 0 | 51 | 8.04 |
| Female | 5 | 22 | 16 | 14 | 10 | 17 | 5 | 10 | 1 | 0 | 100 | 8.29 |
| 1990 Male | 2 | 0 | 1 | 5 | 6 | 2 | 5 | 1 | 0 | 0 | 22 | 9.00 |
| Female | 0 | 6 | 8 | 10 | 7 | 10 | 9 | 3 | 4 | 3 | 60 | 9.40 |
| Total | | | | | | | | | | | | |
| Male | 57 | 31 | 39 | 34 | 24 | 13 | 12 | 2 | 1 | 0 | 213 | 7.19 |
| | [26.8] | [14.6] | [18.3] | [16.0] | [11.3] | [6.1] | [5.6] | [0.9] | [0.4] | [0.0] | [100.0] | |
| Female | 65 | 73 | 88 | 95 | 55 | 44 | 30 | 21 | 5 | 3 | 479 | 7.86 |
| | [13.6] | [15.2] | [18.4] | [19.8] | [11.5] | [9.2] | [6.3] | [4.4] | [1.0] | [0.6] | [100.0] | |

NOTE: The figures in brackets show the row percentages. Year in this Table starts from 1st January.

SOURCE: Same as Table 5.1.

Table 5.12 shows the number of years worked by *umedvars* before fulfilling the conditions for permanent employment. There is no record of the time when *umedvars* entered service in the lists of permanent employees for the years 1984, 1987 and 1988, and as a result the sample for analysis is a little under 700. The average years worked increased at a constant level for both males and females between 1982 and 1990. What greatly affected the number of years worked was the ratio between *umedvars* and permanent employees. When the ratio of *umedvars* was kept low, the AMC had to use them more often as substitute workers and so the number of years of service for becoming permanent workers decreased. On the other hand, when there was a surplus of *umedvars*, the number of years of temporary work increased. Officially, a ratio of 1:6 was regarded as appropriate between *umedvars* and permanent workers, but because the rate of absence among permanent workers was not insignificant, their numbers were generally maintained at a higher level than the official ratio. Table 5.12 shows that the average number of years worked increased by two years between the late 1980s and 1990. From the time of the Thakore Award to the year 1987, the number of *umedvars* were strictly controlled, as they were probably in excess of the official ratio. There is little difference between males and females in the average number of years worked, but the number of females is greater than that of males each year without exception. Further, the variation in the years worked is much greater among females than males. These gender variations probably arise from differences in the range of occupational choice and mobility. Males have a greater chance of finding other kinds of occupations than females. Therefore, males with multiple choices available to them, do not persist as *umedvars* for as long a time as females do. An equally important factor is, whereas males feel compelled to work as the main breadwinner, females by and large work to provide a supplementary income and so are able to remain on a temporary status for a longer period of time. This is the cause of the male/female differential.

*Umedvars* do not necessarily become permanent workers the same year they complete their stipulated period of service. Table 5.13 shows that the average period of wait between 1984-90 was a little less than two years for both sexes, 1.96 years for men and 1.78 years for women. As a result of the employment regulations of 1984, workers who had completed the stipulated period of work were supposed to be promoted to permanent employment from the next month; however, actually a delay grew over the wait for vacancies to appear in the quota. All the same, between 1984 and 1990 there was a slight shrinkage in the average waiting time. There was

TABLE 5.13: DISTRIBUTION OF WORKERS ACCORDING TO THE YEAR THEY GAINED PERMANENT EMPLOYMENT AND THE TIME WAITED BETWEEN PROMOTION CRITERIA BEING MET AND PERMANENT EMPLOYMENT BEING GAINED

*(persons, %)*

| Year | | Years waited | | | | | | | Total | Average no. of years waited |
|---|---|---|---|---|---|---|---|---|---|---|
| | | 0 | 1 | 2 | 3 | 4 | 5 | 6 | | |
| 1984 | Male | – | 18 | 167 | 84 | 6 | – | – | 275 | 2.28 |
| | Female | – | 24 | 106 | 57 | 7 | – | – | 194 | 2.24 |
| 1986 | Male | 5 | 48 | 51 | 22 | 14 | 5 | – | 145 | 2.05 |
| | Female | 6 | 124 | 104 | 16 | 21 | 19 | 1 | 291 | 1.94 |
| 1987 | Male | 6 | 48 | 6 | – | – | 1 | – | 61 | 1.07 |
| | Female | 4 | 75 | 2 | – | – | – | – | 81 | 0.98 |
| 1988 | Male | – | 31 | 1 | – | – | – | – | 32 | 1.03 |
| | Female | – | 73 | – | – | – | – | – | 73 | 1.00 |
| 1989 | Male | – | 11 | 25 | – | – | – | – | 36 | 1.69 |
| | Female | – | 28 | 44 | – | 1 | – | – | 73 | 1.64 |
| 1990 | Male | – | 8 | 18 | – | – | – | – | 26 | 1.69 |
| | Female | – | 27 | 55 | – | 1 | – | – | 84 | 1.75 |
| Total | | | | | | | | | | |
| Male | | 11 | 164 | 268 | 106 | 20 | 6 | – | 575 | 1.96 |
| | | (1.9) | (28.5) | (46.6) | (18.4) | (3.5) | (1.1) | – | (100.0) | – |
| Female | | 10 | 351 | 311 | 73 | 30 | 19 | 2 | 796 | 1.78 |
| | | (1.2) | (44.1) | (39.1) | (9.2) | (3.8) | (2.4) | (0.2) | (100.0) | – |

NOTE: The figures in brackets show the row percentages.
The year period here runs from 1 January to 31 December.

SOURCE: Same as Table 5.1.

little difference between males and females. Taking Tables 5.12 and 5.13 in conjunction, the time from *umedvar* to permanent employment was 9 years for males and 9.5 years for females.

To examine compensatory employment, Table 5.14 shows the distribution by sex and reason for leaving of those whose jobs were the subject of compensatory employment. The figures show the numbers of those by whose death or disability employment permission was given to successors in 1991/2. Since the new employment policy of 1991 was backdated to 1987/8, the table divides death and disability by year.

The proportion of males among the deaths and disabilities is 60 per cent and that of females 40 per cent. Though females outnumber males

TABLE 5.14: DISTRIBUTION OF EX-WORKERS APPEARING IN COMPENSATORY EMPLOYMENT CASES BY SEX AND REASON FOR LEAVING

*(persons, %)*

| Year of application | Death | | | Disability | | | Total | | |
|---|---|---|---|---|---|---|---|---|---|
| | male | female | total | male | female | total | male | female | total |
| 1987/8 | 4 | 5 | 9 | 1 | 0 | 1 | 5 | 5 | 10 |
| 1988/9 | 9 | 7 | 16 | 2 | 0 | 2 | 11 | 7 | 18 |
| 1989/90 | 14 | 5 | 19 | 0 | 1 | 1 | 14 | 6 | 20 |
| 1990/1 | 14 | 11 | 25 | 4 | 5 | 9 | 18 | 16 | 34 |
| 1991/2 | 27 | 16 | 43 | 25 | 16 | 41 | 52 | 32 | 84 |
| Total | 68 | 44 | 112 | 32 | 22 | 54 | 100 | 66 | 166 |
| | (60.7) | (39.3) | (100.0) | (59.3) | (40.7) | (100.0) | (60.2) | (39.8) | (100.0) |

NOTE: The figures in brackets show the row percentages.
SOURCE: Same as Table 5.1.

among permanent employees, males outnumber females in the figures for deaths and disabilities. The chief reasons why the difference is so large are that the average years worked as permanent employees is greater among males than females and that particularly unhealthy work, like rubbish collection and the cleaning of public latrines, is the domain of males. The proportion of deaths in the combined total figure is 68 per cent and that for disability is 33 per cent. There is little difference between males and females.

There are no records relating to the details about disabilities. However, from 1991/2 the Conservancy Department has begun keeping simple records of those who left work because of disability. Here the names of the hospitals and clinics which issued the disability certificates are noted. Table 5.15 is based on this information and gives the distribution of disability by sex and type. Certificates issued by the hospitals specialising in eye related problems indicate problems with sight, while those issued by hospitals specialising in pulmonary tuberculosis indicate tuberculosis. Those issued by general hospitals have been categorized under 'other'. There is every likelihood that disability certificate related to vision problems and tuberculosis might also have been issued by the general hospitals. Of particular note are the figures for tuberculosis. A number of unions with sweepers as members told the author in the course of interviews that sweepers had a particularly high rate of tuberculosis. The table shows that at least 23 per cent of male disabled workers suffered from tuberculosis;

TABLE 5.15: DISTRIBUTION OF SUFFERERS OF DISABILITY BY SEX AND CAUSE (1991/2)

(*persons, %*)

| Sex/ Cause | Vision | Tuberculosis | Other | Total |
|---|---|---|---|---|
| Male | – | 9 | 31 | 40 |
| | – | (22.5) | (77.5) | (100.0) |
| Female | 1 | 2 | 25 | 28 |
| | (3.6) | (7.1) | (89.3) | (100.0) |
| Total | 1 | 11 | 56 | 68 |
| | (1.5) | (16.2) | (82.3) | (100.0) |

NOTE: The figures in brackets show the row percentages.
SOURCE: Same as Table 5.1.

this may be attributed to a still poor working and living environment and to a meagre hygienic situation. The difference in the ratio of tuberculosis sufferers between the sexes can be explained by differences in their working environments.

To examine the beneficiaries of the compensatory employment system, Table 5.16 shows the distribution of *warasdars* by sex and family connection. Males predominate *warasdars* with 89 per cent as against females with 11 per cent. In only a few cases does the husband succeed; the major beneficiaries of compensatory employment are sons. Irrespective of the sex of the ex-worker, the son, as main provider, gets priority for permanent employment. Where the ex-worker is a female, the husband is probably already in employment, or he may perhaps because of his age pass the right of *warasdar* to the other family member. Where the ex-worker does not have a son, or has one who is under-age, or whose son already has a good job, priority would be given to his wife, daughter, and

TABLE 5.16: DISTRIBUTION OF *WARASDARS* BY SEX AND FAMILY CONNECTION (1991/2)

(*persons, %*)

| Sex / Family connection | Male | | Female | | | Total |
|---|---|---|---|---|---|---|
| | son | husband | wife | daughter | daughter-in-law | |
| No. of *warasdars* | 160 | 1 | 13 | 4 | 3 | 181 |
| | (88.4) | (0.6) | (7.2) | (2.2) | (1.6) | (100.0) |

NOTE: The figures in brackets show the row percentages.
SOURCE: Same as Table 5.1.

daughter-in-law. Such a priority system would work to increase the ratio of female workers above thirty and male workers under twenty-nine in the Conservancy Department.

Future trends in compensatory employment are suggested by the ratio of dead and disabled people among ex-workers as a whole. Table 5.17 gives the distribution of ex-workers by sex and reason for leaving employment. It has been constructed from data concerning vacancies in the permanent employee quota. The *umedvar* promotion list of 1991/2 gives, besides details about the new employee, details of the vacancy he or she has filled, including the name of the muster station, the name of the ex-worker, the date the worker left employment, and the reason for leaving. The dates of leaving employment range from 1986 to 1991, and the ratio of ex-employees according to the reasons for leaving should reflect trends during this period.

The proportion of those ex-workers whose successors received compensatory employment is 51 per cent of the total number of ex-workers. As a result of the relaxation of the rules for *niradhars*, applying for compensatory employment has become easier than before, and the annual number of applications has grown greatly compared to the pre-1990 level. This will inevitably raise the ratio of compensatory employment within the permanent quota, and become obstacle to *umedvars* waiting for promotion. There is a possibility that the number of years an *umedvar* works before being promoted will increase substantially.

The main reasons for leaving employment are retirement and death. While there is little difference in the proportions of these two in the total, the differentials between males and females are very high. Death is the main reason males leave employment, and retirement for females. The high

TABLE 5.17: DISTRIBUTION OF EX-WORKERS BY SEX AND REASON FOR LEAVING (1991/2)

(*persons, %*)

| Sex Reason | Death | Disability | Retirement | Quitting | Dismissal | Total |
|---|---|---|---|---|---|---|
| Male | 55 | 4 | 39 | 1 | 0 | 99 |
| | (55.6) | (4.0) | (39.4) | (1.0) | (-) | (100.0) |
| Female | 35 | 8 | 56 | 3 | 1 | 103 |
| | (34.0) | (7.7) | (54.4) | (2.9) | (1.0) | (100.0) |
| Total | 90 | 12 | 95 | 4 | 1 | 202 |
| | (44.6) | (5.9) | (47.0) | (2.0) | (0.5) | (100.0) |

NOTE: The figures in brackets show the row percentages.
SOURCE: Same as Table 5.1.

rate of death among males while in employment results in the male-female differential in the reason for leaving employment. Quitting work is usually the result of changing jobs or moving away from the area. Its proportion is very low. We can see the strong adherence workers have to permanent employment in the AMC. Dismissal arises from the nonperformance of compulsory duties, and one or two cases crop up each year.

### REFUSE DEPARTMENT

The permanent employment list of the Refuse Department includes the date of permanent employment as well as the date of registration on the waiting list. As a result an analysis is possible of the relationship between initial registration age, present age and the age of permanent employment, as well as of the number of years worked as an *umedvar*.

First, Table 5.18 gives the distribution of workers according to present age. Unlike permanent male workers in the Conservancy Department, the proportion of workers under 29 is small and the 30-9 band is comparatively wide. However, the 40+ ratios are similar between the two departments. The smallness of the under 29 ratio is probably due to the AMC's tightening of the employment policy being applied stringently by the Refuse Department.

The correlation between present age and the age of registration on the waiting list is shown in Table 5.19. The proportion of workers who were under 29 when they registered is 77 per cent of the total. The proportion of youths under 19 in that figure is particularly high, 27 per cent. This pattern is probably shared by the male permanent employees of the Conservancy Department. The proportion of workers who registered over 35 is extremely low, and over 45 non-existent.

Table 5.20 shows the correlation between present age and the age of gaining permanent employment. The proportion of workers who were

TABLE 5.18: DISTRIBUTION OF WORKERS BY PRESENT AGE (1991)

(*persons, %*)

| Present age | | | | | | | | Total |
|---|---|---|---|---|---|---|---|---|
| 25-9 | 30-4 | 35-9 | 40-4 | 45-9 | 50-4 | 55-9 | 60+ | |
| 25 (5.2) | 119 (24.6) | 116 (24.0) | 54 (11.1) | 55 (11.4) | 70 (14.4) | 42 (8.7) | 3 (0.6) | 484 (100.0) |

NOTE: The figures in brackets show the row percentages.

SOURCE: Compiled from the permanent workers' list of the Refuse Department, Ahmedabad Municipal Corporation.

TABLE 5.19: CORRELATION BETWEEN PRESENT AGE AND AGE WHEN REGISTERED ON THE WAITING LIST (1991)

*(%, persons)*

| Age at registration<br>Present age | 10-14 | 15-19 | 20-4 | 25-9 | 30-4 | 35-9 | 40-4 | Total |
|---|---|---|---|---|---|---|---|---|
| 25-9 | 14.3 | 50.0 | 21.4 | 14.3 | – | – | – | (14) |
| | 100.0 | 7.8 | 2.9 | 2.8 | – | – | – | 4.0 |
| 30-4 | – | 64.4 | 32.2 | 3.4 | – | – | – | (87) |
| | – | 62.2 | 27.5 | 4.2 | – | – | – | 25.0 |
| 35-9 | – | 18.9 | 54.1 | 24.3 | 2.7 | – | – | (74) |
| | – | 15.6 | 39.2 | 25.0 | 3.6 | – | – | 21.3 |
| 40-4 | – | 2.9 | 22.9 | 34.3 | 34.3 | 5.6 | – | (35) |
| | – | 1.1 | 7.8 | 16.7 | 21.4 | 9.5 | – | 10.1 |
| 45-9 | – | – | 2.2 | 54.3 | 41.3 | 2.2 | – | (46) |
| | – | – | 1.0 | 34.7 | 33.9 | 4.8 | – | 13.2 |
| 50-4 | – | 3.8 | 13.5 | 19.2 | 38.5 | 21.2 | 3.8 | (52) |
| | – | 2.2 | 6.9 | 13.9 | 35.7 | 52.4 | 40.0 | 14.9 |
| 55-9 | – | 27.0 | 40.5 | 5.4 | 5.4 | 16.3 | 5.4 | (37) |
| | – | 11.1 | 14.7 | 2.7 | 3.6 | 28.5 | 40.0 | 10.6 |
| 60+ | – | – | – | – | 33.4 | 33.3 | 33.3 | (3) |
| | – | – | – | – | 1.8 | 4.8 | 20.0 | 0.9 |
| Total | (2) | (90) | (102) | (72) | (56) | (21) | (5) | (348) |
| | 0.6 | 25.9 | 29.3 | 20.7 | 16.1 | 6.0 | 1.4 | 100.0 |

NOTE: The figures in the upper line show the row percentages (the distribution of present age group workers by the age group when registered on the waiting list), while the figures in the lower line present the column percentages (the distribution of age group workers when registered on the waiting list by the present age group workers). The figures in brackets in the Total show the number of workers. Of the 484 workers registered on the list, the records of 136 are missing.

SOURCE: Same as Table 5.18.

under 29 when permanently employed is 62 per cent, 10 points lower than permanent male workers in the Conservancy Department. This difference is probably due to differences in the patterns of compensatory employment in the Conservancy and Refuse Departments. The regulations for compensatory employment are the same, but in the Conservancy Department males, particularly sons, can become *warasdars* for a female ex-worker. This means that the proportion of Conservancy Department workers who gain permanent employment under 29 should therefore be larger than in the Refuse Department.

Table 5.21 shows the interrelationship between the number of years worked between registration on the waiting list and promotion to permanent

TABLE 5.20: CORRELATION BETWEEN PRESENT AGE AND AGE OF PERMANENT EMPLOYMENT (1991)

(*%, persons*)

| Age of permanent employment / Present age | 10-19 | 20-4 | 25-9 | 30-4 | 35-9 | 40-4 | 45-9 | 50-4 | Total |
|---|---|---|---|---|---|---|---|---|---|
| 25-9 | 16.7 | 77.8 | 5.5 | – | – | – | – | – | (18) |
| | 33.3 | 13.2 | 0.9 | – | – | – | – | – | 4.8 |
| 30-4 | 1.1 | 59.3 | 38.5 | 1.1 | – | – | – | – | (91) |
| | 11.1 | 50.9 | 30.2 | 1.6 | – | – | – | – | 24.5 |
| 35-9 | 3.3 | 17.8 | 63.3 | 15.6 | – | – | – | – | (90) |
| • | 33.3 | 15.1 | 49.1 | 20.9 | – | – | – | – | 24.2 |
| 40-4 | – | 5.0 | 20.0 | 55.0 | 20.0 | – | – | – | (40) |
| | – | 1.9 | 6.9 | 32.8 | 16.3 | – | – | – | 10.7 |
| 45-9 | – | 2.3 | 11.6 | 51.2 | 34.9 | – | – | – | (43) |
| | – | 0.9 | 4.3 | 32.8 | 30.6 | – | – | – | 11.6 |
| 50-4 | 3.6 | 10.7 | 7.1 | 14.3 | 37.2 | 23.5 | 3.6 | – | (56) |
| | 22.3 | 5.7 | 3.4 | 11.9 | 42.9 | 72.2 | 33.3 | – | 15.1 |
| 55-9 | – | 40.6 | 18.8 | – | 15.6 | 12.5 | 9.4 | 3.1 | (32) |
| | – | 12.3 | 5.2 | – | 10.2 | 22.2 | 50.0 | 100.0 | 8.6 |
| 60+ | – | – | – | – | – | 50.0 | 50.0 | – | (2) |
| | – | – | – | – | – | 5.6 | 16.7 | – | 0.5 |
| Total | (9). | (106) | (116) | (67) | (49) | (18) | (6) | (1) | (372) |
| | 2.4 | 28.5 | 31.2 | 18.0 | 13.2 | 4.8 | 1.6 | 0.3 | 100.0 |

NOTE: The figures in the upper lline show the row percentages (the distribution of present age group workers by the age group of permanent employment), while the figures in the lower line present the column percentages (the distribution of age group workers of permanent employment by the present age group). The figures in brackets in the Total show the number of workers. Of the 484 workers registered on the list, the records of 112 are missing.

SOURCE: Same as Table 5.18.

employment, and present age. Here both workers who gained permanent employment through compensatory employment and workers who were promoted from *umedvars* are included. Before 1987, beneficiaries of compensatory employment were registered on a special employment list, and received priority in employment when a vacancy in the quota arose. The waiting period could be anywhere between zero and several years. After 1987 employment was made after one year of acting status, which meant that only one year elapsed between registration as a *warasdar* and permanent employment. After 1984, it was stipulated that umedvars who had worked more than 5 years and 900 days would be promoted; before that there were no clear regulations governing promotion.

TABLE 5.21 DISTRIBUTION OF WORKERS BY PRESENT AGE AND THE NUMBER OF YEARS WORKED BEFORE GAINING PERMANENT EMPLOYMENT (1991)

*(persons, %)*

| Years worked<br>Present age | 0-4 | 5-9 | 10-14 | 15-19 | 20+ | Total |
|---|---|---|---|---|---|---|
| 25-9 | 2 | 5 | – | – | – | 7 |
| | (28.6) | (71.4) | – | – | – | (100.0) |
| 30-4 | 8 | 49 | 2 | – | – | 59 |
| | (13.6) | (83.0) | (3.4) | – | – | (100.0) |
| 35-9 | 9 | 39 | – | – | – | 48 |
| | (18.8) | (81.2) | – | – | – | (100.0) |
| 40-4 | 8 | 15 | – | – | – | 23 |
| | (34.8) | (65.2) | – | – | – | (100.0) |
| 45-9 | 25 | 8 | 1 | – | – | 34 |
| | (73.5) | (23.5) | (3.0) | – | – | (100.0) |
| 50-4 | 19 | 11 | 5 | 1 | 2 | 38 |
| | (50.0) | (28.9) | (13.2) | (2.6) | (5.3) | (100.0) |
| 55-9 | 24 | 1 | – | 1 | 2 | 28 |
| | (85.7) | (3.6) | – | (3.6) | (7.1) | (100.0) |
| 60+ | 1 | 1 | – | – | – | 2 |
| | (50-0) | (50-0) | – | – | – | (100.0) |
| Total | 96 | 129 | 8 | 2 | 4 | 239 |
| | (40.2) | (54.0) | (3.3) | (0.8) | (1.7) | (100.0) |

NOTE: The figures in the upper line show the number of workers, while the figures in the brackets present the row percentages. Of the 484 workers registered on the list, the records of 245 are missing.

SOURCE: Same as Table 5.18.

The distribution of workers presently aged 45 and over is very different to that of workers 44 and under. The proportion of workers who had worked under four years is high, but at the same time there were also some who had worked ten years or more. By comparison, the distribution of workers presently aged between 44 and under is limited to under 9 years, and the proportion of the range 5 to 9 years is extremely high. Since generally the higher the present age, the older is the entry time, it can be concluded that the difference in the distribution of the numbers of working years of the two age groups, viz., above and below 45 reflect the transition in the ratio of permanent and temporary workers and also in the compensatory employment system.

The correlation between the age when a worker registered on the waiting list and the number of years it took until he/she gained permanent

TABLE 5.22: DISTRIBUTION OF WORKERS BY AGE OF REGISTRATION AND THE NUMBER OF YEARS WORKED BEFORE GAINING PERMANENT EMPLOYMENT (1991)

*(persons, %)*

| Years worked<br>Age at registration | 0-4 | 5-9 | 10-14 | 15-19 | 20+ | Total |
|---|---|---|---|---|---|---|
| 10-14 | 1 | – | – | – | – | 1 |
| | (100.0) | – | – | – | – | (100.0) |
| 15-19 | 11 | 51 | 2 | 1 | – | 65 |
| | (16.9) | (78.5) | (3.1) | (1.5) | – | (100.0) |
| 20-4 | 28 | 44 | 1 | – | 3 | 76 |
| | (36.8) | (57.9) | (1.3) | – | (4.0) | (100.0) |
| 25-9 | 22 | 16 | 3 | 1 | 1 | 43 |
| | (51.2) | (37.2) | (7.0) | (2.3) | (2.3) | (100.0) |
| 30-4 | 23 | 11 | 2 | – | – | 36 |
| | (63.9) | (30.6) | (5.5) | – | – | (100.0) |
| 35-9 | 8 | 6 | – | – | – | 14 |
| | (57.1) | (42.9) | – | – | – | (100.0) |
| 40-4 | 3 | 1 | – | – | – | 4 |
| | (75.0) | (25.0) | – | – | – | (100-0) |
| Total | 96 | 129 | 8 | 2 | 4 | 239 |
| | (40.2) | (54.0) | (3.3) | (0.8) | (1.7) | (100.0) |

NOTE: The figures in the upper line show the number of workers, while the figures in the brackets present the row percentages. Of the 484 workers registered on the list, the records of 245 are missing.

SOURCE: Same as Table 5.18.

employment is shown in Table 5.22. Two trends can be discerned. First, the older the worker was when he registered, the higher the ratio of the age group of workers who gained permanent employment in 0-4 working years. This indicates that the proportion of those who gained employment as *warasdars* rises with age. It should be noted however that beneficiaries of the compensatory employment system are concentrated in the age range of below 34. Second, the younger the worker was when he registered, the higher the ratio of that group employed as *umedvar.*

Table 5.23 examines the influence on the distribution of the number of years worked until promotion by the compensatory employment system and the ratio of permanent and temporary workers. The compensatory employment system began in 1958 and beneficiaries appeared from the 1960s. The Criteria for authorisation of ex-workers and beneficiaries were

TABLE 5.23: DISTRIBUTION OF WORKERS BY PERIOD WHEN PROMOTED AND THE NUMBER OF YEARS WORKED BEFORE GAINING PERMANENT EMPLOYMENT (1991)

(*persons, %*)

| Years worked / Period when promoted | 0-4 | 5-9 | 10-14 | 15-19 | 20+ | Total |
|---|---|---|---|---|---|---|
| 1950-9 | 20 | – | – | 2 | 4 | 26 |
| | (76.9) | – | – | (7.7) | (15.4) | (100.0) |
| 1960-9 | 18 | 5 | 5 | – | – | 28 |
| | (64.2) | (17.9) | (17.9) | – | – | (100.0) |
| 1970-9 | 56 | 124 | 3 | – | – | 183 |
| | (30.6) | (67.8) | (1.6) | – | – | (100.0) |
| 1980-9 | 1 | – | – | – | – | 1 |
| | (100.0) | – | – | – | – | (100.0) |
| Total | 95 | 129 | 8 | 2 | 4 | 238 |
| | (39.9) | (54.2) | (3.4) | 0.8) | (1.7) | (100.0) |

NOTE: The figures in the upper line show the number of workers, while the figures in the brackets present the row percentages. Of the 484 workers registered on the list, the records of 246 are missing.

SOURCE: Same as Table 5.18

variously revised in 1972, 1984, 1987 and 1991. No reports have come to hand about the actual working of the system, and so we have no clear knowledge of how long it has taken to check applications or about the amount of waiting time between authorisation and permanent employment. The waiting time from registration on the special employment list until permanent employment is thought to be generally in the range of 0 to 4 years. However, as can be seen from the distribution of the number of years worked before promotion to permanent employment in the 1950s, some umedvars too were promoted in 0 to 4 years. It is therefore difficult to get a clear picture of the proportion of warasdars among permanent employees at that time. The analysis of the AMC employment policy suggests that the proportion of *warasdars* among permanent employees was higher in the 1970s (criteria: death, disability, niradhar) than the 1960s (criteria: death, niradhar). From the middle of the 1980s (criteria: death, disability, age limit, niradhar) it fell to its lowest level when employment tightened. However, with the revision in 1991 that broadened the criteria (death, disability, removal of niradhar rules), the proportion of warasdars in the permanent workforce grew appreciably, as in the Conservancy Department.

Let us ncw examine the connections between the ratio between the permanent and temporary workers and the distribution of the number of years worked to gain permanent employment. The proportion of workers gaining permanent employment in 0-4 years decreased between the 1950s and the 1970s. The proportion of workers who had gained permanent employment in 10 or more years also decreased during the same period. Whereas in the 1950s some workers took even 20 years to be permanently employed, during the 1960s there were none who worked more than 15 years. In the 1970s the proportion of workers who had worked 5-9 years rose remarkably. When temporary workers were retained in excess of the official ratio with permanent workers, the proportion of workers who had to work longer before gaining permanent employment rose. In this sense, the proportion between temporary and permanent workers was improved between the 1950s and the 1970s. However, since the proportion of workers working 0-4 years before gaining permanent employment in the 1950s and 1960s was large, we should be able to confirm the existence of groups who were employed permanently in a short time, even where temporary workers were maintained in excess of the standard. We cannot know, however, whether or not this was based on some form of discrimination in employment.

### *An Analysis of Temporary Workers by Sex*

At present there are around 1,200 *umedvars* working in the Conservancy Department. C lists are maintained at every muster station, but because these reports are not centralised, it is not possible to obtain exact figures. The list of casual labourers used in this section was prepared in 1991. It records the names of 319 males and 705 females, making 1,024 altogether. However, it contains information regarding labour days for 137 males and 430 females, 43 per cent and 61 per cent respectively of the names listed. The lists are incomplete because some muster stations report only names. However, the numbers are sufficient for a sample and should not hinder the analysis of the sex differential among workers.

Let us first examine the sex differential in the number of days worked. Table 5.24 gives the distribution of *umedvars* by sex and year and the number of days worked per year. The earliest year which appears on the list is 1976, when two females were employed. The earliest year for males is 1978. The proportion of *umedvars* by sex has been comparatively constant since 1980, around 20 per cent for males and around 80 per cent for females. The table also shows the lowest number of days worked, the maximum

TABLE 5.24: DISTRIBUTION OF *UMEDVARS* BY SEX AND YEAR AND THE NUMBER OF DAYS WORKED

(*persons,days*)

| Year | *Umedvar* numbers | | Days worked per year | | | | | | | |
|---|---|---|---|---|---|---|---|---|---|---|
| | | | minimum | | maximum | | average | | standard deviation | |
| | male | female | male | female | male | female | male | female | male | female |
| 1976 | – | 2 | – | 2 | – | 2 | – | 2.00 | – | 0.00 |
| 1977 | – | 13 | – | 1 | – | 29 | – | 10.15 | – | 9.46 |
| 1978 | 2 | 20 | 1 | 3 | 6 | 45 | 3.50 | 16.95 | 3.54 | 11.27 |
| 1979 | 8 | 37 | 3 | 1 | 26 | 56 | 11.88 | 16.03 | 8.71 | 14.00 |
| 1980 | 17 | 67 | 1 | 1 | 72 | 47 | 17.82 | 15.40 | 18.12 | 11.55 |
| 1981 | 29 | 120 | 1 | 1 | 90 | 117 | 16.48 | 16.23 | 17.43 | 15.34 |
| 1982 | 44 | 167 | 1 | 1 | 99 | 119 | 25.27 | 18.83 | 21.46 | 16.56 |
| 1983 | 74 | 238 | 1 | 1 | 142 | 97 | 28.66 | 22.43 | 25.11 | 16.93 |
| 1984 | 83 | 275 | 5 | 1 | 141 | 124 | 39.60 | 29.10 | 27.80 | 20.38 |
| 1985 | 89 | 297 | 1 | 1 | 143 | 155 | 31.57 | 23.52 | 29.43 | 23.97 |
| 1986 | 107 | 367 | 2 | 1 | 173 | 310 | 46.20 | 35.33 | 35.02 | 30.33 |
| 1987 | 115 | 384 | 1 | 1 | 166 | 227 | 56.55 | 44.84 | 38.18 | 34.35 |
| 1988 | 126 | 398 | 1 | 1 | 288 | 243 | 88.24 | 71.48 | 60.08 | 50.13 |
| 1989 | 132 | 424 | 1 | 1 | 276 | 272 | 116.33 | 102.60 | 69.58 | 61.39 |
| 1990 | 111 | 343 | 2 | 1 | 296 | 299 | 161.18 | 149.68 | 73.01 | 72.50 |

NOTE: The year period here runs from 1 January to 31 December.
SOURCE: Compiled from the temporary workers' list of the Conservancy Deartment of the Ahmedabad Municipal Corporation.

number of days worked, the average number of days worked and the standard deviation.

As we have already seen, between the end of the 1970s and the beginning of the 1980s, 213 males and 479 females were promoted to permanent employment. To complete the stipulated 900 days of work within five years requires an annual average of 180 days of work. The average number of days remained very low from the beginning to the middle of the 1980s, suggesting that *umedvars* were maintained in excess of the ratio with permanent workers. There was a vast improvement in this area after 1988. After 1987 the Conservancy Department placed heavy restrictions on the numbers of *umedvars* employed, and the effects of this policy are very obvious in the trends for both maximum and average days worked.

Variations by sex can be noticed both in the average number of days worked and the standard deviation. After 1980 males worked considerably more days on average than females. The standard deviation too shows that males exceeded females after 1980.

Table 5.25 shows the distribution of the total number of days and years worked according to sex. The number of years worked are divided into three groups, 1-5, 6-10 and 11+. At present the criteria for permanent employment are over five years and 900 days service; therefore the first group does not satisfy the standard for promotion. The second group, 6-10 years, satisfies the requirements in terms of years but not in days. The third group, 11+, is included for examining the proportion of day labourers working for an exceptionally long period of time.

There is a clear differential by sex in the distribution of both the years and days worked. The sexual ratio in the number of *umedvars* recruited

TABLE 5.25: DISTRIBUTION OF DAY LABOURERS BY SEX, NUMBER OF YEARS WORKED AND THE TOTAL NUMBER OF DAYS WORKED

*(persons, %)*

| Number of years / Total number of days | Males | | | | Females | | | |
|---|---|---|---|---|---|---|---|---|
| | 1-5 | 6-10 | 11+ | Total | 1-5 | 6-10 | 11+ | Total |
| 0-89 | 9 | 1 | – | 10 | 28 | 3 | – | 31 |
| | (17.3) | (1.4) | – | (7.3) | (20.0) | (1.3) | – | (7.2) |
| 90-179 | 7 | 2 | – | 9 | 27 | 14 | 2 | 43 |
| | (13.5) | (2.8) | – | (6.6) | (19.3) | (6.0) | (3.4) | (10.0) |
| 180-359 | 12 | 12 | – | 24 | 37 | 56 | 4 | 97 |
| | (23.1) | (16.6) | – | (17.5) | (26.4) | (24.1) | (6.9) | (22.5) |
| 360-539 | 8 | 19 | 5 | 32 | 26 | 74 | 19 | 119 |
| | (15.4) | (26.4) | (38.5) | (23.4) | (18.6) | (31.9) | (32.8) | (27.7) |
| 540-719 | 9 | 26 | 7 | 42 | 15 | 60 | 19 | 94 |
| | (17.3) | (36.1) | (53.8) | (30.7) | (10.7) | (25.9) | (32.8) | (21.9) |
| 720-899 | 5 | 12 | 1 | 18 | 3 | 24 | 14 | 41 |
| | (9.6) | (16.7) | (7.7) | (13.1) | (2.1) | (10.4) | (24.1) | (9.5) |
| 900+ | 2 | – | – | 2 | 4 | 1 | – | 5 |
| | (3.8) | – | – | (1.4) | (2.9) | (0.4) | – | (1.2) |
| Total | 52 | 72 | 13 | 137 | 140 | 232 | 58 | 430 |
| | [38.0] | [52.51 | [9.51 | [100.01 | [32.6] . | [54.0] | [13.4] | [100.0] |

NOTE: The figures in the round brackets show the column percentages, and the figures in square brackets in the Total show the row percentages. Of the 1.024 labourers registered on the list, the records of 457 are missing.

SOURCE: Same as Table 5.24.

each year is comparatively constant; what affects the proportion of workers among the three groups is the speed of promotion. The shorter the average number of years required for promotion, the higher the proportion of promotions among *umedvars*. As a result, the proportion of workers in the long year groups decreases. As has already been confirmed, males exceed females both in the average number of years and the average number of days per year worked before gaining promotion. This means that the proportion of males among workers in the 6+ year groups is smaller than females. In particular, there is a large sex differential in the 11+ group. The figures attained in Table 5.25 agree with the analysis of the distribution of the average number of years taken to reach promotion based on Table 5.12.

## Conclusion

The conclusions in this chapter are drawn from a cross-sectional and diachronic analysis of sweepers, based on the permanent and temporary employees lists of the Conservancy and Refuse Departments of the AMC. The focus of the cross-sectional analysis has been on the sex differential in the distribution of the present age structure, the age structure at the time of permanent employment, and the years necessary from registration on the waiting list to permanent employment, in the case of permanent employees, and in the distribution of the number of years worked, the number of days worked per year, and the total number of days worked, in the case of temporary workers. The sex differential seen in the present age structure and the age structure at the time of permanent employment reveals that females begin sweeping work generally later than males, and that when they begin they are of a wider age span than males. The sex differential in the pattern of beginning work has its main cause in differences of role within the household and range of work choice. The compensatory employment system has also functioned to widen the sex differential in age structure. To verify this point, we have examined the scope and nature of compensatory employment in the 1980s using documents other than the permanent and temporary workers' lists. The main reason for compensatory employment is the death of a worker, followed in a small number of cases by disability. Also, it is noticed that most beneficiaries by far are the ex-worker's son. The proportion of female beneficiaries, such as wives or daughters is small. Thus, compensatory employment system has functioned to raise the proportion of male workers aged under 29. We have seen in specific detail that the scale and nature of the system have been directly affected by periodical changes in employment policy. It is also confirmed that there is a sex differential in favour of males even in permanent employment from the waiting list, as the average number of years of male workers before gaining permanent employment tends to appear smaller than that of females workers throughout the reference period. Analysis of the temporary workers' list has also confirmed the advantageous position of male workers in terms of the distribution of years worked, days worked per year and the total number of days worked. This serves to strengthen the arguments made in the analysis of the permanent workers' list.

The diachronic analysis has focused on the effect of changes in AMC employment policy on the scale of permanent employment in each period, on the distribution of the work years needed to attain permanent employment after registration on the waiting list, and on the sex differentials in these. An analysis of the permanent employees of the Conservancy Department suggests there was discrimination against females in employment until the middle of the 1960. However, as a result of the abolition of discrimination the proportion of female workers among permanent workers rose well above that of males. The move to permanent employment of the auxiliary labour force has made a considerable contribution in raising the income level of Bhangi households in general. The tightening of employment in the early 1970s and the latter 1980s can be verified by the decreases in permanent employment in those years. Based on the employees' list of the Refuse Department, we have examined changes in the scale of compensatory employment, an important pillar of employment policy, and in the proportion of permanent and temporary workers. Compensatory employment broadened in scale in the 1970s, but decreased significantly in the middle of the 1980s. While, the ratio of permanent and temporary workers showed improvement between the 1950s and 1970s.

Chapter Six

# The Socio-economic Condition of Sweepers

## INTRODUCTION

The local bodies are largest employers of sweepers. In addition, the central and state governments also employ sweepers. A large number of them also work in factories, companies, residential areas, shopping precincts and institutes; their exact numbers, however, are difficult to assess. Those sweepers in the private sector are engaged in cleaning and scavenging under the contract or *gharaki* systems. Their working and employment conditions are far worse than those of sweepers employed by the central and state governments; their wage level is low, and they are often out of the legal protection.

The employment and working conditions of sweepers employed by local bodies are in general better than those of sweepers in the private sector, but there are considerable variations among the various local bodies. Those working for large local bodies have virtually the same conditions as those working for the central or state government, while those working for small local bodies are often in much the same situation as workers under private contract, with no access to a labour union or financial facilities.

After Independence, the Indian government set up several committees to investigate the employment and working conditions of sweepers and scavengers. The reports of these committees provide with the most comprehensive and wide-ranging information, available at the time of their compilation, on scavengers and sweepers. However, the reports are deficient in terms of statistical data and analysis. For a better understandings of the employment, working and living conditions of sweepers and scavengers, it is necessary to undertake a broad macro-analysis of the statistics as well as a more minute micro-analysis of individuals and households.

To this end, I made a preliminary survey of the socio-economic condition of sweepers in July 1990, and a full-scale survey between July and September the following year (1991). I selected eight local bodies in

Ahmedabad District, Gujarat State, two local bodies from each of the four Talukas in the northern part of the district (Map. 6.1). The local bodies were selected to examine the influence that such bodies of different sizes exert upon the employment and working conditions of sweepers employed by them. Ahmedabad was selected to represent a large urban municipal corporation (population over 300,000), the cities of Dehgam, Viramgam and Dholka to represent a Municipality/Nagar Palika (population between 25,000 and 300,000), the towns of Sanand, Bareja and Bavla to represent a Nagar Panchayat (population between 10,000 and 25,000) and the village of Sola to represent a Gram Panchayat (population under 10,000). Municipal Corporations were set up under the Bombay Municipal Corporation Act, 1947, municipalities under the Gujarat Municipalities Act, 1963 and Nagar and Gram Panchayats under the Gram/Nagar/Taluka/District Panchayats Act, 1961. Ahmedabad is the site of the District Office for Ahmedabad District and the three cities of Dehgam, Viramgam and Dholka are the sites of the Taluka Offices of their respective talukas. Sola is a rural village on the outskirts of Ahmedabad. Small and medium villages do not generally employ sweepers; even large villages do not employ more than a few. Thus to acquire a statistically viable sample it would been ideal to cover several dozen villages. However, this was impossible due to the exigencies of time and labour, and in Sola I could survey only the educational and occupational structures of a few sweeper households.

Table 6.1 shows the number of sweeper households and persons surveyed in each local body. The number of those sampled from each local body lessens in proportion to the size of the local body. However, the proportion of the sample sweepers to the total sweepers employed by each local body is in inverse proportion to the size of the local body. In the case of municipalities (Nagar Palika) the proportions are around 50 per cent, while they constitute about 80 per cent for Nagar Panchayats.

## Employment and Working Conditions

### *Legal Developments*

Prior to the Barve Committee Report, the Vyas Committee set up by the Saurashtra State Government had already published a report in 1956 concerning sweepers in that state.[1] Though it did not have the same national influence as the Barve Report, it was the first survey on the conditions of sweepers in Gujarat.

The *Vyas Committee Report* consisted of seven chapters: Living

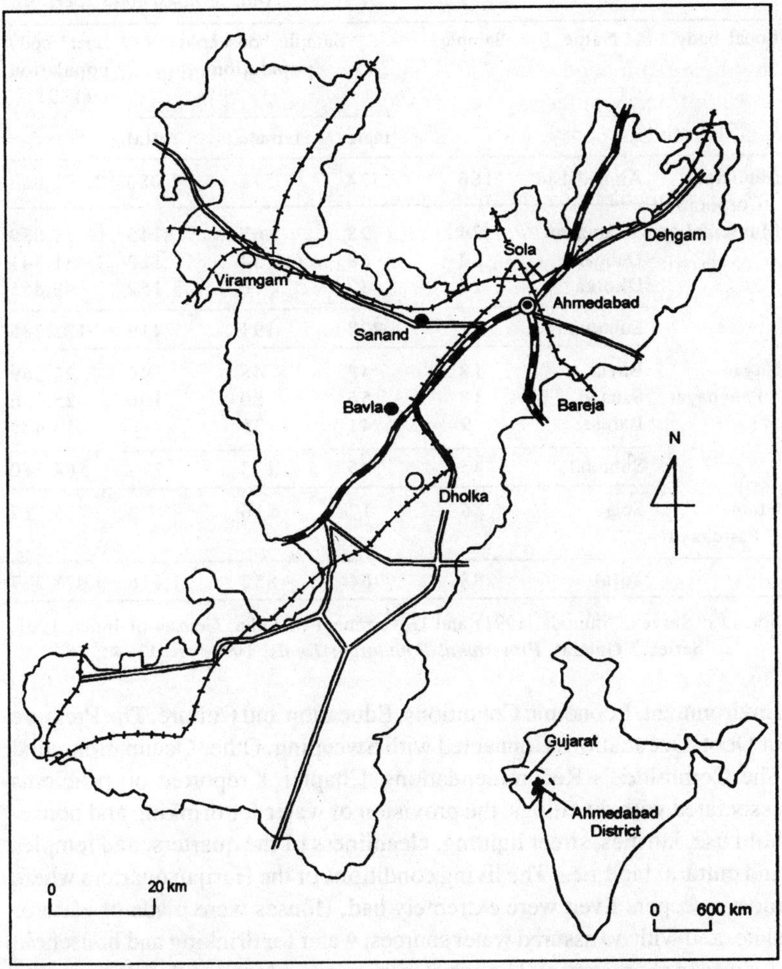


◉ — Municipal Corporation
● — Nagar Panchayat
○ — Municipality / Nagarpalika
X — Gram Panchayat

MAP 6.1: LOCAL BODIES UNDER STUDY

TABLE 6.1: DISTRIBUTION OF SAMPLE HOUSEHOLDS BY LOCAL BODY AND HOUSEHOLD POPULATION

(*no. of households, persons*)

| Local body | Name | Sample | Sample household population | | | Local body population (1991) |
|---|---|---|---|---|---|---|
| | | | male | female | total | |
| Municipal Corporation | Ahmedabad | 166 | 574 | 512 | 1,086 | 2,872,865 |
| Municipality | Viramgam | 24 | 78 | 67 | 145 | 51,089 |
| | Dehgam | 22 | 68 | 54 | 122 | 31,341 |
| | Dholka | 25 | 82 | 70 | 152 | 49,855 |
| | Subtotal | 71 | 228 | 191 | 419 | 132,285 |
| Nagar Panchayat | Bavla | 18 | 48 | 48 | 96 | 25,369 |
| | Sanand | 18 | 56 | 50 | 106 | 25,656 |
| | Bareja | 9 | 41 | 35 | 76 | 13,485 |
| | Subtotal | 45 | 145 | 133 | 278 | 64,510 |
| Gram Panchayat | Sola | 6 | 17 | 16 | 33 | 5,717 |
| | Total | 288 | 964 | 852 | 1,816 | 3,075,377 |

SOURCES: Survey (Shinoda, 1991) and Government of India, Census of India, 1991, Series-7 Gujarat, *Provisional Population Totals*, 1993, pp. 43, 44, 78.

Environment, Economic Conditions, Education and Culture, The Pressure of Debt, Occupations Connected with Sweeping, Other Occupations, and The Committee's Recommendations. Chapter 1 reported on problems associated with dwellings, the provision of water for drinking and household use, latrines, street lighting, cleanliness of the quarters, and temples and cultural facilities. The living conditions of the Harijan quarters where most sweepers lived were extremely bad. Houses were made of earth or slate, and with no assured water sources, water for drinking and household use was in short supply. Though sweepers contributed to the maintenance of municipal sanitary facilities, latrines or street lighting and cleaning services were not provided and the environment was extremely unhealthy. There was also a conspicuous lack of temples and cultural facilities.[2]

Chapter 2 explained the economic impact of the revisions in allowances and the minimum wage legislation (promulgated in May 1952) on sweepers. As a result of this legislation wages of workers for municipal corporations were set at a minimum of Rs. 52 per month and even for those in the smallest local bodies, at Rs. 32.5. The results of the survey conducted by the Vyas Committee showed that when two members of the same family (not household) worked for a local body, their wages combined with the income from other members who worked as day labourers brought the family income on par with other labouring classes. The study found that the economic situation of the Untouchables had improved greatly in recent years.[3]

Chapter 3 pointed out that workers did not utilize their free time for personal development, education or cultural activities. In particular, men would go to a hotel after work and drink alcohol, gamble at cards, and waste their time. Women by contrast had housework and cleaning to do, and children to look after, and they could hardly have time for a bath. Also, because they had to hold down a double workload even during their monthly periods and before and after childbirth, they were susceptible to serious illnesses. The survey clearly indicated a trend among male sweepers employed in local bodies to have unemployed female family members share their work, forcing them to provide auxiliary labour. The report hoped that the workload of women would be reduced, leaving them with more time for child raising, education and cultural activities. The majority of sweeper children did not go to school, and even they did they took their smaller siblings with them and so could not study. Most children accompanied their parents to the workplace and so were not looked after properly or supervised.[4]

Chapter 4 dealt with the problem of debt. A separate survey had showed that as many as 90 per cent of sweepers surveyed had debts. It was pointed out that even labourers who earned less than sweepers did not generally incur this much debts. Debt was incurred through weddings, funerals, other rituals, bad habits like drinking and smoking and ignorance. Whatever the reason for debt, once it had been incurred, the sweeper fell into a debtor's hell, the report stated.[5]

Chapter 5 pointed out that dry latrines were the norm in Saurashtra, and painted a grim picture of the work of scavengers, carting human waste, coming into direct contact with it by carrying it on the head, and the continual insanitary conditions, without the provision of clean water or soap. Since society looked down on latrine cleaning and other communities avoided the work as it was unclean, sweepers had come to regard scavenging as their hereditary work or customary rights. In many local bodies, private contract labourers (*khangi*) performed scavenging work; as a result local bodies could not take the work in hand. And in some, their own sweepers subcontracted scavenging to *khangi*.[6]

Chapter 6 discussed the advantages of other occupations and how the change could be brought about. Since Bhangis have only done sweeping over a long period of time, they were not prepared to enter any other occupation, and as a result could not participate even in relief works, like road construction and dam repairs, that Saurashtra had organized as a way to help the very poor. The report recommended that Bhangi youth be given training for a variety of occupations and that they be provided in the suitable jobs by appropriate departments in the government. The department should, therefore, reserve a certain proportion of jobs for Bhangis, it said.[7]

The Vyas Report recommended that baths, separate for men and women, be provided for sweepers in their colonies: 1 bathroom for less then 20 people, 2 for between 20 and 50 people, and 3 for between 50 and a 100 people. Other recommendations were: provision of soap, street lighting, latrines in proportion to the population, as well as latrine and street cleaning.[8] It suggested that part-time employment be stopped and that existing part-time workers be promoted to permanent status.[9] Based on the evidence from Harijan leaders, the committee revealed that local bodies were in the habit of punishing certain workers without an explanation and asked therefore that local bodies act according to the requirements of the Industrial Employment Act of 1946.[10] It recommended that the Debt Invalidation Act, currently applied to some farmers, should also be applied to sweepers, when the interest exceeded the original loan by 150 per cent to 300 per cent, that every effort be made by local bodies to establish credit associations so as to prevent sweepers from falling into a debtor's hell, and that the government establish a debt invalidation committee to look into the actual state of sweepers' debts. It also urged that, sweepers' children be provided compulsory education till age of 12, schools be set up near sweeper colonies, school fees be waived, and that books and materials be provided free.[11]

The Vyas Report was a pioneer in its analysis of the conditions of the sweepers and recommendations for improving it. However its recommendations, on the whole, were not implemented. Actual improvements in the employment and working conditions of sweepers was to come a little later.

The employment and working conditions of sweepers employed by local bodies were left to the discretion of these bodies. However, improvements in their working conditions were often impeded by the chronic financial problems that local bodies faced. Improvements in employment and working conditions came rather 'from above', through reforms initiated by the state governments.

It would be useful, therefore, to examine the role of state decisions and directives, their contents and frequency over time in bringing about changes in the employment and working conditions of sweepers.[12] Of course, such decisions and directives were not easily accepted by the local bodies; considerable pressure was probably applied on them during periods when there was a strong drive for reform 'from above.'

Table 6.2 shows the distribution of such directives from 1950 to 1970. Their contents can be broadly divided into five areas: employment conditions, working conditions, plans for Bhangi liberation, the provision of latrines and drains, and housing. The time division is a five year period from 1950 to 1970. The documents consisting of directives were published around 1972, and so the final period is irregular, consisting of just two years, 1971-2. In 1950 Saurashtra and Kutch were integrated as Part B and Part C states; the remaining area of Gujarat was incorporated into Bombay state. With the reorganization of states in 1956, Saurashtra and Kutch also became part of Bombay state. In 1960, as a result of the bifurcation of

TABLE 6.2: STATE GOVERNMENT DIRECTIVES BY SUBJECT AND PERIOD

(*no. of directives*)

| Period | Employment conditions | Working conditions | Bhangi liberation plan | Latrines drains | Housing, etc. | Total |
|---|---|---|---|---|---|---|
| 1950-4 | 2 | – | – | – | – | 2 |
| | (100.0) | – | – | – | – | (100.0) |
| 1955-9 | 1 | – | – | – | – | 1 |
| | (100.0) | – | – | – | – | (100.0) |
| 1960-4 | – | 6 | – | – | 1 | 7 |
| | – | (85.7) | – | – | (14.3) | (100.0) |
| 1965-9 | 3 | 1 | 8 | 7 | 5 | 24 |
| | (12.5) | (4.2) | (33.3) | (29.2) | (20.8) | (100.0) |
| 1970-1 | 7 | 2 | 2 | 12 | 2 | 24 |
| | (28.0) | (8.0) | (8-0) | (48.0) | (8.0) | (100.0) |
| Total | 13 | 9 | 10 | 19 | 8 | 59 |
| | (22.0) | (15.3) | (16.9) | (32.2) | (13.6) | (100.0) |

NOTE: Figures in brackets show the row percentages.

SOURCE: Government of Gujarat, Department of Social Welfare, *Bhangi Kasht Mukti Karyakram* (in Gujarati), Ahmedabad, 1972.

Bombay state, the present state of Gujarat came into existence. Thus the Government of Gujarat directives date from 1960, while the earlier years are part of the Bombay state.

The distribution of directives shows that reform 'from above' gained pace after 1965. The *Malkani Committee Report* of 1960, which followed the *Barve Committee Report* of 1956, aroused the interest of the central and state governments in the condition of sweepers and scavengers. But of greater importance was that the Harijan Sevak Sangh declared the Bhangi liberation as a national project commemorating the Gandhi birth centenary celebration on 2 October 1969 and the response it received from the central and state governments.

The three directives that emerged during the 1950s were all demands that the Minimum Wage Act be observed in the case of workers at local bodies. The 1952 directive of the Department of Labour and Backward Classes was to local bodies in Saurashtra, the 1954 directive of the Department of Development was to local bodies in Bombay, and the 1959 directive of the Department of Labour and Social Welfare was to local bodies in Kutch. They all stipulated that a minimum monthly wage be paid to all workers at local bodies based on the Minimum Wage Act of 1948. The 1954 directive ruled that the monthly minimum wage in Bombay city (Division 1) be Rs. 70, in the cities of Ahmedabad, Pune, Sholapur, Surat, Vadodara and Babli (Division 2) Rs. 65, in other towns (Division 3) Rs. 55, and in Gram Panchayats (Division 4) Rs. 45. Children were to receive half the minimum wage (an indication that child labour was still widespread). The daily wage was to be calculated at one twenty-sixth of the monthly minimum wage.[13]

Six of the seven directives of the early 1960s concerned working conditions of scavengers and sweepers. Improving work tools and methods of cleaning was aimed at street sweepers, through the promotion of the distribution of long-handled brooms and dust pans. The old style short-handled broom was considered to encourage a humiliating posture and insanitary conditions, while a long handled broom enabled the sweeper to stand straight. The first directive forbidding the carrying of human waste on the head came out in April 1962. However, the reaction of local bodies was so slow that it was repeated the following June, asserting that human waste should be only transported by a wheelbarrows or trucks, and local bodies should not permit to build dry latrines, and owners of existing dry latrines should be encouraged to convert them into a flush or septic type.[14] Improvement of the working environment was aimed at scavengers. The 1963 directive from the Department of General Administration quoted the recommendations of the state appointed committee headed by N.R. Malkani inquiring into the problems of scavengers. It was reported that as of 1963, 79 of the 147 towns in Gujarat had purchased wheelbarrows with the financial assistance from the central government. Since the wheelbarrows were not standardized their storage was a problem, that most public latrines were of the dry type, around 25 per cent of households used dry latrines, and that *gharaki* was rife throughout Gujarat.[15] The committee recommended standardization and regular purchase of wheelbarrows, ban on the new construction of dry latrines by law, and abolishing the *gharaki* system by absorbing private scavengers into local bodies. The 1964 directive of the Department of Village Development pointed out that even where local bodies had purchased wheelbarrows, scavengers found them difficult to use because of poor construction and bad roads, that some municipalities allowed scavenging by privately contracted labourers, and that the carrying of human waste on the head was observed in some Nagar Panchayats.[16]

In the latter half of the 1960s, 24 directives were sent out. Eight concerned the Bhangi liberation scheme, more properly known as the Bhangi Kasht Mukti Karyakram (scheme to liberate Bhangis from their hardship), which had as its purpose the release of scavengers from their 'traditional' occupation. The first to call for such a plan was Mamasaheb Phadke.[17] The slogan drew the attention of some social workers, but it could not be organized as a social movement before Independence. The scheme was launched on a national scale to abolish dry latrines by 2 October 1969, the centenary year of M.K. Gandhi. Its philosophy and programme are fully set out in J. Jairamdas' *Bhangi Kasht Mukti and Bhangi Mukti*, published as one of the events of the Gandhi centenary celebration.[18]

The Bhangi liberation plan placed great emphasis on improving latrines and sewage facilities.[19] In the second half of the 1960s, seven directives focused on this point. The first directive on the conversion of latrines was issued in February 1965 by the Department of Village Development. It required that latrines in areas with sewage be connected to it, that no new latrines be permitted in areas where there was no sewage, that existing dry latrines in areas where sewage had recently been provided be connected to it within two years, and that in newly developed areas only sewage and flush latrines should be provided.[20] Further, it was strongly urged that the conversion of dry latrines and the eradication of the system of carrying waste on the head be enforced by legislation. The central government encouraged the conversion of latrines by providing 50 per cent of the cost of conversion to owners who undertook conversion work during the Gandhi centenary year (March 1969, Directive, Department of Panchayat and Health).

During the same time, three directives were issued concerning employment conditions. Two of them (1966 and 1969, both by the Department of Education and Labour) were revisions of the minimum wage regulation and the other (1969, Commissioner of Development) concerned the re-training of sweepers. This was to be the responsibility of the Departments of Welfare and beneficiaries between the ages of 15 and 45 could receive up to a year's training.[21] This was the first directive concerning re-training, but at this stage no schemes have introduced. Budgetary measures were not in place until the 1980s. Directives concerning a housing-aid scheme for scavenges and sweepers were issued in 1966 (Department of Conservancy) and 1968 (Department of Education and Labour), which were to provide a maximum of 75 per cent of the cost of construction (up to Rs. 750).

The number of directives increased greatly in the late 1960s, from 6 in 1968 to 11 in 1969. This is a confirmation of the importance placed on putting a Bhangi liberation plan into place by the Gandhi centenary. This impetus continued even after the centenary. And in 1970, 17 directives were issued and 8 in 1971. The directives issued in the early 1970s centred on the improvement of latrines and sewage facilities, essential for the Bhangi liberation plan. At the same time, 5 directives were issued concerning the provision of permanent employment to sweepers. These spoke of bringing as many privately contracted scavengers as possible into the sanitation, general affairs and clerical departments of local bodies, and the directives do suggest that the reforms had achieved a certain amount of success.

The Harijan Sevak Sangh set up the Safai Vidyalaya as a research institute on sweepers in 1963. It acted as a link between the state government and the local bodies, and also contributed a great deal to the education of beneficiaries of latrine conversion and grass-roots level social workers who came into direct contact with them. The role of the Institute was to bring about a reformation in the attitudes of local bodies and the people towards the sweepers community, and even after the enthusiasm of the Gandhi centenary year had cooled down, it continued to adopt a Gandhian approach. The Department of Social Welfare provided funds through the Gujarat Harijan Sevak Sangh to social workers involved in the Bhangi liberation plan.[22]

In the late 1970s, international organizations like the World Bank, the UNDP and UNICEF began taking an interest in public sanitation in Gujarat. The state government also prepared to put into effect a low cost sanitation plan. There were legislative changes as well. The Gujarat Panchayat and

Municipal Law was partially revised in 1980; the Taluka Development Officer was given the powers to order householders with no suitable latrine facilities to build or repair them within a stipulated period of time and, in case they failed to do so, to get the latrine built and charge it to the householder.[23]

In the midst of this new movement, the Gujarat government set up a (low cost) public sanitation scheme for urban areas in 1984 with the aid provided by the World Bank and the UNDP. The international aid organizations recommended to the state government that Ishwarbhai Patel of the Safai Vidyalaya be made an advisor for the implementation of the scheme. The plan was executed through the cooperation of beneficiaries, local bodies, the Gujarat Water Supply and Sewerage Board, and the advisor.[24] By March 1992, 30,000 latrines had been built.[25]

In 1988 a low cost sanitation scheme funded by the World Bank was introduced for rural areas . The Safai Vidyalaya was made a nodal agency. Unlike the low cost sanitation scheme for urban areas, various non-governmental organizations, under the leadership of the Safai Vidyalaya, were expected to undertake responsibility for confirming beneficiary villages and households and putting the scheme into action at site. Many of them had already been involved at the village level and so were considered the most suitable organizations for grassroot level interaction and feed back of problems.[26] The initial plan was to build 20,000 two pit latrines at a cost of Rs.55 million but applications from beneficiaries far exceeded the estimate and the number of latrines was revised to 56,000. By March 1992, 38,000 latrines had been constructed with the cooperation of 108 non-governmental organizations.[27] A commission of 100 rupees for each latrine was given to the nodal agency and the non-governmental organizations. The cost of a latrine was estimated to be Rs.2,700 in 1992. Of this amount, Rs.1,850 was subsidized for beneficiaries from the Scheduled Castes, Scheduled Tribes and Other Backward Classes, and Rs.1,270 for other groups.[28] By September 1991, beneficiaries from these Backward Classes shared 72.5 per cent of the 28,341 latrines built. [29] Besides the World Bank, the Dutch Government collaborated with the Indian government to build 180 latrines in two villages, and UNICEF contributed towards the cost of 5,000 latrines in villages.[30]

The conversion of dry latrines in Gujarat has been promoted under the Bhangi liberation plan, the low cost urban sanitation scheme and the low cost rural sanitation scheme. When the state came into being, there were about 180 thousand dry latrines in existence, mainly in urban areas, with a user population of around 1 million.[31] By 1985/6, most of these had been converted to one-pit improved latrines.[32] Now, with the conversion of dry latrines virtually completed, the Gujarat government is concerned with controlling public defecation and converting one-pit latrines to two-pit latrines where sewage facilities are not developed.

### *Public Sanitation Facilities*

Sanitation facilities and the sanitary environment govern the working conditions and environment of sweepers. Sanitation facilities may be divided broadly into two categories, for liquid and solid wastes.

#### TREATMENT FACILITIES FOR LIQUID WASTE

Liquid waste consists of urine and faeces, other household waste water, factory waste water and rain water. The treatment of liquid waste consists of initial collection, intermediate disposal, transport and final disposal. Facilities for initial collection include various types of latrine, and for intermediate disposal septic tanks and such like. Sewers, various types of drains and pumping stations transport the waste to the final disposal plants. There is a great variation in the provision of facilities among local bodies.

Few dry latrines, which involve direct contact with human waste, remain in Gujarat due to the concerted campaign of eradication by the government and people. In March 1992 there were no more than 1,720 dry latrines in the state (22 of these were public latrines) and only 262 scavengers remained.[33] Gujarat is one of the few Indian states to have almost abolished dry latrines. The remaining dry latrines are confined to five districts; there are none in Ahmadabad District. The most common types of latrine in use are: flush, septic and traditional. The flush type presupposes a sewage system. The septic type allows intermediate disposal of waste, but this must be cleaned out periodically. The traditional type is constructed in such a way that waste flows into a cistern (one-pit type), which must also be emptied regularly. An improved form, devised by a group of Gandhians, consisting of two cisterns (two-pit type); while one cistern is being filled the waste collected in the other can be converted into fertilizer (Fig. 6.1).

The growth of the sewage system can contribute the most to the sanitary collection of human waste. In 1981 out of the 255 cities/towns in the state, 72 had sewerage. The smaller the city population, the lower the ratio of provision of sewerage. Of the places surveyed in this study, only Ahmedabad and Viramgam had sewage facility. In the remaining six local

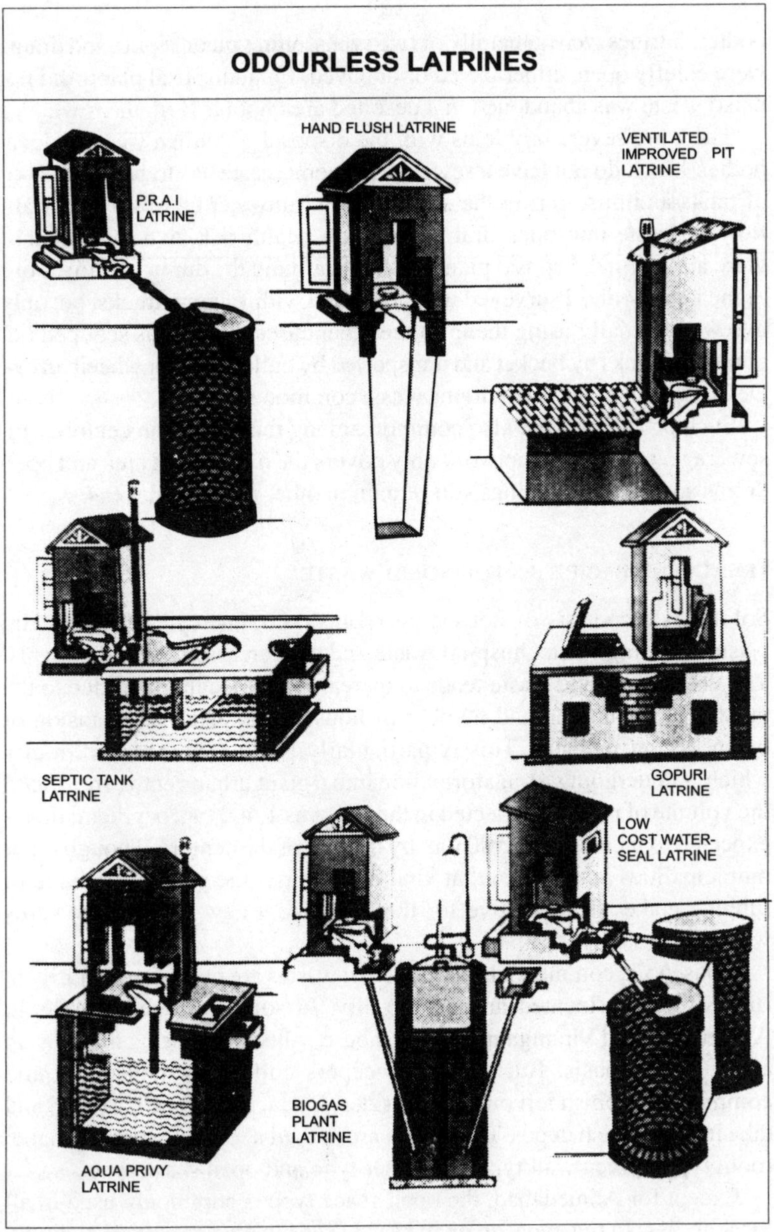


*Source*: Pamphlet of Safai Vidyalaya.

FIG. 6.1: IMPROVED LATRINES

bodies, latrines were generally of two types, either pit or septic, and drains were chiefly open, either paved or unpaved. Final disposal plants did not exist; waste was abandoned in a deserted area not far from the town.

There are severe problems with the disposal of human waste in local bodies which do not have a sewerage system: waste has to be cleared out of tanks and pits, during the rainy season rainwater causes a backward flow of waste into open drains, posing a health risk, and that because there are no final disposal plants, the area around the dump is filthy. Four of the local bodies I surveyed were provided with vacuum trucks, but only two were actually using them. In the other cases, waste was scooped out of pits and tanks by bucket and transported by bullock cart or wheelbarrow. Defecation over the open drains was a common sight.

Such problems were also common among the two urban centres with sewerage, because the network only covers the main urban area and open drains and cistern openings still remain in other residential areas.

## TREATMENT FACILITIES FOR SOLID WASTE

Solid waste consists of household rubbish, commercial and industrial waste, building waste, hospital waste and the carcasses of dead animals. The volume of solid waste tends to increase in all local bodies due to the growth in population and number of households, and the expansion of business and industry. This is particularly true of Ahmedabad, a city which is undergoing a transformation into a giant urban centre. In 1988/9, the volume of rubbish collected in the city was 1,400 ton. per diem; this is expected to increase to 3,500 ton. by the end of the century. Though other municipalities do not face that kind of increase, the growing volume of rubbish makes it imperative for them to take a new approach towards waste disposal.

Household, commercial and industrial wastes are placed temporarily in rubbish depots located around the city. In some residential areas in Ahmedabad and Viramgam, house to house collection is being made on an experimental basis. But usually sweepers collect the household and commercial rubbish left on the roadsides, load it into wheelbarrows, and take it to a rubbish depot. The depots are named according to their shape: room type, screen wall type, container type and open space type.

Except for Ahmedabad, the open space type is commonly used in all local bodies. In this type, an open space is designated as a rubbish dump. It is the most unhygienic among the depots: rubbish is left scattered on the ground to rot, domestic animals roam on it, and the air is filled with the stench of the rubbish. The screen wall type consists of a single wall, which does not provide any protection against animals or rain. The room type has three walls and a roof. It provides some protection against smell and animals though workers come into direct contact with rubbish while removing it for disposal. The most hygienic type of depot is the container, which can be loaded directly onto the truck and unloaded at the dump without the worker coming into direct contact with the waste. The container type is only used in Ahmedabad, where the solid waste management system is being reorganized through mechanization.

Rubbish is either placed in a dump or used as road filling. There are more than ten dumps in Ahmedabad. Some dumping sites have been made into parks or walkways with rubbish and building waste being piled on each other in layers. Only Ahmedabad uses trucks or trailers to take rubbish to the dumps; the other local bodies employ tractors.

### *Employment Conditions*

This section examines the employment condition of sweepers employed by local bodies with special reference to their employment status, wage scale, promotion, and employment method.

Sweepers are either permanent or temporary employees. Day labourers employed by the AMC are divided into *umedvars* (registered workers) and *hangamis* (non-registered workers). There are slight differences in their pay scales and other conditions. Other local bodies do not have *umedvars*. The provisions of the Minimum Wage Act apply to *hangamis* but there are some local bodies which do not observe these.[34]

In cash-strapped small and medium local bodies there is a tendency to save expenditure on sweepers by restricting the number of permanent employees and substituting day labourers. The unions oppose this and demand an extension of the permanent quota. Thus, the employment status of sweepers is conditioned both by the financial situation of the local body and by the power relationship between the local body and labour unions. In such local bodies where there are powerful unions, the employment conditions of workers tend to improve, while in those where the negotiating power of unions is weak, there is a tendency to ignore even the Minimum Wage Act. In Ahmedabad, where the labour unions are strong, 70 per cent of the AMC sweepers are permanently employed, in contrast to small and medium local bodies where permanent employment is very rare.

The wage scale of sweepers also reflects the power relationship between the local body and the unions. Permanently employed sweepers are classified as Class 4 workers in the local body. The wages of sweepers are conditioned by the wage system of workers in the local body as a whole, and cannot be changed arbitrarily. However, the larger the local body the higher the level of the wage paid to sweepers. AMC sweepers move to higher scales after 10, 19 and 28 years of work. In other local bodies, sweepers are placed on a single scale and wage increases end after 10 to 15 years.

A basic demand of sweepers in local bodies has been for a promotion system. Sweepers' unions in Ahmedabad have concentrated their efforts on achieving promotions for sweepers as clerical workers and peons, who are also Class 4 employees. This demand is connected with their desire to move away from the 'traditional' occupation of sweeping. However, not only in Ahmedabad but among other local bodies as well, such promotions have not been realized. The situation is similar even in the central and state governments, which have in general superior employment conditions for sweepers than in local bodies.

Local bodies recruit most of their permanent employees from waiting lists. Applicants placed on waiting lists are employed in order of registration as and when vacancies arise. A few local bodies have made working as day labourer for a particular period of time while on the waiting list a prerequisite for permanent employment. In Ahmedabad over 5 years or 900 days are required. This method avoids nepotism and is comparatively fair for the applicant. However, when there is an excess in the number of registrations over permanent employees, the waiting time becomes very long.

Compensatory employment system is prevalent in a large number of local bodies in India. This system allows a qualified member of the family of a permanent worker who has died or become disabled in service to be his or her successor and be given priority in permanent employment. Its application depends on the reason a worker left work and the suitability of the successor. Death before retirement is considered as an adequate reason, but many local bodies do not accept disability. Some local bodies also have an age limit when confirming the reason for leaving work. Even in the same local body, as in Ahmedabad, the requirements for approval have been revised many times. Regulations governing confirmation of the successor too vary from one local body to another. But if there is no permanent worker in the ex-worker's family, there is no problem about granting permanent employment to one family member as successor. The ratio of sweepers who have entered permanent employment by way of compensatory employment is around 14 per cent in Ahmedabad, and close to 50 per cent in Viramgam. The compensatory employment system was started with the purpose of helping families of sweepers in economic difficulties because of the loss of a worker, since occupations outside sweeping were largely closed to them. However, today when the economic situation of sweepers has largely ameliorated, the system functions to prevent sweepers from finding new avenues of work. Since more sweepers are being employed through compensatory employment, applicants seeking permanent employment through the waiting list are to wait for longer periods of time. The compensatory employment system as it exists today works as a major hindrance towards their socio-economic development.

### *Labour Unions*

Labour unions representing the interests of sweepers existed in four local bodies under study. They were not formed in small local bodies due to lack of collective power and legal support. There were signs of an incipient labour union in Sanand and Bareja, but members fell away because of inadequate leadership and misappropriation of funds. The movement either collapsed or became stagnant. Ahmedabad, on the other hand, has had a long history of unionism, including a large number of unions for sweepers, and a wide experience of union activities, from collective bargaining and demonstrations to disputes in tribunals.

The unions have been generally concerned with improving employment conditions, such as better wages and an enlarged permanent quota of sweepers. Chapter 4 has already discussed in detail the activities of unions in Ahmedabad. Union action in other local bodies can be gleaned from the causes of strikes and disputes in the tribunals. For example, strikes have been held in Viramgam over holiday allowances (1987) and the promotion of *mukadams* (1988), disputes have occurred in Dholka over an increase in the dearness allowance, the introduction of new allowances, and the provision of uniforms, and a dispute has been in progress in Baula over the employment of day labourers and permanent workers and the appointment of *mukadams*. In local bodies with a strong union movement, the employment conditions of sweepers have vastly improved.

However, where there was only a weak union presence or none at all, the number of permanent workers was restricted and the wage levels of both permanent and temporary workers were kept low. In such places the frailty of the sweeper community was exposed in various ways. For example, when Bareja was raised to Nagar Panchayat status in 1985, it announced that it would employ three permanent workers instead of five temporary ones as had been the case; as a result of sweeper opposition, eleven temporary workers were employed at the same cost as the three permanent workers. Before Bareja was raised in status, sweeper households took it in turns on a rotation basis to fill the temporary quota. They regarded sweeping as their customary rights and so chose to enlarge the quota. In Sola, a post of sweeper with the wage of Rs. 100 per month was held in common by 15 households. They were the original sweeper inhabitants of the village; their 'rights' were not shared with an incoming group of 20 households. The amount of Rs. 100 was no more than a nominal wage; the *gharaki* rights still seemed to dominate the thinking of sweepers.

### *Working Conditions*

Cleaning work in local bodies is usually looked after by the Conservancy Department, the Sanitary Department and/or the Refuse Department. At places, where there is sewerage and where mechanization is advanced, the Sewage Department and the Transportation Section work in concert with the other departments. In large local bodies cleaning is divided into variously ranked jobs. For example, the Conservancy Department in Ahmedabad has ten ranks, whereas the Sanitary Departments in Viramgam and Sanand have only five and four job rankings respectively.

The placement and the number of workers in the cleaning section vary considerably among local bodies. In Ahmedabad, there are 9,500 workers broadly defined as sweepers. Of these, 5,800 clean streets and latrines, 500 transport waste, 1,000 work in drains and sewerage, and 2,200 are attached to hospitals. In Viramgam, of 98 sweepers, 78 clean roads and latrines, 11 transport waste, 5 clean drains and 4 are with hospitals. In places like Bareja, where there are no sewers, public latrines or rubbish collection trucks, all the 11 day workers are engaged in cleaning streets.

The ratio of sweepers that are assigned by local bodies to different tasks varies, but in all street cleaning involves the majority of work force. Street cleaners have their own beat. In Ahmedabad, the area differs according to the density of population, but in a place like Viramgam the area assigned to each beat is constant. In all local bodies, the area of the beat is between 3,000 and 10,000 sq. m.

Rubbish collection methods (for example, whether house to house or not) differ according to the management system, but almost all street cleaners feel some dissatisfaction. Their complaints are centred on the number of roll calls and its location, the shift system, the difficulty in using the tools provided, the irregular provision of tools, and the distance to rubbish depots and dumps. Because of the exigencies of labour management (verifying the presence and absence of workers, and arranging relief workers, etc.) all local bodies have between two and four roll calls a day. These frequently take place at the muster station but there is resentment among workers if that involves traveling long distances. Cleaning is usually done in two shifts, morning and afternoon, and lunch is taken at home. When the time needed to reach the roll call point is long, the lunch period is necessarily shortened. Some sweepers want the favour of a single shift system, but this would mean working seven to eight hours continuously, which would be very hard.

Local bodies provide sweepers with uniforms, brooms and dust pans, though usually behind schedule, and quite often sweepers have to wear their own clothes and work with inadequate equipment (Fig. 6.2). Women sweepers have been particularly dissatisfied with the wheelbarrows. When fully loaded, women find it very difficult to push because of the weight. When men and women work together in groups, the men tend to push the wheelbarrows and the women collect the rubbish. When women are working it is usual that family members, including young children, come to help. The standard distance between the beat and a depot or dump is supposed to be within 500 m., but this is no small distance keeping in mind the method of transportation.

Despite various problems associated with the working conditions, sweepers have not taken the initiative in reforming the solid waste management system. Rather, sweepers have tended to oppose to any reform in their working conditions including the introduction of mechanization, if it would be a threat to their jobs. Thus, their adherence to a monopolized labour market constituted the main reason for the lack of improvement in their working conditions.

### Occupational Structure

We will first examine the occupational structure of the sample households. Table 6.3 shows the distribution of male workers by age and the type of local body they work for. Table 6.4 gives the distribution of female workers by age.

A special feature of the male workers is that the work participation ratio (WPR) for the 20-9 age class is considerably low, or in others words, there is a high incidence of unemployment in this age group. This is because of their pursuit of higher education, search for a better job, or waiting as a

*Source*: Pamphlet of Safai Vidyalaya.

FIG. 6.2: MODERN SANITATION IMPLEMENTS

TABLE 6.3: DISTRIBUTION OF MALE WORKERS FROM SAMPLE HOUSEHOLDS BY AGE GROUP AND LOCAL BODY

*(persons, %)*

| Age group | Municipal Corporation | Municipality | Nagar Panchayat | Gram Panchayat | Total |
|---|---|---|---|---|---|
| 10-14 | – | – | 1 | – | 1 (0.9) |
| 15-19 | 4 | 9 | 4 | 1 | 18 (11.2) |
| 20-4 | 37 | 20 | 10 | 2 | 69 (48.3) |
| 25-9 | 21 | 12 | 9 | – | 42 (62.7) |
| 30-4 | 33 | 15 | 8 | – | 56 (80.7) |
| 35-9 | 25 | 11 | 9 | 1 | 46 (88.5) |
| 40-4 | 26 | 7 | 6 | 2 | 41 (91.1) |
| 45-9 | 25 | 6 | 2 | 1 | 34 (91.9) |
| 50-4 | 21 | 6 | 3 | – | 30 (78.9) |
| 55-9 | 7 | 3 | 2 | – | 12 (75.0) |
| 60+ | 3 | – | – | – | 3 (13.6) |
| Total | 202 | 89 | 54 | 7 | 352 (36.5) |

NOTE: The figures in brackets show the work participation ratio by age group.
SOURCE: Survey (Shinoda, 1991).

successor under the compensatory employment system. It is also caused by the relative smallness of the permanent and temporary quotas in the cleaning service.

A second feature is that the male WPR after age 50 falls below the corresponding WPR for females, probably as a result of the higher incidence of physical unfitness and voluntary retirement among male workers in this age class. Thirdly, the WPR of the 10-19 age group is lower in the Municipal Corporation than in medium or small local bodies, because of the relatively higher school attendance rates for this age group in the former.

The WPR pattern for females varies considerably from that of males. There is a much lower WPR in the 10-20 age group, due to the prevalence of primary and lower secondary education, participation in housework

TABLE 6.4: DISTRIBUTION OF FEMALE WORKERS BY AGE GROUP

(*persons, %*)

| Age group | Number of workers |
|---|---|
| 15-19 | 5 (4.1) |
| 20-4 | 18 (16.1) |
| 25-9 | 37 (52.1) |
| 30-4 | 37 (68.5) |
| 35-9 | 37 (75.5) |
| 40-4 | 38 (80.9) |
| 45-9 | 39 (88.6) |
| 50-4 | 24 (85.7) |
| 55-9 | 16 (84.2) |
| 60+ | 6 (25.0) |
| Total | 257 (30.2) |

NOTE: The figures in brackets show the work participation ratio by age group.
SOURCE: Survey (Shinoda, 1991).

before marriage, and child birth and care after marriage. However, the WPR goes up to 80 per cent in the 40-plus age group, and the high ratio continues beyond age 50. The female WPR pattern is characterized generally by later entry into the work force than males, with a peak in the middle and later years, and a small drop-out ratio in the later years. Whereas about 50 per cent of female workers belong to the 40-plus age group, only 34 per cent of mlaes do so. This female pattern is largely determined, not only by the employment policies of local bodies, but also by the role females are expected to play in the household.

There is little difference between males and females in the status of their employment. The proportion of permanent workers among all workers is 59 per cent for males and 62 per cent for females. Workers other than permanent are clubbed together as temporary; these include day labourers employed by local bodies, workers under private contract to other institutions, and sweepers under the *gharaki* system. In general, their working conditions are far worse and their wage levels are much lower. However some, like the *umedvars* in Ahmedabad, receive wages which are in no way inferior to those of permanent workers.

The distribution of temporary and permanent workers according to age shows a sharp contrast. Whereas both males and females predominate in the middle and higher age groups among permanent workers, the age group below 30 is dominated by the temporary workers of both sexes, though female workers are more evenly distributed over the other age groups than males. The male-female variable can be explained by the female role allocation within the family and the priority male successors receive at the time of compensatory employment.

A pattern of occupational mobility among Bhangi workers is evident from the changes in their working status. Table 6.5 shows the distribution of 'present' and 'previous' working status of workers. Only those workers who have had a change in occupation or status are included under previous employment. If there are two or more changes, only the most recent case is shown. Of the workers who have not reported any change, either in occupation or status, 132 are males and 109 are females. The overwhelming majority of these workers entered the cleaning service as temporary workers and still remain so. Occupational mobility is essentially in terms of movement from temporary to permanent status; the 210 male and 142 female workers, who were temporary workers in their previous occupation, seem to have changed their employment status within the cleaning section with a few exceptions caused by transfer. The movement of Bhangis from the cleaning section to other sections is very rare. Their occupational

TABLE 6.5: DISTRIBUTION OF WORKERS BY PRESENT AND PREVIOUS WORKING STATUS AND BY SEX

*(persons, %)*

| Employment status | Present Status | | Previous Status | |
|---|---|---|---|---|
| | male | female | male | female |
| Permanent | 220 | 161 | 29 | 8 |
| | (59.3) | (62.2) | (12.1) | (5.3) |
| Temporary | 151 | 98 | 210 | 142 |
| | (40.7) | (37.8) | (87.9) | (94.7) |
| Total | 371 | 259 | 239 | 150 |
| | (100.0) | (100.0) | (100.0) | (100.0) |

NOTE: The figures in brackets show the column percentages.
SOURCE: Survey (Shinoda, 1991).

mobility is confined to 'promotion' within the cleaning section.

The range of occupational choice among Bhangi workers is very narrow. Tables 6.6 and 6.7 show that 80 per cent of male workers and 93 per cent of female workers are classified as sweepers. There are some differences in the type of work allocated to male and female sweepers. Whereas women mainly are involved in street cleaning, men are allocated the more unhygienic and dangerous tasks, too, like cleaning latrines, and sewers, removing and disposing the carcasses of dead animals, and disposing of human waste.

TABLE 6.6: DISTRIBUTION OF MALE WORKERS BY OCCUPATION AND TYPE OF LOCAL BODY

*(persons, %)*

| Occupation | Municipal Corporation | Municipality | Nagar & Gram Panchayats | Total |
|---|---|---|---|---|
| Sweepers (including *mukadams*) | 196<br>(81.3) | 81<br>(84.4) | 48<br>(70.6) | 325<br>(80.2) |
| Clerks & Teachers | 6<br>(2.5) | 7<br>(7.3) | 2<br>(2.9) | 15<br>(3.7) |
| Other workers | 39<br>(16.2) | 8<br>(8.3) | 18<br>(26.5) | 65<br>(16.1) |
| Total | 241<br>(100.0) | 96<br>(100.0) | 68<br>(100.0) | 405<br>(100.0) |

NOTE: The figures in brackets show the column percentages.
SOURCE: Survey (Shinoda, 1991).

TABLE 6.7: DISTRIBUTION OF FEMALE WORKERS BY OCCUPATION AND TYPE OF LOCAL BODY

*(persons, %)*

| Occupation | Municipal Corporation | Municipality | Nagar & Gram Panchayats | Total |
|---|---|---|---|---|
| Sweepers (including *mukadams*) | 157<br>(95.2) | 53<br>(91.4) | 53<br>(86.9) | 263<br>(92.6) |
| Clerks & Teachers | 3<br>(1.8) | 1<br>(1.7) | –<br>– | 4<br>(1.4) |
| Other workers | 5<br>(3.0) | 4<br>(6.9) | 8<br>(13.1) | 17<br>(6.0) |
| Total | 165<br>(100.0) | 58<br>(100.0) | 61<br>(100.0) | 284<br>(100.0) |

NOTE: The figures in brackets show the column percentages.
SOURCE: Survey (Shinoda, 1991).

TABLE 6.8: DISTRIBUTION OF THE LAST OCCUPATION OF RESPONDENT'S PARENTS AND PATERNAL GRANDPARENTS

(*persons, %*)

| Occupation | Father | Mother | Grandfather | Grandmother | Total |
|---|---|---|---|---|---|
| Sweeper | 254 | 200 | 146 | 101 | 701 |
| | (90.7) | (95.2) | (93.6) | (95.3) | (93.2) |
| *Mukadam* | 5 | 3 | 2 | 1 | 11 |
| | (1.8) | (1.4) | (1.3) | (0.9) | (1.5) |
| Technical worker | 8 | 2 | 3 | – | 13 |
| | (2.9) | (1.0) | (1.9) | – | (1.7) |
| Clerical worker | 4 | 2 | 2 | – | 8 |
| | (1.4) | (1.0) | (1.3) | – | (1.1) |
| Teacher | – | – | – | 1 | 1 |
| | – | – | – | (0.9) | (0.1) |
| Singer | – | 1 | – | – | 1 |
| | – | (0.4) | – | – | (0.1) |
| Other miscellaneous | 9 | 2 | 3 | 3 | 17 |
| workers | (3.2) | (1.0) | (1.9) | (2.9) | (2.3) |
| Total | 280 | 210 | 156 | 106 | 752 |
| | (100.0) | (100.0) | (100.0) | (100.0) | (100.0) |

NOTES: The last occupation is the one at retirement or the one held at the time of the survey.
The figures in brackets show the column percentages.

SOURCE: Survey (Shinoda, 1991).

Occupations other than sweeping consist of clerical, teaching, and other miscellaneous works. Only 20 per cent of male workers and 7 per cent of female workers are employed in these occupations. Though all these works are so-called 'clean' works, the only prestigious ones are the clerical and teaching occupations.

This occupational immobility among Bhangis is not confined to the present generation. Table 6.8 shows the distribution of the last reported occupation of parents and paternal grandparents of the respondents of this survey. The table clearly indicates that there has not been any visible improvement in the occupational mobility of the Bhangis as a whole over three generations. This occupational immobility is the very factor which restrains the socio-economic development of the Bhangis.

## EDUCATION

Education is of strategic importance to the socio-economic development of the Bhangis both at the household and community level. As a result of the diffusion of primary and lower secondary education in recent years, the emphasis has moved from the eradication of illiteracy to the upgrading of the educational structure. Nevertheless, primary and lower secondary education still needs to reach more women as well as the Scheduled Tribes and the some of the backward communities.

The educational structure of the Bhangis surveyed indicates that the enrollment ratio at the primary and middle school level has been shooting up in both sexes though illiteracy is still dominant among the adult females. Since schooling has spread rapidly, illeteracy is expected to be minimized sooner or later. An important feature of their educational structutre, in comparison with other Scheduled Castes, is that they have fewer number of graduates. Graduation is a minimum qualification for a 'white collar' job which may attribute to the upliftment of the community as a whole. In this sense, the Bhangis lag far behind the other communities of the Scheduled Castes.

Several factors discourage a rise in the number of Bhangi graduates: poor financial position to support higher education, tough competition with other Scheduled Castes for reserved seats in higher educational institutions, and social discrimination against the employment of the Bhangi graduates. In Gujarat 7 per cent of the seats are reserved for the Scheduled Castes, based on their population ratio in the state. It is not easy for the Bhangis, who constitute only 13 per cent of the Scheduled Castes population and are the most backward educationally among them, to compete with other Scheduled Castes for the reserved quota.

Entering a higher educational institution is the first handle that the youth of this community encounter. It is even more difficult for Bhangi graduates to take advantage of the reservation quota to enter government work. Also, it is very difficult for them to get a 'white collar' job in the private sector, where both merit system and social discrimination work. Thus, there is not much scope for them to gain remunerative employment through higher education.

Table 6.9 examines the correlation between educational level and occupation among male Bhangi workers. Though the literacy rate appears high, there are many who have dropped out of primary school. This accounts for the educational backwardness of adult males. Also, the fact that the two graduates both work as sweepers shows the dilemma of the Bhangis that higher education is not necessarily linked to a good job.

Since most of occupations in which the Bhangis are engaged do not require any educational qualifications, the educational pattern of workers by occupation does not suggest much variation. The educational structure

TABLE 6.9: DISTRIBUTION OF MALE WORKERS BY OCCUPATION AND EDUCATIONAL LEVEL

*(persons, %)*

| Occupation | Illiterate | <Primary | Primary | Lower secondary | Higher secondary | University | Total |
|---|---|---|---|---|---|---|---|
| Sweepers | 53 | 74 | 85 | 53 | 21 | 2 | 288 |
| | (18.4) | (25.7) | (29.5) | (18.4) | (7.3) | (0.7) | (100.0) |
| | [94.6] | [83.2] | [80.2] | [88.3] | [80.8] | [100.0] | [85.0] |
| *Mukadam* | 2 | 5 | 6 | 1 | 2 | – | 16 |
| | (12.5) | (31.2) | (37.5) | (6.3) | (12.5) | – | (100.0) |
| | [3.6] | [5.6] | [5.7] | [1.7] | [7.8] | – | [4.7] |
| Peon | – | 4 | 5 | 5 | – | – | 14 |
| | – | (28.6) | (35.7) | (35.7) | – | – | (100.0) |
| | – | [4.5] | [4.7] | [8.3] | – | – | [4.1] |
| Clerk | – | – | – | – | 1 | – | 1 |
| | – | – | – | – | (100.0) | – | (100.0) |
| | – | – | – | – | [3.8] | – | [0.3] |
| Compounder | – | – | 1 | – | – | – | 1 |
| | – | – | (100.0) | – | – | – | (100.0) |
| | – | – | [0.9] | – | – | – | [0.3] |
| Mechanic | 1 | – | 4 | | – | – | 5 |
| | (20.0) | – | (80.0) | | – | – | (100.0) |
| | [1.8] | – | [3.8] | | – | – | [1.5] |
| Watchman | – | – | – | 1 | – | – | 1 |
| | – | – | – | (100.0) | – | – | (100.0) |
| | – | – | – | [1.7] | – | – | [0.3] |
| Ward boy | – | 1 | – | – | 1 | – | 2 |
| | – | (50.0) | – | – | (50.0) | – | (100.0) |
| | – | [1.1] | – | – | [3.8] | – | [0.6] |
| Petrol pump operator | – | 1 | – | – | – | – | 1 |
| | – | (100.0) | – | – | – | – | (100.0) |
| | – | [1.1] | – | – | – | – | [0.3] |
| Other labourers | – | 4 | 5 | – | 1 | – | 10 |
| | – | (40.0) | (50.0) | – | (10.0) | – | (100.0) |
| | – | [4.5] | [4.7] | – | [3.8] | – | [2.9] |
| Total | 56 | 89 | 106 | 60 | 26 | 2 | 339 |
| | (16.5) | (26.2) | (31.3) | (17.7) | (7.7) | (0.6) | (100.0) |
| | [100.0] | [100.0] | [100.0] | [100.0] | [100.0] | [100.0] | [100.0] |

NOTE: The figures in round brackets show the row percentages, while the figures in square brackets show the column percentages.

SOURCE: Survey (Shinoda, 1991).

of the Bhangis is, to a considerable extent, reflected through the educational distribution of sweepers, since sweeping is their major occupation. Interestingly, the *mukadam*, who is the supervisor of the sweepers, is not better-educated than his fellow sweepers. Thus, the education of the Bhangis is quite irrelevant to their occupation. As long as sweeping remains the dominant occupation of the Bhangis, they may lack the motivation to achieve higher educational qualifications.

Table 6.10 looks at the correlation between educational level and occupation among Bhangi females. Illiteracy is high among female workers and their educational level is considerably lower than that of the male workers. Those who have completed lower secondary education or above are confined to the younger generation. There is one graduate who works as a sweeper in Ahmedabad. Though she has applied for public service jobs on five occasions, she has not met with any success. She decided to take up the work of sweeping because of economic difficulties. Social restrictions on occupation are even more severe for female Bhangis than male, and their dilemma, that higher education does not lead to 'clean' work, is even more pressing.

TABLE 6.10: DISTRIBUTION OF FEMALE WORKERS BY OCCUPATION AND EDUCATIONAL LEVEL

(*persons, %*)

| Occupation | Illiterate | <Primary | Primary | Lower secondary | Higher secondary | University | Total |
|---|---|---|---|---|---|---|---|
| Sweeper | 140 | 43 | 43 | 4 | 6 | 1 | 237 |
| | (59.1) | (18.1) | (18.1) | (1.7) | (2.6) | (0.4) | (100.0) |
| | [94.6] | [95.6] | [91.4] | [100.0] | [100.0] | [100.0] | [94.4] |
| Compounder | – | 1 | – | – | – | – | 1 |
| | – | (100.0) | – | – | – | – | (100.0) |
| | – | [2.2] | – | – | – | – | [0.4] |
| Domestic | 2 | – | 2 | – | – | – | 4 |
| worker | (50.0) | – | (50.0) | – | – | – | (100.0) |
| | [1.3] | – | [4.3] | – | – | – | [1.6] |
| *Gharaki* | 6 | 1 | 2 | – | – | – | 9 |
| and other | (66.7) | (11.1) | (22.2) | – | – | – | (100.0) |
| labourers | [4.1] | [2.2] | [4.3] | – | – | – | [3.6] |
| Total | 148 | 45 | 47 | 4 | 6 | 1 | 251 |
| | (59.0) | (17.9) | (18.7) | (1.6) | (2.4) | (0.4) | (100.0) |
| | [100.0] | [100.0] | [100.0] | [100.0] | [100.0] | [100.0] | [100.0] |

NOTE: The figures in round brackets show the row percentages, while the figures in square brackets show the column percentages.

SOURCE: Survey (Shinoda, 1991).

The correlation between employment status and educational level among workers in the sample households is shown in Tables 6.11 and 6.12. It is interesting to note that the educational level of temporary workers is slightly higher than that of permanent workers for both sexes. This tendency is observed both among sweepers as well as those in other occupations. This is because temporary workers mainly consist of the younger generation that has a close association with middle or higher level of education.

Another important point is that the occupation of three graduates is confined to sweeping. One female graduate is a permanant sweeper and two male graduates are temporary sweepers. An intensive interview with them revealed that they have succumbed to social as well as family pressure

TABLE 6.11: CORRELATION BETWEEEN EMPLOYMENT STATUS AND EDUCATIONAL LEVEL AMONG MALE WORKERS

*(persons, %)*

| Educational level | Permanent worker | Temporary worker | Total |
|---|---|---|---|
| Illiterate | 39<br>(68.4)<br>[18.4] | 18<br>(31.6)<br>[13.6] | 57<br>(100.0)<br>[16.6] |
| <Primary | 58<br>(65.2)<br>[27.3] | 31<br>(34.8)<br>[23.5] | 89<br>(100.0)<br>[25.9] |
| Primary | 68<br>(63.6)<br>[32.1] | 39<br>(36.4)<br>[29.6] | 107<br>(100.0)<br>[31.1] |
| Lower secondary | 33<br>(54.1)<br>[15.6] | 28<br>(45.9)<br>[21.2] | 61<br>(100.0)<br>[17.7] |
| Higher secondary | 14<br>(50.0)<br>[6.6] | 14<br>(50.0)<br>[10.6] | 28<br>(100.0)<br>[8.1] |
| University | –<br>–<br>– | 2<br>(100.0)<br>[1.5] | 2<br>(100.0)<br>[0.6] |
| Total | 212<br>(61.6)<br>[100.0] | 132<br>(38.4)<br>[100.0] | 344<br>(100.0)<br>[100.0] |

NOTE: The figures in round brackets show the row percentages, while the Figures in square brackets show the column percentages.

SOURCE: Survey (Shinoda, 1991).

TABLE 6.12: CORRELATION BETWEEEN EMPLOYMENT STATUS AND EDUCATIONAL LEVEL AMONG FEMALE WORKERS

*(persons, %)*

| Educational level | Permanent worker | Temporary worker | Total |
|---|---|---|---|
| Illiterate | 100 | 49 | 149 |
| | (67.1) | (32.9) | (100.0) |
| | [61.7] | [54.5] | [59.1] |
| <Primary | 29 | 16 | 45 |
| | (64.4) | (35.6) | (100.0) |
| | [17.9] | [17.8] | [17.9] |
| Primary | 27 | 20 | 47 |
| | (57.4) | (42.6) | (100.0) |
| | [16.7] | [22.2] | [18.6] |
| Lower secondary | 2 | 2 | 4 |
| | (50.0) | (50.0) | (100.0) |
| | [1.2] | [2.2] | [1.6] |
| Higher secondary | 3 | 3 | 6 |
| | (50.0) | (50.0) | (100.0) |
| | [1.9] | [3.3] | [2.4] |
| University | 1 | – | 1 |
| | (100.0) | – | (100.0) |
| | [0.6] | – | [0.4] |
| Total | 162 | 90 | 252 |
| | (64.3) | (35.7) | (100.0) |
| | [100.0] | [100.0] | [100.0] |

NOTE: The figures in round brackets show the row percentages, while the Figures in square brackets show the column percentages.

SOURCE: Survey (Shinoda, 1991).

and taken up the broom after several failed efforts to get a 'clean' job. The rest of the eleven unemployed graduates are also involved in the struggle to find a 'clean' job. If their educational qualifications remain unconnected to 'clean' occupations, families with graduates and the community as a whole will lose faith in the benefits of raising their educational standards. This will only serve to inhibit the efforts of the community from raising its educational standards and breaking the shackles of a monopolistic labour market.

## INCOME

Income level and its distribution pattern in a community is generally associated with the level of economic development of the community as a whole. The income distribution pattern of Bhangi household particularly attracts our attention as they are at the lowest of the social hierarchy. Table 6.13 gives the distribution of the annual income of the sample households according to the local body. It reveals that 55 per cent of the sample households earn more than Rs. 20,000 per year. This income group has nothing to do with poverty in economic terms and is better off than other labour classes of urban Gujarat. The Bhangi household income is positively correlated with the number of permanent workers (mainly sweepers) per household. Since the monthly wage of a permanent sweeper is in the range of Rs. 800 to 1,500 the annual household income would be around Rs. 10,000 to 20,000 with one permanent worker; an annual income

TABLE 6.13: DISTRIBUTION OF HOUSEHOLDS BY ANNUAL INCOME AND TYPE OF LOCAL BODY

*(no. of households, %)*

| Annual income (Rs.) | Municipal Corporation | Municipality | Nagar Panchayat | Gram Panchayat | Total |
|---|---|---|---|---|---|
| <5,000 | 6 | 5 | 3 | – | 14 |
| | (42.9) | (35.7) | (21.4) | – | (100.0) |
| | [3.6] | [7.0] | [6.7] | – | [4.9] |
| 5,001-10,000 | 9 | 6 | 5 | 2 | 22 |
| | (40.9) | (27.3) | (22.7) | (9.1) | (100.0) |
| | [5.4] | [8.5] | [11.1] | [33.3] | [7.6] |
| 10,001-20,000 | 41 | 32 | 21 | 1 | 95 |
| | (43.2) | (33.7) | (22.1) | (1.1) | (100.0) |
| | [24.7] | [45.1] | [46.7] | [16.7] | [33.0] |
| 20,001-30,000 | 33 | 17 | 6 | 2 | 58 |
| | (56.9) | (29.3) | (10.3) | (3.4) | (100.0) |
| | [19.9] | [23.9] | [13.3] | [33.3] | [20.1] |
| 30,001-50,000 | 65 | 11 | 6 | 1 | 83 |
| | (78.3) | (13.3) | (7.2) | (1.2) | (100.0) |
| | [39.2] | [15.5] | [13.3] | [16.7] | [28.8] |
| >50,001 | 12 | – | 4 | – | 16 |
| | (75.0) | – | (25.0) | – | (100.0) |
| | [7.2] | – | [8.9] | – | [5.6] |
| Total | 166 | 71 | 45 | 6 | 288 |
| | (57.6) | (24.7) | (15.6) | (2.1) | (100.0) |
| | [100.0] | [100.0] | [100.0] | [100.0] | [100.0] |

NOTE: The figures in round brackets show the row percentages, while the figures in square brackets show the column percentages.

SOURCE: Survey (Shinoda,1991).

of lower than Rs. 10,000 would suggest that the household had no permanent worker among its members. The latter generally falls into the category of urban poor. With well developed legal protection and active trade unions, the household income of the municipal sweepers is higher than those of other local bodies. There is hardly any difference in the income distribution pattern of households between the Municipalities and Nagar Panchayats owing to the similar conditions of legal protection and trade unions.

Per capita income, in the context of the present survey, is a useful criterion to assess the distribution of actual economic power and to demarcate the urban poor. Since per capita income is calculated by dividing the annual household income by the number of family members, let us first examine the distribution of households by family size. As Table 6.14 shows, the distribution of household members ranges from 2 to 18. The average household size in the sample is 6.3, which is 1.2 persons larger than the Gujarat state urban average of 5.1 (44th National Sample Survey, 1989). Thus, the distributed per capita income is lower than it appears to be. In

TABLE 6.14: DISTRIBUTION OF HOUSEHOLDS BY FAMILY SIZE

*(no. of households, persons, %)*

| Family size | Households | | | Persons | | |
|---|---|---|---|---|---|---|
| | Number | Percentage | Cumulative percentage | Number | Percentage | Cumulative percentage |
| 2 | 6 | 2.1 | 2.1 | 12 | 0.7 | 0.7 |
| 3 | 12 | 4.2 | 6.3 | 36 | 2.0 | 2.6 |
| 4 | 34 | 11.8 | 18.1 | 136 | 7.5 | 10.1 |
| 5 | 62 | 21.5 | 39.6 | 310 | 17.1 | 27.2 |
| 6 | 60 | 20.8 | 60.4 | 360 | 19.8 | 47.0 |
| 7 | 50 | 17.4 | 77.8 | 350 | 19.3 | 66.2 |
| 8 | 24 | 8.3 | 86.1 | 192 | 10.6 | 76.8 |
| 9 | 19 | 6.6 | 92.7 | 171 | 9.4 | 86.2 |
| 10 | 6 | 2.1 | 94.8 | 60 | 3.3 | 89.5 |
| 11 | 7 | 2.4 | 97.2 | 77 | 4.2 | 93.7 |
| 12 | 3 | 1.1 | 98.3 | 36 | 2.0 | 95.7 |
| 13 | 2 | 0.7 | 99.0 | 26 | 1.4 | 97.1 |
| 17 | 2 | 0.7 | 99.7 | 34 | 1.9 | 99.0 |
| 18 | 1 | 0.3 | 100.0 | 18 | 1.0 | 100.0 |
| Total | 288 | 100.0 | 100.0 | 1,818 | 100.0 | 100.0 |

SOURCE: Survey (Shinoda, 1991).

the light of the criterion of the Planning Commission for the urban poor during the Seventh Five-Year Plan, the urban poor may be referred to a group whose annual per capita income does not reach Rs. 1,500. Table 6.15 shows that, according to this criterion, 9.4 per cent of the sample households can be classified as urban poor. This is a very low figure for the backward groups, confirming that urban Bhangis as a community no longer fall into the category of urban poor. Here again, the percentage of the urban poor in the Municipal Corporation is relatively smaller than those in other local bodies. Also there is not much difference in the distribution pattern of per capita income between the Municipalities and the Nagar Panchayats.

TABLE 6.15: DISTRIBUTION OF HOUSEHOLDS BY ANNUAL PER CAPITA INCOME AND TYPE OF LOCAL BODY

*(no. of households, %)*

| Per capita income (Rs.) | Municipal Corporation | Municipality | Nagar Panchayat | Gram Panchayat | Total |
|---|---|---|---|---|---|
| <1,500 | 13 | 7 | 7 | – | 27 |
| | (48.2) | (25.9) | (25.9) | – | (100.0) |
| | [7.8] | [9.9] | [15.6] | – | [9.4] |
| 1,501-2,500 | 21 | 15 | 6 | 2 | 44 |
| | (47.7) | (34.1) | (13.6) | (4.6) | (100.0) |
| | [12.7] | [21.1] | [13.3] | [33.3] | [15.3] |
| 2,501-4,000 | 41 | 26 | 21 | 2 | 90 |
| | (45.6) | (28.9) | (23.3) | (2.2) | (100.0) |
| | [24.7] | [36.6] | [46.7] | [33.3] | [31.2] |
| 4,001-6,000 | 50 | 16 | 3 | 1 | 70 |
| | (71.4) | (22.9) | (4.3) | (1.4) | (100.0) |
| | [30.1] | [22.6] | [6.7] | [16.7] | [24.3] |
| 6,001-8,000 | 29 | 4 | 6 | – | 39 |
| | (74.3) | (10.3) | (15.4) | – | (100.0) |
| | [17.5] | [5.6] | [13.3] | – | [13.5] |
| >8,001 | 12 | 3 | 2 | 1 | 18 |
| | (66.7) | (16.7) | (11.1) | (5.5) | (100.0) |
| | [7.2] | [4.2] | [4.4] | [16.7] | [6.3] |
| Total | 166 | 71 | 45 | 6 | 288 |
| | (57.6) | (24.7) | (15.6) | (2.1) | (100.0) |
| | [100.0] | [100.0] | [100.0] | [100.0] | [100.0] |

NOTE: The figures in round brackets show the row percentages, while the figures in square brackets show the column percentages.

SOURCE: Survey (Shinoda, 1991).

### DEBT

Together with income, debt is a useful criterion to assess the financial position of sweepers. Previous studies refer to the heavy burden of debt that sweepers bear.[35] Officials in the cleaning services and social workers familiar with Bhangi customs also confirm that sweepers are captured by debts due to their low income and high expenditure on religious and social occasions and also, through gambling and drinking.[36] Debt, therefore, is one of the factors contributing to the economic and social backwardness of Bhangis.

It is generally difficult to obtain accurate information about debt. As debt is a symbol of dependency for backward groups, respondents naturally find it hard to discuss it. As a result the survey probably underestimates the number of households in debt, its frequency and its amount. Since the survey focuses on major debts, smaller debts are totally unreported. Further, most respondents tend to give only one reason for their debts, so that the distribution of reasons for debt is somewhat distorted. Despite these limitations, it is still possible to trace the broad trends in debt among the sample households.

Table 6.16 shows that 187 households (65 per cent) have received loans from institutional lending bodies, which include the various types of credit unions and banks. Though advances taken out against the provident fund are not considered as debts, it is included here under debt for convenience, since it is one way of raising money to make ends meet. A major source of institutional debt are the credit unions, which account for 82.9 per cent of such finance. Loans from banks are less common than from credit unions, because of the severity of the guarantees and the higher interest rates, and account for 13.4 per cent of the loans. Loans drawn against the provident fund are rarer than expected, there are only seven cases altogether. Institutional liability is very common in the Municipal Corporation, accounting for 72.3 per cent of the surveyed households. In the municipalities it is less common with a share of 47.9 per cent of households. The ratio of Nagar Panchayats falls in between.

The range of institutional loans is between Rs. 300 and 70,000 for a single loan; the average is Rs. 8,474. This average varies with the local body; it is Rs. 9,770 in the AMC, Rs. 6,917 in the Municipalities and Rs. 5,715 in the Nagar Panchayats. Nothing is wrong in getting a loan if it is for productive purposes, such as education or business. However, as Table 6.17 shows, the reasons for debt have no such productive purpose. The performance of marriage is given as supposed, the main reason for

TABLE 6.16: DISTRIBUTION OF HOUSEHOLDS BY THE SOURCE OF INSTITUTIONAL LOANS AND TYPE OF LOCAL BODY

*(no. of households, %)*

| Source | Municipal Corporation | Municipality | Nagar Gram Panchayat | Total |
|---|---|---|---|---|
| Credit union | 99<br>(82.5) | 27<br>(79.4) | 29<br>(87.9) | 155<br>(82.9) |
| Bank | 18<br>(15.0) | 4<br>(11.8) | 3<br>(9.1) | 25<br>(13.4) |
| Provident fund | 3<br>(2.5) | 3<br>(3.8) | 1<br>(3.0) | 7<br>(3.7) |
| Total | 120<br>(100.0)<br>[64.2] | 34<br>(100.0)<br>[18.2] | 33<br>(100.0)<br>[17.6] | 187<br>(100.0)<br>[100.0] |

NOTE: The figures in round brackets show the column percentages. The figures in square brackets show the row percentages.

SOURCE: Survey (Shinoda, 1991).

borrowing money, accounting for 44 per cent of the cases of institutional loans. Marriage ceremonies seem to be a heavy burden on the finances of sweepers,[37] and this is confirmed by the present survey. The average marriage expense for a man is around Rs. 10,000 and for a woman Rs. 15,000. Since the average monthly income of the sample households is around Rs. 2,000, this represents five months earnings in the case of a man and eight months in the case of a woman. In proportion to the annual income this does not seem too heavy, being much smaller than that of the urban middle classes. But in order to assess the impact of wedding expenses it is also necessary to take into consideration their average family size and weak financial base. Family size generally corresponds with the frequency of marriage and a fresh debt is likely to be a burden on a household whose financial base is already weak. The second major reason for debt is household expenditure, including medical and child delivery expenses, which accounts for 21 per cent of the loans. This large proportion indicates the lack of savings and the chronic financial weakness among the sweeper households. The third reason is the construction and repair of houses, amounting to 17 per cent of the total. Of particular importance is the 9 per cent which is used to settle other loans.

In general the terms and conditions of institutional loans are better than those of private loans, but all the same they have a number of limitations, the main being the unfamiliarity of workers with procedures,

TABLE 6.17: DISTRIBUTION OF REASONS FOR INSTITUTIONAL LOANS

| Reason | Frequency | Percentage |
|---|---|---|
| Wedding | 81 | 44.0 |
| Other religious events | 9 | 4.9 |
| Household expenditure | 33 | 17.9 |
| Medical treatment | 4 | 2.2 |
| Childbirth | 2 | 1.1 |
| House construction | 17 | 9.2 |
| House repair | 14 | 7.6 |
| Settling other debts | 16 | 8.7 |
| Others | 8 | 4.4 |
| Total | 184 | 100.0 |

SOURCE: Survey (Shinoda, 1991).

the resultant intervention by middlemen, and the relatively longer waiting period for the loan to be processed. Another limitation is that only a small segment of the society is able to have access to institutional loans. By contrast private loans are easy to access and are available immediately, although their interest rates are higher.

As Table 6.18 presents, the main source of private loans is the *mahajan*, the professional money lender. It accounts for 72 per cent of the total cases of private loans, followed by relatives and private loan institutions. Since the private liability of small amounts is totally unreported, the actual number of cases of private loans would surpass that of institutional loans.

The average amount of a private loan is Rs. 5,479 which is lower than the average amount of institutional loan by Rs. 3,000. It varies from Rs. 6,465 in the Municipal Corporation to Rs. 5,150 in the Municipalities, and Rs. 4,187 in the Nagar Panchayats. Here again, the average amount of the Municipal Corporation surpasses the amount of other local bodies. However, the frequency of private loans is much less than that of the institutional loans in the Municipal Corporation, while in the Municipalities and Nagar Panchayats, the sweeper households make frequent use of private loans as institutional loans are not easily accessible.

The interest rate of private loans varies from 2 to 15 per cent per month. The average monthly rate is 5.95 per cent, which is equal to a simple interest rate of 71.4 per cent per year. Since it takes more than one year to repay the amount in most of the cases, the prevalence of private loans tends to further deteriorate the financial basis of sweeper households.

The major reason for private loans differs from that of the institutional loans. As Table 6.19 shows, household expenditure in a broad sense shares

TABLE 6.18: DISTRIBUTION OF HOUSEHOLDS BY THE SOURCE OF PRIVATE LOANS AND TYPE OF LOCAL BODY

*(no. of households, %)*

| Source | Municipal Corporation | Municipality | Nagar Gram Panchayat | Total |
|---|---|---|---|---|
| Relatives | 7<br>(14.9) | 4<br>(10.5) | 7<br>(21.9) | 18<br>(15.4) |
| Mahajan | 30<br>(63.8) | 30<br>(79.0) | 24<br>(75.0) | 84<br>(71.8) |
| Private loan institution | 10<br>(21.3) | 4<br>(10.5) | 1<br>(3.1) | 15<br>(12.8) |
| Total | 47<br>(100.0)<br>[40.2] | 38<br>(100.0)<br>[32.5] | 32<br>(100.0)<br>[27.3] | 117<br>(100.0)<br>[100.0] |

NOTE: The figures in round brackets show the column percentages. The figures in square brackets show the row percentages.

SOURCE: Survey (Shinoda, 1991).

nearly 44 per cent of the total cases of private loans. Thus, the basic maintenance of a family is the major reason for private loans. Wedding comes scond in the frequency of reasons with its share slightly less than 30 per cent, followed by construction and repair of houses. Again there are several cases of private loans for setting other private debts to escape the immediate threat and pressure.

## CONCLUSION

As regards the institutional climate, there is a considerable gap between the large and small local bodies. The level of wages and various allowances, the availability of labour unions and financial institutions are in favour of the large local bodies, while the workers in the small local bodies suffer from low wages, unstable service conditions and less accessibility to labour unions and financial institutions.

The household survey reveals a high concentration of the Bhangi workers in sweeping work. Most of them are employed by the local bodies either as permanent or temporary workers, while a few work as sweepers or scavengers under private contract or the *gharaki* system. The male occupational structure is slightly more diversified than that of the female worker, but that diversification is quite limited even compared with the other Scheduled Castes.

Occupational mobility among Bhangis centres on promotion from

TABLE 6.19: DISTRIBUTION OF REASONS FOR PRIVATE LOANS

| Reason | Frequency | Percentage |
|---|---|---|
| Wedding | 33 | 28.2 |
| Other religious events | 1 | 0.9 |
| Household expenditure | 37 | 31.6 |
| Medical treatment | 11 | 9.4 |
| Childbirth | 3 | 2.6 |
| House construction | 12 | 10.3 |
| House repair | 3 | 2.6 |
| Settling other debts | 3 | 2.6 |
| Others | 14 | 11.8 |
| Total | 117 | 100.0 |

SOURCE: Survey (Shinoda, 1991).

temporary to permanent status as sweepers employed by local bodies. The occupational mobility for a better job is rarely observed due to social, occupational discrimination and their lack of competitive drive.

The debt survey shows that a large number of Bhangi households are ensnared by debt, caused by the weakness of their financial base and undue expenditure on weddings and funerals. The household dependence on private lending institutions is destructive as it depletes the family income.

The argument that the local bodies should raise the level of wages of the sweepers to encourage their socio-economic development holds good for the sweepers employed by small local bodies. However, it is less applicable to the sweepers employed by large local bodies. It is a serious issue that those employed by large local bodies still remain backward inspite of having relatively better institutional climate and service conditions.

The sweepers have been downtrodden for quite long and their consciousness is thus moulded. Any improvement of the institutional climate and their service and working conditions may surely provide them a material basis for their socio-economic development. However, actual development may take place in the wake of a massive movement to overcome their internal weakness and social contradictions.

## NOTES

1. Government of Saurashtra, *Saurashtra Safai Kamdaro Angeni Rivyu Samitino* (Vyas Samiti) Aheval (in Gujarati), 1956.
2. Ibid., pp. 105-7.

3. Ibid., p. 109.
4. Ibid., pp. 111-12.
5. Ibid., p. 114.
6. Ibid., pp. 115-16.
7. Ibid., p. 117.
8. Ibid., p. 126.
9. Ibid., p. 127.
10. Ibid., p. 129.
11. Ibid., pp. 129-30.
12. Government of Gujarat compiles documents of various departments regarding sweepers and scavengers circulated among local bodies. See Government of Gujarat (Department of Social Welfare), *Bhangi Kasht Mukti Karyakram* (in Gujarati), Ahmedabad, 1972.
13. Ibid., pp. 11-13.
14. Ibid., p. 26.
15. Ibid., pp. 27-8.
16. Ibid., p. 30.
17. Oral information from Ishwarbhai Patel, the Director, Safai Vidyalaya (August 1991). The first Gujarat Political Conference, chaired by M.K. Gandhi was held at Godhra, Panch Mahals in 1917. Gandhi, after coming to know that the children of sweepers were not allowed to attend school, decided to set up a school for the children of the Untouchables. He opened the Harijan Ashram at Godhra in 1919, and entrusted its management to Phadke. At present, the Ashram is run by the Harijan Sevak Sangh.
18. J. Jairamdas, *Bhangi Kasht Mukti and Bhangi Mukti*, New Delhi: National Committee for Gandhi Centenary, 1969.
19. Government of Gujarat, op. cit., p. 35.
20. Ibid., pp. 34-5.
21. Ibid., p. 84.
22. National Sanitation Improvement Foundation, *Organizing Voluntary Action for Promotion of Low Cost Sanitation in Gujarat*, New Delhi: Consortium of Rural Technology, 1991, p. 5.
23. Government of India (Ministry of Rural Development), *Status of Rural Sanitation Programme in States and UTs*, New Delhi, 1992, p. 13.
24. National Sanitation Improvement Foundation, op. cit., p. 6.
25. Government of India (Ministry of Rural Development), op. cit., p. 10.
26. National Sanitation Improvement Foundation, op. cit., p. 8.
27. Government of India (Ministry of Rural Development), op. cit., p. 11.
28. Ibid.
29. National Sanitation Improvement Foundation, op. cit., p. 10.
30. Government of India (Ministry of Rural Development), op. cit., p. 11.
31. National Sanitation Improvement Foundation, op. cit., p. 1.
32. Ibid., p. 5.
33. Oral information from the Department of Social Welfare (August 1992).
34. It is common among small and medium local bodies to employ sweepers as part time workers to bypass the Minimum Wage Act. Out of the eight local bodies surveyed, Bareja and Sola had no permanent sweepers.

35. Besides Vyas Committee, Pandya Committee also supports the argument that debt was so common among the Bhangis.
36. Both P.U. Asnani, Deputy Commissioner, The Ahmedabad Municipal Corporation and Ishwarbhai Patel, Safai Vidyalaya confirm that sweepers are captured by debt traps.
37. Oral information from P.U. Asnani and Ishwarbhai Patel (August 1991).

Chapter Seven

# Epilogue: Social Development of Sweepers: Prospects and Challenges

## Scope of the Present Study

The approach that this study uses is made up of the weft of institutional reform and the warp of the analysis of group and individual mobility. By doing so it attempts grasp the direction in which the Scheduled Castes, and the Bhangis in particular are moving.

A special feature of this work as a analytical study of institutional reform is that it gives priority to reforms at the municipal level. Institutional reform within local bodies, the chief employers of sweepers, directly regulates the employment and working conditions of sweepers, and thus their living standards. In this sense, the most important institutional reforms as far as the Bhangis are concerned are those which occur at the municipal level. Moves by local bodies in these areas have actually determinèd the direction of Bhangi liberation.

The acquisition of political power is of great importance for the social development of backward groups, since the extent to which those groups were able to gain educational and occupational opportunities and other benefits derived from the various institutional reforms and their political power. The political backwardness of the Bhangis is the primary factor in the growing developmental differential between them and the other advanced groups of the Scheduled Castes.

An internal reform movement provides an important opportunity to overcome factors which might act as obstacles in the social development of a backward group as well as to mobilize resources important to that development. Following the growth of the trade union movement in Gujarat, trade unions have emerged as the strongest pressure group for the Bhangis. However, trade union activities have been restricted to improving employment conditions. The improvement of working conditions has been limited to areas which do not hinder the betterment of employment conditions. Like a large number of unions, the Bhangis themselves have not tended to look beyond immediate objectives, and they have not promoted their own associations for internal reform.

The unions have not called for group mobility, but Bhangi household income has risen as a result of increases in sweeper employment quotas by local bodies and the improvement of employment conditions. Of course, there is a large differential among local bodies depending on whether or not a union exists and how active it is, but over all the unions have played an extremely important role in improving the employment conditions of Bhangis as a whole.

Household income is the most important factor in limiting the educational or occupational mobility of household members. Though the level of Bhangi household income does not compare unfavourably with the average household income of the advanced groups of the Scheduled Castes, a great difference can be seen between them in terms of educational and occupational mobility. Despite the fact that Bhangi household income has improved, a number of structural reasons exist that encourage the continuation of their backwardness. Their high dependence on private moneylenders suggests a constant seepage from their income and the resources that could otherwise be mobilised for social advancement. Their adherence to their traditional occupation prevents from diversifying their occupational structure. Further, the development of the compensatory employment system encourages the continuation of their traditional occupation, which actually holds Bhangis to the lowest level of educational and occupational mobility.

The socio-economic condition of sweepers, and particularly the employment and working conditions of those employed by local bodies, have greatly improved since Independence. The development of employment policies among local bodies, the bettering of public hygiene facilities, the provision of legislation and the growth of the labour union movement, as well as the promotion of the Bhangi liberation movement, have all contributed to the improvement in employment and working conditions of sweepers. In Gujarat, the fruits of the Bhangi liberation movement have been particularly significant, and in the conversion of dry latrines it is far more advanced than other states.

Particularly interesting in terms of historical studies of the pre-Independence period are questions regarding the emergence and customs of scavengers. Dry latrines came into use under the Mughals, which suggests that scavengers also emerged at that time. Under British rule dry latrines proliferated in urban areas. At the same time, in northern and western India, customary rights came into being among scavengers. There was also a great deal of movement by the sweeper caste into areas where such castes had not emerged spontaneously. Customary rights of scavengers gave rise to various abuses, such as a lowering of service standards by scavengers and a subcontracting system. In addition, the participation of the sweeper caste in scavenging greatly lowered the sweepers' social position. The municipalization of customary rights by local bodies was promoted after Independence by means of compensatory payments for holders and their employment as cleaners by local bodies.

An historical process by which the scavenger class formed proves that scavengers were no more than a product of early modern society. Though there is a severe lack of documentary evidence, historical research can be a stimulus for social reform for the sweeper caste, in the same way as Phule's studies provided a stimulus for the Mahar social liberation movement.

### Prospects for the Bhangi Liberation Movement

This study is based on materials that were available hand up till 1993. However, a number of important materials concerning the Bhangi liberation movement were made public after that year. I will bring my study to an end by considering the latest trends within the movement as seen in these documents and comment on its future prospects.

The central and state governments have established since 1950 a number of investigatory committees with the intent of abolishing scavenging. While their briefs and recommendations differed slightly from one another, their recommendations stimulated improvements in the employment and working conditions of scavengers with legislative support for the conversion of dry latrines. In the early 1980s, much aid was received from international organizations for low cost sanitation programmes for both urban and rural areas. Despite variations among states, the conversion of dry latrines and the absorption of scavengers into the ranks of sweepers have proceeded to a certain extent throughout India.[1]

The *Basu Task Force Report* of 1991 looked at what had been achieved in the 1980s and made recommendations. Its main points were the abolition of the many remaining dry latrines and the provision of other forms of employment to scavengers. In response, the Ministry of Welfare introduced the National Scheme of Liberation and Rehabilitation of Scavengers and Their Dependents to confirm its strategy in the Eighth Five-Year Plan (1992-7).[2] The purpose of the National Scheme was to completely abolish dry latrines, and incorporate all scavengers and their dependents into other forms of work in the course of the Eighth Five-Year Plan. Conversion of dry latrines to flush latrines was to be carried out under the supervision of the Ministry of Urban Development and the re-employment of scavengers was to be under the Ministry of Welfare.[3]

The National Scheme estimated, based on the *Basu Task Force Report*, that in 1989 there were 400,000 scavengers in India. The distribution was 83 per cent in urban areas and 17 per cent in rural areas, with the proportion of women being 21 per cent in rural areas, 38 per cent in urban areas, and 35 per cent of the total scavenger population. These are the estimated numbers of workers from the Scheduled Castes; the total scavengers including non-Scheduled Caste scavengers are estimated to be around 500,000.[4] The National Scheme defined a scavenger as 'one who is partially or wholly engaged in the obnoxious and inhuman occupation of manually removing night soil and filth'.[5] Ordinary sweepers not engaged in the removal of night-soil from dry latrines were also included in the scope of the definition.

Scavengers and their dependents were the subjects of the re-employment scheme, including those who did not belong to the Scheduled Castes. The rehabilitation of those employed by local bodies was to be the responsibility of the local bodies. Re-training was restricted to workers in the 15-50 age group.[6]

The National Scheme indicated that it would organize a simple survey to ascertain the desires of scavengers and their dependents regarding the type of work they would like to move into; and that this would be completed by 30 June 1992. The survey questionnaire consisted of eight basic items: name of respondent; whether or not it belonged to a Scheduled Caste; name, age and marital status of family members; education; whether or not it engaged in scavenging work; yearly wage; desired occupation; and remarks.[7] A list of the types of possible occupations was attached to the questionnaire. The occupations covered four sectors: agriculture, small industries, service and business. The agricultural sector listed 10 types of work, including dairying and sericulture; the small industries sector listed 16 types, including flour milling and power looms; the service sector listed 33 types, including vehicle repair and tailoring, and the business sector listed 26 types, including tea-shops and furniture manufacture.[8] The survey was carried out at the district level. District level Scheduled Castes and Scheduled Tribes Corporations made estimates of potential beneficiaries, and the information was filled in with the help of District Collectors.

The survey was carried out in all but two districts of Gujarat state. The results are shown in Table 7.1. Unfortunately, those surveyed were not

TABLE 7.1: RESULTS OF THE OCCUPATIONAL CHOICE SURVEY, GUJARAT (1993/4)

(*persons %*)

| District | Wanting occupational retraining | | | | | | | | Not Wanting | Total |
|---|---|---|---|---|---|---|---|---|---|---|
| | Tailor | Driver | Car repair | Embr-oidery | Radio repair | Weav-ing | Other | Sub-total | | |
| Jamnagar | 152 | 89 | 97 | 48 | 6 | 0 | 32 | 424 | 1,086 | 1,510 |
| Rajkot | 164 | 121 | 98 | 22 | 7 | 21 | 14 | 447 | 768 | 1,215 |
| Surendranagar | 356 | 288 | 35 | 30 | 14 | 0 | 46 | 769 | 1,840 | 2,609 |
| Bhavnagar | 399 | 390 | 176 | 156 | 96 | 333 | 220 | 1,770 | 2,519 | 4,289 |
| Amreli | 315 | 238 | 233 | 213 | 13 | 10 | 88 | 1,110 | 3,412 | 4,522 |
| Junagadh | 36 | 20 | 19 | 17 | 19 | 0 | 28 | 139 | 5,799 | 5,938 |
| Kutch | 55 | 115 | 20 | 60 | 5 | 1 | 28 | 284 | 1,205 | 1,489 |
| Banaskantha | 32 | 113 | 32 | 62 | 5 | 82 | 36 | 362 | 3,370 | 3,732 |
| Sabarkantha | 333 | 343 | 91 | 60 | 35 | 3 | 83 | 948 | 2,407 | 3,355 |
| Mehsana | 125 | 332 | 51 | 58 | 45 | 0 | 49 | 660 | 2,406 | 3,066 |
| Gandhinagar | 149 | 78 | 25 | 6 | 3 | 0 | 14 | 275 | 388 | 663 |
| Ahmedabad (R) | 95 | 184 | 92 | 83 | 18 | 0 | 30 | 502 | 3,462 | 3,964 |
| Ahmedabad (U) | 5,232 | 1,101 | 28 | 10 | 542 | 0 | 238 | 7,151 | 5,750 | 12,901 |
| Kheda | 176 | 356 | 20 | 26 | 14 | 2 | 48 | 642 | 6,250 | 6,892 |
| Panchmahals | 34 | 34 | 63 | 2 | 1 | 0 | 35 | 169 | 1,293 | 1,462 |
| Surat | 21 | 23 | 2 | 1 | 1 | 0 | 6 | 54 | 271 | 325 |
| Valsad | 17 | 33 | 2 | 0 | 4 | 0 | 5 | 61 | 122 | 183 |
| Total | 7,691 | 3,858 | 114 | 1154 | 8211 | 452 | 1,000 | 15,767 | 42,348 | 58,115 |
| | (48.8) | (24.5) | (6.9) | (5.4) | (5.3) | (2.9) | (6.2) | (100.0) | | |
| | – | – | – | – | – | – | – | [27.1] | [72.9] | [100.0] |

NOTES: The survey was not completed in the districts of Panchmahals and Bharuch. (R) refers to rural areas, (U) to urban.
The figures in round brackets show those who wanted a particular type of work as a percentage of all those who wanted work.
The figures in square brackets show those who wanted work and those who did not want work as a percentage of the persons surveyed.

SOURCE: Gujarat Scheduled Caste Economic Development Corporation Ltd., *National Scheme of Liberation & Rehabilitation of Scavengers and Their Dependents Survey Report*, Gandhinagar, 1993/4, pp. 1-2.

distinguished by sex, or, other than in Ahmedabad District, by area-whether rural or urban. Nor was there any distinction between scavengers and their dependents among those who wished for retraining. Despite these shortcomings, we may trace the overall trend of those who had wanted re-training, according to occupation. Of the 58,115 people who had responded, 15,767 (27 per cent) wanted re-training and 42,348 (73 per cent) did not. The high proportion of sweepers not wanting re-training is revealing. Since changing jobs involves a high risk, it may be surmised that the majority of those not wanting to change jobs must have been permanent employees of local bodies.

The National Scheme suggested a variety of occupations for re-training, but the Gujarat survey results show a trend that is restricted to a few areas, notably tailoring and driving (four-wheeled vehicles and rickshaws), accounting for the choice of 73 per cent of the aspirants. Table 7.1 lists only 6 types of occupations, though 18 were reported in the survey. These were omitted for lack of space. The remaining 12 occupations had the following number of aspirants: video and photo shops (261), typing and shorthand (180), car repair (154), carpentry (121), furniture manufacture (63), clock repair (51), welding (51), printing (33), toy manufacture (28), diamond cutting (27), screenprinting (18) and copying (13). The objective of training was the acquisition of technical skills. The occupations chosen by women were likely to be limited to sewing and tailoring, embroidery, weaving and screen printing. There were also considerable regional variations in the choice of occupation.

The National Scheme stipulated that those interested in re-training be given between one and six months of training at the nearest government or private facility. The cost of training was estimated to be Rs. 500 per month for each person, including an allowance of up to Rs. 150 per month for the trainee.[9] Table 7.2 shows projections of the number of trainees and costs of the scheme for the Eighth Five-Year Plan. During the plan period, 350,000 people were to be trained at a cost of Rs. 1 billion.

Besides, as Table 7.3 shows, a special subsidy/loan plan was prepared for the self-employed who did not need any occupational training. During the five years, 400,000 beneficiaries were anticipated, and Rs. 8 billion budgeted. This plan included subsidy and loan to the tune of Rs. 50,000 for those who wished to be self-employed. It included 50 per cent of running costs (up to Rs. 10,000) in subsidy and 15 per cent of running costs at a yearly interest of 4 per cent (margin money); the rest was to be provided by a bank loan. The Scheduled Castes Development Corporation was to be the chief provider of low interest finance. Subsidy and loan for

TABLE 7.2: THE PLANNED RETRAINING SCHEME BY YEAR

(*persons, Rs. 10,000*)

| Year | Planned numbers of persons to be trained | Total costs |
|---|---|---|
| 1992/3 | 42,000 | 12,600 |
| 1993/4 | 100,000 | 30,000 |
| 1994/5 | 100,000 | 30,000 |
| 1995/6 | 108,000 | 32,400 |
| Total | 350,000 | 105,000 |

SOURCE: Government of India, Ministry of Welfare, *National Scheme of Liberation & Rehabilitation of Scavengers and Their Dependents*, New Delhi, 1991/2, p. 11.

the average running costs of a business were calculated at Rs. 20,000.[10]

Costs for training and subsidy for the self-employed were to be borne by the central government. In the provision of low interest finance, the central and state governments were responsible for 49 per cent and 51 per cent respectively. Thus, the central government was the financial pillar of support.[11]

The National Scheme was organized at three administrative levels: the central government, the state governments and the districts. The Ministry of Welfare was the organizing facility at a national level, and it had the responsibility for putting the scheme into action throughout the country.

TABLE 7.3: THE PLANNED TRAINING SCHEME FOR THE SELF-EMPLOYED BY YEAR

(*persons, Rs. 10,000*)

| Year | Planned numbers of beneficiaries | Subsidies, loans | | | |
|---|---|---|---|---|---|
| | | Subsidies | Low interest loans | Bank loans | Total |
| 1992/3 | 42,000 | 42,000 | 12,600 | 29,400 | 84,000 |
| 1993/4 | 65,000 | 65,000 | 19,500 | 45,500 | 130,000 |
| 1994/5 | 80,000 | 80,000 | 24,000 | 56,000 | 160,000 |
| 1995/6 | 100,000 | 100,000 | 30,000 | 70,000 | 200,000 |
| 1996/7 | 113,000 | 113,000 | 33,900 | 79,100 | 226,000 |
| Total | 400,000 | 400,000 | 120,000 | 280,000 | 800,000 |

SOURCE: Government of India, Ministry of Welfare, *National Scheme of Liberation & Rehabilitation of Scavengers and Their Dependents*, New Delhi, 1991/2, p. 14.

A Central Monitoring Committee was also set up to monitor implementation of the scheme and to make necessary adjustments. The National Scheduled Castes and Scheduled Tribes Finance and Development Corporation was responsible for the day-to-day running of the scheme and maintained close links with its state representatives. At the state level, Welfare Departments for the Scheduled Castes were responsible for the running of the scheme and remained in close contact with departments dealing with urban development, industrial development, rural development, labour, technical education and institutional financing, and with the central government. A State Monitoring Committee consisted of representatives from the concerned departments, local bodies, the scavengers, and leading banks. The State Scheduled Castes Finance and Development Corporation was chiefly responsible for the running of the scheme and for re-training sweepers. District Collectors had the main responsibility at the local level. Monitoring included two scavenger representatives and members from related departments. The district managers of the District Scheduled Castes Finance and Development Corporations looked after the everyday running of the scheme. Other than the above three strata, areas where the scavenger population of a local body or a mohalla exceeded 100 persons, a small municipal or mohalla level committee was also formed with scavenger representatives to assist in the identification of scavengers and to hold public discussions.[12]

The National Scheme stipulated that the role of the various organs at the three levels of national, state and district government be interrelated, with the Ministry of Welfare as the central authority. However, as there were no scavenger or scholarly representatives at the ministry, it was predicted that this would cause difficulties in the determination and revision of the scheme, and in its supervision. Already the National Commission for the Scheduled Castes and Scheduled Tribes had been set up to plan and monitor various programmes concerning the Scheduled Castes and Tribes, and there was a great concern to establish a separate legal national commission for sweepers.[13] This came into being with the National Commission for Safai Karamcharis Act of 22 April 1993. The Act defined a sweeper as 'a person engaged in or employed for manually carrying human excreta'.[14] The Act acknowledged the fact that a large number of sweepers, besides the narrow category of scavengers, had to deal with excreta in one or other ways. Accordingly, it included in its scope of 'sweeper' all workers engaged in any kind of cleaning activity.[15] The Act, its purpose being the liberation and rehabilitation of all sweepers in the course of the eighth Five Year Plan, gave the National Commission sweeping authority to recommend special plans of action to the central government, assess the functioning of the scheme and recommend improvements in collaboration and coordination between the central and state governments, investigate complaints regarding the scheme and to issue warnings about non-performance, and collect various reports about the plan from the government, local bodies and other interested parties.[16] In addition, the National Commission was entrusted with preparing periodic reports on the functioning of the scheme, and communicate any problems that might arise to the central and state governments.

The National Commission was to consist of a chairman, a deputy chairman and five delegates, appointed by the central government. These individuals were to be knowledgeable in the area of socio-economic development and welfare of sweepers. At least one member was to be a woman.[17] It was accordingly inaugurated on 12 August 1994 with seven members. Five of these, including Mangi Lal Arya, the chairman, and I. P. D. Salappa, the deputy chairman, were of Scheduled Caste background. The lone woman delegate was Maya Devi of the All India Safai Mazdoor Congress. Ishwarbhai Patel of the Safai Vidyalaya was appointed as of the non-Scheduled Caste members.[18]

With the setting up of the National Commission, the structure was in place to promote the liberation and rehabilitation of sweepers as a time-bound programme to be completed in the course of the eighth Five Year Plan. As the current programme is under central government jurisdiction, the impact of the scheme should be more or less uniform among states. While the National Scheme is expected to have far reaching results, certain questions have emerged about the Scheme and its practicality. We shall now consider some of the important aspects of the National Scheme meant to improve the prospects of the sweepers in the coming decades.

First is the maintenance of records. The accurate keeping of records is indispensable not only for a correct evaluation of the Bhangi liberation movement but also for the setting of practical targets by the National Scheme. Unfortunately, some of the essential data have been unreliable, especially data on dry latrines that have been converted and the number that still remains to be done, and the population of scavengers and sweepers. Local bodies have no interest at all in collecting and maintaining such records. As a result, estimates by state government departments are considered to be public records.[19] The National Scheme has no plans to collect basic data or maintain and manage records. It is necessary that local bodies be organized as a matter of priority to collect information and maintain records in order to raise their efficiency in the functioning and monitoring of the National Scheme.

The second issue concerns the use and definition of the term 'scavenger'. All committees, from the Barve to the Basu Task Force, have defined scavengers as collectors of human waste as distinct from sweepers as street cleaners. On the other hand, the national census maintains a broad definition of 'scavenger', including it with sweepers, which invites confusion in a variety of ways. 'Scavengers' as used in the census is sometimes understood as scavengers in the narrow sense. The National Scheme, unlike the various committees that preceded it, includes in its definition of scavenger both workers who collect human waste and those who clean roads, who are normally known as sweepers. Thus, it follows the usage of the national census. The National Scheme's usage reflects a perceived need to make sweepers as a whole the object of the scheme. Furthermore, the scheme has broadened its concern to non-Scheduled Caste sweepers, including them too in its re-training and financial aid programmes. Its concern is thus broader than that of the preceding committees.

The third is the impact of the National Scheme on sweepers employed by local bodies. Though there are considerable differences in the employment and working conditions of sweepers among local bodies, permanent employment generally ensures a stable income. There are many instances where two or more members of the same household are employed by local bodies and their average household income is of a level that is more than sufficient for social development. However, social development of the group as a whole has not been realized so far. Because of this, the National Scheme has placed the responsibility for the rehabilitation of the local body workers on the local bodies themselves. However, they need to maintain the requisite number of sweepers and are in no position to encourage changes in occupation among sweepers. Those employed by local bodies, especially permanent workers are strongly inclined to cling to the benefits they already have and do not want to undertake the high risks involved with changing jobs. Temporary workers, virtually the reserve troops for permanent employment, are bound to their position by the compensatory employment scheme and the waiting list. It is difficult to think that under such conditions municipal sweepers will be inclined to make the move to alternative employment.

The fourth aspect is the role of private organizations. The National Scheme does not clearly stipulate the role of such bodies. The Safai

Vidyalaya in Gujarat, the Sulabh International in Bihar and the Gandhi Smarak Nidhi in Maharashtra have all played an important role in promoting the Bhangi liberation policy in their respective states. They have urged local bodies to develop alternative forms of latrines and to encourage owners of dry latrines to convert them, and have contributed in the training and education of officials and social activists at the grass-roots level. Such groups have tended to be based on Gandhian ideals. However, for the National Scheme's plans of rehabilitation to be effective, the cooperation of private organizations outside the Gandhi orbit is also required. The nature of the relationship between private organizations and the National Scheme would depend on local conditions, but at the same time it is important that those which have already proved effective in the Bhangi liberation movement be used as models in terms of their organization, and management. Their cooperation should be sought to develop mutual relationships at the state and local level.[20]

The fifth is the setup and reliability of the survey. The survey has a role of great importance within the scheme, since the determination and registration of beneficiaries is based upon it. Despite its importance, there are a number of problems concerning its setup and reliability. The main drawback of the survey has been that no prior information on the various occupations was provided to the respondents.[21] Sweepers had no practical knowledge of work outside their own jobs. Thus they based their selection of jobs on unreal expectations or attractive-sounding jobs. This is apparent in Gujarat's survey results, which were concentrated in a small number of occupations. Though the wishes of the people concerned are important in the selection of their occupation, at the same time the chances of their being absorbed into the occupation of choice must be examined. For example, the results of the survey in the Ahmedabad District and City showed that 5,232 sweepers wanted to become tailors and 1,101 sweepers wanted to become drivers. Even if the occupational training given was successful, such large numbers would hardly find employment. Thus before wishes of beneficiaries are assessed, it is necessary to provide information on the relevant occupations and job opportunities. Private organizations would be more suitable for this work than government departments.

The sixth is the crucial issue of provision of financial assistance and training for those who wish to be self-employed. People who have been forcibly isolated within society by their work based on the long-standing system of Untouchability and social restrictions on occupation will not find it easy to be independent in businesses, which require the fostering of new social relationships. The lack of know-how and capital will also make their entry into business difficult. The Gujarat results of the survey do not show in detail the distribution of the types of self-employment which were most favoured. The scheme intends to provide a maximum of Rs. 50,000 as financial aid to those who wish to set up an independent business. This amount could be regarded as the initial fixed capital. The scheme makes no mention at all of any benefits or help besides finance. Since it has no plans about marketing, it can be expected that many of the beneficiaries will have difficulties in the management of their business. To encourage sweepers to start business, protection would be necessary, which will necessitate further budget provisions.

The seventh issue concerns the revision of the reservation and promotion systems. This is not a subject taken up by the National Scheme. However, in order to diversify the occupational structure of sweepers and the Sweeper caste, an improvement in these two areas is essential. There is a need for reviewing the reservation policy in terms of removal of castes which as groups have already gained sufficient socio-economic growth for the benefit of other Scheduled Castes including the Bhangis. Likewise, there is the need to revise the promotion system for sweepers employed by the central and state governments and local bodies. The present system is confined to rises in the salary scale, not in job ranking, and sweepers cannot change departments even within the Class 4 jobs. If sweepers could be promoted to 'clean' work in a different department, the diversification of their occupational structure would be promoted on a larger scale. Because the National Scheme does not address the issues of reservation and promotion, the social effects of its occupational change programme and its promotion of self-employment will be severely circumscribed.

Finally, there is a connection between the National Scheme and the much needed internal reform of the Sweeper caste. The various institutional reforms which occurred after Independence strengthened the movements based on caste and caste associations. Advanced groups even within the Scheduled Castes organized themselves internally and mobilized their resources to gain an advantageous political position, and received full benefits of the reservation policy and other institutional measures aimed at the Scheduled Castes and economically weaker groups. After Independence, the most important factor in the widening of differences in the internal development of a caste was whether or not it had been able to respond successfully as a group to institutional reforms. The income level of the Sweeper caste has generally improved, but it has not been able to mobilize its resources as a group and so continues in a condition of isolation, both socially and politically. Labour unions have contributed in improving the employment and working conditions of sweepers, but they have not been able to act as a centripetal force in promoting internal reforms. The socio-economic development of the sweeper caste would be very difficult without such an organized reform movement.

The National Scheme is a plan to rehabilitate the individual. Surely it would be more effective to rehabilitate the group through development. One such way would be through a cooperative union, which would not only be conducive to occupational change and rehabilitation, but would act as the basic unit to strengthen the collective power of the Sweeper caste and mobilize it for internal reform and the acquizition of political power. A cooperative union would not be able to subsume all those who wanted a change in occupation, because of geographical and other limitations, but as a focus for rehabilitation and internal reform, it would certainly be able to play a part in releasing the Sweeper caste from its backwardness. Plans for occupational change and rehabilitation in the sweeper communities have long been emphasized by the Bhangi liberation movement, but it was only with the introduction of the National Scheme that any large-scale action had been taken. Because of the enormity of the problems and the attendant difficulties it will be difficult to reach the desired target in the course of the plan period. It is to be hoped that it will be continued as a national project even after the completion of the Plan, incorporating revisions as and when required. We have already seen that there are many troublesome issues that need to be rectified in the National Scheme, but it must be evaluated positively for its stated purpose of raising the Bhangi liberation movement to a new level.

## NOTES

1. The Council for Social Development evaluated the performance of the Low-Cost Sanitation Programmes in some states, which revealed that the number of substituted dry latrines amounted to 140,000 (83 per cent of the total dry latrines) in Maharashtra, 158,000 (51 per cent) in Andhra Pradesh, 108,000 (46 per cent) in Rajasthan and 19,000 (37 per cent) in Orissa. See B.D. Sinha, P.S.K. Menon and A.K. Ghosh, *Restoration of Human Dignity: Impact of Development Programmes on Scavengers*, New Delhi: Arnold Publishers, 1994, p. 58; B.D. Sinha and A.K. Ghosh, *Evaluation of Low Cost Sanitation: Liberation, Training & Rehabilitation of Scavengers*, New Delhi: Arnold Publishers, 1990, p. 44.
2. Government of India, Ministry of Welfare, *National Scheme of Liberation and Rehabilitation of Scavengers and Their Dependents*, New Delhi, 1991/2.
3. Ibid., p. 2.

4. Ibid., p. 3.
5. Ibid., p. 4.
6. Ibid., pp. 3-4.
7. Ibid., p. 26.
8. Ibid., pp. 27-30.
9. Ibid., pp. 4-5.
10. Ibid., p. 13.
11. Ibid., p. 14.
12. *National Scheme*, pp. 14-17.
13. The National Commission for Safai Karamcharis Bill (Bill No. 56 of 1993), 1993, p. 6.
14. Ibid., p.2.
15. As a term to denote various workers who are engaged in sweeping, scavenging and related works, the term Safai Karamcharis is better than the term scavengers.
16. The National Commission for Safai Karamcharis Bill, op. cit., pp. 3-4.
17. Ibid., p. 2.
18. A list of the members appeared in Government of India (Ministry of Welfare), Notification S.O. 592(E), 12 August 1994.
19. It is reported that the records are not well-maintained even in Gujarat, where the Bhangi Liberation Movement brought some positive changes. See B.D. Sinha and A.K. Ghosh, *Sanitation and Environment: Evaluation of Low-Cost Sanitation in Gujarat*, New Delhi: Arnold Publishers, 1994, p. 73.
20. One of the main reasons that Gujarat was taken up in the foregoing study was to examine whether Gujarat could be a good model for other states. The answer is in the negative according to Sinha and Ghosh. See ibid., pp. 7-73.
21. Oral information from Dr. Ishwarbhai Patel (August 1994).

# Bibliography


1. GOVERNMENT, SEMI-GOVERNMENT PUBLICATIONS

Ahmedabad Municipal Corporation, *Report on Census of Slums in Ahmedabad 1976*, Ahmedabad, 1977.

——, *Statistical Outline of Ahmedabad City 1988/89*, Ahmedabad, 1990.

Census of India 1931, Vol. 8, *Bombay Presidency*, Part 2, *Statistical Tables*, Bombay, 1933.

Government of Bombay, *Report of the Scavengers' Living Conditions Enquiry Committee*, Bombay, 1958.

Government of Gujarat, Directorate of Economics and Statistics, *Socio-Economic Review: Gujarat State 1993-94*, Gandhinagar, 1994.

Government of Gujarat, *District Gazetteer*, 19 vols, 1968-84.

——, *Eighth Five Year Plan 1992-97*, Gandhinagar, 1992.

——, *Handbook of Basic Statistics: Gujarat State 1969 to 1976*, Vol. 1, Gandhinagar, 1978.

——, Industries Commissionerate, *Industries in Gujarat* (Some Statistics), Gandhinagar, 1992.

——, *Perspective Plan of Gujarat 1974-84*, Vol.1, Ahmedabad, 1972.

——, *Report of the Gujarat State Land Commission*, 1979.

——, *Report of the Socially and Educationally Backward Classes Commission*, 2 vols., 1976.

——, *Report of the Socially and Educationally Backward Classes [Second] Commission*, 2 vols., 1983.

——, *Seventh Five Year Plan 1985-90*, Gandhinagar, 1986.

——, *Statistical Outline of Gujarat State 1987*, Gandhinagar, 1988.

——, Department of Social Welfare, *Bhangi Kasht Mukti Karyakram* (in Gujarati), Ahmedabad, *c*. 1972.

Government of Haryana, *Report of the Commission to Enquire into the Living Conditions of Safai Mazdoors Employed by Local Bodies and Private Scavengers Working in Haryana State, 1969-72*.

Government of India, Census of India 1961, Vol. V Gujarat, Part V-A, *Tables on Scheduled Castes and Scheduled Tribes*, 1964.

——, Census of India 1961, Vol. V Gujarat, Part IX, *Census Atlas*, 1965.

——, Census of India 1961, Vol. V Gujarat, Part V-B, No. 2, *The Shenvas: A Scheduled Caste of Gujarat*, 1972.

——, Census of India 1971, *Indian Census in Perspective*, New Delhi, 1971.

——, Census of India 1981, Series-5 Gujarat, Part III-A, *General Economic Tables*, 1986.

——, Census of India 1981, Series-5 Gujarat, Part IX (i), *Special Tables for Scheduled Castes*, 1988.

——, Census of India 1981, Series-5 Gujarat, Part IX (ii), *Special Tables for Scheduled Tribes*, 1988.

——, Ministry of Home Affairs, *Report of the Scavenging Conditions Enquiry Committee*, New Delhi, 1960.

——, Ministry of Rural Development, *Status of Rural Sanitation Programme in States and UTs*, New Delhi, 1992.

——, Ministry of Welfare, *National Scheme of Liberation and Rehabilitation of Scavengers and Their Dependents*, New Delhi, 1991-92.

——, National Commission on Labour, *Report of the Committee to Study the Working and Service Conditions of Sweepers and Scavengers*, Delhi, 1969.

——, Planning Commission, *Report of the Task Force for Tackling the Problems of Scavengers and Suggesting Measures to Abolish Scavenging with Particular Emphasis on Their Rehabilitation*, New Delhi, 1990-91.

——, *Reservation for Backward Classes: Mandal Commission Report of the Backward Classes Commission, 1980*, Delhi: Akalank Publications, 1991.

Government of Karnataka, *Report of the Committee on Improvement of Living and Working Conditions of Sweepers and Scavengers*, 1976.

Government of Saurashtra, *Saurashtrana Safai Kamdaro angeni Rivyu Samitino* (*Vyas Samiti*) *Aheval* (in Gujarati), 1956.

## 2. OTHER PUBLICATIONS

Aikara, Jacob, *Scheduled Castes & Higher Education: A Study of College Students in Bombay*, Poona: Dastane Ramchandra & Co., 1980.

Bailey, F.G., *Caste and the Economic Frontier*, Bombay: Oxford University Press, 1957.

Baker, C.J., *The Politics of South India 1920-1937*, New Delhi: Vikas Publishing House, 1976.

Bakshi, P.M. (comp. & ed.), *The Constitution of India with Comments*, Delhi: Universal Book Traders, 1991.

Benjamin, Joseph, *Scheduled Caste in Indian Politics and Society*, New Delhi, Ess Ess Publications, 1989.

Beteille, Andre, *Caste, Class and Power*, Berkeley: University of California Press, 1965.

Bhatt, Anil, *Caste, Class and Politics: An Empirical Profile of Social Stratification in Modern India*, Delhi: Manohar, 1975.

Bhattacharya, V.R., *New Strategy of Development in Village India: Progress under Revised 20 Point Programme*, New Delhi: Metropolitan Book Co., 1983.

Breman, Jan, *Of Peasants, Migrants and Paupers: Rural Labour Circulation in West India*, Delhi: Oxford University Press, 1985.

Briggs, G.W., *The Chamars*, Delhi: Low Price Publications, 1990 (1st published 1920).

Campbell, J.M. (ed.), *Hindu Castes and Tribes of Gujarat*, 2 vols., Gurgaon: Vintage Books, 1988 (1st published 1901).

—— (ed.), *History of Gujarat: Ancient, Medieval, Modern, Gurgaon*, Vintage Books: 1989 (1st published 1896).

Chatterjee, P.G. Pandey (eds.), *Subaltern Studies* VII, Delhi: Oxford University Press, 1992.

Chaudhary, S.N., *Changing Status of Depressed Castes in Contemporary India*, Delhi: Daya Publishing House, 1988.

Chavda, Vijaysingh, *Modern Gujarat: Reflections on Sources, Historiography, Society, Economy and Culture*, Ahmedabad: New Order Book Co., *c*. 1967.

——, *A Select Bibliography of Gujarat: Its History and Culture 1600-1857*, Ahmedabad: New Order Book Co., 1972.

Commissariat, M.S., *A History of Gujarat*, Vols. I and II, Bombay: Orient Longman, 1938, 1957.

Crook, W., *The Tribes and Castes of the North Western India*, Vol. I, Delhi: Cosmo Publications: 1974 (1st published 1896).

Dahiwale, S.M., *Emerging Entrepreneurship among Scheduled Castes of Contemporary India: A Study of Kolhapur City*, New Delhi: Concept Publishing Company, 1989.

Dastur, A.J. et al. (eds.), *Studies in the Fourth General Elections*, Bombay: Allied Publishers, 1972.

Desai, A.R. (ed.), *Rural Sociology in India*, Bombay: Popular Prakashan, 1969.

Desai, I.P., *Water Facilities for the Untouchables in Rural Gujarat*, New Delhi: ICSSR, 1973.

——, *Untouchability in Rural Gujarat*, Bombay: Popular Prakashan, 1976.

Desai, I.P. et al., *Caste, Caste Conflict and Reservation*, Delhi: Ajanta Publications, 1985.

Desai, M.B., *The Rural Economy of Gujarat*, Bombay: Oxford University Press, 1948.

——, *Tenancy Abolition and the Emerging Pattern in Gujarat*, Baroda: M.S. University, 1971.

Desai, M.H., *A Righteous Struggle: A Chronicle of the Ahmedabad Textile Labourers' Fight for Justice*, Ahmedabad: Navajivan Publishing House, 1968.

Dosabhai, Edalji, *A History of Gujarat: From the Earliest Period to the Present Time*, New Delhi: Asian Education Services, 1986 (1st published 1894).

Dube, S.C., *Indian Village*, London: Routledge and Kegan Paul, 1955.

Dube, S.C. (ed.), *Social Sciences and Social Realities: Role of the Social Sciences in Contemporary India*, Simla: Indian Institute of Advanced Study, 1976.

Dumont, Louis, *Homo Hierarchicus: The Caste System and Its Implications*, Chicago: The University of Chicago Press, 1980 (1st published 1970).

Enthoven, R.E., *The Tribes and Castes of Bombay*, 3 vols., Delhi; Cosmo Publications, 1975 (1st published 1920, 1922).

Galanter, Marc, *Competing Equalities: Law and the Backward Classes in India*, Delhi: Oxford University Press, 1984.

Gandhi, M.K., *The Removal of Untouchability*, Ahmedabad: Navajivan Publishing House, 1954.

Ghurye, G.S., *Caste, Class and Occupation*, Bombay: Popular Book Depot, 1961.

Gillion, K.L., *Ahmedabad: A Study in Indian Urban History*, Berkeley and Los Angeles: University of California Press, 1968.

Guha, Ranajit (ed.), *Subaltern Studies*, Vols. I-VI, Delhi: Oxford University Press, 1982-90.

Hardiman, David, *Peasant Nationalists of Gujarat: Kheda District 1917-1934*, Delhi: Oxford University Press, 1981.

——, *The Coming of the Devi: Adivasi Assertion in Western India*, Delhi: Oxford University Press, 1987.

Hazari, *I Was An Outcaste: The Autobiography of An 'Untouchable' in India*, New Delhi: The Hindustan Times, 1957 (1st published 1951).

ICSSR, *A Survey of Research in Sociology and Social Anthropology*, 3 vols, Bombay: Popular Prakashan, 1972, 1974.

——, *Survey of Research in Sociology and Social Anthropology 1969-1979*, 3 vols, New Delhi: Satvahan Publications, 1985.

Issacs, H.R., *India's Ex-untouchables*, Bombay: Asia Publishing House, 1974.

Jairamdas, J., *Bhangi Kasht Mukti and Bhangi Mukti*, New Delhi: National Committee for Gandhi Centenary, 1969.

Johnson, G., *Provincial Politics and Indian Nationalism: Bombay and the Indian National Congress 1880 to 1915*, Cambridge: Cambridge University Press, 1973.

Kothari, Rajni (ed.), *Caste in Indian Politics, New Delhi*: Orient Longman, 1986 (1st published 1970).

Kothari, Rajni et al., *Context of Electoral Change in India: General Elections 1967*, Bombay: Academic Books, 1969.

Kothari, V.N., *A Study of Economic Profiles of the Scheduled Castes in Gujarat*, Baroda: M.S. University, 1976.

Kumar, Dharma (ed.), *The Cambridge Economic History of India*, Vol. 2: *c. 1757-c. 1970*, Cambridge: Cambridge University Press, 1982.

Lakdawala, D.T. (ed.), *Gujarat Economy: Problems and Prospects*, Ahmedabad: SPIESR, 1983.

Lewis, O., *Village Life in Northern India*, Urbana: University of Illinois Press, 1958.

Mac, M.R., *Select Bibliography on Scheduled Tribes*, Surat: Centre for Social Studies, 1982.

Mac, M.R., G.V.S. Reddy, *Select Bibliography on Scheduled Castes*, Surat: Centre for Social Studies, 1983.

Majmudar, M.R., *Cultural History of Gujarat from Early Time to Pre-British Period*, Bombay: Popular Prakashan, 1965.

Malabari, B.M., *Gujarat and the Gujaratis*, Delhi: Mittal Publications, 1983 (1st published 1889).

Malkani, N.R., *Clean People and an Unclean Country*, Delhi: Harijan Sevak Sangh, 1971 (1st published 1965).

Mandelbaum, D.G., *Society in India*, Bombay: Popular Prakashan, 1987 (1st published 1972).

Marriott, M., *Village India*, Bombay: Asia Publishing House, 1955.

Masvi, M., *Gujaratna Harijano* (in Gujarati), Ahmedabad: Tribal Research and Training Institute, 1982.

Masvi, M., C. Upadhyay, *Gujaratna Harijano-2* (in Gujarati), Ahmedabad: Tribal Research and Training Institute, 1983.

——, *Gujaratna Harijano-3* (in Gujarati), Ahmedabad: Tribal Research and Training Institute, 1984.

Misra, S.C., *Muslim Communities in Gujarat: Preliminary Studies in Their History and Social Organization*, New Delhi: Munshiram Manoharlal, 1985.

Muley, D.M., *Rural Development Administration: Problems and Prospects*, Allahabad: Chugh Publications, 1987.

National Sanitation Improvement Foundation, *Organising Voluntary Action for Promotion of Low Cost Sanitation in Gujarat*, New Delhi: Consortium of Rural Technology, 1991.

Nightingale, P., *Trade and Empire in Western India 1784-1806*, Cambridge: Cambridge University Press, 1970.

O'Hanlon, Rosalind, *Caste, Conflict and Ideology: Mahatma Jotirao Phule and Low Caste Protest in Nineteenth-Century Western India*, Cambridge: Cambridge University Press, 1985.

Pandya, Bhanuprasad, *Striving for Economic Equality*, Bombay: Popular Book Depot, 1959.

Parvathamma, C., *Scheduled Castes and Tribes: A Socio-Economic Survey*, New Delhi: Ashish Publishing House, 1984.

Patel, B.B., *The Structure of Inter-District Inter-Sectoral and Inter-Industry Wage Differentials in Gujarat*, Baroda: M.S. University, 1976.

——, *Report on the Implementation of Minimum Wages for Sweepers in Village Panchayats in Saurashtra*, Ahmedabad: Gandhi Labour Institute, 1990.

Patel, G.D., *The Land Revenue Settlements and the British Rule in India*, Ahmedabad: Gujarat University, 1969.

——, *The Land Systems of Union Teritories of India*, Anand, Charotar Book Stall, 1970.

Patel, Ishwarbhai, *Safai-Marg Darshika* (A Guide Book on Sanitation), Delhi: Harijan Sevak Sangh, 1970.

Patel, Sujata, *The Making of Industrial Relations: The Ahmedabad Textile Industry 1918-1939*, Delhi: Oxford University Press, 1987.

Pathak, Bindeshwar, *Road to Freedom: A Sociological Study on the Abolition of Scavenging in India*, Delhi, Motilal Banarsidass, 1991.

Pathak, D., P. Sheth, *Sardar Vallabhbhai Patel: From Civic to National Leadership*, Ahmedabad: Navajivan Publishing House, 1980.

Pathak, D.N., M.G. Parekh, K.D. Desai, *Three General Elections in Gujarat*, Ahmedabad: Gujarat University, 1966.

Pathy, Jaganath, *Tribal Peasantry Dynamics of Development*, New Delhi: Inter-India Publications, 1984.

Pearson, M.N., *Merchants and Rulers in Gujarat*, New Delhi: Munshiram Manoharlal, 1976.

Phadke, Y.D. (ed.), *Mahatma Phule Samagra Vangmaya*, Bombay: Maharashtra Rajya Sahitya ani Sanskriti Mandal, 1980 (1st published 1969).

Pocock, D.F., *Kanbi and Patidar: A Study of the Patidar Community of Gujarat*, Oxford: Oxford University Press, 1972.

Punalekar, S.P., J. Ranadivi, *Tribal Education: An Inter-State Study*, Surat: Centre for Social Studies, 1984.

Rajput, K.C. (comp.), *Award, Judgement, Pay Commission Report & Important Circulars by Shri G.S. Barot*, Ahmedabad: The Gujarat Municipal & Panchayat Kamdar Association, 1992.

Rajyagor, S.B., *History of Gujarat*, New Delhi, S. Chand & Co., 1982.

Ram, Nandu, *The Mobile Scheduled Castes: Rise of a New Middle Class*, Delhi: Hindustan Publishing Co., 1988.

Randeria, Shalini, 'The Politics of Representation and Exchange among Untouchable Castes in Western India (Gujarat)', Ph.D. dissertation, Freien Universtat Berlin, 1992.

Rao, M.S.A., *Social Movements and Social Transformation: A Study of Two Backward Classes Movements in India*, New Delhi: Manohar, 1987.

Raval, R.L., *Socio-Religious Reform Movements in Gujarat during the Nineteenth Century*, New Delhi: Ess Ess Publications, 1987.

Selvanathan, S., *Status of Scheduled Castes*, New Delhi: Ashish Publishing House, 1989.

Shah, C.H. et al., *Second Resurvey of Matar Taluka*, Ahmedabad: The Gujarat Institute of Area Planning, 1987.

Shah, Ghanshyam, *Caste Association and Political Process in Gujarat: A Study of Gujarat Kshatriya Sabha*, Bombay: Popular Prakashan, 1975.

——, Politics of *Scheduled Castes and Tribes: Adivasi and Harijan Leaders of Gujarat*, Bombay, Vora & Co. Publishers, 1975.

——, *Economic Differentiations and Tribal Identity: A Restudy of Chaudhris*, Delhi: Ajanta Publications, 1984.

Shah, Ghanshyam et al., *Tribal Education in Gujarat*, Delhi: Ajanta Publications, 1985.

Shah, Vimal, C.H. Shah, *Resurvey of Matar Taluka*, Bombay: Vora & Co., 1974.

Shah, Vimal, Tara Patel, *Who goes to Colleges? Scheduled Caste and Scheduled Tribe Post-Matric Scholarships in Gujarat*, Ahmedabad: Rachna Pratishthan, 1977.

Sharma, S.K., *Social Movements and Social Change: A Study of Arya Samaj and Untouchables in Punjab*, Delhi: B.R. Publishing Co., 1985.

Sharma, S.K., *The Chamar Artisans: Industrialisation, Skills and Social Mobility*: New Delhi: B.R. Publishing Co., 1986.

Sheth, Pravin, *Patterns of Political Behaviour in Gujarat*, Ahmedabad: Sahitya Mudranalaya, 1976.

Sheth, Pravin and Ramesh Menon, *Caste and Communal Timebomb*, Ahmedabad: Golwala Publications, 1986.

Shinoda, Takashi, *Indo no Seisonin Kasuto Kenkyu* (in Japanese), Tokyo: Shunjusya, 1995.

Shyamlal, *The Bhangis in Transitions*, New Delhi: Inter-India Publications, 1984.

——, *The Bhangi: A Sweeper Caste Its Socio-Economic Portraits with Special Reference to Jodhpur City*, Bombay: Popular Prakashan, 1992.

Silverberg, James (ed.), *Social Mobility in the Caste System in India: An Interdisciplinary Symposium*, The Hague: Mouton Publishers, 1968.

Singer, Milton (ed.), *Traditional India*, Philadelphia: American Folklore Society, 1959.

Singer, Milton and Bernard S. Cohn (eds.), *Structure and Change in Indian Society*, Chicago: Aldine Publishing Co., 1968.

Singh, Yogendra, *Social Stratification and Change in India*, Delhi: Manohar, 1977.

Sinha, B.D., A.K. Ghosh, *Evaluation of Low Cost Sanitation: Liberation, Training & Rehabilitation of Scavengers*, New Delhi: Arnold Publishers, 1990.

——, *Sanitation and Environment: Evaluation of Low Cost Sanitation in Gujarat*, New Delhi: Arnold Publishers, 1994.

Sinha, B.D., P.S.K. Menon, A.K. Ghosh, *Restoration of Human Dignity: Impact of Development Programmes on Scavengers*, New Delhi: Arnold Publishers, 1994.

Sinha, R.K., *Alienation among Scheduled Castes*, Delhi: Manas Publications, 1986.

Srinivas, M.N. (ed.), *Religion and Society among the Coorgs of South India*, Bombay: Oxford University Press, 1952.

——, *India's Villages*, Calcutta: West Bengal Government Press, 1955.

——, *Social Change in Modern India*, Bombay: Orient Longman, 1972 (1st published 1966).

——, *The Dominant Caste and Other Essays*, Delhi: Oxford University Press, 1987.

The Times Research Foundation, *Seminar on Ahmedabad 2001: Imperative Now Towards A New Metropolitan Management Strategy*, Vol. 10, Calcutta, 1988.

Upadhyay, C., D. Parmar, *Gujaratna Harijano-4* (in Gujarati), Ahmedabad: Tribal Research and Training Institute, 1985.

Vyas, Rajnee, *The Glory of Gujarat*, Ahmedabad: Gurjar-Anada Prakashan, 1988.

Washbrook, D.A., *The Emergence of Provincial Politics: Madras Presidency 1870-1920*, Cambridge: Cambridge University Press, 1976.

Watson, J.W., *History of Gujarat*, New Delhi: Cosmo Publications, 1983 (1st published 1876).

Wiser, W.H., *The Hindu Jajmani System: A Socio-Economic System Inter-Relating Members of a Hindu Village Community in Services*, Lucknow: Lucknow Publishing House, 1958 (1st published 1936).

# Index

Ahmedabad
  Borough Municipality (ABM) 146, 174
  City 92, 117, 123, 135
  Municipal Corporation (AMC) 28, 109, 117, 126, 141, 144-5, 147-69, 171-7, 181-4, 186, 189, 193, 197, 202, 207, 211-12, 227-8, 246
  Urban Agglomeration 117
Ahmedabad City Sweepers' Association 153, 166-8, 170-1
Ahmedabad City Sweepers' Credit Co-operative Society 171
Ahmedabad Municipal Co-operative Bank 169, 171
Ahmedabad Municipal Kamdar Karamchari Union 167, 172
Ahmedabad Municipal Nokar Mandal 167-73, 177
Ahmedabad Municipal Servants' Association 166
Ahmedabad Municipal Servants' Consumers Co-operative Society 169-70
All India Safai Mazdoor Congress (Gujarat Branch) 173-4
allowances 63-4, 66, 138, 149-50, 154-8, 165-7, 172, 175, 216, 229, 249
  dearness 64, 66, 146-7, 149, 156, 159, 229
  special 146, 156
  grain 146-7
  house rent 147
  interim 147
  compensatory city 149, 156, 158-9
  unclean 64, 66, 153, 157
  night-soil 157
Ambedkar, Bhimrao Ramji 11, 24
Anti-Untouchability League 41
Arya Samaj 24-5

backwardness 12, 16, 18-19, 83, 88, 110, 140, 238, 246, 253-4, 265
bad habits/custom 48, 166, 170, 217
Baleshahi 23
bamboo basket 56-9, 148
Baniya 14, 16, 98
Bareja 214, 229-30
Barot Award 154-5, 166-7, 175
Barot, G.S. 154
Barve Committee 44, 46, 48, 50-2, 59, 63-4, 66-7, 71, 73-4, 79, 150, 214, 220, 262
Barve, V.N. 44-5
Basu Task Force 49, 62, 74, 79, 255-6, 262
Bavla 214
beat 184, 230-1
Bhangis (over a wide area of north-western India) 23-8, 36, 43-4, 52-4, 88, 90-6, 99-107, 109-10, 122, 139-40, 218, 221, 235, 237-8, 240, 245-6, 249, 253-4, 264 (*see also* Baleshahi, Bhuimalia, Chuhra, Domra/Dumra, Heddish, Lal Begi, Madiga, Mehtar, Thoti, and Valmiki)
Bhangi liberation movement/plan (Bhangi Kasht Mukti Karyakram) 23-7, 29, 221-3, 254-5, 261, 263, 265
Bhangi Mukti Samitee 42
  derivation of the word 23
Bharuch 14
Bhuimalia 23
Bombay 14, 150, 220
  Presidency 13, 23, 41

State 13, 43-5, 59, 98, 116, 146, 149, 219-20
Brahmans 14, 22, 88, 98, 100
British East India Company 3, 15, 116-17, 121-2, 184

caste 11-17, 19-23, 25, 43, 52-53, 69, 85, 88, 98, 105, 255, 264
association 12, 19, 21, 264
federation 12, 21
Hindu 11, 17, 19, 43, 88, 100
Panchayat 25
system 11-12, 22, 43
census 20-1, 23, 27, 78, 85, 87, 90, 95, 105, 125, 262
cesspool 36, 51, 57-8, 108, 121-2, 125-8, 130, 157, 172, 182
Chamars 19-20, 23, 87-8, 90, 92, 95-6, 98-100, 103-6, 110, 176
chawl 130, 132-3, 136, 152, 159
Chhotalal, Ranchhodlal 111, 117, 121-2
Chuhra 23
community bin 133-4, 136-7
Constitution of India 11, 29
customary rights 52-4, 60, 62, 66, 70, 72-5, 77, 79-81, 217, 230, 254-5
*gharaki* (*gharagi*) 52-3, 213, 221, 230, 234, 249
*jagirdari* 52
*dastoori* 52
*virat* 52

Dalit, Adivasi, Baxi Panch Municipal Kamdar Karamchari Mandal 167
debts 70, 217-18, 246-50
Dehgam 214
Delhi 42, 52, 75, 116, 150, 173
Deoginkar, Mamasaheb 42
Department
of Conservancy 137-40, 149, 164, 171-2, 181-6, 193, 199, 201-3, 207-9, 211-12, 230
of Refuse 136-8, 181-2, 185, 202-3, 211-12, 230
Depressed Classes 16, 31
Dholka 214, 229
differentials 55, 64, 88-90, 95, 99-100, 102-3, 128, 147, 156, 158, 186, 189, 193, 197, 201-2, 208, 210-12
among the states 64
among the local bodies 64, 254
among the jatis 88-9, 92-3, 95- 6, 99-102, 253
Dominant Caste 21, 36
dumping sites 227
Dumra/Domra 23

education 12, 18-19, 23-4, 45, 70, 79, 83, 98-102, 118, 136, 140, 173, 177, 184, 217-18, 222, 237, 240, 242, 246, 253-4, 256, 261, 263
formal 102
primary 98, 102, 238
secondary 18, 100, 153, 233, 238, 240
higher 11, 16, 21, 99, 102, 104, 231, 238, 240-1
level of 79, 99-100, 102, 104, 238, 240-1, 254
structure of 24, 27, 29, 88, 102, 105, 214, 238
employment 19, 61, 66, 69-70, 74, 79, 90, 144, 148, 150, 153, 161-2, 164, 171, 175, 181, 186, 189, 193, 197, 201-2, 204, 206, 211-12, 227, 235, 238, 241, 254-5, 263
conditions 24, 27-8, 43, 63, 69-72, 79, 98, 141, 159-61, 164, 166, 170, 172-4, 176, 182, 213-14, 218-19, 222, 227, 229, 253-5, 262, 265
temporary (part-time) 66, 218
permanent (full-time) 69, 148, 160-2, 168-9, 171-2, 181, 185-6, 189, 193, 197-8, 200, 202-4, 206-12, 222, 227-9, 262
compensatory 159, 161-4, 173-5, 186, 189, 198, 200-1, 204-6, 211-12, 228-9, 233, 235, 262

policy 28, 140, 159, 162, 186, 189, 198, 202-3, 207, 212, 234
discrimination in (against) 193, 208, 238
ethnographic survey 20, 23

financial
aid (help/assistance) 17, 26, 46, 60, 62, 74, 221, 262-4
problem (weakness/constraint) 136, 149, 174, 218, 247
institution, 180, 249
situation (base) 152-3, 227, 247, 249
Gambling (gamble) 70, 217, 246
Gandhi centenary 221-2
Gandhi, Indira 31, 50
Gandhi, Mohandas Karamchand 15, 165, 221
Gandhi Smarak Nidhi 26, 42, 263
Ganga Action Plan 61
garbage (rubbish) 43, 58, 72, 108, 132-7, 139-40, 172, 182-4, 226-7
collection of 28, 54, 58, 108-9, 115, 123, 132-3, 135-7, 139, 173, 176, 184, 199, 230-1
disposal of 43, 121, 123, 133, 137, 139-40, 182, 226, 231
Garodas 88, 91-2, 95, 98, 100-3
Gujarat 13-15, 19, 23, 25-8, 47-8, 52-53, 60, 64, 73, 75, 83-9, 104-8, 116, 118, 162, 164, 171, 174, 214, 219, 220-4, 238, 243-4, 253-4, 256, 258, 263-4
Gujarat Municipal and Panchayat Kamdar Association 167, 169, 171

*hangamis* 152, 159-60, 164, 171, 227
Harijan Sevak Sangh 24, 26, 44-5, 51, 220, 222
Haryana 64, 67
Heddish 23
house to house collection 133-4, 226

income 18, 28, 52, 85, 162-3, 197, 212, 217, 242-3, 246, 262, 264
household 140, 243-4, 247, 254, 262
per capita 244-5
Industrial Disputes Act of 1947 70, 144, 164-5, 168, 170, 177

*jajmani* system 21, 35-6, 53
*jati* 11-12, 14, 27, 43, 85, 87-9, 91-3, 95-6, 99-105, 110
Jeejeebhoy Award 147-9, 153, 161, 166, 170, 175
Jeejeebhoy, F. 147, 161

Karnataka 52-3, 75
Kerala 47, 60, 75
*khadi* 151, 178
*khalkuva* 121-2, 157
Kheda 14, 117
Kolis 15, 88
Kutch 88-9, 99, 219-20

labour
conditions 9, 24, 27-8, 43, 46-7, 60, 70-1, 174
exchanges 159
management 72, 128, 139-40
land reforms 12, 15, 18, 21
latrine 23-4, 26-7, 43-4, 47, 50-9, 61-2, 66, 75, 77, 109, 122, 130, 132, 216-19, 221-4, 226, 230, 236, 263
basket 55
Bhanoli-type 59
chawl 130, 132
community 130
dry 43, 51-2, 54-62, 73-8, 217, 220-1, 223-4, 254-6, 261, 263
flush 59, 60-1, 221, 256
Gopuri-style 44-5
improved 25-7, 224
public 61-2, 125, 128, 132, 139, 157, 176, 182, 199, 221, 224, 230
receptacle 56
septic 55, 60, 73
service 56

trench 46, 59
literacy 18, 83, 98-103, 238
local bodies 17, 28-9, 46, 52-4, 58-60, 62-4, 66-7, 69-74, 78-9, 109, 117, 123, 127, 141, 144-5, 159, 161, 171-4, 176, 213-14, 217-24, 226-31, 233-4, 244-5, 248-50, 253-6, 258, 260-4
municipal corporation 28, 109, 117, 126, 141, 144, 181, 214, 216, 233, 245-6, 248
municipality 117, 122, 132, 137-8, 140-1, 146-7, 150, 152-4, 161, 174, 176, 184, 214, 221, 226, 244-6, 248
nagar palika 214
village panchayat 17
low cost sanitation programme/scheme 61, 222-3, 255

Madhya Pradesh 47, 52, 64, 75-6
Madiga 23
Madras 47, 52, 64
*mahajan* 248
Maharashtra 13, 44, 47, 52-3, 60, 64, 76, 164, 263
Mahars 24, 52
Malkani Committee 27, 45-8, 50, 55, 59-60, 63-4, 66, 73-4, 79, 150, 220
Malkani, N.R. 24, 47-8, 220
means of settling industrial disputes
court of enquiry 145
industrial (labour) court 145, 169, 172
industrial tribunals 70, 145, 163, 173, 177, 229
national tribunals 145
Mechanization 133-5, 137, 140, 175-6, 227, 230-1
Meghvals 88, 92, 99-100
Mehtar 23-4
*mukadam* 69, 139-40, 146-8, 151, 168-9, 171, 186, 229, 240
municipalization 74, 255
muster station 149, 151, 159-160, 164, 185, 201, 208, 231

National Commission for the Scheduled Castes and Scheduled Tribes 260
National Scheme of Liberation and Rehabilitation of Scavengers and Their Dependents 255-65
*niradhars* 161-3, 201, 207

occupational
regulations 18, 112
structure 23, 27, 29, 87, 90-98, 105, 214, 231, 249, 254, 264
Orissa 23, 26, 47, 57, 66

Panchayati Raj 17, 21, 32, 37
Pandya Committee 47-50, 63-4, 66-7, 69, 71-72, 74, 79, 150, 159
Pandya, Bhanuprasad 48
Patel, Ishwarbhai 26, 42, 223, 261
Patel, Vallabhbhai Jhaverbhai 15, 117, 121
Pathak, Bindeshwar 25-6
Patidars 15-16, 88
Patwardhan, Appasaheb 42, 44
pensions 63, 66, 156, 168
provident fund 63, 66, 149, 159, 168, 246
retirement age 162, 186
Phadke, Mamasaheb 221
Phule, Jotirao Govindrao 22, 255
pressure groups 12, 24-5, 28, 164-5, 176, 253
promotion 63, 69, 145, 148-9, 152, 157, 160, 164, 168-9, 171-2, 174, 186, 189, 193, 201, 203-4, 206-7, 210-11, 220, 227-9, 236, 249, 254, 264
promotion system (policy) 154-5, 157-8, 167, 175, 264
pumping stations 121, 125, 157, 224
Punjab 23, 47, 52, 55, 58, 64, 67, 75

quarters 70, 147, 152-3, 176, 216

Rajasthan 23, 47, 52, 66, 75
Rajputs 14-15, 51, 88
Reference Group 22, 38
reorganization of states 219
reservation policym (system) 11-12, 16-19, 21, 79, 104, 153, 238, 264

Safai Kamdar Nokar Mandal 168
Safai Vidyalaya 26-7, 42, 51, 222-3, 261
Sanand 214, 229-30
Sanskritization 14, 22, 35, 38-9
Sarabhai, Ansuyaben 165
Saraswati, Dayanand 42
Saurashtra 13-14, 52, 214, 217-20
scavengers 23, 27, 43-6, 50-6, 58-64, 66-8, 70-5, 78-9, 107, 144-6, 148, 150, 161, 173, 213, 217, 220-2, 224, 249, 254-6, 258, 260-2
  definition of 43, 256, 262
  rehabilitation of 74, 79, 255-6, 260-1, 263, 265
  living conditions of 44, 47, 49, 144-5
  working conditions of 43, 45-9, 59-60, 71-2, 144-5, 213, 220, 255
Senvas 88, 90, 92, 99-101
septic tank 125, 130, 182, 224
sewage disposal 115, 127-8
sewerage 55, 59-60, 73, 108, 125, 224, 226, 230
Shah Adjudication 147
Shah Award 147, 165, 168
Shah, M.C. 146
social groups
  Other Backward Classes 11, 31-2, 223
  Scheduled Castes 11-12, 15-22, 27, 43, 48, 72, 79, 83-5, 86-96, 99, 102-6, 110, 140, 153, 167, 170, 176, 223, 238, 249, 253-4, 256, 258, 260, 264
  Scheduled Tribes 11, 14, 19, 29, 83, 85, 99, 167, 223, 238, 256, 260
  Socially and Educationally Backward Classes 111
Sola 214, 230, 251
solid waste management system (programme) 133, 227, 231
subcontracting system 55, 139-40, 217, 255
Sulabh International 25-6, 51, 263
Surat 13-14, 73, 85, 116, 118, 220
sweepers
  basic pay of 64, 66, 137-8, 156
  compensatory appointment of 161
  definition of 78, 183, 239, 256, 260, 262
  institutional reforms of 12, 21-2, 175, 253, 264
  internal reforms of 24, 70, 170, 177, 253-4, 264-5
  living conditions of 49, 144-5, 167, 170, 173, 176, 213
  minimum wages of 44-5, 63-4, 74, 146-7, 149, 155, 173-4, 220, 222, 227
  pay scale of 146-7, 155, 158
  rehabilitation of 74, 79, 260-3, 265
  service conditions of 47, 159-60, 249-50
  strikes by 170, 175, 180, 229
  uniforms for 74, 99, 145, 147, 151, 157, 174, 176, 229, 231

temple entry 17
Thakore Award 149-56, 160, 162, 166-8, 170, 172, 175, 193, 197
Thakore, Indrajit G. 149-50, 160
The National Commission for Safai Karamcharis Act 260
Thoti 23
Trade Union Act of 1926 70, 164, 177
trade union movement 64, 70, 117, 164, 177, 253
traditional occupation 23, 43, 85, 87-8, 93, 100, 104-5, 110, 254
tuberculosis 152, 173, 199-200

*umedvars* 152, 159-60, 164, 168-9, 171, 175, 186, 193, 197-8, 201-2, 204, 206-11, 227, 235
UNDP 26, 222-3
UNICEF 26, 222- 3
untouchables 16-17, 20, 23-4, 217
Uttar Pradesh 23, 45, 47, 52, 55, 66, 75-8

Vadodara (Baroda) 14, 74, 85, 116, 118, 220
Valmiki 23
Vankars 19, 52, 85, 88, 90, 92, 95-6, 98-101, 103-4, 110, 176
*vatan* 53-4, 74
*vatandar* 52-3
Viramgam 214, 224, 226, 229-30
Vyas Committee 214, 217-18
*warasdars* 161, 164, 168-9, 171, 174-5, 193, 200, 203-4, 206-7
West Bengal 23, 47, 76, 78
Westernization 35, 38
wheelbarrows 46, 59-60, 133-4, 169, 171, 220-1, 226, 231
white collar job 18, 105, 238
workers
  temporary 149, 152, 169, 205-6, 208, 211-12, 229-30, 235, 241, 249, 262
  permanent 138, 152, 159, 161-2, 171, 182, 184-6, 189, 193, 197, 208-9, 212, 228-30, 234-5, 241, 243-4, 262
World Bank 133, 222-3